THE LIVES OF THE
KINGS & QUEENS
OF ENGLAND

THE LIVES OF THE
KINGS & QUEENS
OF ENGLAND

REVISED AND UPDATED

EDITED BY

ANTONIA FRASER

University of California Press

Berkeley   Los Angeles   London

University of California Press
Berkeley and Los Angeles, California

University of California Press, Ltd.
London, England

Published by arrangment with Weidenfeld & Nicolson

ISBN 0-520-21938-4

Designed by Peter Butler
Printed and Bound in Italy

Page one: *Elizabeth I in coronation regalia, by an unknown artist*
Page two: *Queen Anne presents the plans of Blenheim Palace to the figure of Military Merit , by Sir Godfrey Kneller*
Page three: *Charles I with his second son the Duke of York, later to be James II, by Sir Peter Lely, c. 1647*
endpapers*: Richard Coeur de Lion embarks on the Third Crusade in 1190, from the chronicle of David Aubert*

1   3   5   7   9   10   8   6   4   2

CONTENTS

INTRODUCTION   6
BY ANTONIA FRASER

COATS OF ARMS   14
BY J. P. BROOKE-LITTLE
Richmond Herald of Arms

LIST OF COATS OF ARMS   15

THE NORMANS
BY JOHN GILLINGHAM
WILLIAM I 1066–87   20
WILLIAM II 1087–1100   27
HENRY I 1100–35   30
STEPHEN 1135–54   36

THE ANGEVINS
BY JOHN GILLINGHAM
HENRY II 1154–89   42
RICHARD I 1189–99   54
JOHN 1199–1216   62

THE PLANTAGENETS
BY PETER EARLE
HENRY III 1216–72   72
EDWARD I 1272–1307   79
EDWARD II 1307–27   87
EDWARD III 1327–77   94
RICHARD II 1377–99   103

THE HOUSE OF LANCASTER
BY ANTHONY CHEETHAM
HENRY IV 1399–1413   114
HENRY V 1413–22   120
HENRY VI 1422–71   128

THE HOUSE OF YORK
BY ANTHONY CHEETHAM
EDWARD IV 1461–83   142
RICHARD III 1483–5   152

THE TUDORS
BY NEVILLE WILLIAMS
HENRY VII 1485–1509   162
HENRY VIII 1509–47   171
EDWARD VI 1547–53   185

MARY I 1553–8   191
ELIZABETH I 1558–1603   198

THE STUARTS
BY MAURICE ASHLEY
JAMES I 1603–25   216
CHARLES I 1625–49   224
CHARLES II 1660–85   234
JAMES II 1685–8   240
WILLIAM III 1688–1702 AND MARY II 1688–94   247
ANNE 1702–14   254

THE HOUSE OF HANOVER
BY JOHN CLARKE
GEORGE I 1714–27   264
GEORGE II 1727–60   272
GEORGE III 1760–1820   280
GEORGE IV 1820–30   288
WILLIAM IV 1830–7   294

BY JASPER RIDLEY
VICTORIA 1830–1901   299

THE HOUSE OF
SAXE-COBURG-GOTHA
BY JASPER RIDLEY
EDWARD VII 1901–10   320

THE HOUSE OF WINDSOR
BY ANDREW ROBERTS
GEORGE V 1910–36   330
EDWARD VIII 1936   340
GEORGE VI 1936–52   349
ELIZABETH II 1952–   358

INDEX   376
ACKNOWLEDGMENTS   384

GENEALOGICAL TABLES
THE NORMANS AND ANGEVINS   18–19
THE PLANTAGENETS   70–71
THE HOUSES OF LANCASTER AND YORK   136–7
THE TUDORS AND STUARTS   214–15
THE HOUSE OF HANOVER   262–3
THE HOUSES OF SAXE-COBURG-GOTHA
    AND WINDSOR   326–7

INTRODUCTION

I N ONE SENSE A VOLUME OF THE LIVES OF THE kings and queens of England needs no introduction. The popularity of biography among the reading public is a byword of contemporary publishing. Royal biography, if anything, leads the field. It is not difficult to see why this should be so. Most people learn history early on in terms of the reigns – if not the lives– of the sovereigns, for the simple reason that otherwise history to the young can seem all too open-ended. The reigns of the monarchs provide natural frameworks for this vast apparently amorphous mass of material. At the same time there is the perennial appetite for a story provided by the lives. And on one level the biographies of the kings and queens are certainly stories, the stories of great, or at least prominent, men and women. Once again, history told in the form of stories (the German language actually equates the two words in *Geschichte*) is most palatable to us in childhood . . . the death of Prince William in the *White Ship* and the King who never smiled again, the rescue of King Richard with the aid of the minstrel Blondel, a girl Queen who vowed 'I will be good', such tales have a habit of lingering in our imagination. H. A. L. Fisher once said that history is 'one damn thing after another': in the seemingly endless chronicle of events in English history, the reigns of individual kings and queens provide a convenient memorable pattern.

It is then the theory of history via biography of royal personages which needs defending, not the practice of it: its perennial popularity will certainly ensure the practice.

An early sample of the popular taste is provided by the success, from the 1840s onwards, of the *Lives of the Queens of England* by Agnes Strickland. The series received instantaneous acclaim and ran through many editions. *The Lives of the Tudor Princesses*, *The Stuart Princesses* and *Lives of the Queens of Scotland* followed, with equal public support, even if one reverse should be recorded, when, led on by her enthusiasm, Agnes Strickland embarked on the *Lives of the Bachelor Kings of England*, only to find that there was a singular dearth of authentically unmarried sovereigns. Yet the lessons of Agnes Strickland's work can still be learned today. She combined sympathy for her subjects with meticulous scholarship and research, praised by such authorities of the time as the historian Guizot. And her zeal for research was particularly commendable in an age when state papers were largely uncalendared; moreover when the State Paper Room was finally opened, women were at first not admitted, reversal of this decision only being secured by prolonged protests on Miss Strickland's part. It was the measure of her fame that when, as an old lady, Agnes Strickland went down to Oxford, she was acclaimed by the undergraduates with the merry cry: 'The Queens! The Queens! Three cheers for the Queens!'

Of course it is true that the professional historians of the nineteenth century were also often best-sellers, and incidentally very often chose biography as their mode of telling history. In any case they wrote, in general, the kind of wide and sweeping books which both carried away the public and were easily assimilated by them. In contrast, the modern view of history, like the truth, is rarely so pure and certainly never simple; it might be summed up as implying that things are frequently more complicated, more fragmented than has been thought heretofore. Fernand Braudel, for example, who was the leading exponent of the mighty modern French school of history, observed in his own great work on the Mediterranean: 'Thus confronted by man, I am always tempted to see him as enclosed in a destiny which he scarcely made, in a landscape which shows before and behind me the infinite perspectives of the *longue durée.*' Inevitably, in expounding such views, some professional historians today write in more obscure terms, less easily assimilated by the non-professional public. Yet this very public is increasingly highly educated in a basic way, a development which might be dated from the 1940s; increasingly it is fed with facts, brought up to expect information, not only via books, but also other media. The very word beloved of television, the 'documentary', presupposes the existence of and the use of documents, even if there is none to be seen, and what there might be have not necessarily been used. An educated and voracious public fed by these tendencies, unable to read the work of professional historians with great ease, turns to biography to fill the gap and satisfy its appetite.

Popular demand, however explicable, is not of course in itself a justification. It still needs to be demonstrated for the purposes of this volume how far the history of England can actually be usefully told through the lives of its sovereigns. In sheer sweep, our history can certainly be told in this mode (as that of the United States might be told in terms of presidents but for a far shorter span) with the sole exception of the eleven-year interlude of the Commonwealth and Protectorate. Even that interregnum is in effect covered by the life of King Charles II, who although not officially restored until 1660, was after all hailed by legitimists immediately after his father's death. This sweep is in itself a remarkable progression. But how far is this segmentation historically justified? How far indeed are we justified in studying individual lives of monarchs as a method of understanding our history? Which last question is rooted in the further question as to how far, if at all, the individual lives of monarchs have actually affected the course of events. These are the legitimate enquiries which the protagonists of biography have to answer, if they are to justify the theory as well as the practice.

Let us take the last question first: it will be obvious to all but the most dedicated supporters of the Marxist theory of history that the personalities and peculiar characteristics of various sovereigns played at least some part in the shaping of events. For this view, the present volume certainly provides ample evidence. It is not only the more obvious examples which spring to mind, although it is easy to cite such: the innate weaknesses of King Charles I undoubtedly affected the course of the Civil War period, just as the coincidental inability of George I to speak English or understand England unarguably allowed ministerial politics to develop freely during his reign. The highly moral family life of Queen Victoria gave its character to an entire British age, which not for nothing bore her name. It is inconceivable that the English Reformation would have taken precisely the form it did had not the personality of Henry VIII been shaped as it was. England in the age of Elizabeth would surely not have developed as it did, under the aegis of a different sovereign, as for example under her cousin Mary Queen of Scots, a woman of totally conflicting nature to say nothing of religion. It hardly needs pointing out along these lines that the religion of England changed with the death of Edward VI, and again with the death of Mary Tudor.

But there are subtler points, if we look deeper into our chronicles. Did the amiability of Stephen, compared with the arrogance of Matilda, affect their respective fortunes? How much did the likes and dislikes of Queen Anne, which at first sight had a strong effect on the changing fortunes of the newborn political parties, actually do so? The madness of King George III has been much stressed, yet it is possible that his personal integrity during the long years of his sane rule contributed to the preservation of the English throne in an age of European revolution. The personality of King George VI might not at first thought appear one of the most striking in our long line of monarchs. Yet his particular combination of courage and devotion to his people, albeit quietly expressed, enabled the House of Windsor to survive in the Abdication what was surely the greatest crisis of the monarchy since the flight of James II. Once again, in the 1930s, monarchy was under general examination in an age of changing values, and the dutifulness of George VI, continues into wartime, was a factor which cannot be ignored in its survival.

In this volume appear the biographies – albeit told briefly – of each of the men and women who have inherited, or who have seized possession of, the Crown of England since 1066, the most famous date in English history. It was then, with the battle of Hastings, that England came under the sway of Norman kings; and, because of the early establishment of the hereditary principle, the Crown has since that time remained with a succession of ruling families which have changed only when there was no undisputed heir or when there was a violent usurpation. Such changes of dynasty have marked important epochs in English history, and in this book we have followed the course of each from the Normans to the present-day House of Windsor.

More than nine hundred years of monarchy present widely different problems of scope and perspective for the historian. For medieval times records are relatively few and the personalities of the sovereigns, in a period when their actions were decisive in shaping the course of events, remain on the whole shadowy and insubstantial. In later times there is a wealth of material and we know far more about the characters of the monarchs; but their roles become more difficult to interpret as the scope of government widened and the Crown's role within it changed. In this book we have not attempted to impose any artificial uniformity or pattern of approach; rather, we have invited individual historians to write their own interpretations of the lives of the sovereigns in their own specialist field of interest. What emerges is, I trust, a book which is not only a biographical guide to England's kings and queens but also a contribution to the understanding of the overall development of English history.

Such a volume inevitably calls into question the interesting subject of hereditary kingship. It is a topic on which time's revolutions have brought about some striking changes in general thinking. The death of Charles I caused a *frisson* of horror in Europe, and understandably so, since the execution of an anointed king threatened in theory every crowned head. And from the time of the French Revolution onwards, despite the restoration of the English hereditary principle under Charles II, it might be said to have been heavily under fire. In this attack, the history of the United States under elected presidents certainly made a notable contribution. After the American Declaration of Independence, England was often seen as being weighed down by a hereditary monarchy and a hereditary royal family of princes and princesses. Recently, however, as Americans tend to create their own 'royal families' out of the families of their presidents, and as European presidents come and go, not always with the ceremonial grace of the hereditary British royal family, it is notable that there has been some rethinking on the subject: if the desire for ceremony is inherent in human nature, then at least our royal family is trained for the job. In the eighteenth century Gibbon had some wise words to say on the subject: 'Of the various forms of government which have prevailed in the world, an hereditary monarchy seems to present the fairest scope for ridicule. Is it possible to relate without an indignant smile, that, on the father's decease, the property of a nation, like that of a drove of oxen, descends to his infant son, as yet unknown to mankind and to himself; and that the bravest warriors and the wisest statesmen, relinquishing their natural right to empire, approach the royal cradle with bended knees and protestations of inviolable fidelity . . .' Nevertheless, 'The superior prerogative of birth, when it has obtained the sanction of time and popular opinion, is the plainest and least invidious of all distinctions amongst mankind . . . To the firm establishment of this idea we owe the peaceful succession and mild administration of European monarchies.' These words, if not totally apposite to the present situation, would at least find more echoes today than in time gone by.

The strengths and weaknesses of the hereditary principle are fully demonstrated in the pages which follow. One observes how it has in fact, *pace* Gibbon, not infrequently been breached, when the incumbent was not up to the task before him, for one reason or another: like animals, the herd have tended to drive out their leader when they considered him too weak to tame them or hold them in check. Edward II is rightly described here as 'a standing indictment of hereditary monarchy', just as his father, the mighty Edward I, with his extreme toughness in any situation which demanded it, could be claimed as a justification for it. But one would have to admit that Edward III, that unlikely son of his *fainéant* father, was another witness for the defence, so that at least the wretched Edward II propagated the right type of species to rule, if he could not rule himself. Of Henry VI, it is rightly observed that 'if the man was a saint, the King was a political simpleton'. James II, Richard III, and in a manner of speaking Edward VIII, for different reasons could not hold their position. Henry VII, a strong man but without any particularly strong hereditary claim and, like George I, living in an age when there were others whose purely hereditary claims were preferable, survived through strength to found a dynasty. Charles II provides an interesting example of the ambivalence at the heart of the question: as a monarch he undoubtedly fortified the succession politically, and yet by failing to provide a legitimate heir, condemned the country on his death to the care of his unsatisfactory brother, a king who was almost bound to undermine by his personality all his elder brother had achieved.

How much of this is, historically speaking, distortion? Obviously no one is suggesting that history should be studied entirely through the lives of kings and queens. One ignores social history at one's peril; economic history is a rich field in itself, if full of unsuspected quagmires, and few would go as far as Emerson in postulating that 'there is no history, only biography'. In a certain sense, all written history is a form of distortion, and biography is merely imposing one of a number of possible patterns. Yet it does have a particular use, not only in its own right, but also as the groundwork for more generalised studies. After all, the most brilliant generalisations can properly only be made on the basis of biographical studies of much detail: Emerson's point is a valid one, taken from the angle that the most sweeping statement can only be historically valid if the accumulated biographies of the people concerned support the theory. The relative influence of each monarch, the personal involvement of Henry VIII in the Reformation, the interplay of his desires and his statecraft, all this must be taken into account before any kind of remarkable generalisation about the trends of the age is brought to birth.

The value of biography is surely just this specificity. In his *Poetics*, Aristotle contrasted the function of the historian and the poet – 'The true difference is that one relates what has happened, the other what may happen . . . poetry tends to express the universal, history the particular.' One might adapt Aristotle's distinction nowadays to the relative functions of the historian and the biographer. There are obvious traps lying in wait for those historians who aim to propound a general theory of history, particularly if it leads them into predictions which are not fulfilled or a highly stylised series of abstractions. It is just this sort of trap which is avoided by the specific nature of biography. Aristotle, distinguishing once again between poetry and history, wrote that 'the poet should prefer probable impossibilities to improbable possibilities'. The biographer interests himself or herself in improbable actualities.

It still has to be considered whether such reigning men and women as lie within the confines of the present study are being inflated beyond their deserts, simply on grounds of their royal birth. In a challenging article, 'Fiction in History', A. J. P. Taylor took the medieval historian Bruce Macfarlane to task for describing Henry V as 'the greatest man that ever ruled

England'. He questioned not only whether the famous warrior king was great compared to Churchill, let alone Cromwell, before going on to state more categorically: 'I doubt whether he was much improvement on Ramsay MacDonald. Looking around the crowned heads who have bestrewn the European stage over the centuries, I cannot see any other than Frederick the Great as a man of more than common abilities, and even his abilities were on the thin side. Of course many kings conducted the affairs of state in a reasonably competent way just as the wealthy man who inherits a great industrial undertaking makes a tolerable chairman of the board. But we cannot be content with that. We manufacture heroes simply because they occupy great position . . .' This of course is an extreme statement of the view. I am convinced that the present volume demonstrates not only that with kings and queens – as with family firms – there were heroes as well as anti-heroes, and of course mediocrities as well, but also that these individuals, whatever their precise nature, did have a profound effect on our history.

Of course, had these biographies all been written by Carlyle, who considered that the history of the world was but the history of great men, we should have been presented with a gallery of heroes. Lytton Strachey would have endowed us no doubt, if not with anti-heroes, at least with heroes or heroines whose whole bodies, to say nothing of their feet, were made of clay. But it is to be hoped that we live in a cooler age when neither extreme of attitude is necessary. In contrast, it cannot be denied that in the nineteenth century, heroism was an important putative element in any chosen biographical subject. A. J. Cockshut pointed out in his study of nineteenth-century biography, *Truth to Life*, that throughout the period there was 'a persistent attempt to establish heroism' and even if it were not successful, 'the assumption remained that the fundamental reason for writing a man's life was that he was admirable'. It is easy to understand how George Eliot was brought to the opinion that biographies were the disease of English literature. It was exactly this assumption which Lytton Strachey intended to extinguish with the cold water of his lively criticism, or as he put it himself, to replace the two thick hagiographical volumes in which reputations were so often interred.

It is pleasant to record that in our own day we seem to have benefited from the corrective influence of Lytton Strachey in terms of style and presentation, without inheriting, it is to be hoped, his somewhat wayward treatment of historical truth. What are the other elements which go to make up excellence? Another important element might seem to be sympathy, such as the Stricklands possessed – and yet on second glance that is not necessarily so, and as this volume shows, it is possible to sum up some unsympathetic monarchs with equal verve. If sympathy were always an essential, or for that matter self-identification, then it would be impossible to write about Henry VIII, in terms of the latter, without six wives, an arduous assignment for any practising historian, or in terms of the former, to attempt an analysis of William II in the first place.

No, the real essential virtue of biography, if it is to succeed as an art, is surely that of balance. There are two aspects to this quality of balance. In the first place, there is the vital assessment of the evidence, or as Professor Elton put it, in *The Practice of History*: 'there is a single question which the researcher must ask himself in assessing his evidence: how and why did this come into existence?' and he goes on to divide the evidence into two categories, 'that produced specifically for the historian's attention, and that produced for some other purpose'. It is, concretely put, the distinction between chronicles, memoirs, notes of self-justification and letters intended for publication on the one hand, and state papers and law reports on the other. Secondly – and this is always crucial with regard to sovereigns – there is the proper balancing of the subject in relation to the age in which he lived, in order that the reproaches of A. J. P. Taylor can be anticipated and avoided.

It seems to me that even in a brief biography the point of view of the monarch concerned should be given, along with his political setting. And then there are other standards by which a reign should be judged, other than those of pure politics. Henry III, Richard II and George IV might all be cited as examples of monarchs under whose auspices the arts flourished in our country, and civilisation itself was enhanced, even if they were not politically successful. Kings and queens should never be allowed to degenerate into mere hierarchical figures, otherwise this segmentation by reigns will tend to fall into the category of artificial division. Should the biographer take it upon him or herself to judge the subject? There is always an inherent danger in moral judgements, made about another age, whose moral standards were undoubtedly, for better or for worse, so very different from our own. Nor do these standards stand still after a hundred years or so: there is always the potentiality of further change, which will leave the historian's over-strident moral condemnation stranded and out of fashion even with his own time. The homosexuality of James I provides a case in point. It used to be much condemned by biographers whose disapproval sometimes extended to every aspect of the King's career. A blanket condemnation, based on tastes outside 'normal' family life, was clearly too extreme. The attitude of our own day to these matters is certainly permissive, in the sense that it attempts to be based on understanding how such developments should come about. Yet it would be quite wrong for any biographer writing now to ignore the widespread damage done to King James's career by the political – as opposed to sexual – status of his male favourites. It was the political phenomenon which preoccupied King James's own contemporaries.

There is one respect in which the biographer of royal personages should find it an easier task to maintain balance than those who delineate the more lowly born. For such, the period of childhood is often a very difficult field to till, since the words 'obscure origins' only too often mean exactly what they say. Before 1500, kings and queens are in the fortunate but small class of those about whom we know at least something of their dates and the details of their personal appearance. In the same way, the enormous problem that other biographers face of how to keep their subject in the centre of the book, at a moment when he was not in the centre of the stage in his own time, is in some measure solved for the royal biographer. Monarchs tended to be central, at any rate for large periods of their lives, giving their biographers a natural advantage.

There is another asset at their command. It has always appeared to me very much the duty of the biographer to discuss, analyse and if necessary dismiss the myths which gather about the subject. Sovereigns, because they represent their people, gather more myths than those rolling stones, their subjects. Biography does not consist totally in the selection of the facts. Nor should these myths be dismissed out of hand, even if demonstrably untrue, since the legends with which a people surrounds its ruler can tell us much about the age, the nature of monarchy at the time, and finally the man himself. Analysing these myths in *The Undergrowth of History*, Robert Birley wrote that such apocryphal stories generally survive because they encapsulate a true facet of a historical period, however false the facts on which they are based. Thus the story of Alfred and the cakes expresses the extreme destitution of the monarchy at that date, just as the story of Elizabeth, Raleigh and the cloak illustrates the chivalrous hold on her subjects' imagination which the Virgin Queen had been careful to cultivate as a measure of government.

Is there some further merit to the reading of biography other than the pleasure it gives, and the information it provides? Perhaps there are lessons to be learned, as Machiavelli thought the ancient Romans could teach his age of the Renaissance via *The Discourses* and Gibbon too believed something could be learned from ancient Rome. I myself am constantly struck by the insights to be derived from the perusal of history – the reign of William I for example is an apposite study in an age which has seen Britain's entry into the Common Market. The ultimate effects of the Conquest, whether good or bad, are still discussed, followed by a prolonged and at times fierce Euro debate; but at least the ruthless suppression of the previous English ruling class, with its subsequent loss of culture and richness, at the hands of the Normans, must be seen to be bad, however highly – or lowly – continental involvement is rated. So that from the reign of William I one lesson at least can be learned: that integration should never mean the exclusion for the future of a native culture.

There are many other obvious parallels according to individual taste. One is from the position of Queen Elizabeth I as a woman in a world previously dominated by men and holding her own most successfully, a topic that has risen to the fore again. Then there is the loss of America in the reign of George III, when our present Queen also has presided over the disintegration of an empire, although even here, as Andrew Roberts points out in the final chapter, with a monarch who reigns but does not rule, Queen Elizabeth II's personal enthusiasm for the Commonwealth played its part. In a very different time, the debatable character of Richard III provides at least an example of a career in which much administrative good work was fatally vitiated by one alleged evil deed. There will be favourite parallels, as there will be favourite monarchs – there always have been. One might quote Pieter Geyl, the great historian of *Napoleon – For and Against*, who said that history is an argument without an end. In the course of this argument, the biography of kings and queens has an honourable place, and can be said perhaps to be a study without an end, and an enjoyable one.

COATS OF ARMS

by J. P. Brooke-Little
Richmond Herald of Arms

ONE OF THE FASCINATIONS OF ROYAL HERALDRY IS the way in which the development of the royal arms reflects the story of the kings and queens who bore them. Territorial claims and acquisitions, conquests and sometimes changes of dynasty have been mirrored in the arms of the sovereigns. To call heraldry 'the shorthand of history' is perhaps an extravagant claim but it certainly adds another and colourful dimension to the study of history.

Looked at from another angle, a knowledge of royal heraldry enables the student of history to identify and so date innumerable artefacts for, understandably, representations of the royal arms are manifold. To a great extent arms are used wherever they can beautify or identify. As no one boasts greater possessions nor wider patronage than the Crown, so the mark, that is the arms, of the Crown is to be found everywhere, from on a mouldering thirteenth-century tomb to a jar of the Queen's favourite marmalade.

I have always maintained that heraldry was originally a haphazard way of decorating shields and flags, which was moulded into an ordered form of personal symbolism by the ceremonial officers of the Crown, the heralds. Hence the study of coats of arms came to be called heraldry; the principal business of the heralds.

We know, from the evidence of tombs and seals, that the early Norman kings and nobles used decorated shields but, from the same evidence, we also know that these were not used consistently and do not appear to have been inherited. Yet, by the beginning of the thirteenth century, a system of hereditary symbolism, obeying definite canons of design, was everywhere in use by the nobility. Not only that but the nobles jealously guarded both their right to use certain devices and the right of the whole noble caste to be distinguished from lesser men by the bearing of arms. Obviously order could not have emerged from chaos so swiftly if the process had not been accelerated by someone and it is my contention that it was the heralds who did this. After all, it was very much in their interests to do so, for they marshalled the feudal host and the great tournaments and so needed to know who was who. A well-designed coat of arms freely displayed on the coat armour (the coat worn over the mail; hence the term coat of arms for that which was shown on it), shield, flag and horse trappings made it easy to recognise a man from a distance. The advent of heraldry must have made the job of the medieval herald much less arduous. All he had to do was to remember who bore what arms; this he did by making rolls and books of arms, many of which are still extant.

As I have suggested, an important aspect of heraldry is its hereditary character. A coat of arms is inherited, in much the same way as a surname, by the legitimate descendants of the person to whom the arms were first assigned or allowed. Another characteristic of heraldry is that no two people shall bear the same coat. How is this apparent contradiction resolved? By the use of brisures for cadency or, in layman's terms, the adding by junior members of a family of small marks, such as a star or crescent, to the arms of the head. In medieval times, when it was necessary to recognise these distinctive marks from afar, they were more dramatic and could involve a change of colour or of a fairly major feature in a coat, but when heraldry left the battlefield for the book plate the need for such changes disappeared and more modest distinctions were used. Today the rule that junior members of a family must add an appropriate mask of difference to their arms is often more honoured in the breach than the observance, except in the royal family.

Royal heraldry differs from ordinary, familial heraldry in that the arms of the monarch are not personal arms but arms of dominion or sovereignty. If it were otherwise the Queen would bear a most complicated shield containing the various coats borne by her paternal family of Saxe-Coburg-Gotha and the Prince of Wales would bear his father's not his mother's arms. The sovereign bears arms to represent his possessions and his children bear them likewise but with such differences as shall be assigned to them. According to heraldic law a woman bears her father's arms on a lozenge (a diamond shape) without helmet crest or mantling until she marries, when she bears her husband's arms in conjunction with her own. In royal heraldry this is not the case. The sovereign is always regarded as masculine and never bears arms conjoined in any way with those of his or her wife or husband. If the sovereign is a woman then her children will be assigned her royal arms and will not, as in familial heraldry, automatically inherit their father's arms at birth.

In the pages accompanying the coats of arms I shall trace how, when and why the royal arms have, from time to time, been altered to symbolise the dominions over which the English kings have reigned or, in one noted case, have hoped to reign.

List of Coats of Arms

Some Attributed Arms of Pre-Norman Kings *44*
The Arms of the Norman Kings *46*
The Arms of Edward III and Richard II *96*
The Royal Arms in the Fifteenth Century *150*
The Arms of Henry VII and Henry VIII *180*
The Arms of Philip and Elizabeth I *192*
The Arms of the Stuarts *226*
The Royal Arms 1707–1837 *242*
The Royal Arms *318*

THE NORMANS
1066–1154

WILLIAM I 1066–87
WILLIAM II 1087–1100
HENRY I 1100–35
STEPHEN 1135–54

Opposite: A fourteenth-century genealogical tree of
William the Conqueror and his Norman successors.

THE NORMANS AND ANGEVINS

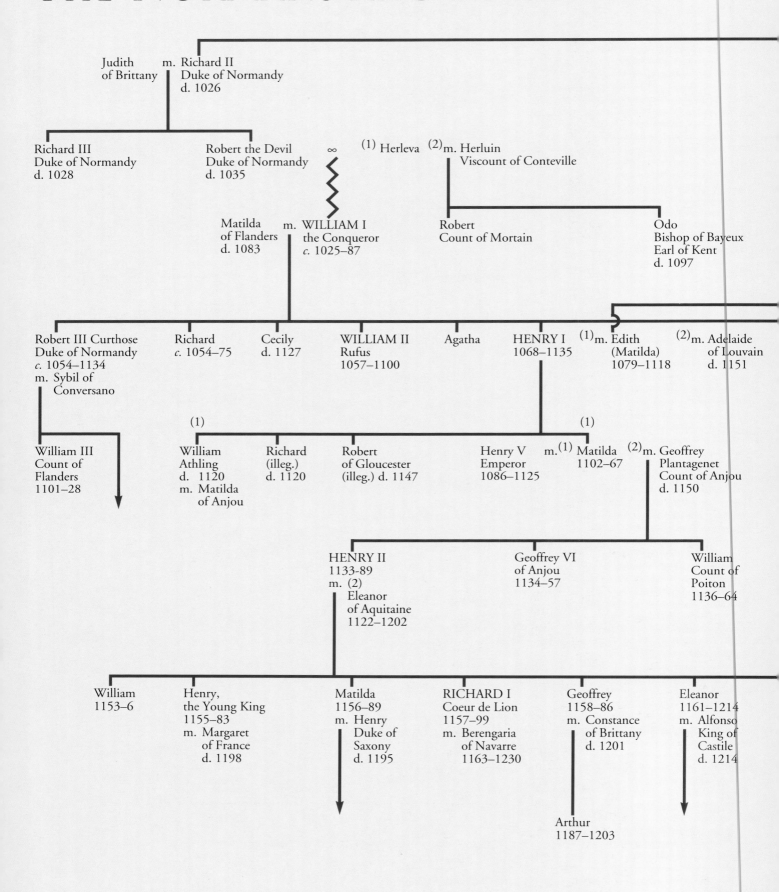

Judith of Brittany — m. Richard II, Duke of Normandy, d. 1026

Richard III, Duke of Normandy, d. 1028

Robert the Devil, Duke of Normandy, d. 1035 ∞ (1) Herleva — (2) m. Herluin, Viscount of Conteville

Matilda of Flanders, d. 1083 — m. WILLIAM I the Conqueror, c. 1025–87

Robert, Count of Mortain

Odo, Bishop of Bayeux, Earl of Kent, d. 1097

Robert III Curthose, Duke of Normandy, c. 1054–1134, m. Sybil of Conversano

Richard, c. 1054–75

Cecily, d. 1127

WILLIAM II Rufus, 1057–1100

Agatha

HENRY I, 1068–1135 (1) m. Edith (Matilda), 1079–1118 (2) m. Adelaide of Louvain, d. 1151

William III, Count of Flanders, 1101–28

(1) William Athling, d. 1120, m. Matilda of Anjou

Richard (illeg.), d. 1120

Robert of Gloucester (illeg.), d. 1147

(1) Henry V, Emperor, 1086–1125 — m. (1) Matilda, 1102–67 — (2) m. Geoffrey Plantagenet, Count of Anjou, d. 1150

HENRY II, 1133-89, m. (2) Eleanor of Aquitaine, 1122–1202

Geoffrey VI of Anjou, 1134–57

William, Count of Poiton, 1136–64

William, 1153–6

Henry, the Young King, 1155–83, m. Margaret of France, d. 1198

Matilda, 1156–89, m. Henry Duke of Saxony, d. 1195

RICHARD I Coeur de Lion, 1157–99, m. Berengaria of Navarre, 1163–1230

Geoffrey, 1158–86, m. Constance of Brittany, d. 1201

Eleanor, 1161–1214, m. Alfonso King of Castile, d. 1214

Arthur, 1187–1203

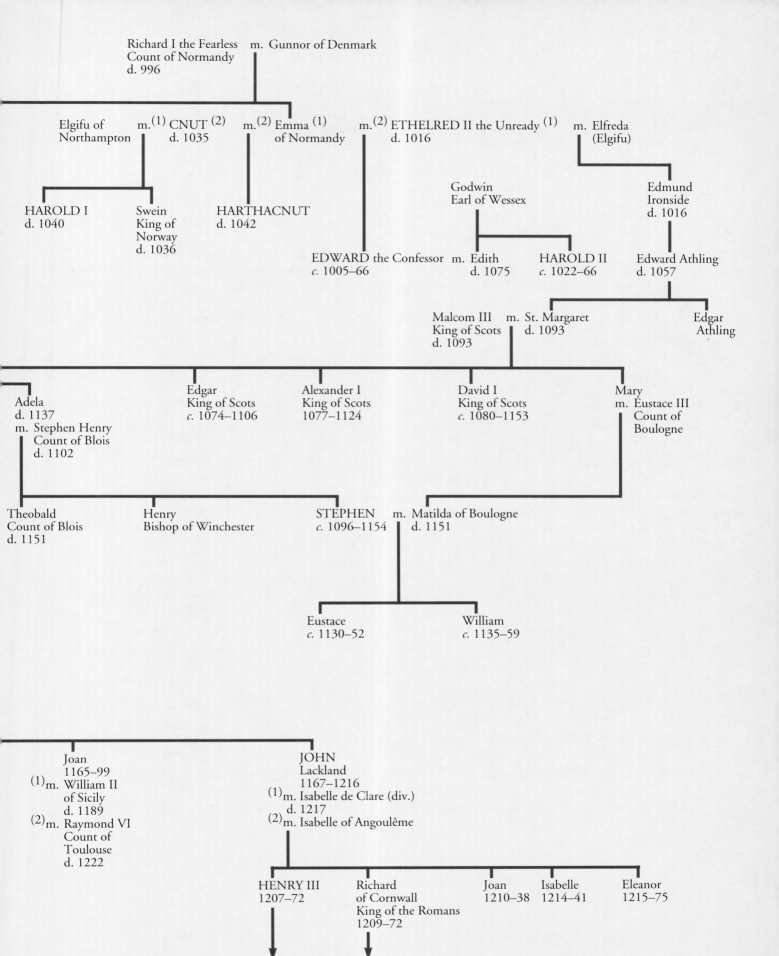

Richard I the Fearless m. Gunnor of Denmark
Count of Normandy
d. 996

Elgifu of   m.(1) CNUT (2) m.(2) Emma (1)   m.(2) ETHELRED II the Unready (1)   m. Elfreda
Northampton   d. 1035   of Normandy   d. 1016   (Elgifu)

HAROLD I   Swein   HARTHACNUT   Edmund
d. 1040   King of   d. 1042   Godwin   Ironside
                  Norway   Earl of Wessex   d. 1016
                  d. 1036

                                   EDWARD the Confessor m. Edith   HAROLD II   Edward Athling
                                   c. 1005–66   d. 1075   c. 1022–66   d. 1057

                                                           Malcom III m. St. Margaret   Edgar
                                                           King of Scots   d. 1093   Athling
                                                           d. 1093

Adela   Edgar   Alexander I   David I   Mary
d. 1137   King of Scots   King of Scots   King of Scots   m. Eustace III
m. Stephen Henry   c. 1074–1106   1077–1124   c. 1080–1153   Count of
    Count of Blois   Boulogne
    d. 1102

Theobald   Henry   STEPHEN m. Matilda of Boulogne
Count of Blois   Bishop of Winchester   c. 1096–1154   d. 1151
d. 1151

                                            Eustace   William
                                            c. 1130–52   c. 1135–59

Joan   JOHN
1165–99   Lackland
(1)m. William II   1167–1216
    of Sicily   (1)m. Isabelle de Clare (div.)
    d. 1189   d. 1217
(2)m. Raymond VI   (2)m. Isabelle of Angoulême
    Count of
    Toulouse
    d. 1222

HENRY III   Richard   Joan   Isabelle   Eleanor
1207–72   of Cornwall   1210–38   1214–41   1215–75
                   King of the Romans
                   1209–72

WILLIAM I

r. 1066–87

WILLIAM WAS BORN AT ABOUT the time that his father, Robert, became Duke of Normandy (1028). William's mother was Herleva, daughter of a wealthy citizen of Falaise. Not long after William was born she was given in marriage to one of Duke Robert's followers and by him she had two more sons: Robert, who became Count of Mortain, and Odo, who was made Bishop of Bayeux in 1049 when he was not yet twenty years old. William therefore was illegitimate and most contemporary writers refer to him as William the Bastard. But he was his father's only son and shortly before Duke Robert went on a pilgrimage to Jerusalem (1034), he persuaded the Norman barons to recognise William as his heir. On the way home Robert died in Asia Minor and so, in 1035, young William found himself Duke of Normandy.

In practice this meant that for the next ten years Normandy was without a ruler and a great deal of disorder went unchecked. William was lucky to survive these years. Several of his cousins would have preferred to see him out of the way. He had some narrow escapes, but survive he did – largely thanks to the support of his mother's kinsmen. William's boyhood was spent among scenes of violence and intrigue. As a result he learned that not many men could be trusted, and those few in whom he did place his trust were mostly the friends he made in childhood.

In the mid-1040s William began to govern for himself. He was almost continuously at war, either against Norman rebels or neighbouring princes, or both. He became a hard and ruthless campaigner – though flatterers liked to say that he was the best knight in the world. His most powerful neighbours were King Henry of France, Count Geoffrey of Anjou and Count Baldwin of Flanders. Between 1052 and 1060 two of these, France and Anjou, were hostile to Normandy so it was well for William that he could count on the friendship of Flanders. He had asked Count Baldwin for the hand of his daughter Matilda, but in 1049 the Pope forbade the marriage, presumably on the grounds that William and Matilda were too closely related. Despite this William went ahead; the Flemish alliance was more important than papal disapproval. William and Matilda must have been an odd-looking couple. The evidence of the bones found in their graves suggests that he was about five foot ten inches tall and she about four foot two inches. But by all accounts it was a successful marriage. She bore at least nine children (four of them sons) and most contemporaries believed that William was never unfaithful to her.

In 1060 both King Henry and Count Geoffrey died. The heir to France was a small boy and in Anjou there was all the trouble of a disputed succession. The consequent weakness of his neighbours left the way clear for William to conquer the county of Maine in 1063 and then turn his eyes on England.

Although William was only a distant cousin of Edward the Confessor, in 1051, perhaps to win Norman support in a quarrel with his powerful father-in-law, Earl Godwin, Edward dangled before William the prospect of succeeding to the English throne. Edward himself was childless and since mon-

Illuminated manuscript of Norman warriors at sea in readiness for battle

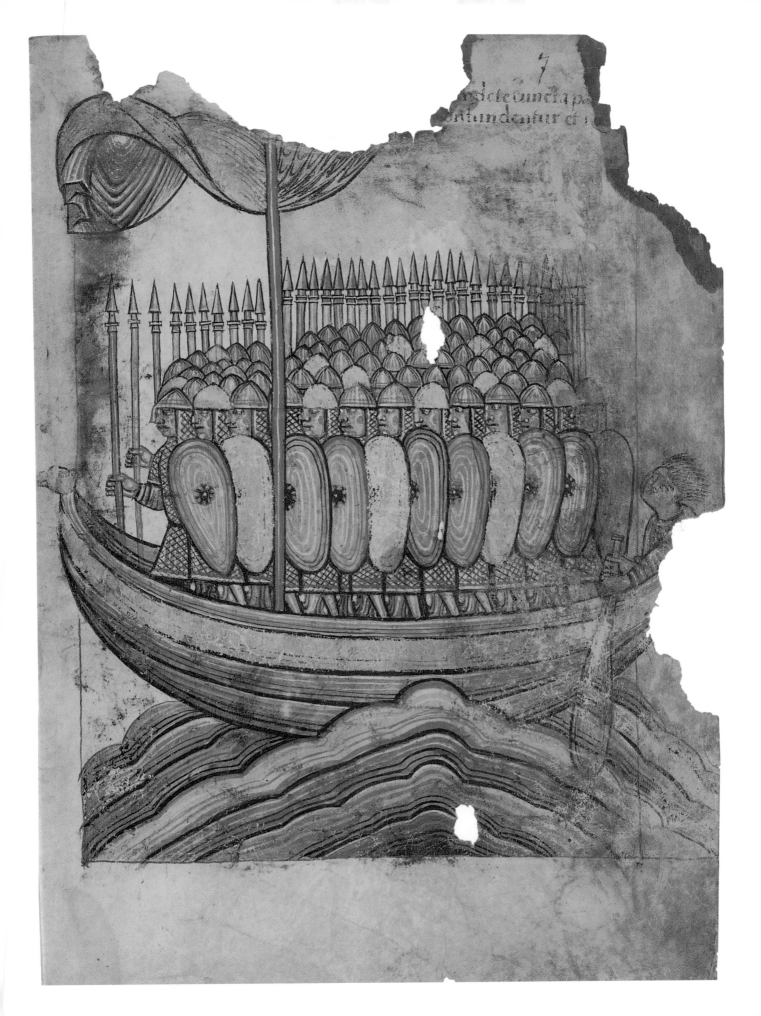

archs were not yet chosen in strict order of heredity, there were several candidates for the succession. Among these was Harold, son of Earl Godwin and brother of Edward's wife Edith. By 1066 Edward was reconciled with the Godwin family, and on his deathbed he nominated Harold, the chief magnate of the kingdom, as his heir.

William felt cheated and prepared at once for an invasion of England. He insisted that Edward had promised him the throne and that, on a visit to Normandy in 1064, Harold had sworn an oath to support his accession; he claimed that Harold was thus both usurper and perjurer and so won papal approval for his expedition. In the careful preparations for invasion William showed himself at his best. It was an enterprise far beyond the resources of his duchy and so he recruited soldiers from all over northern France and Flanders. The prospect of laying hands on the wealth of England, its land and its silver, attracted thousands to his banner. Throughout the spring and summer of 1066 ships were built and military supplies assembled. But however meticulous his preparations, William cannot have expected anything like the rapid and overwhelming success he in fact achieved. It must have seemed likely that he was facing many years of hard campaigning against an enemy whose wealth and military resources were greater than his own. But an extraordinary series of lucky chances brought things to a swift and dramatic conclusion.

By August 1066 William's expeditionary force was ready. If he had sailed when he wanted to he would have found Harold and an English fleet waiting to receive him. If he had managed to defeat the English he would then have had to face another contender for the throne, Harold Hardrada, the King of Norway and a famous Viking warrior. But, as it happened, throughout August and most of September the wind was against William. Merely to

Edward the Confessor on his deathbed in 1066, from the Bayeux Tapestry. This famous tapestry, 231 feet long and 91 inches wide, tells the full story of the Norman Conquest in over seventy scenes. It also offers the Norman case for the legitimacy of William's conquest of England.

hold his waiting army together was, in these circumstances, a great achievement, yet while he impatiently kicked his heels some of his greatest problems were being solved for him. In September Harold Hardrada, accompanied by one of his wives and several of his children, reached the Tyne and then defeated the northern levies in a pitched battle near York. As soon as he heard of the Viking landing Harold Godwinsson marched north and routed Hardrada and his allies at Stamford Bridge on 25 September 1066. Two days later the wind in the Channel changed direction. William set sail and was able to make an unopposed landing at Pevensey. During the next two weeks his soldiers fortified their beachhead and pillaged the area. But what then? Would William dare march far inland, losing

contact with his fleet and the line of communication with Normandy? Fortunately the problem was solved by Harold who came rushing back from the north and allowed William to challenge him to battle. If Harold had held aloof it is hard to see what William could have done, but Harold was confident of his military prowess and, as a new king with an uncertain title, he wished to see the matter settled once and for all. Thus on 14 October 1066 the two armies met at Hastings.

After a long and desperately hard struggle William's skilful handling of a combined force of archers and cavalry enabled him to break down the English shield wall. The fact that Harold and his brothers died fighting meant that after Hastings there was no leader capable of organising further resistance.

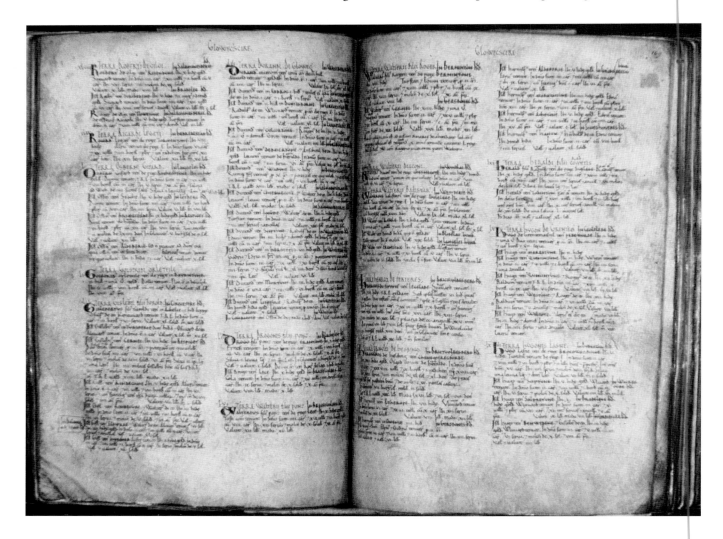

The English earls and bishops hesitated, took a few indecisive steps and then decided to submit. On Christmas Day 1066 William was crowned in Westminster Abbey. In February 1067 he returned to Normandy leaving his half-brother Odo of Bayeux, now Earl of Kent, in charge. Apart from the destruction of the Godwinsson dynasty he left the English scene much as he had found it. All this, however, was to change as a result of the events of the next four years. All over England revolts broke out. They were unplanned and unco-ordinated. Some of the leaders, like Hereward the Wake, passed into legend, but none of them was capable of more than local action. Thus William was able to deal with one minor uprising after another and by 1071 he had subdued the whole country. The turbulent north had been devastated. Several hundred castles had been built and within their walls the outnumbered Normans could sleep safely. William punished rebels by confiscating their estates and giving them to Normans. Thus the native English aristocracy was wiped out. Within the areas covered by the Domesday Book only two English landowners of any note survived the Norman flood.

The English Church suffered the same fate as the English nobility. At William's request papal legates deposed five English bishops in 1070. They were replaced by men from the continent. Outstanding among them was Lanfranc, the new Archbishop of Canterbury. From now on whenever a bishop or an abbot died the same policy was pursued. By 1096 there was not a single bishopric or important abbey in English hands. The traditional learning and liturgy of the English Church was treated with contempt by men educated in the schools of Europe. Probably no other conquest in European history ever had such disastrous consequences for the defeated ruling class. This had not been intended, for William was a conservative by temperament; but he was also ruthless and when events pushed him to destroy then he destroyed thoroughly. His own prestige and power were of course tremendously enhanced. He was able to bestow huge gifts of land upon his followers without impoverishing himself. As for England, that was now ruled by a French-speaking aristocracy and although the broad outline of the social structure

Opposite: *Pages from the Domesday Book, a list of every major landowner and their sources of revenue that was compiled by commissioners, who started work in 1086 on William's orders. He had this enormous task undertaken to enable him to assess the wealth of the kingdom that he had conquered as he needed to know what resources were available to him.*
Above: *Illuminated manuscript of William, bearing the royal arms, riding with his soldiers. From the Liber Legum Antiquorum Regum, c. 1321.*

remained unchanged, there was an entirely new and alien ruling class; the language barrier only served to widen the gulf between it and the peasantry.

After 1071 William's hold on England was fairly secure and he came to regard it chiefly as a source of revenue. The extensive royal estates and the sophisticated English financial machinery brought in huge sums. The Welsh and the Scots gave him little trouble; Scandinavian rulers continued to look greedily towards England but the ever-present threat of another Viking invasion never quite materialised. From 1071 to 1084 most of William's attention was taken up by war and diplomacy on the continent. Normandy was his homeland and far more vulnerable to sudden attack than was his island kingdom. Moreover the King of France and the Counts of Anjou and Flanders were alarmed by William's newly acquired power and took every opportunity to diminish it. Their best opportunities were provided by William's eldest son Robert (born 1054). Recognised as the heir to Normandy as long ago as 1066 he had never been permitted to enjoy either money or power and from 1078 onwards he became involved in a series of intrigues, a tool in the hands of William's enemies. In one skirmish William was actually wounded by his son.

Then in 1085 William returned to England with a huge army of mercenaries ready to counter the invasion planned by King Swein of Denmark. The administrative effort involved in catering for this army seems to have persuaded William that he ought

to have more precise information about the distribution of wealth among his barons. So in 1086 commissioners were sent from shire to shire and the results of their inquiries are now enshrined in the Domesday Book. It listed the major landholders in each county and provided William with a remarkably full description of their sources of revenue. But although the book has been of great value to historians, it seems unlikely that William was able to make much use of it. Before the end of the year he had been recalled to Normandy. Once again he found himself campaigning against the King of France and, as usual, the war was concentrated in the Vexin, a disputed territory lying between Rouen and Paris. In July 1087 William launched a surprise attack on Mantes and took it, but during the sack of the town he received the injury from which, on 9 September, he died. His body was carried to the church of St Stephen at Caen for burial. Unfortunately during the last few years he had grown very fat. King Philip of France used to say that he looked like a pregnant woman. When the attendants tried to force his body into the stone sarcophagus it burst and filled the church with a foul smell. It was an unpleasant ending, but unlike many kings he had unquestionably lived more successfully than he died. Few kings can have enjoyed so much luck as William the Bastard, but few took such full advantage of their good fortune as William the Conqueror, founder of a new royal dynasty.

WILLIAM II

r. 1087–1100

WILLIAM, THE THIRD SON OF William of Normandy and Matilda, was born about 1057. Almost nothing is known of his youth, but it is at least clear that the time he spent in the household of Archbishop Lanfranc made little impression upon him. He was deeply attached to his father and while Robert rebelled, William never wavered in his loyalty. When Richard, the second son, died in a hunting accident in the New Forest it seemed possible that William might take Robert's place as chief heir. William, moreover, was at the bedside of the dying King to hear his last wishes while Robert remained at the court of his father's enemy, Philip of France. But the custom which gave the ancestral lands, the patrimony, to the first-born son proved too strong. Robert succeeded to Normandy. To William, however, the old King gave his newly conquered land, England. Following the instructions of the old King's will, Lanfranc crowned William at Westminster on 26 September 1087. Like his father, William was inclined to stoutness. He had fair hair, piercing eyes, a red face (thus his nickname Rufus) and a tendency to stutter when excited.

The division of the Conqueror's lands created political difficulties. Many Norman lords held estates on both sides of the Channel. Their dilemma was summed up by the greatest of them, the new King's uncle, Odo of Bayeux. 'How can we give proper service to two mutually hostile and distant lords? If we serve Duke Robert well we shall offend his brother William, and he will deprive us of our revenues and honours in England. On the other hand if we obey King William, Duke Robert will deprive us of our patrimonies in Normandy.' By 1088 it was already plain that some barons, inspired by Odo, would prefer to have Robert as their lord on both sides of the sea. But Robert failed to appear in England, William acted firmly and the revolt soon collapsed. Now it was the younger brother's turn. In 1089 he laid claim to Normandy. With English silver he was able to buy support in Normandy. Gradually

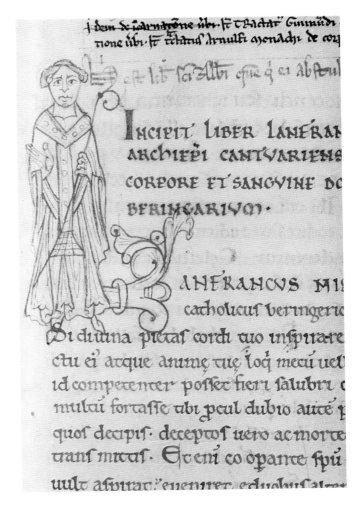

The opening of a surviving manuscript of the Book of Lanfranc, Archbishop of Canterbury, in whose house William Rufus spent some of his youth and who crowned him.

Robert's position became more and more difficult until in 1096 he was glad to join the crusade preached by Pope Urban II. In order to equip himself and his retinue for the long march he pawned Normandy to William for 10,000 marks.

The new Duke's main task was to recover Maine and the Vexin, lost during Robert's slack rule. By 1099 he had successfully accomplished this. In England meanwhile he had, in 1095, suppressed a rebellion led by Robert Mowbray, Earl of Northumberland. In Wales and Scotland the Normans were on the march again. On every front William's combination of diplomacy, bribery and war proved effective; an archbishop of Lyons referred to him as 'the victorious King of the English'.

Yet for all his success as a generous leader of soldiers William's reputation has remained consistently low. Unfortunately for him the history of the time was written almost entirely by monks and they did not like him; nor did he respect them. On one occasion when a monk came to him to report a dream in which he had foreseen William's death, the King dismissed him mockingly – 'he is a monk and so, of course, he dreams for money'. After the death of Lanfranc in 1089 Rufus seemed to throw off all restraints. Serious-minded churchmen, accustomed to the conventional piety and sober discretion of his father's court, were appalled by the gaiety and licentiousness which prevailed under his son. Since neither mistresses nor illegitimate children are ever mentioned in connection with William it is possible that he was a homosexual. He never married. He was sceptical of religion's claims and treated the Church purely as a rich corporation which needed taxing. He was never in a hurry to appoint bishops and abbots, for during vacancies he could help himself to the Church's revenues. In carrying out these profitable policies Rufus relied on the ingenious aid of the quick-witted and worldly clerk Ranulf Flambard, whom he eventually made Bishop of Durham.

Above all, William's reputation has suffered because in 1093 when he thought he was dying he appointed a saint as Archbishop of Canterbury (after keeping the see vacant for four years). What made this appointment so disastrous from William's point of view was the fact that it occurred at a time when a European movement for Church reform was creating an atmosphere in which saints were only too likely to become political radicals. The new Archbishop was Anselm, a scholar monk who had previously been Abbot of Bec. As a Norman abbot Anselm had already sworn to obey Urban II; but in England neither Urban II nor his rival Clement III were recognised as Pope. William, following in his father's footsteps, preferred to remain uncommitted and he was angry when Anselm took it for granted that Urban was the rightful Pope. In 1095 the King called a council at Rockingham in order to settle this and other matters which were in dispute between him and Anselm. But to the consternation of all, Anselm appealed to Rome, claiming that as Archbishop of Canterbury he could not be judged in a secular court. This was too much for Rufus who now determined to rid himself of the Archbishop. He would even recognise Urban if the Pope, in his turn, would depose Anselm. A papal legate was sent to England and Urban was publicly proclaimed as the canonical Pope; but this achieved, the legate would make no move against Anselm. Dismayed by the failure of his plot William continued to harass the Archbishop and he never showed any sympathy for his attempts to reform the Church. Eventually Anselm could bear it no longer. In 1097 he sailed from Dover, leaving the Canterbury estates to be taken into the King's hands.

Besides helping to blacken William's reputation, the quarrel with Anselm is a significant indication of the growing importance of the papacy. For centuries no one had taken much notice of the bishops of Rome but now, as a result of the eleventh-century Gregorian reform movement (named after its most zealous advocate, Pope Gregory VII), they began to wield an influence which not even Rufus could entirely ignore. In the short run, however, William II had gained from the quarrel. In 1100 he enjoyed the revenues of three bishoprics and twelve abbeys. Nor was there as yet any sign that the conflict had tarnished men's belief in the potency of royal magic. Even Eadmer, the Canterbury monk who wrote the *Life of Anselm*, noted that 'the wind and the sea seemed to obey him. Whenever he wished to cross from England to Normandy or back again every storm – and sometimes the storm was raging wildly –

Pope Urban II preaches the First Crusade at the Council of Clermont in 1095. In order to join the crusade William I's eldest son Robert pawned Normandy to his brother William II.

was stilled so that his crossings were always attended by a wonderful calm.' Indeed, Eadmer went on, 'in war and in the acquisition of territory he enjoyed such success that you would think the whole world smiling upon him.'

But on 2 August 1100, at the height of his success and full of plans for further conquests, William was struck down by an arrow while out hunting in the New Forest. It may have been an accident, or murder. His body was carried to Winchester and interred in the cathedral directly below the main tower. In the following year the tower collapsed – though, as one monk wrote, 'it might have collapsed anyway, even if he had not been buried there'.

HENRY I

r. 1100–35

HENRY, THE FOURTH SON OF William and Matilda, was born in England in 1068. He was better educated than his brothers and felt at ease in the company of learned men. From this time onwards the Kings of England were normally able to read. From his dying father he received no land, but was given instead £5,000 in silver – an enormous sum. At once he left the old King's bedside and hurried to the Treasury to supervise the weighing out of the money. When his elder brothers, Robert of Normandy and William of England, quarrelled, he flitted from side to side, always seeking his own advantage and eventually making himself thoroughly distrusted by both. In 1091 they were temporarily reconciled and marched together against Henry. They made a treaty whereby they agreed that if either died without leaving a legitimate son he would be succeeded by the other. This was to disinherit Henry.

When Robert went on crusade Henry's hopes naturally rose. Should the childless William die now, he was the man on the spot and the obvious heir. But by the summer of 1100 everyone knew that Robert was on his way home, accompanied by a rich and beautiful wife and basking in the prestige due to a man who had fought his way into Jerusalem. Henry's chance seemed to be slipping away from him. Perhaps it was just coincidence that William died when he did and where he did – for Henry too was hunting in the New Forest on 2 August 1100. As soon as he knew that his brother was dead Henry moved fast; it was as though he had been prepared for this to happen. He rode to Winchester and took possession of the Treasury. From there he went straight on to Westminster where he was crowned on 5 August. On the same day he issued his coronation charter, in which he renounced the oppressive practices of his brother and promising good government.

A few weeks later Robert arrived back in Normandy. Henry had to prepare to meet the inevitable invasion. His policy was to buy support by granting favours and making wide-ranging concessions along the lines laid down in the coronation charter. 'If they ask for it given them York or even London' was the advice given to Henry by his shrewdest counsellor Count Robert of Meulan. By inviting Anselm to return to England he hoped to win over both the English church and the papacy; by marrying (in November 1100) Edith, sister of King Edgar of Scotland, he was ensuring that he would not be attacked in the north while he had his hands full in the south. He secured the alliance of France and Flanders, neither of whom wanted to see England and Normandy united under one all-too-powerful ruler. Thus when Robert landed at Portsmouth in July 1101 he found he could make little headway. With Anselm as the intermediary a treaty was arranged. Henry was to keep England and pay his brother an annual pension of £2,000.

But not for one moment did Henry trust those who had hoped to protect their Norman estates by aiding Duke Robert in 1101. Above all he distrusted the rich and brutal Earl of Shrewsbury, Robert of Bellême, and he systematically set about the task of breaking him. This he accomplished in 1102. He captured Robert's chief strongholds in the Welsh Marches and then banished him. But Robert, like others in his position, found in his Norman properties a safe base from which he could hope to organised the recovery of his English lands. By perpetuating the division of the Conqueror's lands the treaty of 1101 had ensured the continuance of political instability. So the pattern of the previous reign was repeated as Henry gradually manoeuvred himself into a commanding position in Normandy. In 1106 the issue was decided by the battle of Tinchebrai. The knights in Henry's vanguard dismounted in order to beat off the charge of Duke Robert's cavalry. Robert himself was captured in the battle and spent the last twenty-eight years of his life as his brother's prisoner. Other great barons who fell into Henry's hands, including Robert of Bellême, were also condemned to life imprisonment.

Although in the first years of his reign Henry was preoccupied with Norman affairs, he was not as free to concentrate on them as he would have liked. Traditional royal rights over the church were threatened by the new ideas associated with the Gregorian reform movement. The reformers did not only wish to purify the moral and spiritual life of the clergy; in order to do so they believed that it was necessary to free the church from secular control. The most hated symbol of this control was lay investiture, a ceremony in which a new abbot or bishop received the ring and staff of office from the hands of the secular prince who had appointed him. Although the first papal decree against lay investiture had been issued as long ago as 1059 and many more prohibitions had been published since, no one in England seems to have been aware of their existence until Anselm returned in the autumn of 1100. While in exile he had attended papal councils at Bari (1098) and Rome (1099). There he learned of the papal attitude to lay investiture. Thus although he himself had been invested by Rufus in 1093 he now refused either to do homage to Henry or to consecrate those prelates whom Henry had invested. This placed the King in a difficult position. Bishops and abbots were great landowners and key figures in central and local administration; he needed their assistance and had to be sure of their loyalty. On the other hand, unlike Rufus, he was unwilling to provoke a quarrel, so for years he found it more convenient to postpone the problem rather than try to solve it. Henry's delaying

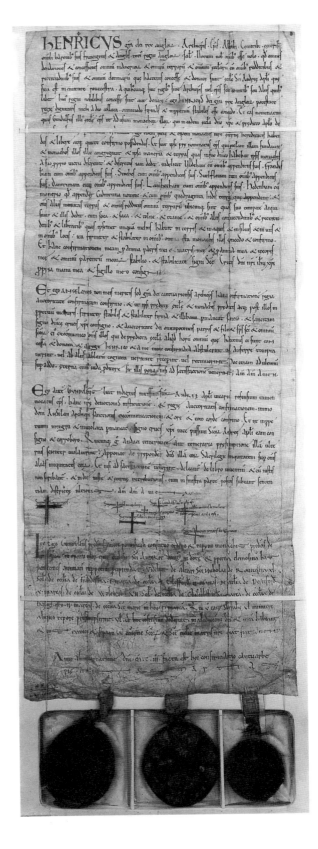

In his coronation charter Henry I promised his subjects good government. From left to right the signatures are: Henry I, Archbishop Anselm, Gilbert, Lord of Tonbridge, Queen Matilda, the Bishop of Rochester, Count Robert of Meulan and Henry, Earl of Warenne.

tactics were intolerable to Anselm and in 1103 he once again took the path into exile.

But then, in 1105, at a critical moment in Henry's Normandy campaign, the Pope threatened to excommunicate him so the King hastened to come to terms. Agreement was reached in 1106 and ratified at a council in London in 1107. Henry renounced lay investiture, but prelates were to continue to do homage for their fiefs. In practice the King's wishes continued to be the decisive factor in the making of bishops. To some extent it can be said that Henry gave up the form but preserved the reality of control. When Anselm died in 1109 he kept the see of Canterbury vacant for five years. Yet he had lost something and he knew it. In the fierce war of propaganda which accompanied the 'Investiture Contest' the Gregorians had insisted that the King was a layman, nothing more, and as such he was inferior to all priests, for priests were concerned with the soul and the King only with the body. The Church could no longer tolerate the old idea that anointed kings were sacred deputies of God. In giving up lay investiture Henry was acknowledging the merely secular nature of his office. It was an important moment in the history of kingship. And yet it is precisely at this time that we first come across the claim that kings possessed a healing magic. It was said that if a person suffering from scrofula were touched by a king, the disease – known as the 'king's evil' – would at once be cleared up. Whatever learned churchmen might say, in popular thought there was still something miraculous in kingship.

Once Normandy had been conquered and a compromise solution found to the investiture dispute, Henry's main concern was to hold on to what he had. Few kings ever did this more tenaciously or effectively. He was a hard man who knew how to keep men loyal; he may not have won their hearts but they looked forward to the rewards he had to offer and they certainly feared his wrath. In 1090 he had pushed a man off the top of Rouen Castle for betraying the oath of allegiance which he had sworn to Duke Robert. With this example before them men took seriously the oaths which they swore to King Henry. The most famous of the King's servants was Roger of Salisbury, the archetypal bureaucrat, competent and discreet. Under his direction there are clear signs of the development of the English civil service, notably the rise of the court of the Exchequer.

Normandy, of course, was the most vulnerable part of his empire and after 1106 Henry spent more than half the remainder of his reign there facing the traditional enemies of the Norman dukes. The year 1118, as described by the Anglo-Saxon Chronicle, was typical. 'King Henry spent the whole of this year in Normandy on account of the war with the King of France, Count of Anjou and Count of Flanders . . . England paid dearly for all this in numerous taxes from which there was no relief all year.' By 1119 all seemed well. Henry, who never risked battle until he had already won the diplomatic war which preceded it, beat King Louis VI of France in the battle of Brémule. Angevin friendship had been secured by the marriage of his only legitimate son, William, to the daughter of the Count of Anjou. But the whole carefully contrived edifice came tumbling down when William was drowned in the wreck of the *White Ship* (November 1120).

From then on the succession problem dominated the politics of the reign. Less than three months after William's death Henry married Adelaide of Louvain (his first wife, Edith, had died in 1118), but the hoped-for heir was never born. So although Henry acknowledged more than twenty bastards he was survived by only one legitimate child, his daughter Matilda. When her husband, the Emperor Henry V of Germany, died in 1125 Henry recalled her to his

Illuminated manuscript page showing the king, top right, sitting on his throne. The French fleur du lys have been incorporated into the background, to the left of the king. Below him is the White Ship *in some distress; it foundered and Prince William, the heir to the throne, was drowned, throwing the king's dynastic ambitions into some disarray.*

Cui successit Henricus frater
eius z regnauit annis xxxvi.
Hic erat pastor ferax z custos
nemor. fuit z sapiens z stre
nuus Dux normannie que
Gayrsinus ambrosius Leonem iusticie
in historia Regum nõiauit ffectr qᷓ eᷟ
iusticium z iusticiam in terra. Duxit qᷓ
vxorem generosam z optimam de
nobili genere anglor. z Ditionu p
quam multum sibi confederauit reg
num scilicet filiam pncipis sui Alba
nie Vita z morib; ornatam sororem
scilicet Alexandri principis sui Scotie
z dauitis scotie qui postea fuit pnceps
Albanie. Qui uero Rex Henricus psa
tus sedit honorem de huntingdon
cum agathilda cognate sua que erat
vxor prius pmi simonis de scenliz
comitis de huntingdon z norhmp
ton cum custodia puero suoᷓ et dic
concordes ad muicem demde ffecti
fuerunt quia prestus Alexander ven
sicauit sibi uir hereditario corona
z monstrecham totius Regni presta
sicut uerus heres z iustus de uir bon
Regis Edwardi ultimi. Alexn qᷓ dn
sup omnia sitauit qᷓ scdm ecclesiam in
multis p sola. ffectr qᷓ bonu in emeu
totum malum qᷓ descruit uocabitur
gyatild Regina optima (Obiit uo
predictus henricus in normannia
apud S. dones. sepultus enim fuit
in anglia apud Redynges in Alba
thia quam construxerat. gyatilda
uero Regina predicta sepulta fuit
in anglia apud Westmonasteriu
cuius anime spicietur deus.

Hernia nati pelago peunt adañ
ffilia que remanet Impiale tenet.

AL Henricus primus genuit

Willm
qui periit
in mari

Ricm
qui piit
in mari

Matil
dam Im
patrice

Ricardi
qᷓ obiit

Hernia
Regis se
cunda

court and made the barons swear to accept her as their ruler in the event of his dying without a male heir. Somewhat against her will Matilda was then in 1128 married to a sixteen-year-old boy, Geoffrey of Anjou, for Henry was determined to continue the Angevin alliance. But the prospect of being ruled by an Angevin did not please the Norman barons and Geoffrey was well aware of this fact. Thus he asked to be given custody of some key Norman castles while Henry was still alive and able to help. But the old King refused to give up any of his power. The result, in summer 1135, was war. In these melancholy circumstances Henry died, supposedly of a surfeit of lampreys, in December 1135.

Although he ruled for thirty-five years few English kings are as little known as Henry I. Careful, sober, harsh and methodical he chose his servants from men of a similar stamp. When compared with Rufus and Ranulf Flambard, Henry I and Roger of Salisbury are drab and colourless characters. But from 1102 until the end of his reign there was no revolt in England. A king who could keep the peace for over thirty years was a master of the art of government.

The effigy of Robert Curthose, Duke of Normandy, in Gloucester Cathedral. Robert died as his brother William's prisoner after his capture twenty-eight years before in the battle of Tinchebrai.

STEPHEN

r. 1135–54

STEPHEN WAS A YOUNGER SON OF Stephen, Count of Blois and Champagne, and of Adela, daughter of William the Conqueror. He was born about 1096, some half-dozen years earlier than his cousin and rival for the Crown, Henry 1's daughter Matilda. Stephen's mother was a formidable woman. When her husband returned early from the First Crusade she sent him away again. As a result he was killed in the Holy Land in 1102 and responsibility for seeing that young Stephen was properly looked after fell upon his uncle the King of England. King Henry provided for him on a grand scale. He granted him estates on both sides of the Channel and by 1130 Stephen was the richest man in his uncle's empire. Henry 1 also looked after Stephen's younger brother, Henry of Blois, making him both Abbot of Glastonbury and Bishop of Winchester, and thus the wealthiest churchman in England. By his generosity Henry made sure that Stephen's elder brother, Count Theobald of Blois, did not join the Norman coalition organised by France and Anjou. In 1125 Stephen married Matilda, the heiress to the county of Boulogne. Her loyalty and energy were to be a great help to Stephen in later years and meanwhile the acquisition of her territories, which included the port of Wissant, meant that Stephen was profitably placed to dominate cross-Channel trade.

Inevitably Henry 1's death in 1135 was followed by a dispute over the succession. There were very few Anglo-Norman lords who wished to be ruled by his daughter and her Angevin husband. One group of Norman barons wanted to elect Count Theobald of Blois but their deliberations were cut short by the news that Theobald's younger brother Stephen had already been crowned (22 December 1135). Advised by Henry of Blois and acting with great decisiveness Stephen had crossed the Channel and taken control of England. Count Theobald at once dropped his claim to the crown, but he still hoped to become Duke of Normandy. The Norman lords, however, were not prepared to face again the problem of divided loyalties; to Theobald's disappointment they transferred their allegiance to Stephen.

For two years Stephen had little trouble, but in 1138 Geoffrey of Anjou invaded Normandy, King David of Scotland (Matilda's uncle) invaded the north, and Robert of Gloucester (Matilda's half-brother) raised the standard of rebellion in the west country. Initially Stephen was able to weather the storm, but he then made three fatal mistakes. In December 1138 he offended Henry of Blois by not making him Archbishop of Canterbury. In the summer of 1139 he arrested three influential 'civil-

36

Opposite: *A coin depicting Stephen and his Queen, Matilda of Boulogne, who supported her husband energetically during the years of bloody rivalry with Empress Matilda.*
Above: *Illuminated manuscript showing King Stephen, with a hawk and prey, sitting on his throne. He managed to keep hold of the English throne, but the death of his son Eustace meant that it eventually fell in Angevin hands.*

service' bishops, including the great Roger of Salisbury, and thus enabled Henry of Blois to claim that ecclesiastical liberties had been infringed. In the autumn, when Matilda fell into his hands, he allowed her to go free when the ruthless, if unchivalrous, thing to do was to keep her in prison. From now on there were always two rival courts in England, though Stephen was generally in a better position than the Empress who rarely held more than a few west country shires. Their relative strengths are indicated by the number of surviving charters: 720 issued by Stephen, only 88 by Matilda. But at one stage Matilda had a clear-cut chance of victory. In February 1141 Stephen rashly accepted battle at Lincoln and fought on bravely when he might have escaped. As a result he was captured and put in prison in Bristol. Henry of Blois, now acting as papal legate, openly went over to the Empress's side and in the summer she was able to enter London. But she spurned the peace terms worked out by the legate and offended the Londoners with her high-handed and tactless behaviour. When Stephen's Queen, Matilda of Boulogne, advanced towards the city the Londoners took up arms and drove the Empress out. Thus the planned coronation at Westminster never took place. Matilda never became Queen of England.

*A fifteenth-century picture of Matilda in the history of England written by the monks of St Albans.
Though never able to realise her ambition of becoming Queen of England, through her marriage to
Geoffrey Plantagenet, Duke of Anjou, she bore Henry II, founder of the royal Plantagenet dynasty.*

A few months later Robert of Gloucester was captured and as he was the mainstay of her party Matilda had to agree to an exchange of prisoners: Stephen for Robert. Her chance of winning the crown was lost and the status quo in England was restored.

In 1142 Robert left England on a mission to Geoffrey of Anjou. But Matilda's husband had his hands full in Normandy and Anjou and refused to disperse his forces still further. Taking full advantage of Robert's absence Stephen moved rapidly and after a skilful diversionary move laid siege to Oxford Castle where Matilda was in residence. This time he was determined not to let her go and pressed the siege relentlessly. But once again the Empress escaped. One December night she was lowered by rope from the castle walls, and with just four companions – all of them wrapped in white cloaks, for there was snow on the ground – she crossed the frozen river on foot, passed through the King's pickets and made her way to safety. After the violent see-saw of fortunes in 1141–2, the civil war settled down into a kind of routine. Stephen's habit of arresting without warning men who were supposed to be his supporters tended to lose him friends, but neither side could make much headway at a time when the art of war revolved around castles and the defenders generally held the advantage. In October 1147 Robert of Gloucester died. Disheartened, the Empress left England early in 1148, never to return. Next year the struggle was taken up by Matilda's son Henry fitzEmpress, but the sixteen-year-old youth simply did not have the resources to alter the balance of power, and while he remained in England, in danger of being captured, he put the whole Angevin cause in jeopardy. It was better that he should return to Normandy and consolidate his position there.

If Stephen ever felt confident that he was going to win the civil war then a glance at Normandy should have made him realise that he would not. The Normans had been thrown into confusion by the news of Stephen's capture at Lincoln and Geoffrey of Anjou had at once taken advantage of the situation. By the time of Stephen's release he had clearly gained the upper hand and few Normans were prepared to fight a losing war on behalf of a king who took so little interest in them – only once in his entire reign, in 1137, did he even visit Normandy. In 1144 Rouen fell and Geoffrey was solemnly proclaimed Duke. From now on those English barons who also held land in Normandy had good cause not to offend the Empress and her son. The result was a stalemate which Stephen was unable to break.

In the last years of his reign Stephen's chief ambition was to secure the throne for his elder son, Eustace. He planned to have him crowned King in his own lifetime and for this he required the co-operation of Theobald, Archbishop of Canterbury. But since 1148 the Archbishop had shown that he had a mind of his own, and although he was prepared to recognise Stephen as king he would do nothing which would tend to prolong the civil war. So, with papal backing, he refused to grant Stephen's request.

In January 1153 Henry fitzEmpress returned to England. He was now a great man: lord of Anjou and Normandy and, in the right of his wife, Eleanor, ruler of Aquitaine. By now it was generally accepted that peace would come only if Henry was recognised as Stephen's heir. The baronial class as a whole was never in favour of long-drawn-out hostilities; their landed estates were too vulnerable to the ravages of war. The problem was to make Stephen see it in the same light. The task was made unexpectedly simple

when Eustace died in August 1153. Stephen's second son, William, had never expected to be King and so the way was opened for a negotiated peace. By the Treaty of Westminster it was agreed that Stephen should hold the kingdom for his life and that he should adopt Henry as his son and heir. William was to inherit all Stephen's baronial lands. This, in essence, was a repeat of the peace terms proposed by Henry of Blois in 1141. Matilda's intransigence then had cost the country another twelve years of civil war. Now, at last, Stephen could rule unchallenged and at peace, but he was a tired man and he did not live long to enjoy it. On 25 October 1154 he died and was buried by the side of his wife and elder son in the monastery they had founded at Faversham.

It is clear that Stephen must take some responsibility for the troubles of his reign. It is true that he was faced by a disputed succession, but then so were William I, William II and Henry I. Stephen was a much more attractive character than any of these Kings, but he lacked their masterfulness. Without it he was unable to dominate either his court or his kingdom. Yet he was no fool and occasionally he made the mistake of trying to be too clever. But it was hard not to like Stephen. Even a chronicler who wrote under the patronage of Robert of Gloucester had to concede that 'by his good nature and by the way he jested and enjoyed himself even in the company of his inferiors, Stephen earned an affection that can hardly be imagined'. He was a competent commander and a gallant knight – too brave perhaps for his own good. Basically he was a kind and amiable man whose friends would not abandon him when he was in trouble.

Above all, of course, he owed much to the courage of his wife in the critical months after the battle of Lincoln. In sharp contrast, Matilda's marriage to Geoffrey of Anjou was an unhappy one, and in 1141 her tactlessness and arrogance provided an object lesson in how to lose friends. Thus Stephen was unlikely to lose the war, but lacked the qualities which were needed to win it. Yet he never lost heart, remaining cheerful and buoyant until the day when the sudden death of his son Eustace made the whole nineteen years seem pointless. Then he resigned himself to the inevitable.

THE ANGEVINS
1154–1216

———❦———

HENRY II 1154–89

RICHARD I 1189–99

JOHN 1199–1216

———❦———

Opposite: From Matthew Paris's chronicles, the Norman Kings of England are represented as patrons of the church – each is holding a model of a church he founded. Left to right, top row: William 1 and William 11. Bottom row: Henry 1 and Stephen.

THE ARMS OF
THE NORMAN KINGS

THE FIRST FIVE POST-CONQUEST KINGS witnessed the birth of heraldry and there is evidence to suggest that they favoured the use of a lion as a symbol.

The coat of two gold lions *passant guardant* on a red shield is frequently attributed to the early Norman kings, although Matthew Paris backdates the coat of three lions and makes it do for all the Norman kings including Stephen. Others attribute a quite different coat to Stephen, presumably because he was not of the House of Normandy, although Henry II, the first Angevin king, is accorded the lions. Stephen's arms are illustrated beside those of the Normans and consist of a gold sagittary on red. This coat is given in College of Arms manuscript L14 but a coat consisting of three sagittaries firing over their shoulders is also frequently used and is mentioned in a treatise on heraldry written by Nicholas Upton *c.* 1400.

Henry II's Queen, Eleanor of Aquitaine, lived until 1204 and the reverse of her seal, cut after her husband's death, shows a shield bearing the three lions. This coat later appears on the second great seal of Richard I and thereafter is universally recognised as the royal arms of England and was used by succeeding monarchs until, in about 1340, Edward III styled himself King of France and assumed the royal arms of France, quartering them with English arms.

The beasts in the arms of England are frequently referred to as leopards. This is not because they were ever shown as or regarded as leopards but because the early heralds described a lion when rampant (rearing up aggressively) as a *lion*, but when walking along, whether looking to his front or looking out of the shield, as a *leopard*, really a contraction for leopard-like lion. Later, to avoid confusion, this term was dropped in favour of *passant*. Later still refinements in the blazon of a lion *passant* were adopted, the simple term *passant* being used simply for a lion looking ahead. When he looked out of the shield, like a lion of England, he became *passant guardant* and when he was shown looking over his shoulder he was *passant reguardant*.

Above: *A stone gargoyle from the outside of Toddington Manor in Gloucestershire, depicting Archbishop Thomas Becket.*
Opposite: *Scenes from an illuminated manuscript showing the murder in 1180 of Thomas Becket in Canterbury Cathedral, an act which scandalised the Christian world and led to Becket's swift canonisation.*

son and heir. Thus when Stephen died in October 1154 Henry took over without difficulty; it was the first undisputed succession to the throne since the Conquest. Henry was now the greatest prince in Western Europe, lord of an empire which stretched from the Scottish border to the Pyrenees. But it is important to remember that although England provided him with great wealth as well as a royal title, the heart of the empire lay elsewhere, in Anjou, the land of his fathers.

In England his first task was to destroy those baronial castles which had been built without royal licence and make good the losses suffered during Stephen's reign. By 1158 these two aims had been achieved. In addition the English King's overlordship of Scotland and Wales had been restored. But it was naturally his continental dominions which took up most of his attention. They were always more vulnerable than the island kingdom and more interesting too, since socially and culturally England was a bit of

a reinep̄ rois elop̄

ex.h. iunior · · · · · · · · · · · · · ex hur pz̅ · · · · ex hur iuur eur

En pes se tient e pacience
He remaundit̅ grundist ne rece
Un de ses clers li dut ben sure
Le muls bad nun martire
Fu tiute hut de tuucode
Ke ala uerite se accode
Kar par martire ert taue
Bien le tuis deuin tiuie
Par uie mort seinte iglise
Cunquert ta pes e ffanchise
Larceuesq̄ a co respunt
Co plese a deu ki fuble muund
Pur sa tie seure · · · ·
Le tut sun regne tonfiner
Sun fiz kert eir albernust̅
Heur li tuit uieut corunes
Icun plusur uit h greuez
ftiudre e enfamtes
La bonture e la franchise
A larceuesq̄ e sa iglise
Grant gent teidott baine
De clerge e de cheualerie

Li ruit henrit grant e diue
De engleterre la curune
A sun fiz esne henri
Repentant fu puis e marri
Li prelat deuer bie roger
A tort lempuit a cirniper
Roger deuer bie isu
Li arcevesques ci neu
Cuesq̄ fu de luudres la
Cist de societe iua
Li cuesq̄ de salesbure
Cuntre loiur de cantrebire
Que larceuesq̄ cert tiut tui
Furent a coruner le rui
Henri le roine las liue
Que en auuir mesauentue
a feste furt plenerement
du mang̅ euieut grant gent
Le pere fist aufiz grant feste
He oimes en chantun neu geste
Fi fuit de riche hom seruit
Cum fu li roine rois henri

Li peres li fut ioie si grant
Ka cu uui li fu sergaut
Oiant plusurs gei
e sul fu tuit iofne henri
Re mie cist ki diue seruu
Dunt mut apres se repenti
Que s'endolut en aprés
Kar poi dura lamur epes
A pres poi dure sen diflut̅
Kil aupere guerre mut
Co fu au cumencement
Le pmer entuchement
Du perche lui rui henri
Ki seint thomas tant pur su
uant li plat de cantrebure
Loi reuuter e diue
Que se tint desp̄sone
e mut sun honur blesce
La dignete de sa iglise
Qut descuucalbree e maumise
Sez les entis chastier
e par la pape amonester

a backwater compared with France. Henry spent twenty-one of the thirty-four years of his reign on the continent. He began by re-asserting his overlordship of Brittany. Then in 1159 he launched a major campaign against Toulouse, a county he claimed was rightfully part of his wife's inheritance. But outside the walls of Toulouse Henry suffered his first real setback. King Louis hurried to support his brother-in-law the Count of Toulouse and rather than attack his overlord Henry decided to withdraw. It did not take him long to get his own back. In 1158 he had betrothed his eldest surviving son Henry to Margaret, Louis VII's daughter by his second wife. Her dowry was to be the Vexin castles so long disputed between France and Normandy but as she was only six months old at the time of the betrothal Louis naturally did not expect to see the Vexin in Henry's hands for many years to come. In 1159, however, there was a disputed election to the papacy and as the price for agreeing to accept Alexander III as the rightful Pope, Henry persuaded Alexander's legates to marry the two children in November 1160. Louis VII was furious but there was nothing he could do about it.

A few months later Archbishop Theobald of Canterbury died. The see was kept vacant for more than a year and then, in June 1162, Thomas Becket was consecrated as his successor. In the eyes of respectable churchmen Becket, who had been Chancellor since 1155, did not deserve to be Archbishop. He was too worldly and too much the King's friend. Wounded in his self-esteem Becket set out to prove, to an astonished world, that he was the best of all possible archbishops. Right from the start he went out of his way to oppose the King who, chiefly out of friendship, had made him an archbishop. Inevitably it was not long before Henry began to react like a man betrayed. In the mid-twelfth century Church–state relations bristled with problems which could be, and normally were, shelved by men of goodwill but which could provide a field-day for men who were determined to quarrel. Henry chose the question of criminous clerks as the issue on which to settle accounts with his Archbishop. Like many laymen Henry resented the way in which clerks who committed felonies could escape capital punishment by claiming trial in an ecclesiastical court. At a council held at Westminster in October 1163 Henry demanded that criminous clerks should be unfrocked by the Church and handed over to the lay courts for punishment. In opposing this Becket carried his episcopal colleagues with him in defence of the privileges of their order, but when Pope Alexander III asked him to adopt a more conciliatory line he indicated his willingness to do so. In order to press home his advantage Henry summoned a council to Clarendon (January 1164). He presented the bishops with a clear statement of the King's customary rights over the church – the Constitutions of Clarendon – and required from them a promise to observe these customs in good faith. Taken by surprise Becket argued for two days and then gave in. But no sooner had the rest of the bishops followed his example than Becket repented of his weakness. Thoroughly exasperated, Henry now decided to break Becket. He summoned him before the royal court to answer trumped-up charges. The Archbishop was found guilty and sentenced to the forfeiture of all his estates. In a hopeless position Becket fled across the Channel and appealed to the Pope for protection. By taking a stand on principle and then wavering Becket had reduced the English Church to confusion.

Once he had succeeded in driving Becket into exile Henry concentrated on more important matters for the next five years: Brittany was conquered and the English judicial system overhauled. Then in 1169 the question of the coronation of the heir to the throne, Prince Henry, led to the interminable negotiations between King, Pope and Archbishop being treated as a matter of urgency. In 1170 Becket returned to England determined to punish those who

Opposite: *The coronation of the Young King, Henry II's eldest son, by Archbishop Roger of York in 1170, from Vie de St Thomas written in England in the mid-thirteenth century. On the right Henry is shown serving his son at table.*

had taken part in the Young King's coronation. His enemies lost no time in telling Henry of the Archbishop's ostentatious behaviour. 'Will no one rid me of this turbulent priest?' Henry's heated words were taken all too literally by four of his knights. Anxious to win the King's favour they rushed off to Canterbury; and there, on 29 December 1170, Becket was murdered in his own cathedral. The deed shocked Christendom and secured Becket's canonisation in record time. In popular memory the Archbishop came to symbolise resistance to the oppressive authority of the state, but in reality everyone, churchmen as well as princes, was better off with him out of the way. Once the immediate storm of protest had died down it became apparent that the King's hold on the resources of his vast empire had in no way been shaken by the Becket controversy. In the early 1170s Henry stood at the height of his power.

The real threat to Henry's position was to come from within his own family. The Angevin Empire was a family possession, not an indivisible state. Henry had no hesitation in planning to partition it among his sons. But his schemes aroused expectations which, while he retained all power in his own hands, he could not satisfy. For example, the Young King (in the whole of English history the only heir to the throne crowned during his father's lifetime) wanted something more than just a royal title. Thus from 1173 onwards Henry was plagued by rebellious sons. Each new scheme caused new discontents since there was always at least one son who felt hard done by. The rebels, moreover, could always count on a warm welcome at the court of the King of France. After 1180 this was a serious matter for in that year the mild-mannered Louis VII was succeeded by his son Philip II, a shrewd and unscrupulous politician who was determined to destroy the Angevin Empire. The deaths of two of his sons, the Young King Henry in 1183 and Geoffrey in 1186, ought to have simplified Henry's problems, but this was offset by the old

King's obvious preference for John, a preference which alarmed Richard. In the autumn of 1188 Richard and Philip came to terms. Throughout the winter the King's health deteriorated and by next summer he was in no condition to resist their invasion. On 4 July 1189 he was forced to accept a humiliating peace. When he was given a list of those who had fought against him he was shocked to find John's name on it. For John's sake he had pushed Richard to the point of rebellion and now John had silently joined the winning side. On 6 July the old King died at Chinon.

Only in the last weeks of his life had the task of ruling his immense territories been too much for Henry. A man of boundless energy, he rode ceaselessly from one corner of his empire to another. He travelled so fast that he gave the impression of being everywhere at once – an impression which helped to keep men loyal. He never seemed to be still; when he was not working, he was out hunting. He cared little for appearances; he dressed simply and enjoyed plain food. Although the central government offices, the Chancery, the Chamber and the Constabulary, travelled around with him, the sheer size of the empire inevitably stimulated the growth of localised administrations which could deal with routine matters of justice and finance in his absence. In England, where there was a strong administrative tradition going back to Anglo-Saxon days, government became increasingly complex and bureaucratic.

This development, taken together with Henry's interest in rational reform, has led to him being regarded as the founder of the English common law, and as a great and creative king. There is much to be said for this view of Henry, but in his own eyes these matters were of secondary importance – whatever their consequences in the long run may have been. To him what really mattered was family politics and he died believing that he had failed. But for over thirty years he had succeeded.

Opposite: *The tomb of Henry II, built of polychrome stone, in the Abbey of Nôtre-Dame-de-Fontevraud.*

RICHARD I

r. 1189–99

RICHARD, THE SECOND surviving son of Henry II and Eleanor of Aquitaine, was born on 8 September 1157. He spent most of his youth at his mother's court at Poitiers - a court famous for its troubadours and their songs of chivalry and courtly love. Here he was sufficiently well educated to be able to speak Latin and to write verse in French and Provençal. But above all he was educated in the art of war. To this end he took an active part in tournaments and knightly exercises.

In 1169 he did homage to Louis VII for Aquitaine and was betrothed to the French King's daughter, Alice. As the second son Richard was to have his mother's inheritance while the patrimony was to go to his elder brother. But Henry II was still only in his thirties and had no intention of allowing his young sons to govern for themselves. Frustrated, Henry, Richard and Geoffrey rebelled in 1173. In May 1174 Richard took command of his first serious campaign but at the age of sixteen he was still no match for his father and he was soon forced to ask pardon. For the next few years Richard concentrated on bringing to heel the unruly barons of Aquitaine. The unstable political situation and the numerous hilltop castles made it a hard school of warfare, but Richard came out of the course with flying colours. In 1183 the Young King died leaving Richard as heir to the throne. Henry II hoped that Richard would be willing to pass Aquitaine on to John, but Richard had spent too long subduing Aquitaine to give it up now. Whenever these tensions flared up into open hostility, Richard could count on the support of the new King of France, Philip II. In the summer of 1189 Richard and Philip battered Henry II into submission and then, in his moment of defeat, the old King died. On 3 September 1189 Richard was crowned at Westminster.

He stayed in England only long enough to make the necessary financial arrangements for his crusade. In 1187, under the impact of the news of Saladin's advance into the Holy Land, he had taken the Cross. For two years family feuds had prevented him from going on crusade and he was impatient to be off. He

Opposite: *A page from a Latin chronicle describing the coronation of Richard I.*
Above: *Two knights jousting from the Luttrell Psalter of 1340. The knight on the left bears the arms of Richard I, while the shield of the knight on the right represents the infidel Saladin.*

and Philip II agreed to travel together and to divide equally any conquests they might make. They set out in the summer of 1190 but transport difficulties led to the decision to spend the coming winter in Sicily. Not surprisingly, the new King of Sicily, Tancred, was somewhat alarmed by the prospect of having a large army encamped for months outside the walls of Messina, but since they were crusaders he could hardly deny them. He and Richard were not on the best of terms. Richard felt that Tancred had been less than just in his treatment of Richard's sister Joan, the

widow of the previous King of Sicily. When fighting broke out between the crusaders and the people of Messina Richard stepped in and took the city by storm. He now held a counter with which to bargain with Tancred and he exacted very profitable terms from the hapless Sicilian. But during the enforced idleness of that winter Richard and Philip quarrelled. In Philip's view it was high time that Richard married his sister, Alice of France, but Richard, who may have believed that the girl had been his father's mistress, refused. His mother then arrived in Sicily with an alternative bride, Berengaria of Navarre, so in anger Philip sailed on ahead to the Holy Land.

When Richard left Sicily (April 1191) he took Berengaria and Joan with him. Unfortunately the ship carrying the two Princesses became separated from the main fleet and was nearly captured by the Greek ruler of Cyprus. Richard came up in the nick of time and then became involved in fighting which ended, less than a month later, with the whole of Cyprus in his hands. Militarily it was a brilliantly successful operation; strategically Cyprus was to be invaluable to future generations of crusaders. While at Limassol the wedding of Richard and Berengaria took place. Early in June 1191 Richard completed the short sea trip from Cyprus to Acre where a Muslim garrison had been under siege since August 1189. The army outside Acre was the only Christian force of any size in the whole of Outremer, yet it was itself hemmed in by a still larger Muslim army commanded by the great Saladin. If there was to be any hope of recovering Jerusalem it would first of all depend upon the outcome of the siege of Acre. Encouraged by Richard's arrival the besiegers pressed harder and a month later Acre fell. The moment of triumph was, however, clouded by the quarrel over the spoils which broke out between Richard and Duke Leopold of Austria. The crusaders suffered a further setback when Philip decided to return home.

Richard ordered the slaughter of prisoners taken at Acre and then led the army down the coast to Jaffa. They were harassed all the way by Saladin's troops even though Richard did manage to relieve the pressure slightly when he won a fine victory at Arsuf. From Jaffa it was possible to advance

Right: *Illuminated manuscript of Richard I watching the beheading of Turkish prisioners in 1191 after the capture of Acre. The slaughter was considerable and the artist has depicted the gruesome pile of bodies beneath the scaffold in some detail*
Overleaf: *Illuminated manuscript of Richard the Lionheart setting off on the Third Crusade in 1190, from the Chronicle of David Aubert. Throughout his reign crusading against the Infidel was his main preoccupation, and he was by the standards of his time a model of kingship.*

cautiously inland towards Jerusalem. But neither then in January 1192, nor later in June 1192, could the crusaders come any nearer to the Holy City than Beit Nuba, some twelve miles away. Richard's crusade ended when he and Saladin made a three years' truce in September 1192. Inasmuch as Jerusalem had not been recaptured the crusade had failed. On the other hand Richard had probably done as much as was possible. The reconquest of the coastal strip and the settlement of the chaotic political affairs of the kingdom of Jerusalem were unquestionably very considerable military and diplomatic achievements.

Disturbing news from home had forced Richard to curtail his crusade and return as quickly as possible. But a combination of shipwreck and anxiety to be on his way ended with the King falling into the hands of Leopold of Austria in December 1192. For more than a year Richard remained in prison while kings and princes bargained for possession of his person. Eventually the Regents of England were able to free him in return for a ransom of £100,000 but not before his treacherous brother John had joined forces with King Philip. As a result some of the most important castles on the borders of Normandy and Touraine were lost. After a second brief visit to England from March to May 1194, Richard devoted the next five years to the hard grind of recovering the territory lost so rapidly while he was in prison. By 1199 this had been accomplished, and with the building of fortresses like Château-Gaillard the

defences of Normandy were in better shape than ever. Richard had won back the initiative against Philip when, in an obscure sideshow at the little castle of Chalus in the Limousin, he received a fatal wound. On 6 April 1199 he died.

His nearest male relative was his brother John, for his marriage to Berengaria had been unsuccessful and he had left no legitimate children. By the standards of his own day he had been an ideal king, preoccupied above all with the crusade and the defence of his ancestral lands. For this reason he spent only a few months of his reign in England. Unlike his father and younger brother he was uninterested in the judicial and financial detail of government, but on his return from Germany he found a minister of outstanding ability, Hubert Walter, justiciar and Archbishop of Canterbury, a man who stood for harmonious co-operation between Church and state. In Hubert Walter's hands the domestic business of the empire was efficiently and profitably administered. It was he who raised the money to pay for Richard's ransom and Richard's wars – and vast sums were needed. A generous lord and a shrewd politician Richard was, above all else, a great soldier. His own individual prowess in battle was an inspiration to his men. In the end his indifference to his own safety cost him his life, yet it was precisely this reckless quality which added the attributes of legendary heroism to a man who was also a competent king and a prudent general.

Opposite: The grave of Richard I in the Abbey of Nôtre-Dame-de-Fontevraud. The great castles that the king built stand with this effigy as his memorials.

JOHN

r. 1199–1216

JOHN WAS BORN ON CHRISTMAS EVE 1167, the last of the children born to Henry II and Eleanor of Aquitaine. After his birth his parents drifted apart. He was brought up partly in the household of his eldest brother, so that he could learn to be a knight, and partly in the household of his father's Justiciar, Ranulf Glanvil, presumably in order to learn something of the business of government. As the fourth son it was not easy to provide for him, thus the nickname 'Lackland'. Henry II's attempts to remedy this situation usually drove one or more of his other sons into rebellion. Richard's refusal to hand over Aquitaine in 1184 led to the first armed clash between John and his elder brother. Not surprisingly John came off much the worse. Then the old King devised a more promising scheme. In 1185 he sent John to rule Ireland, but although none of John's brothers had any prior rights to Ireland, the expedition ended in fiasco within six months. John and the other, equally frivolous, young men in his train were out of their depth. They rapidly alienated both the native Irish and those Anglo-Norman conquistadors who were in the process of carving out new lordships for themselves. In September 1185 John crawled back home, blaming others for his failure.

Despite everything which his affectionate father had done for him, John seems to have been in no way grateful. When, in 1189, it at last became clear that the old King was a beaten man, John secretly and cynically betrayed him, bringing despair as well as defeat to his father's last days. Then, in the hope of keeping him quiet while he was away on crusade, Richard gave him vast estates: the Norman county of Mortain, the honour of Lancaster, the revenues of six English counties, and the heiress to the earldom of Gloucester. The bribe did not work. As soon as Richard was at a safe distance John began scheming to overthrow William Longchamp, the man whom Richard had placed in charge of the administration. But news of these intrigues reached Richard while he was in Sicily and he sent back Walter of Coutances, Archbishop of Rouen, to investigate and if necessary to take over. To John's dismay this is precisely what Walter of Coutances did and by October 1191 John, who had enjoyed himself as leader of the opposition to an unpopular minister, found himself left out in the cold.

He began to conspire with King Philip of France. Their discussions began to have a real point when they heard that Richard was a prisoner in Germany. John went to Paris to do homage to Philip and then returned to stir up rebellion in England, while Philip launched his armies against Normandy. John's revolt went badly yet he still hoped for success, indeed he and Philip nearly persuaded the German Emperor to sell them Richard for £100,000.

But in February 1194 Richard was released and John was forced to sue for pardon. It was granted at once, casually and contemptuously. 'Don't be afraid, John. You are a child. You have got into bad company and it is those who have led you astray who will be punished.' (The 'child' was now twenty-seven years old.) For the next five years John remained very

Opposite: A fourteenth-century illuminated manuscript of King John at a stag hunt. In youth John had a reputation for frivolity and he was treacherous to his father. However, he was preoccupied with detail and he paid close attention to administration and the activities of the law courts in his kingdom.

Neustria Johis huit inde fensa sub annis
Cum que reliquit; gallis possessa reliquit

Johannes rex genuit videlicet

*Pope Innocent III, who in 1208 suspended all church services in England and
Wales for six years, following a disputed election to the see of Canterbury.*

much in his brother's shadow, but he conducted himself well enough for the dying King to nominate him as his heir in April 1199.

Richard's wishes were respected in England and Normandy, but not in Anjou, Maine and Touraine. There the local barons chose John's twelve-year-old nephew, Arthur of Brittany, as their lord. John had to pay a high price in order to persuade King Philip to abandon the young Prince but by May 1200 he had ousted Arthur and was lord of all the Angevin dominions. Later that year he had his marriage to Isabella of Gloucester annulled and married instead Isabella of Angoulême, an heiress whose estates would help to knit together the northern and southern parts of his empire. Yet this apparently sensible marriage set in train the events which were to lead to the loss of Normandy. Isabella had been betrothed to Hugh of Lusignan; he protested against the sudden loss of his fiancée and when he got no justice from John he appealed to the court of King Philip. When John refused to answer Philip's summons, the French King declared all of his continental fiefs forfeit in April 1202.

It now remained to carry out the sentence, but at first John put up a stiffer resistance than had been expected. Indeed, by displaying an astonishing turn of speed he was able to capture Arthur of Brittany and several of the leading rebels, including the Lusignans. Arthur vanished into one of John's prisons, never to emerge again. Men had already learned to distrust John and as rumours of Arthur's fate began to percolate through Normandy and Anjou, the suspicion and the fear mounted. In this atmosphere no effective defence was possible. In December 1203 John abandoned the attempt and crossed over to England, leaving his castellans to make the best terms they could. By spring 1205 the last of his strongholds in Normandy and Anjou had fallen; Poitou also stood on the verge of surrender. These humiliating military reverses earned for John a new nickname; he became 'Soft-sword'.

From now on John's one overriding aim was to recover the lost territories. An expedition to Poitou in 1206 proved sufficient to stop the slide, but also showed John that it would require careful preparation and an immense concentration of resources before he could tackle the French King directly. For the next eight years he made his preparations, and force of circumstances meant that most of the work was carried out in England. Not since 1066 had a king of England spent so long in the country. The weight of John's presence was even felt in the north where men were not accustomed to seeing English kings. The extent of their resentment can be measured by the number of northerners who opposed John in 1215–16. But it was not just in the north that John's rule seemed to be oppressive. Scutage, which had been levied eleven times in the forty-five years between 1154 and 1199, was imposed eleven times in the sixteen years up to 1215. A recently devised tax on rents and chattels brought in huge sums. Levied at the rate of one thirteenth it yielded £60,000 in 1207 – perhaps twice the total annual revenue of the Crown in the twelfth century. The forest laws were tightened up, and also proved very profitable. The King was exerting more pressure than ever before –

and all this at a time of economic and social uncertainty when prices were rising at a rate never before experienced. Many families and religious houses were in deep financial trouble and they found it easier to blame the King than to understand the underlying economic forces.

The tension spilled over into the sphere of Church–state relationships. A disputed election to the see of Canterbury in 1205 led to a clash between John and the most masterful of popes, Innocent 111. In 1208 Innocent laid an interdict on England and Wales; all church services were suspended and remained so for six years. In 1209 John himself was excommunicated. Neither John nor lay society in general seems to have been very worried by this state of affairs; indeed since John's response to the interdict was to confiscate the estates of the Church it even helped to ease his financial problem. But in 1212 a baronial plot and Philip's plans to cross the Channel served to remind John that an excommunicated king was particularly vulnerable to rebellion and invasion. So he decided to make peace with the Church in order to have a free hand to deal with his more dangerous enemies. By agreeing to hold England as fief of the papacy in May 1213 he completely won over Innocent and assured himself of the Pope's support in the coming struggles.

All now turned on the result of the two-pronged attack on Philip launched by John and his heavily subsidised allies in 1214. At first all went according to plan but then, in July 1214, Philip won the vital battle of Bouvines. When news of this defeat reached England discontent turned to rebellion. Only success in war could have justified the measures which John had taken in the last eight years, and that success was still denied him. In May 1215 the rebels captured London, forcing John to make peace. In June, at a meeting with the rebel lords at Runnymede, he agreed to the terms laid out in a document later to be known as Magna Carta. In essence it was a hostile commentary on some of the more objectionable features of the last sixty years of Angevin rule – and as such clearly unacceptable to John who regarded it merely as a way of buying time. The attempts to implement the terms of this peace treaty only led, in fact, to further quarrels and the renewal of war.

Above: The head of the effigy of King John on his tomb in Worcester Cathedral.
Opposite: Magna Carta, in which John agreed peace terms with the rebel lords at Runnymede in 1215.

Seeing that they could get no more from John the rebels elected Louis of France, King Philip's son, as an anti-king of their own. In May 1216 Louis invaded and made an unopposed entry into London. When John died in October, the country was torn in two by a civil war which was going badly for the Angevins.

John possessed some good qualities. Few kings took such a close interest in the details of administration and the daily business of the law courts, but in his own day this counted for very little. John was suspicious of other men and they of him. He inspired neither affection nor loyalty and once he had shown that, no matter how hard he tried, he lacked Richard's ability to command victory in war, then he was lost. 'No man may ever trust him', wrote the troubadour Bertrand de Born, 'for his heart is soft and cowardly.' Not even the Angevin governmental machine could sustain him against that damning verdict.

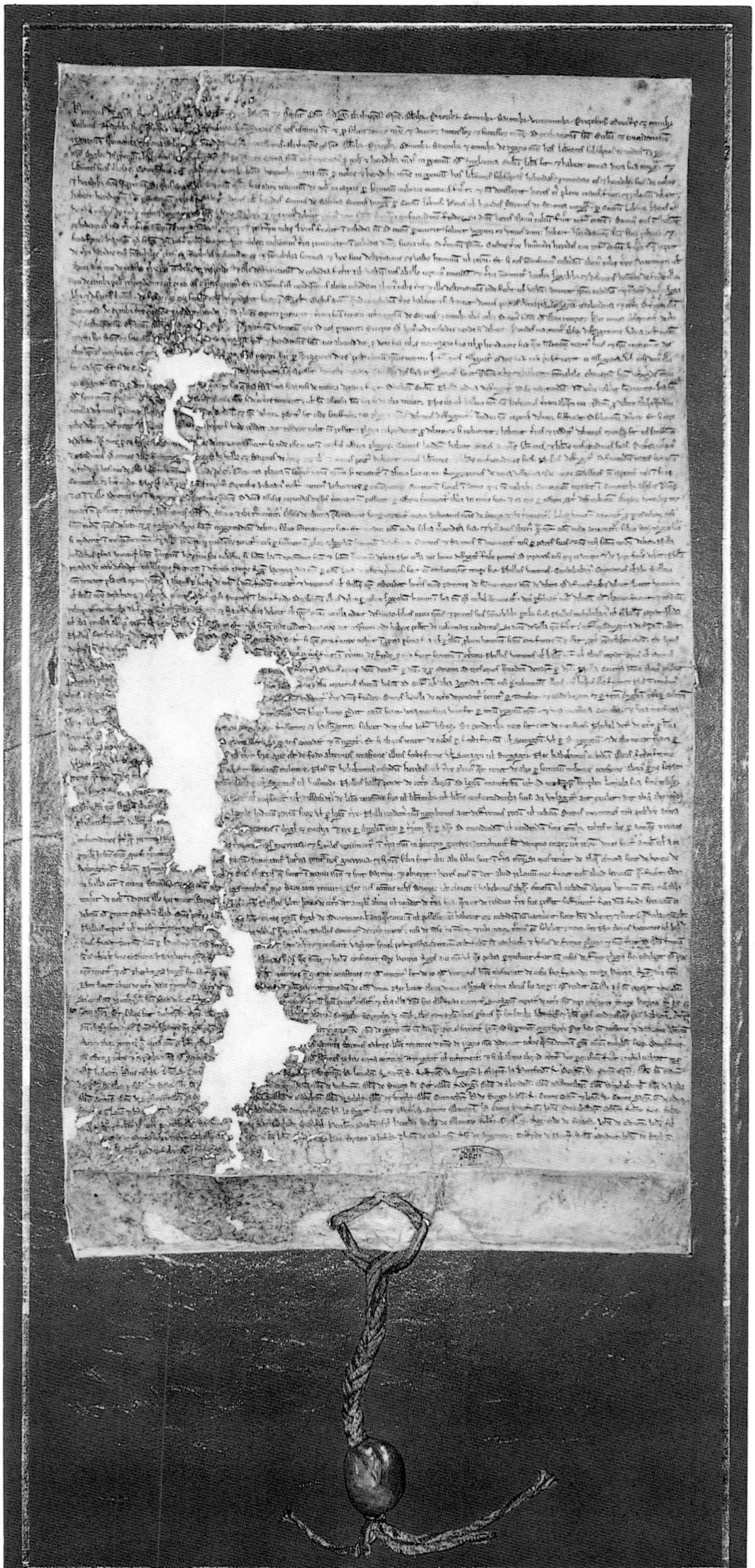

THE PLANTAGENETS
1216–1399

HENRY III 1216–72

EDWARD I 1272–1307

EDWARD II 1307–27

EDWARD III 1327–77

RICHARD II 1377–99

Opposite: Edward III, pictured here receiving a sword from St George, carefully cultivated the knightly image enshrined in the cult of St George and King Arthur

THE PLANTAGENETS

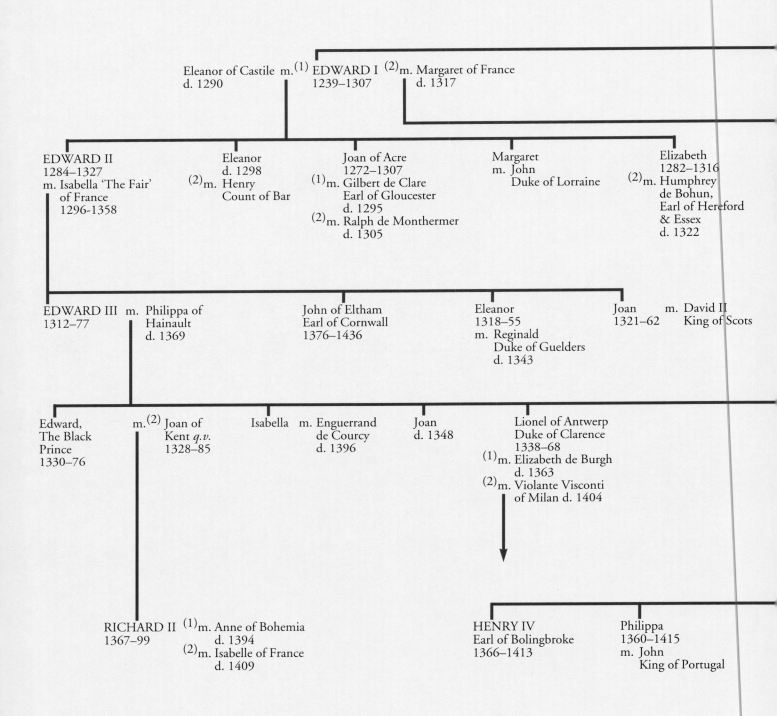

Eleanor of Castile m.(1) EDWARD I (2)m. Margaret of France
d. 1290   1239–1307   d. 1317

EDWARD II
1284–1327
m. Isabella 'The Fair'
   of France
   1296-1358

Eleanor
d. 1298
(2)m. Henry
Count of Bar

Joan of Acre
1272–1307
(1)m. Gilbert de Clare
   Earl of Gloucester
   d. 1295
(2)m. Ralph de Monthermer
   d. 1305

Margaret
m. John
Duke of Lorraine

Elizabeth
1282–1316
(2)m. Humphrey
de Bohun,
Earl of Hereford
& Essex
d. 1322

EDWARD III   m. Philippa of
1312–77   Hainault
                         d. 1369

John of Eltham
Earl of Cornwall
1376–1436

Eleanor
1318–55
m. Reginald
Duke of Guelders
d. 1343

Joan   m. David II
1321–62   King of Scots

Edward,   m.(2) Joan of
The Black   Kent q.v.
Prince   1328–85
1330–76

Isabella   m. Enguerrand
                 de Courcy
                 d. 1396

Joan
d. 1348

Lionel of Antwerp
Duke of Clarence
1338–68
(1)m. Elizabeth de Burgh
   d. 1363
(2)m. Violante Visconti
   of Milan d. 1404

RICHARD II   (1)m. Anne of Bohemia
1367–99   d. 1394
                    (2)m. Isabelle of France
                          d. 1409

HENRY IV
Earl of Bolingbroke
1366–1413

Philippa
1360–1415
m. John
King of Portugal

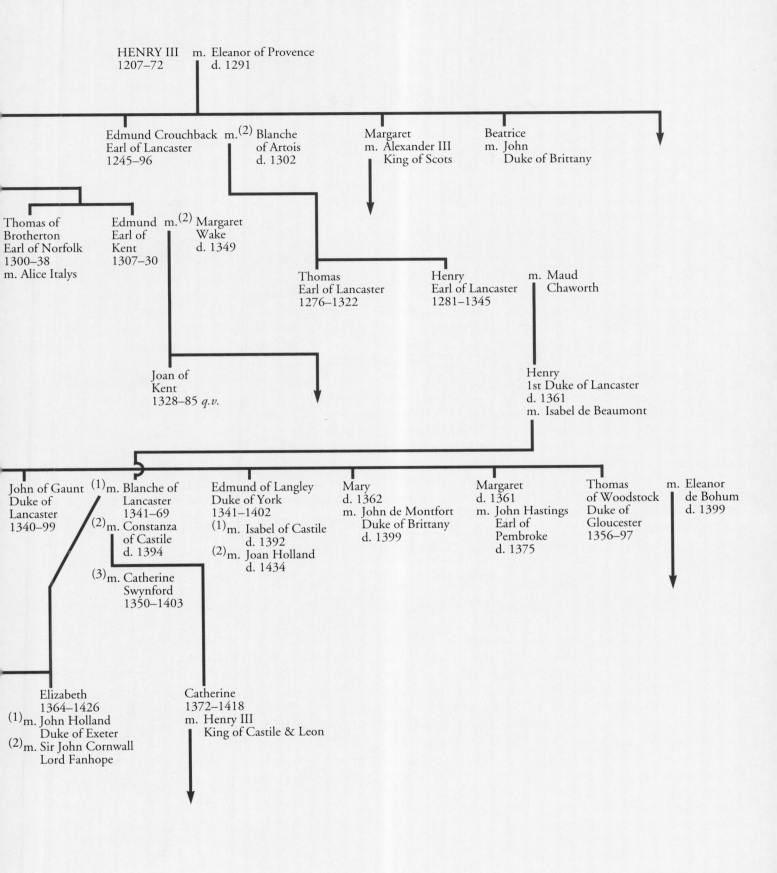

HENRY III
1207–72

m. Eleanor of Provence
d. 1291

Edmund Crouchback
Earl of Lancaster
1245–96

m.(2) Blanche
of Artois
d. 1302

Margaret
m. Alexander III
King of Scots

Beatrice
m. John
Duke of Brittany

Thomas of
Brotherton
Earl of Norfolk
1300–38
m. Alice Italys

Edmund
Earl of
Kent
1307–30

m.(2) Margaret
Wake
d. 1349

Thomas
Earl of Lancaster
1276–1322

Henry
Earl of Lancaster
1281–1345

m. Maud
Chaworth

Joan of
Kent
1328–85 q.v.

Henry
1st Duke of Lancaster
d. 1361
m. Isabel de Beaumont

John of Gaunt
Duke of
Lancaster
1340–99

(1)m. Blanche of
Lancaster
1341–69
(2)m. Constanza
of Castile
d. 1394
(3)m. Catherine
Swynford
1350–1403

Edmund of Langley
Duke of York
1341–1402
(1)m. Isabel of Castile
d. 1392
(2)m. Joan Holland
d. 1434

Mary
d. 1362
m. John de Montfort
Duke of Brittany
d. 1399

Margaret
d. 1361
m. John Hastings
Earl of
Pembroke
d. 1375

Thomas
of Woodstock
Duke of
Gloucester
1356–97

m. Eleanor
de Bohum
d. 1399

Elizabeth
1364–1426
(1)m. John Holland
Duke of Exeter
(2)m. Sir John Cornwall
Lord Fanhope

Catherine
1372–1418
m. Henry III
King of Castile & Leon

HENRY III
r. 1216-72

HENRY III, WHO SUCCEEDED HIS father John as King of England in 1216, inherited, apart from a passion for lampreys and a perhaps connected tendency to plumpness, a very disorganised kingdom. Much of the magnificent Angevin Empire of his grandfather Henry II had disappeared in the reign of his father and in England itself the nine-year-old boy could claim little as his own. London and most of the south-east was in the hands of the French Dauphin Louis, while much of the north of the country was occupied by rebellious barons. Only in the south-west and a broad belt of the Midlands were there supporters prepared to recognise the child as King. Yet within a year he was undisputed King of England and at his death fifty-six years later he was to leave to his son a kingdom more united, more prosperous and more prepared to accept the rule of an autocratic king than anyone in 1216 could have imagined possible. And this in spite of the fact that he has been almost universally castigated by historians as fickle, cowardly, incompetent and totally lacking in wise judgement. Indeed most writers are happy to describe Henry in Dante's words as 'the simple king who sat apart' and then to hurry on to his more glorious son, Edward I.

Henry's ultimate success owes little to his own character. He maintained his kingdom as a boy because he had good men to help him and he handed over a strong kingdom to his son because, in the long run, most people preferred a legitimate king to anarchy or usurpation, and because virtually every institution and everybody with any real power in thirteenth-century Europe was behind him. The English had not yet acquired that remarkable habit of killing their kings in the name of progress and good government which was to make them so notorious to later generations of Europeans, and although it is with Charles I that it is easiest to compare Henry III, he was never in any danger of suffering his descendant's fate.

Even in 1216 when the boy was crowned at Gloucester with his mother's chaplet, things were not as bad as they seemed. The death of King John had taken much of the point out of the baronial revolt and had made the Dauphin's presence in the country take on the appearance of a usurpation. The Pope and the Church were on the young King's side and crusading vows could be commuted to fighting to restore his inheritance. And the boy King had good men to fight for him. Foremost amongst these was the aged and loyal William the Marshal, now in his seventies, who swore when he agreed to take on the office of Rector of the kingdom that 'if need be, he would carry the King on his shoulders from land to land, rather than give in'. But this was not to be necessary. In two battles, one at Lincoln and the other at sea off Sandwich, William and the Justiciar, Hubert de Burgh, were able to destroy the opposition. The subsequent Treaty of Kingston provided for a general amnesty, very liberal terms for the former rebels and a handsome bribe to the Dauphin to leave the country.

The old Marshal died in 1219 and the government of the country largely devolved on Hubert de Burgh. A few years more were necessary to bring the

Opposite: *Illuminated manuscript of the crowned Henry III. Henry was a cultivated mornarch who commissioned the creation of a significant number of ecclesiastical buildings, most notably Westminster Abbey. He is shown holding one of his churches*

pres son regna henry le terz sun fiz. lvi. aunz. si
fuit de .ix. aunz de age quant fuit corone [et en]
tens fuit la bataylle de Euesham. ou fuit occys syr
Symund de munfort. e sun fiz henry. e syre hugh le des
penser e muz des barons e des cheualers de Engle
tere. puis mouist cyl henry le roy. e gist a Westmuster.

Above: *One of the so-called Eleanor Crosses, built in memory
of his queen by the grieving Edward I at every place where
her body rested on its final journey from Nottingham to
Westminster*
Opposite: *The funeral effigy of Eleanor of Castile in Westminster
Abbey.*
Following pages: *Edward I returning from battle in Gascony
with his troops.*

Henry III's struggle with the barons between 1258
and 1265. He changed sides twice, broke his sworn
promise on more than one occasion and was at least
partly responsible for the royal disaster at Lewes.
Commanding the right of the royal forces he was faced
by an ill-armed body of Londoners, against whom he
felt he had a particular grievance, as his mother had
formerly been insulted in the city. Breaking their
ranks, he chased them miles up the hill outside Lewes,
only to discover when he returned to the battle that
the royal cause had been lost. In the following year,
after escaping from the custody of the barons, he
emerged as the royalist leader, and it was his quick
thinking that cut off Simon de Montfort from his
reinforcements and brought him to the end of his
adventure in the murderous battle of Evesham. But
even there the young Lord Edward sullied his honour
by the unchivalrous trick of displaying as his own the
banners of some baronial supporters who had recently
been captured, and thus luring Simon de Montfort to
his doom. After the defeat of the barons much of the
work of government fell on Edward but he showed
little of that leniency which had healed wounds so
quickly after the defeat of the barons in Henry III's
minority. Leading rebels were savagely fined, as was
Edward's bête noire, the City of London, and confis-
cations from the de Montforts and the Earl of Derby
went to build up the enormous patrimony of Edward's
brother, Edmund of Lancaster.

With the kingdom secure and his ageing father
safe in his royal office, Edward was free in 1270 to
fulfil a long ambition and set off on crusade with the
French King, St Louis. Louis himself died that same
year of fever in Tunis and Edward's crusade achieved
very little, but it is during his four-year absence from
England that Edward's somewhat chequered youth is
forgotten and he emerges with an international reputation as a great man and a fine warrior, the 'greatest
lance in the world'.

Edward received news of Henry III's death in
Sicily on his way home from the Holy Land, but he
made no haste to return to his inheritance, once
assured of his peaceful proclamation as King. After a
magnificent passage through Italy he proceeded to
Paris to visit the new French King, Philip III. Here
he did homage for his French lands but he phrased

his submission in the vague formula 'I do you homage for all the lands which I ought to hold of you'. Twenty years of somewhat uneasy peace were to follow before a new burst of expansionist policy in France led to a fresh outbreak of warfare in Gascony. This was to cause Edward great embarrassment as it coincided with his Scottish wars. A settlement finally came after a truce in 1297 and was later confirmed by Edward's second marriage to the French King's sister, Margaret, and by the betrothal of his son, Edward of Caernarvon, to Philip's daughter, Isabella.

On 2 August 1274 Edward landed at Dover after his four years of travel and adventure. His first task was to reassert the royal authority. Commissioners were appointed to tour the whole country to obtain evidence on such matters as the abuse of the law and local power. After so many years of weak central government, they found plentiful evidence of corruption and extortion, and many royal officers, especially sheriffs, found that their careers of easy pickings had come to an end. Although Edward's inquiry was concerned with abstract justice, its main function was to determine more clearly the boundaries between royal and private power and thus to maximise both royal authority and revenue. He disliked in particular the widespread powers in private hands, with no better warrant than long custom. Edward was unable to do much about such entrenched privileges, but he was able to define the 'time immemorable', in which so many people claimed their rights had been granted, as before the accession of Richard 1. Anything granted after then needed rigid proof. All rights now had to be clearly defined and it was shown that their extension without grant was not to be tolerated. Edward followed up his investigations in the country by considerable legislative activity, mainly under the direction of his Chancellor, Robert Burnell. In doing this he was careful to carry the great council or Parliament with him and the result was a considerable extension and clarification of the law, which has earned him the somewhat inflated title of the English Justinian.

Edward's programme of reform was interrupted in 1277 by a long-standing problem of the English monarchy, trouble in Wales. Welsh independence and power depended on the control of the inaccessible area of Snowdonia and the island of Anglesey which served

as a granary. From here raids could be made south and east into the more settled areas occupied by Welsh and Anglo-Norman alike. To control this potentially explosive force the King of England depended on the Marcher lords who, in their castles in South Wales and the border counties, enjoyed a state of near independence of the English Crown in return for keeping North Welsh tendencies to expansion in check. Relations between the two cultures ebbed and flowed, depending on the strength of the lords of Snowdonia, the political condition of England and the chronic state of private war existing between the Marcher lords. Edward had had a somewhat unsatisfactory apprenticeship into the gangster politics of the region as a young man and, now that he was feeling his strength as a king, he was reluctant to allow the former state of near anarchy to continue. By the time of his accession to the throne Welsh power was in the ascendant. The Lord of Snowdonia, Llewelyn ap Gruffydd, had taken advantage of the political disturbances of the previous reign to build up a position of considerable strength and, by the Treaty of Montgomery in 1267, had been acknowledged as Prince of Wales and lord of nearly all the Welsh chieftains.

He now sought a greater degree of independence and refused repeatedly to do homage to Edward, on the grounds that the King had refused to hand over for justice his brother David, suspected of a plot against him. Edward, aware of the problems of Welsh campaigns, was at first reluctant to take action against this challenge to his feudal overlordship, but in 1277 he decided to exert his authority. In a remarkably well-organised campaign he cut off the Prince from his supply base in Anglesey and forced him to surrender. The settlement was very mild. Llewelyn lost his lands outside Snowdonia and Anglesey, but retained his title as Prince of Wales.

Five years later the Welsh were up in arms again and Edward was forced to repeat his previous campaign. This time he was at first not so successful and the attempted invasion of Snowdonia from Anglesey was foiled. However, the death of Llewelyn after a skirmish led to the collapse of Welsh resistance and the complete conquest of North Wales. Edward took this opportunity to reorganise completely the government of this troublesome area. By the Statute of Wales of

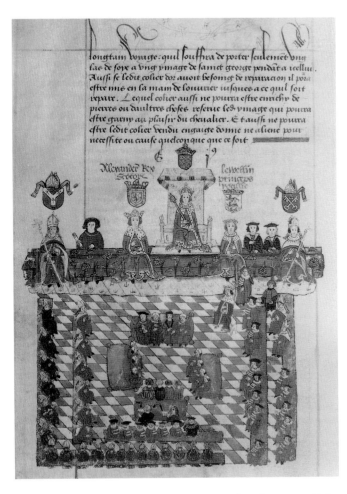

Above: *Illuminated manuscript depiction of Parliament, which began to meet on a more regular basis during the reign of Edward I*

on efficient organisation, both of supply and of recruitment. During his Welsh and Scottish wars he was able to bring into the field armies which were not to be exceeded in size in England till the Civil War of the seventeenth century. Admittedly, most of these men were infantry, poorly armed and eager to desert, but their sheer numbers were often sufficient to intimidate the enemy, and they included large numbers of Welsh archers whose skill foreshadowed the English military success of Edward III's reign. Most battles, however, were still won by cavalry, not archers. The Crown still had the right to unpaid feudal service for forty days but this was now often more of an embarrassment than an asset. Both the King and his magnates began to supplement their feudal levies with paid retainers with whom they had made contracts specifying the nature and length of service and the rate of pay that they should receive.

Edward's wars and the large armies with which he fought them put an enormous strain on the royal revenue. His reign sees a considerable expansion of taxation which resulted, as so often in the reigns of financially embarrassed kings, in a parallel expansion of the effectiveness of the Parliaments which granted the extra taxes. Regular meetings of Parliament became an established feature of British political life in Edward's reign and sometimes knights and burgesses were summoned to attend, following the precedent set by Simon de Montfort.

However, taxation was not enough for Edward's needs. The traditional source of extra revenue was to tallage the Jews but, by Edward's reign, past extortions had so impoverished them that this was hardly worth the effort. In 1290 he killed the golden goose for good, expelling the Jews from England and seizing most of their remaining assets. Their place as royal creditors was taken by Italians, papal bankers and wool exporters, who exchanged loans for trading privileges and left Edward at his death in considerable debt.

The arena in which most of this money was spent during the last decade of Edward's reign was Scotland. Relationships between England and Scotland in the thirteenth century were similar to those between England and Wales, although the Scots had a far greater degree of real independence. Nonetheless the King of England claimed the overlordship of the

1284, the area was transferred to the King's dominion and divided up into shires on the English pattern. Although the basis of law and custom under the new administration continued to be Welsh, those features which the English did not like were removed and in fact during the next century the whole region underwent a steady process of anglicisation. To secure his new dominion Edward ordered the building of that great ring of castles on the coast surrounding the mountains of Snowdonia that remains today as an impressive, if somewhat grim, monument to his most successful enterprise.

Edward I's successes as a general depended heavily

northern kingdom, a claim which at times the Scots were preprared to accept. A chance for Edward to exercise this claim, and if possible to reinforce it, came in 1286 when King Alexander III of Scotland died, leaving as heir his six-year-old granddaughter, the Maid of Norway. Edward's first plan, which was accepted by the Scots and would have saved much bloodshed, was to marry the girl to his son Edward, born at Caernarvon in 1284. But sadly, in 1290, the girl died in the Orkneys on her way from Norway to Scotland, leaving the Scots with the horrors of a disputed succession. Edward, as overlord, was called in to adjudicate between the three main claimants. After careful consideration, he chose John Balliol, a decision which most historians have considered to be fair and just. What was less fair was the advantage Edward took of the needs of the Scots and the weakness of Balliol to establish his supremacy over the northern kingdom. Ultimately Edward's demands pushed the Scots into accepting in 1295 an alliance with Philip of France with whom Edward was now at war. This clever move came just a little too late. The Welsh too had tried to take advantage of Edward's troubles in France and had risen in the winter of 1295. But Edward had time to quell the Welsh rebellion and then in the spring of 1296 to strike at Scotland. Berwick was stormed and sacked by the King in March, and in late April the main Scots army was crushed by Earl Warenne of Surrey at Dunbar. Edward made a grand passage through Scotland, accepted the submission of the great men and the abdication of Balliol, seized the Stone of Destiny from Scone Abbey and was back in Berwick in August. As a contemporary put it, he 'conquered the Kingdom of Scotland and searched it through in twenty-one weeks'. He then left the country to be ruled by Earl Warenne and went home.

Edward had seriously underestimated the Scots. His contemptuous treatment of them led to bitter hatred of their English conquerors which flared up in the year after Dunbar into a war of independence which was long to outlast his reign. Such hatred was soon matched by the English who were subjected to the horrors of continuous raiding and whose instinctive dislike of their northern neighbours was fed by stories of savage atrocities.

In the face of English military superiority, much of the Scots resistance took the form of guerrilla fighting from bases in the hills and forests. The first great leader to emerge was the gigantic outlaw William Wallace, whose dramatic exploits play such a large part in Scots legend. Supported mainly by peasants and outlaws like himself, Wallace was able in 1297 to score a decisive victory over Earl Warenne at the battle of Stirling Bridge. Although Edward had his revenge in 1298, when he returned with the greatest army he had ever assembled to destroy Wallace at the battle of Falkirk, the outlaw himself was not captured till 1305 and was succeeded in the following year by a new leader who was ultimately to inflict on England the most devastating defeat in her history.

Robert Bruce was the grandson of one of the claimants to the Scots throne at the death of the Maid of Norway. Like most of the nobles he had made his peace with King Edward, but in 1306, after putting himself beyond the law by murdering a rival for the forfeit throne, he decided to make a bid for popular support and had himself crowned King of Scotland. His early career as king was a disaster and he spent most of that summer hiding in the heather from Englishman and Scot alike. But he remained alive and his threat was sufficient to force the ailing King of England to undergo one last campaign to conquer Scotland. The old King never got there. On 7 July 1307, aged sixty-eight, the 'hammer of the Scots' died at Burgh-on-Sands within sight of the Scottish border. His last command was that his son should carry his bones at the head of his armies until the last Scotsman had surrendered.

The assessment of Edward's expansionist policy depends ultimately on one's view of the benefits of the union of the whole island. Traditional English historiography, with its firm roots in the British world empire of the nineteenth century, saw such a union as part of England's manifest destiny. Today opinion is not so unanimous. Edward's legal justification for his attempt to bring both Wales and Scotland under the direct dominion of the English Crown is dubious and his failure in Scotland was to give rise to three hundred years of intermittent warfare and almost continuous border-raiding. In return for this devastation and mutual slaughter it can hardly be said that either kingdom received much benefit.

EDWARD II
r. 1307–27

N O KING OF ENGLAND HAS HAD such a consistently bad press as Edward II. Squeezed in between his two warrior namesakes he seemed to justify contemporary suspicion that he was a changeling. Yet the outward appearance was quite clearly that of a Plantagenet. He was as tall, strong, golden-haired and good-looking as his father in his prime, but inside this magnificent shell there was no king as the fourteenth century understood that word. He made no effort to rule or impress his subjects. He cared nothing for the duties of a king. His only desire was to use the advantages of his position to enrich his friends and amuse himself. Such behaviour of course was not all that uncommon among kings, but in addition both Edward's friends and his amusements were themselves suspect. The King had no taste for jousting and the other martial pursuits of his class. Instead he preferred to test his strength in activities of a distinctly plebeian sort, such as digging or rowing, or to learn and practise the manual crafts of his subjects like thatching and farming. Today we would hardly condemn such activities with the intensity that Edward's contemporaries did, but even now they hardly fit our conception of a medieval king. Edward compounded his faults by the low company he kept in pursuing his rural amusements. But even worse was the company he kept at court. He systematically avoided his natural counsellors, the magnates of the land, and gave his heart and all the spoils that flowed from the royal office to upstarts. Edward was a very good friend and his loyalty to his friends is one of the most attractive features of his character, but a policy of continually antagonising the magnates was certain to lead to trouble.

The amateur psychologist which lurks within most historians has made much of Edward's upbringing to explain his unroyal behaviour, which could well

Above: *Edward II holding the symbols of kingship, the orb and sceptre, and standing on a royal lion. However, he did not behave in a way recognised by his contemporaries as kingly, and he alienated many of his subjects.*

87

la royne dangleterre ysabel
arriua en angleterre ez mes
sire Jehan de hannau. v.e C

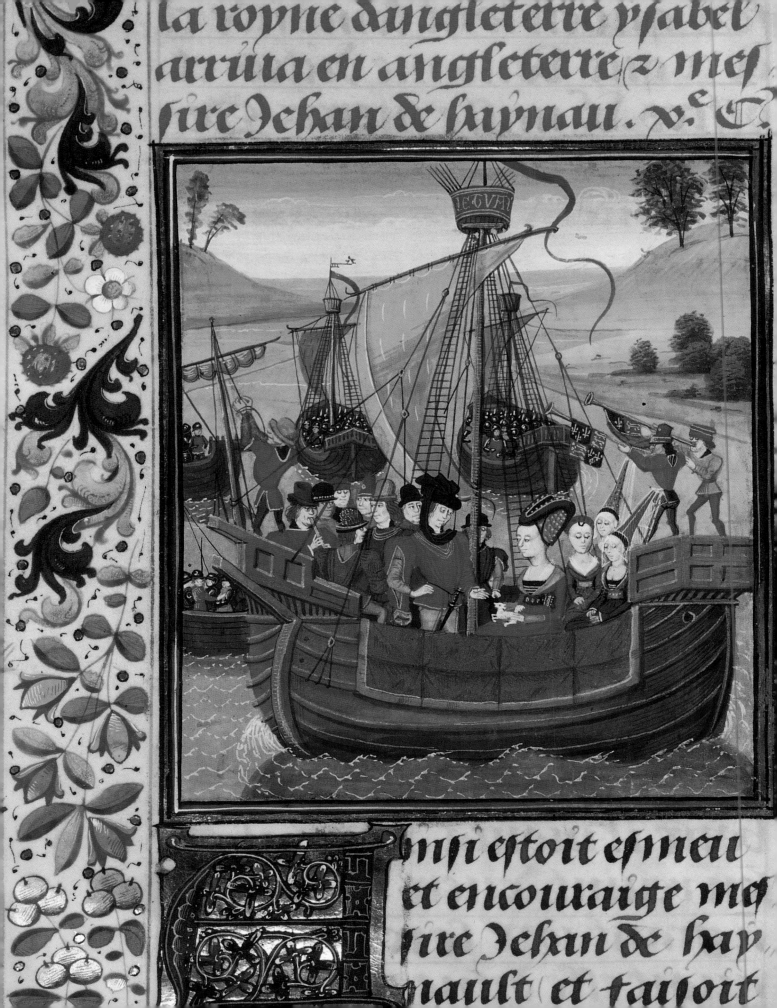

nsi estoit esmeu
et encouraige mes
sire Jehan de hay
nault et faisoit

have been in part the reaction of a weak son to a strong-willed and increasingly tyrannical father. If Edward I bears some responsibility for his son's character he certainly left him other problems which such a character would be unable to solve. His powerful personality had been able to subdue a serious threat to his autocracy in 1297, but there were many of the magnates who felt that the spirit of the royal concessions of the earlier thirteenth century had been forgotten and who were now only waiting for the death of the terrifying old man to impose themselves on his son. More immediate was the chaotic legacy in Scotland of a war which already looked as if it would never be won. The young King's reaction to his father's last command that he should pursue the Scottish war to the bitter end was very much in character. After a perfunctory march across the border, he gave up the north to civil war and the triumph of Robert Bruce and returned to London to enjoy himself.

Here he was joined by the best of his friends, Piers Gaveston, a handsome Gascon knight with an eye to the main chance, who had been his close companion since childhood. So extravagant were Edward's demonstrations of affection for his 'brother Perrot' that it is generally assumed that there was a homosexual relationship between the two young men. It is clear that Edward I shared these suspicions and Gaveston had twice been banished by the old King. But now there seemed nothing to stop Edward II from showing to the world how much he loved his favourite. Less than a month after Edward I's death, Gaveston was made Earl of Cornwall, a title formerly held only by the sons of kings. Shortly afterwards he was married to the King's niece, and a further insult to the magnates came early in 1308 when the King left Gaveston as Regent when he went over to Boulogne to bring home his young bride, Isabella of France. Edward soon made it plain that the delights of marriage were not going to cool his love for Gaveston. Many of his wedding presents were given away to the favourite and at his coronation he shocked the court by demonstrating that he preferred the couch of Perrot to that of the Queen.

Gaveston did nothing to quell the hatred and jealousy that the King's generosity aroused in the hearts of the magnates. Indeed he went out of his way to ridicule them, inventing derisive nicknames for them and, even worse, inviting them to a tournament and then demonstrating that his sword was as keen as his tongue by decisively defeating them.

Edward and Gaveston were playing a dangerous game. No king had the military resources to fly in the face of the united opposition of the earls in those days of private armies. Total unity was, of course, unlikely and the number of opponents of the King ebbed and flowed, but the King's behaviour ensured that they were usually sufficient to put very considerable pressure on him. Within a year of Edward's accession, the threat of force from a strong baronial group drove the King to agree to the exile of Gaveston. Edward made strenuous efforts to appease and divide his opponents but had to agree to a programme of reform undermining the royal prerogative before his favourite was reinstated. However, Gaveston's insufferable arrogance speedily reunited the nobility against him. A committee calling itself the Lords Ordainers enforced Edward's agreement to detailed reforms and the perpetual exile of Gaveston. But Edward had no intention of implementing anything or honouring any of his promises. All he wanted was to go on as he had before with Gaveston by his side. Within two months of his second exile the favourite appeared openly at the Christmas court at Windsor. This was too much for the earls. After a short struggle, Gaveston was captured and murdered by his enemies, despite a promise that he should be allowed to plead his case before Parliament.

In many ways the murder of Gaveston was a tactical mistake, since it removed the main focus of opposition and, by marshalling opinion against the murderers, put Edward in a stronger position than he had so far enjoyed as King. This royalist reaction,

Opposite: *Manuscript illumination of Queen Isabella in conversation with John of Hainault during her return from France to invade her husband's kingdom.*

Above: *The intense personal relationship between the handsome Gascon knight Piers Gaveston and Edward II, pictured here, caused such animosity it led to Gaveston's murder.*
Opposite: *Jean Froissart's chronicles of the exploits of the nobles of England and France include this illumination of Hugh Despenser the Younger, the Marcher lord and favourite of Edward being brutally executed in 1326 on the orders of Queen Isabella.*

his career the idealism involved in opposition to the King was tarnished by his only too obvious desire to divert the benefits that the King was giving elsewhere to himself. To make matters worse, when power did come into his hands he seemed incapable of using it, preferring to stay within his castles and leave the country in a state near to anarchy.

Lancaster's defiance of the Crown came out into the open in 1314 when he and three other earls refused to accept the King's summons to military service against Scotland, on the grounds that the expedition had not been approved by Parliament. It proved to be a wise decision. Edward had hoped to lead his disgruntled barons to a great victory and bring a little glory to his reign but his efforts brought only disaster and the triumph of the stay-at-home Lancaster. On Midsummer Day 1314, after a display of incredible incompetence by both the King and his military advisers, the English were totally defeated at the battle of Bannockburn by Robert Bruce and a Scottish army only one-third their strength. In one day Bruce had assured the independence of Scotland. Edward was to make other expeditions to Scotland but none had any real success.

The next three years must be amongst the worst in English history. After the disaster of Bannockburn, Edward II gave up even the pretence of ruling and became a mere puppet in the hands of Lancaster. But as the royal power collapsed, Lancaster did little to replace it. The Scots ravaged the north of England, levying ransoms from the towns, while private warfare broke out in many other parts of the kingdom. Providing a grim background to this situation of chaos was the worst famine in European history.

In 1318 some semblance of normality returned. A measure of reconciliation between Edward and Lancaster was engineered by the so-called middle party under the leadership of the Earl of Pembroke, the most honourable and competent of the earls. But Edward still remained a king in name only, his every act to be controlled by a standing council. Nonetheless by exchanging one master for many he had returned to the position of being able to play them off against each other. For, despite his weakness, Edward was still determined to reassert the royal prerogative and avenge himself on his enemies.

however, was only superficial and there still existed an opposition movement determined to reduce the King to a mere figurehead to carry out their wishes. The leader of this group and the most consistent opponent of the King was his first cousin, Thomas of Lancaster. The fortunes of his house had been built up on the confiscated estates of the de Montforts after the battle of Evesham in 1265. By 1311 Lancaster had become a classic over-mighty subject with five earldoms in his possession and an immense private army at his command. In a rather fanciful way he now saw himself as a second Simon de Montfort who would control the King in the interest of his greater subjects. There are of course parallels between the two situations but Lancaster was unfortunately no de Montfort. By all accounts he was a thoroughly nasty man, grasping and vicious, and on many occasions in

auecques luu.

Comment messire huon le
despensier fut justicie. Le
xviij. Chapitre.

uant la feste fut
passee les messe
huon qui point
nestoit ame la

Any hopes that Edward had been tamed for ever were quashed by the rise of new favourites at court. The two Despensers, father and son, were Marcher lords whose greed and ambition were as great as those of Gaveston, but whose ability and sense of political responsibility were far greater. To begin with their story was a repetition of the events of the early part of the reign. Supported by the Despensers the King cast off the control of the magnates and in return for their support they were rewarded with a flow of estates and hard cash. Jealousy led to an inevitable baronial reaction, particularly from the other Marcher lords who resented the expansion of the Despensers' power in South Wales. In 1321 a combination of the Marcher lords and Lancaster forced Edward to agree to the exile of the new favourites.

Here the similarity to the story of Gaveston ends. For in the following year Edward was to act with more resolution than ever before in his reign and completely break the main centres of opposition to royal power. Supported by a movement of moderate opinion in his favour, Edward was able to strike at the Marchers in Wales and force them to surrender. Then he turned his attention to Lancaster whose failure to support his allies had been the major cause of their defeat. The now isolated Lancaster ruined his chances by asking Robert Bruce to come to his aid with a Scottish army. This treachery made him a target for the hatred of the long-suffering northcountry men who defeated what was left of Lancaster's great private army at Borough-bridge. At last Edward had the chance to revenge the murder of Gaveston ten years earlier and to pay back his cousin for the years of humiliation after Bannockburn. Lancaster's head was hacked off and the King and the returned Despensers ruled the land.

The long tale of deceit, incompetence, treachery and violence which is the story of the reign of Edward II has a fitting end. The key figure was that of the Queen, Isabella of France. We have seen how shabbily she was treated at her marriage and in the days of Gaveston, but from his death until the early 1320s there seems to have been little discord between the royal couple. They had certainly done their duty in providing for the succession. The future Edward III was born in the year of Gaveston's murder and he was followed by a second son and two daughters. The Queen herself was well looked after and her occasional interventions into politics were those of a peacemaker. But after the defeat of Lancaster in 1322 there were increasing rumours of troubles in the marriage and the Queen emerges as the focus of a new opposition movement determined to overthrow the Despensers. The Despensers returned the Queen's dislike but seem to have been too confident of their own security and power to do much to check her political ambitions. In 1325 they made a very bad mistake. Relations between England and France had once again come to a head and it was suggested that Isabella, sister of the King of France, might be the best person to re-establish peace. Edward and the Despensers unwisely agreed and the lady who became known as the 'she-wolf of France' sailed away to find her rather sordid place in the history books.

Isabella's court in Paris became a centre for exiles eager to destroy the regime of the Despensers. Amongst these, one of the most powerful was Roger Mortimer, a great Marcher lord, who had been defeated by the King in 1322 but had later escaped from the Tower. To the horror of her brother, the King of France, Isabella openly took Mortimer as her lover and the couple prepared for the invasion of England. The Queen's position was strengthened by the arrival of her eldest son, Edward, to do homage for Aquitaine in the name of his father. Isabella now refused to allow him to return to England and openly defied Edward II and the Despensers.

In 1326 Isabella was forced to leave France as her brother was no longer prepared to put up with the scandal of her liaison with Mortimer. Undismayed, Isabella and Mortimer went to Hainault whose count was persuaded to support her cause with a body of mercenaries by the proposal that his daughter Philippa should marry the young Prince Edward. At last all preparations had been made and, on 23 September, the Queen, her son and Mortimer sailed to Suffolk to invade her husband's kingdom.

That kingdom, long tired of the rule of the King and his favourites, welcomed the Queen with open arms. There was virtually no resistance and Edward II retired with the Despensers to the main base of their strength in the west. The tragedy was slowly played out. One by one the Despensers and

Above: *The tomb of Edmund Crouchback, Earl of Lancaster and the King's younger brother, who was one of the knights instrumental in the final defeat of the Scots. He went to the crusades with Edward I and his body is buried to the left of the high altar in Westminster Abbey.*

the other supporters of the King were captured and executed in various horrible ways.

The King himself was not so easy to deal with. After his capture on 16 November he was persuaded to hand over the great seal of England so that writs could be issued in his name for a Parliament. But Parliament without a king is no Parliament and, in order to give some semblance of legality to the deposition on which nearly everyone was set, it was necessary to persuade the King to renounce the Crown in favour of his son. Edward at this time was a well-treated prisoner of Lancaster's brother, the Earl of Leicester, at Kenilworth Castle. He put up a spirited resistance to the deputation who came to see him, but the threat that his son might be repudiated persuaded him at last to agree to the terrible demand.

The continued existence of the deposed King was both an embarrassment and a threat to the Queen and Mortimer. Mortimer's solution was to have him

secretly and shamefully murdered in the dungeon of Berkeley Castle. Here his gaolers, having failed to starve him to death, satisfied their orders to leave no mark on his body by thrusting a red-hot spit into his bowels. Two months later he was buried in Gloucester Abbey in a lavish ceremony which was attended by both the Queen and the new King.

Edward must always arouse sympathy for the horror of his death and indeed it is easy to feel some sympathy for his whole predicament as King. He is really a standing indictment of hereditary monarchy. He clearly did not have the ability to be a king but yet simply because he was his father's eldest surviving son England had to endure twenty years of his reign. Since these two decades were years when the monarchy was faced with particularly difficult problems and when most of the great earldoms were filled with particularly unpleasant men, the reign of Edward II was one that most people would be glad to forget.

EDWARD III

r. 1327–77

ENGLAND EXPECTS HER MONARCHY to produce at least one great king each century. But even chauvinists like a surprise. Who would have thought that the pathetic Edward II, who presided over England's fortunes for two decades of military failure and baronial quarrels, could have spawned such a magnificent son? And who could have foreseen that this son, the pawn of his scandalous mother and the grasping Mortimer, would not only restore harmony to the English upper classes but would also become the greatest warrior king in Christendom who, thirty years after his accession, was to entertain two captive kings at a series of feasts which were said to be the most splendid since the days of his model, King Arthur?

Edward III was fourteen when he was crowned King of England in 1327, the first king to rule by a Parliamentary title. The child who had been born a few months after the murder of his father's favourite, Gaveston, showed no signs that he had inherited his father's low tastes. In every way he appeared to be a conventional representative of his class and there is no evidence that he had any reluctance in joining with his mother to forward his father's deposition. Later he was to make a rather half-hearted attempt to bolster up the royal dignity by building a splendid tomb over his father's grave and encouraging the cult which brought simple pilgrims to the last resting place of a king who had been brought so low, but there seems little doubt that Edward could feel little respect for the man who had brought the English monarchy to its lowest ebb.

Edward's first task was to restore once more the shattered dignity of that monarchy. At first, still a boy, he found himself under the dual control of a regency council of barons led by Henry of Lancaster and a court dominated by the arrogant Mortimer, his mother's lover, who was clearly angling for the throne himself. But Edward grew up fast. By 1330 he was ready to strike. With Lancaster's connivance, the King's servants seized Mortimer at Nottingham Castle, as he lay in the Queen Mother's chamber. His supporters disappeared and he was charged before his peers in Parliament with an appalling range of crimes, of most of which he was quite clearly guilty, and executed. Isabella was forgiven and allowed to retire to live a quiet life on a reduced income at Castle Rising in Norfolk.

Following his successful coup Edward pursued a very sensible policy of toleration. There was no wholesale slaughter of Mortimer's followers and most of them were absorbed without difficulty into the life of the kingdom. Mortimer's grandson was later restored to all his grandfather's titles and was to prove a faithful supporter of the King. In this he was no exception for everyone was a faithful supporter of Edward. It was his most remarkable achievement that he was able to turn the baronage into one great happy family with himself as their leader and their friend. It was in fact a family in more senses than one, for Edward strengthened his position by marrying many of his children to the sons and daughters of magnates, thus tying great houses such as Mortimer and Lancaster to his own dynastic ambitions.

(continues on page 98)

Opposite: *Manuscript illumination of the coronation of Edward III at the age of fourteen.*
The son of the weak Edward II, he was
destined to become the greatest warrior king in Christendom.

Pres que les plꝰ
des compaignons
de haynault se
furent partiz.

THE ARMS OF EDWARD III
AND RICHARD II

OPPOSITE ARE ILLUSTRATED THE ARMS OF Edward III (top) and Richard II. It will at once be apparent that a new element has been introduced into the simple heraldry of their predecessors. This is the crest.

At the beginning of the fourteenth century it became fashionable to have a modelled device affixed to the top of the helm. This was called the crest. It was not long before this, like the arms, came to be regarded as a hereditary symbol. When a man's full armorial bearings were displayed, as in a picture or on a seal, it became customary to show the arms on the shield surmounted by the crest on the helm. As the helm had a short cloak or mantle attached to it, possibly to deaden the effect of sword blows on the neck, this too was depicted. It is referred to as the 'mantling'.

The third seal of Edward III shows an equestrian figure with a crested helm. The crest is a golden lion *statant* (standing, as opposed to walking) *guardant*, crowned with an open crown and standing within a chapeau. The chapeau is an ancient cap of dignity, the royal chapeau being of crimson velvet lined with ermine. The royal mantling was also red and ermine.

It may seem curious that the lion in the crest is *guardant*, whereas if modelled in the round it would naturally look forward over the front of the helm. This must be regarded as early artistic licence. The seal engraver must have wanted the lion to look as it did in the arms and so committed a solecism which has continued down the centuries. In fact, as the helm of Edward, Prince of Wales, the eldest son of Edward III, has been preserved at Canterbury Cathedral, we know that in reality the lion looked forward and not over his shoulder as he does symbolically in heraldry.

In 1337 Edward laid claim to the throne of France. He symbolised this claim in his royal style, *Rex Angliae et Franciae*, and by assuming the blue field powdered with gold fleurs-de-lys, which was the arms of France. He quartered his shield and placed the French arms in the first and last (France was the senior kingdom in the medieval hierarchy) and the English in the second and third quarters.

I have mentioned that Richard II used the attributed arms of St Edward. This he did in personal rather than formal representations and in the manner illustrated.

peninsula in Normandy. The orgy of burning and destruction which followed, as Edward moved through France's most prosperous province on his way to link up with his allies in Flanders, was too much for even Philip VI to ignore. The flower of French chivalry was summoned, the oriflamme unfurled and on 26 August Edward III, after crossing the Somme with great difficulty, was brought to bay in a defensive position at Crécy. Confident in their enormous superiority in numbers the French attacked just as the sun was beginning to set. But then 'the English archers stept forth one pace and let fly their arrows so wholly together and so thick that it seemed snow'. Attack after attack broke down under the hail of fire and the steadiness of the dismounted men-at-arms until, by midnight, there was a great wall of dead before the English lines and Philip fled from the field with the remnant of his army. It was the end of the old wars of chivalry.

After the battle Edward led his victorious army to Calais, which after a long siege surrendered in the face of starvation and thus gave the English a base for further assault much nearer to home. The final seal on English triumph came with news from the north. The Scots had taken advantage of Edward's departure to march across the border, only to be crushed by the fighting Archbishop of York, William de la Zouche, in a terrible battle in thick fog at Neville's Cross near Durham. Amongst the prisoners was King David who was taken to London as the most convincing evidence of the might of English arms.

The next three years are dominated in European history by the first onslaught of the Black Death which is estimated by many historians to have killed one-third of the population of Western Europe. The social changes brought about by such a calamity were ultimately to pose new problems for the English monarchy, but its immediate impact on the biography of Edward III was surprisingly small. Normal history did not stop in the face of such clear evidence of God's displeasure with man. The truce made after the battle

Right: *The battle of Poitiers from the Froissart chronicles. The resounding French defeat led to the collapse of the government and the breakdown of law and order.*

of Crécy was extended till 1350, but then, with the death of Philip VI and the accession of the optimistic King John, hostilities broke out once more. The English strategy was similar to that of the Crécy campaign. Large-scale raids from both Gascony and Calais filled English pockets and at last drew the French once again to battle. This time success was to fall to the King's eldest son, Edward, the Black Prince, already at the age of twenty-six a warrior with an impressive military reputation. In 1356 he won his astonishing victory at Poitiers in which King John himself was captured and sent back to England to join King David of Scotland in captivity.

After Poitiers the government of France broke down and the country dissolved into virtual anarchy. Peace could still not be made on terms acceptable to both sides and in the winter of 1359–60 Edward III sailed to France to try to impose his will in one last terrible raid. Edward's men suffered dreadfully in what were appalling climatic conditions and the expedition was a military failure. But it was enough to force the issue. In 1360, by the Treaty of Brétigny, all Edward's original claims were satisfied. His sovereignty over Calais and the whole of Aquitaine, nearly a quarter of France, was recognised and in return he renounced his claim to the French Crown.

This remarkable recovery of the English position in France after the disappointments of the last century and a half marks the peak of Edward's achievement as King. As if to demonstrate the vanity of such triumphs the plague returned in 1361 and from then onwards the English hold on French territory was steadily undermined. Delay and incompetence meant that the most important term of the treaty, French acceptance of English sovereignty in Aquitaine, was never ratified. The position was wide open once again. And in 1364 the Dauphin, a very different man from his father, came to the throne as Charles V. He was determined to recover all that had been lost, not in the glory of a great battle, but by steady erosion as English taxation and the indignity of being ruled by Englishmen led the French in Aquitaine to take up arms against their new masters. Castle by castle, town by town, all that the English had won was lost again. English numbers were now too small to hold so great

a territory and there was little loot left to attract new adventurers. Many of the great captains were dead and the King's fourth son, John of Gaunt, was a poor military replacement for the ailing Black Prince. By 1374 all that was left was Calais and a coastal strip of south-west France which was smaller than that in English hands at Edward's accession.

Military failure was paralleled at home by a breakdown in the harmony which had been such a characteristic feature of Edward's long reign. The King himself had lost the will to control his kingdom and, as he grew older, sank into a long dotage and increasing dependence on his able but grasping mistress, Alice Perrers. So great a king was still regarded with respect, but popular dislike of the mismanagement of the war and the high taxation which it involved led to increasing criticism of his advisers. The discontent exploded in 1376 with a successful attack by the Commons of the 'Good' Parliament on the King's servants and his mistress who were accused of corruption and peculation. Later that year this unprecedented seizure of initiative by the Commons was reversed and punished by John of Gaunt, now head of the great House of Lancaster, and with the death of his brother the Black Prince in the same year by far the strongest man in the kingdom. Many felt him to be too strong and feared that he planned to disinherit the Black Prince's son, Richard of Bordeaux, and seize the Crown himself at his ageing father's death.

Gaunt's loyalty was soon to be put to the test for Edward III died the following year. His fortunes had sunk low after the glories of the middle years of his reign but the least which could be said for him was that his reign was one of the few half centuries of the later Middle Ages which saw no civil war in England. Unfortunately his recipe for harmony was to leave a dangerous legacy. His policy of curbing aristocratic restlessness by leading the barons to war was to involve England in hostilities for many years to come. And his policy of building up the fortunes of his sons was to create a new generation of over-mighty subjects who would attempt to subdue his grandson, Richard II, just as Thomas of Lancaster had tried to subdue his father.

RICHARD II
r. 1377–99

AN UNEASY HARMONY LAY OVER the country when Richard of Bordeaux came to the throne at the age of ten. Court, Commons, Lords and Londoners had played out a somewhat undignified power game as authority slipped from the hands of his ageing grandfather, Edward III, in his long dotage. Umpire of this game had been Richard's eldest uncle, John of Gaunt, unpopular but all-powerful, once suspected of coveting the Crown himself but now apparently the most loyal supporter of his young nephew's hereditary rights. For the next two decades Gaunt lies like a dark shadow over the land, always suspected of ulterior ends, but always in fact a loyal prop to the Crown, a man whose absence from London was a sure harbinger of trouble. Now, in 1377, it was Gaunt, as Steward of England, who organised Richard's coronation, an impressive affair specifically designed to emphasise the sanctity and magnificence of the hereditary monarchy and to usher in a new period of harmony. The chronicler Walsingham described it as 'a day of joy and gladness . . . the long-awaited day of the renewal of peace and of the laws of the land, long exiled by the weakness of an aged king and the greed of his courtiers and servants'. This was to prove a rather optimistic prediction, since the new King, being a minor, was bound to be weak and there was little likelihood that his courtiers and servants would give up that greed which was the hallmark of their trade. Moreover these were troubled times. Forty years of intermittent warfare had left their mark. Great lords now had large private armies tempered in battle which they were prepared to use against other enemies than France. The country was full of disbanded soldiers skilled in the use of the longbow and keenly aware of its power to lay low the mighty. But the war itself had been going badly for a decade. The French celebrated Richard's coronation by raiding the English coast and the people grumbled at the incompetence of their leaders and even more at the mounting cost of that incompetence. Some were soon to go even further and question the assumption that there should be leaders at all. For had not God made all men equal in his own image?

The boy who had just been crowned was to go the furthest of all England's medieval kings in trying to assert the opposite contention – that God had sent the king to rule the people – a belief which was to cost him his life at the age of thirty-three. Perhaps he could have been successful if he had carried the people behind him as a great warrior. But Richard, son of the Black Prince, inherited only his father's outward appearance and none of his skills at war. Not that he was the coward or weakling of legend – on many occasions in his reign he was to display outstanding courage – but his was the courage of pride, not military prowess.

After his father's death in 1376 the main influences on the young Richard were his gentle and much-loved mother, the thrice-married Joan of Kent, and his tutor, Robert Burley, a knight of his father's household. Soon these influences for moderation and sense were to be overshadowed by his great admiration for his hereditary chamberlain, Robert de Vere,

Following pages: The Wilton Diptych, showing Richard II kneeling before the Virgin. He is being presented by St Edmund (king and martyr), St Edward the Confessor and St John the Baptist, and round his neck is the white hart insignia that he adopted in 1390. The angels are wearing his insignia too.

Earl of Oxford, who as the recipient of the King's affection and bounty was to play a part in Richard's reign similar to that of Piers Gaveston in the reign of Edward 11. For the moment, however, the influence of the King's court was effectively shackled by the appointment of a regency council chosen specifically so that no one person or group could gain permanent control of policy. Not of the council, but supervising this recipe for weak government, was John of Gaunt.

In 1381 the council was faced with the terrifying challenge of the Peasants' Revolt. This threat to the establishment was extremely well timed. Most of the army was far from London, in Scotland, France or Wales, and John of Gaunt himself was absent in Scotland negotiating a truce. As the two main armies of peasants marched on London from Kent and Essex, there was therefore little readily available force to resist them. The council had no option but to play for time by appeasing the rebels and standing aside as they took their vengeance on those who seemed to be the authors of their grievances. The young King, 'very sad and sorry', shut up in the Tower with his council and watching his city go up in flames from a garret window, makes a pathetic picture. But in reality he was in no personal danger and the watchword of the rebels was 'King Richard and the True Commons'. This misguided faith in the King as the champion of the people against the cruel hand of authority was to last the whole reign.

Richard, still only fourteen, rose to the occasion. With a great company of nobles he rode out to Mile End to meet the rebel spokesman Wat Tyler, face to face. Here he carried out his council's policy of appeasement by consenting to every one of Tyler's demands – the abolition of serfdom, a fixed, low rent for all land, and a general amnesty for the rebels. Satisfied, many of the rebels now went home but a hard core of more desperate men remained. There still seemed to be no plan to disperse the rebels by force. The government's only action was to summon yet another meeting with the rebels.

Here at Smithfield Richard played the most dramatic part of his life. Wat Tyler, puffed up with earlier successes, rode out from the main body of the rebels and in an insulting manner made further demands of the King. But he had gone too far, and the King's retinue attacked and killed him. Realising that they had been betrayed, his supporters began to string their bows, when the young King rode out straight towards the rebels. 'Sirs, will you kill your King?' he cried. 'I am your King, I your captain and your leader. Follow me into the fields.' And the King rode out of the square, followed by the rebels.

The death of Tyler marked the end of the Revolt in London – and ultimately in England. The sheeplike men who had followed their King were rounded up and for the most part sent home. None of the King's promises was fulfilled, though some of the rebels' demands were later implemented by the pressure of economic realities. For the King himself, apart from the huge boost to his reputation, the Revolt had two lessons. The power of deceit in dispersing trouble had been quite clearly demonstrated, and the almost mystical faith of the rebels in their King was later to stir memories in a man who was to have an almost mystical faith in his own ability to rule.

But the King was not yet a ruler and later in the year an attempt was made to bring some more order to his household. Two experienced men, Richard, Earl of Arundel, and Sir Michael de la Pole, were appointed to attend the King and to counsel and govern his person. This sensible move was to have little effect. The King was growing up and, with the encouragement of de Vere, was beginning openly to resent his leading reins. Very soon there developed an almost inevitable polarisation between the immediate court circle and the magnates which was reflected even between the King's two counsellors; de la Pole winning his friendship, while Arundel, whom he had always disliked, became the leading critic of the court.

Such criticism took a familiar form. The court group were monopolising the King's ear and the flow of bounty from the royal office. They were effeminate, preferring love to war, and were indifferent to the prosecution of the struggle against France and Scotland. The King himself did little to win respect. He threw out insults on all sides, on one occasion threatening the Archbishop with his sword and on another telling the Earl of Arundel to go to the devil when he complained of misgovernment. His reputation sank even lower when in 1385 he led the one

Above: *manuscript illumination from the chronicles of Jean Froissart, showing Richard II, aged ten, holding court after his coronation. Much of his minority was safeguarded by the protection and good counsel of John of Gaunt.*

major military expedition of his reign to Scotland. The result was a fiasco in which the Scots army was never encountered and Richard returned to England after about a fortnight, tired of the whole business. The only factor preventing an open break was the continued presence of John of Gaunt and Richard had even had a quarrel with him.

In 1386 events moved to a climax when Gaunt sailed from Plymouth to try to make good a claim to the throne of Castile. In his absence the critics of the court moved into action and demanded the dismissal of de la Pole, the Chancellor. Richard's high-handed answer was to say that he would not dismiss a single man from his kitchen at their insistence. But power lay in his critics' hands and a thinly-veiled threat of deposition from their leaders, Arundel and Thomas

of Gloucester, the King's youngest uncle, was sufficient. De la Pole was impeached and the government was placed in the hands of a commission of thirteen.

Richard's first instinct was to try to thwart the opposition by getting the impeachment declared illegal and at the same time raising retainers to fight for him if the situation developed into civil war. This advance notice of his intentions brought matters to a head. Late in 1387, Gloucester and Arundel, now joined by the Earl of Warwick, mustered their men to the north of London and forced Richard to agree to the trial of five of his friends, including de Vere and de la Pole, at a Parliament to be held in the New Year. Richard may have agreed, but he did nothing to arrest his friends and de Vere immediately fled to the northwest where he raised an army to impose the King's will on his critics. But to no avail. On 20 December de Vere's army was trapped at Radcot Bridge in Oxfordshire by the forces of the magnates, now augmented by Gaunt's son, Henry Bolingbroke, and Thomas Mowbray, Earl of Nottingham. De Vere escaped in the mist to die in exile, but others of the King's friends were not so lucky and now had to face the vengeance of their victorious critics.

The Merciless Parliament of 1388 was dominated by the five Lords Appellant, as the leaders of the opposition were called, who, dressed in golden surcoats, led a full-scale attack on the King's household. Those of their original five victims who had not fled suffered the hideous penalties for treason and this fate was shared by other members of the court party, including the King's old tutor, Sir Robert Burley. The King was stunned by this judicial murder of his friends. For the moment there was little he could do but obey the Lords Appellant, now the real sovereigns of the land, but it is clear that for the rest of his reign his deepest wish was to avenge himself for his loss. He was, however, quite prepared to take his time.

The first move came in the following year when the King, now aged twenty-two, announced his

Left: *During his Irish campaign Richard knights Henry of Monmouth (the future Henry V), son of the exiled Henry Bolingbroke who took advantage of Richard's absence to return to England and usurp the throne.*

intention to rule as a monarch of full age. No one could query his right to do so and indeed the King made no attempt at this stage to be provocative. Minor changes were made in the household but there was no victimisation and the King went out of his way to be friendly with the Appellants. A further sign of the return to normality came with the arrival of John of Gaunt back from Spain. This atmosphere of peace was to last for six years.

During this period Richard as a statesman had some success. In 1394 he scored a personal triumph by bringing a settlement to anarchic Ireland and in 1396 he concluded a very successful twenty-eight years' truce with France.

As the quiet years passed by, Richard was surreptitiously building up his power as King. The most obvious illustration of this was in his creation of a magnificent court, designed to soothe the great and to impress his lesser subjects with his own regality. It was rather different from previous English courts and owed much to continental example, partly as a result of Richard's two foreign marriages, to Anne of Bohemia in 1382 and after her death in 1394 to Isabella of France. Earlier English courts had tended to be geared to war; Richard's court was more peaceful, and although the knightly ideals remained, they tended to be more those of the courtly knight than of the knight in the field. Presiding over everything was an increasingly flamboyant and dilettante king.

There was nothing dilettante about Richard's activities outside the court, however. For while faction was hushed in luxury at court, Richard was preparing for future trouble by recruiting in Ireland, Wales and Cheshire a substantial private army which received his pay and wore his famous badge of the white hart.

In 1397 he was ready to strike. Without warning, Gloucester, Arundel and Warwick were arrested, Gloucester being sent to Calais where he was quietly strangled. In September Richard's old enemies were tried before Parliament in a deliberate parody of the Merciless Parliament. Arundel was executed, but Warwick, who pleased the King greatly by making an abject confession of his guilt, was banished for life to the Isle of Man. Now it was the turn of the two younger Appellants, Bolingbroke and Mowbray, to

fear for their safety. Both of them had recently been the recipients of the King's favour but they must have been uneasy. In 1398 Mowbray confided his uneasiness to Bolingbroke and the latter, on the advice of his father, John of Gaunt, reported Mowbray's treasonable remarks to the King. Mowbray stoutly denied the accusation of treason and, since there had been no witnesses to the conversation, it was decided that the truth could only be determined by trial by combat. For Richard it seemed a god-sent opportunity to rid himself of the last two of his old enemies at one go. Elaborate preparations had been made for such an exciting contest and the battle was just about to begin, when Richard in the most dramatic way stopped the combat and exiled both the contestants, Bolingbroke for ten years and Mowbray for life.

Now Richard was free to act as he liked. With his enemies dead or in exile and with a large private army at his command, he began to demonstrate the powers of an absolute king. Those who offended him were forced to purchase pardons at a high price. Arbitrary taxes were demanded. The records of Parliament were altered to condemn his enemies as traitors. The rule of law was overridden. Richard himself took on megalomaniac airs, spending recklessly and building a great throne from which on feast-days he could look down on his guests – any who caught his eye being forced to kneel to his majesty. Hatred of the King's Cheshire archers and fear of his power were widespread but there was little that anyone could do. Armed power was controlled by the King and by a group mainly of his kinsmen who had been rewarded with the forfeit estates of Arundel and Gloucester.

In February 1399 John of Gaunt died. In his last years he had been once again a loyal prop to Richard; as Steward he had been in the forefront of the procedure which led to the destruction of Gloucester, Arundel and Warwick, and when in turn his own son was banished he had said not a word. Gaunt's death would have been a good opportunity to pardon his son and maintain the power of Lancaster as a support to the Crown. Instead Richard took the step which was to lead to the rapid curtailment of his arbitrary exercise of power. Bolingbroke's exile was increased to life and his inheritance was seized. No longer could any magnate feel secure in possession of his lands and the determination of the lords to resist the King now only awaited a leader.

Richard was still sublimely confident of his power and that summer he set off to Ireland where the settlement of 1394 had once more dissolved into rebellion. With him he took nearly all his supporters, leaving behind his last remaining uncle, the incompetent Edmund of York, as keeper of the realm. A few weeks later Bolingbroke sailed from Boulogne to claim his inheritance. As he made his triumphal progress from Ravenspur on the Humber across the middle of England, all resistance disappeared and his small number of followers was soon swollen by the retinues of lords eager to greet him. Richard's Cheshire archers, whose arrogance and depredations had been the prop of his power, slunk off to their homes, stripping off their white hart badges as they went. Richard himself, whose personal courage had never been in doubt, left Ireland for the region in which he had most personal support, North Wales. It was a hopeless mission. Betrayed and deserted, he soon found himself a prisoner of Bolingbroke in the Tower, later to be removed to the fatal safety of Lancastrian Pontefract.

So successful had Bolingbroke's enterprise been that he decided himself to seize the throne. The precedent of 1327 could be used to depose King Richard, though he proved more difficult to coerce into abdicating than Edward II. Somewhat more tricky was the fact that Bolingbroke was not the heir of the childless Richard, whose most plausible successor was the eight-year-old Earl of March. But this was no time for a minor, and after much debate Bolingbroke successfully challenged the Crown, 'through the right that God of his grace hath sent me, with the help of my kin and of my friends'. Richard, like Edward II, was now too dangerous to live, a fact which was made self-evident when on Twelfth Night 1400, a group of Richard's friends tried to murder Henry IV and all his family preparatory to restoring their captive King. So Richard was secretly murdered in Pontefract Castle and for the rest of his life Henry IV was to be haunted by guilt and doubt – guilt for the murder of an anointed king, and doubt on the part of interested persons that Richard was really dead. It was left for Henry V to lay the bogy for ever when, secure in his Lancastrian inheritance, he removed the remains of the murdered King from their inglorious resting place to the tomb which Richard had built for himself in Westminster Abbey.

THE HOUSE OF LANCASTER
1399–1471

HENRY IV 1399–1413
HENRY V 1413–22
HENRY VI 1422–71

Opposite: Henry Bolingbroke (Henry v) enters London to
take the throne from Richard ii, from Jean Froissart's Chroniques
de France et d'Angleterre.

HENRY IV
r. 1399–1413

IN SHAKESPEARE'S PLAYS HENRY IV is a king condemned to a sterile reign, beset by rebellious barons and an ailing body, punished by divine retribution for his usurpation of Richard's throne. This view is not far off the mark. The King who ruled England and Aquitaine for thirteen troubled years from 1399 to 1413 was a sad contrast to the brilliant, energetic and chivalrous figure of Henry Bolingbroke, Earl of Derby.

Henry was born in April 1366 at Bolingbroke Castle in Lincolnshire, the only son of John of Gaunt and his first wife, Blanche of Lancaster, to survive infancy. His parents were cousins: John was the third surviving son of Edward III and Blanche was the great-great-granddaughter of Henry III. She brought to her husband the vast estates and ducal title of Lancaster, as well as the earldoms of Derby, Lincoln and Leicester. It was in Blanche's memory that Chaucer wrote his *Book of the Duchesse*. She died in her early twenties when Henry was only three.

With his mother dead and his father usually absent on affairs of state, Henry's upbringing was entrusted largely to a group of Lancastrian retainers, some of whom remained his most trusted servants when he became King. He proved himself an able pupil, well equipped to fulfil the ideals of chivalry. With his stocky build and vigorous health he excelled at the martial arts; he was also devout, well read, a pleasant talker and an accomplished musician. Since he was so clearly destined to play an important role in the affairs of state, Henry was not permitted the obscurity of childhood. When Edward III died in 1377, he bore the sword of mercy at the coronation of his young cousin, Richard II, and was afterwards styled Earl of Derby. Three years later, at the age of fourteen, he was married to Mary de Bohun, co-heiress of the late Earl of Hereford and Essex, a match

which cost his father 5,000 marks. Mary bore him four sons and two daughters, the first being the future Henry V who was born at Monmouth in 1387; the last was Philippa whose birth in 1394 brought about her mother's death. Like Henry's own mother, Mary was in her early twenties when she died.

In the year which saw the birth of his first son, Henry also made his precocious entry into the political arena. By joining his name to the cause of the Lords Appellant in their semi-treasonable enterprise to unseat the King's closest counsellors, and by taking arms to block the crossing of the Thames at Radcot Bridge to Richard's special favourite, Robert de Vere, Henry sowed in his royal cousin's mind the mistrust and the thirst for vengeance which was to cost Richard his Crown and his life. Indeed there is some evidence that the Appellants meant to depose Richard after Radcot Bridge, but changed their minds when they failed to agree whether Henry or his uncle, Thomas, Duke of Gloucester, should replace him. Instead the Appellants concentrated on the persecution of Richard's servants at the Merciless Parliament of 1388. Here Henry showed a more generous spirit than his fellows by speaking up for at least one of the luckless victims, Sir Simon Burley.

Henry's initiative cannot have pleased his father who remained until his death a faithful servant of the Crown, and it would never have taken place unless Gaunt had been absent in Spain, pressing his claim to the throne of Castile. When Gaunt returned to England late the following year (1389) his son retired to the wings and occupied himself for a while with the administration of his estates. But the conventional life of an itinerant nobleman could not contain his energies for long, and the autumn of 1390 saw Henry in command of a privately mounted expedition – part adventure, part crusade – to distant Lithuania, where

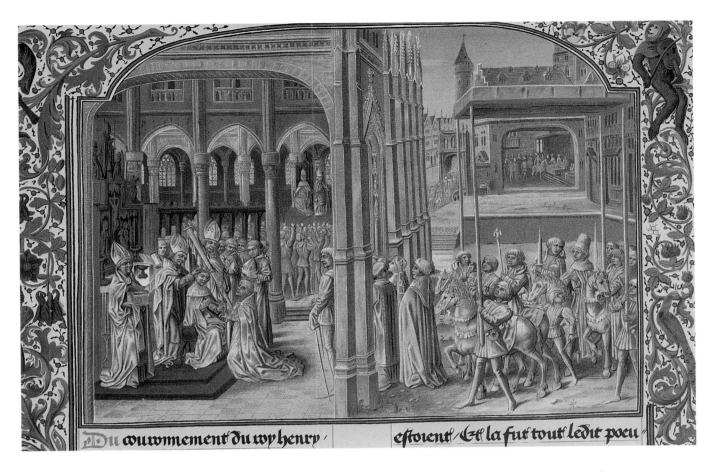

Du couronnement du roy henry / estoient / Et la fut tout ledit poeu

The coronation of Henry IV, after the imprisoned Richard II's abdication, from the Froissart chronicles.
According to one report the service was marred by three bad omens for the future.

he fought side by side with the Teutonic Knights at the siege of Vilna. The campaign was not arduous – Henry's band of two hundred lost only one knight killed and two captured before returning to Königsberg for Christmas, and he was accompanied throughout by a band of six minstrels. All embarked safely for England in the spring of 1391. In 1392 Henry undertook a more ambitious journey to Jerusalem, travelling overland through Frankfurt (Oder), Prague, Vienna and Venice, and then by ship to Jaffa by way of Corfu and Rhodes. On the return journey he visited Cyprus, Rhodes, Venice, Milan and Paris. This grand tour occupied nearly a year and gave Henry the opportunity to enjoy the hospitality of King Wenceslas of Bohemia, Duke Albert of Austria, the Doge of Venice, the Grand Master of the Knights

Hospitaller of St John, King James I of Cyprus (who presented him with a leopard) and the Visconti Duke of Milan. Along the road he impressed his hosts with his handsome appearance, his courtesy and his fluency in English, French and Latin. Now at the age of twenty-seven he could boast the European reputation of a seasoned warrior and courtier.

The five years between Henry's return from Jerusalem and his banishment in 1398 gave little scope for the exercise of those talents. There are signs that he grew restive, for in 1396 it was said that his father forbade him to accept an invitation from William of Hainault, a distant cousin, to join him in a campaign against Friesland. More serious is the story – admittedly unsubstantiated – that Henry was party to the conspiracy, concocted by Gloucester, Arundel and

The abdication of Richard II and the proclamation of Henry IV as King of England in
Westminster in September 1399.

Warwick in July 1397, to imprison both Gaunt and the King for life. Whatever the facts about Henry's complicity, he stood by the King when the three former Appellants were subsequently convicted of treason in Parliament, and shortly afterwards, in September 1397, he was created Duke of Hereford. The motives behind the events which followed are equally obscure. Henry's own account is that Thomas Mowbray (Earl of Nottingham and Duke of Norfolk), the man who apprised King Richard of the conspiracy, told Henry that the two of them were marked men, whom the King would bring down just

as he had already brought down the other three Appellants. Mowbray apparently went on to reveal another conspiracy aimed at eliminating all the barons close to the King, including Gaunt and Henry himself. Henry then reported the conversation to his father, who in turn repeated everything to the King. In February 1398 Henry accused Mowbray of treason to his face in the King's presence: in April a court of chivalry at Windsor ordained that the two Dukes should resolve their dispute in a trial by battle, to take place at Coventry in September.

The contest never took place, for Richard decided

at the last moment to banish both parties, Henry for ten years, Mowbray for life. Although Henry's sentence was subsequently reduced to six years, he now had ample reason for believing Mowbray's warning that the King meant to undo him. Nevertheless, while Gaunt lived he had no choice but to go. In Paris he was warmly greeted as one of royal rank and resided at the Hôtel Clisson. Henry had only been there for four months when he heard the news, in February 1399, of his father's death. It was then that Richard made his literally fatal mistake of altering Henry's sentence to perpetual banishment and declaring all the possessions of the House of Lancaster forfeit to the crown.

This decision opened Henry's path to the throne. No man could feel safe when the laws of inheritance could be so arbitrarily flouted, and the lifelong service of the father so shoddily repaid in the punishment of the son. Henry's prospects were enhanced by two other recent demises: that of his uncle Gloucester who had reputedly fancied himself as Richard's replacement in 1387 and again in 1397; and that of Roger Mortimer, Earl of March, whom the childless King had recognised as his heir. Mortimer's heir was a seven-year-old boy, Edmund.

When Richard compounded his error by leaving on a punitive expedition to Ireland at such a critical juncture (May 1399), Henry gathered his followers and struck. Early in July three small ships bore him and perhaps three hundred men to Ravenspur in Yorkshire. His progress to Pontefract was more of a triumph than a campaign, for he met no opposition, and while the Duke of York, Richard's ineffectual uncle and Viceroy, dithered in the south, Henry's ranks grew with Lancastrian retainers and, more significantly, the heads of the two baronial dynasties who dominated the north, the Percys and the Nevilles. The Percys later claimed that Henry swore an oath at Doncaster declaring that he had come only to claim his inheritance, not to molest the King. If this is true it was more probably a stratagem to broaden the base of his support than a statement of real intent.

When the Duke of York, with a small royalist army, gave in to the inevitable and threw in his lot with Henry at Berkeley Castle on 27 July, the outcome was no longer in doubt. Richard, returning from Ireland on the same day, allowed himself to be gulled by assurances that Henry would be content with the restitution of his duchy, and fell into an ambush laid by the Earl of Northumberland's men near Flint. In less than six weeks Henry had made himself master of England. It now remained to take the giant step from de facto master to anointed King.

The manner in which Henry presented his claim was all-important, for any loopholes would quickly be seized upon by Richard and his heirs or by any malcontent baronial clique seeking a respectable pretext for rebellion. Many of Henry's subsequent misfortunes stemmed from precisely the fact that his claim was paper-thin by any measure. He could give out that Richard, now a prisoner in the Tower, had abdicated of his own free will and designated Henry his successor by giving him his signet ring, but how could the story be proved? He could claim by right of conquest, but such a right found no sanction in law. He could claim to have been elected by Lords and Commons, but then he might find his prerogative shackled by conditions imposed in return. He could even fall back on the old wives' tale that his Lancastrian ancestor Edmund was the elder, not the younger, brother of Edward 1, and the Crown was being restored to the senior branch of the Plantagenets. In the event, a deliberately vague mixture of all these claims was put before Parliament at the end of September 1399.

Henry's coronation on Monday, 13 October – the feast of the translation of Edward the Confessor – was celebrated in the traditional form, with his eldest son, Henry of Monmouth, bearing the sword of mercy which the new King had himself borne at Richard's crowning. If we are to believe Adam of Usk, a Welsh councillor who wrote a history of Henry's reign, the ceremony was attended by three ill omens for the future: 'First, in the procession, he lost one of his coronation shoes: whence, in the first place, the Commons who rose up against him hated him ever after his whole life long. Secondly, one of the golden spurs fell off: whence, in the second place, the soldiery opposed him in rebellion. Thirdly, at the banquet a sudden gust of wind carried away the crown from his head: whence, in the last place, he was set aside from his kingdom and supplanted by Prince Henry.'

It was the soldiery, or rather the barons whose badges they wore, who struck first. Barely three months of the new reign had elapsed before Henry had to flee from Windsor to London to escape from a rebel coup plotted by the Earls of Kent, Huntingdon and Salisbury and Lord Despenser. All were closely associated with the deposed King and three had recently been deprived of the titles conferred on them by Richard in 1397. But their cause was not yet a popular one and they were beheaded by the mob before they fell into Henry's hands. Some thirty other rebels were executed after the King had presided over their trial at Oxford. Their corpses were chopped up and carted to London in sacks. The ferocity of Henry's response bears witness to the near-panic caused by the revolt of the Earls, a revolt which came so soon after an almost bloodless usurpation. It proved that it was easier to win the throne than to keep it. It also sealed Richard's fate. Although we do not know exactly how or when he died, it must have been with Henry's connivance, if not at his orders. In February 1400 the Council recommended that the body should be publicly exposed in London to scotch any rumours of escape.

The autumn of 1400 saw the start of an intractable guerrilla war in Wales. It began just as a local quarrel between a Welsh squire, Owen Glendower, and his English neighbour, but quickly flared into a national uprising. Glendower's successful resistance was certainly one of the causes of a far more serious crisis which erupted in 1403 with the revolt of Henry's hitherto most powerful supporters, the Percys. The Earl of Northumberland's son, Henry Percy, better known as Hotspur, had taken umbrage when the King refused him the ransom of an important Scottish prisoner, the Earl of Douglas. He also had some grievances about the lack of support he had received while serving as Henry's lieutenant in North Wales. These seem slender grounds for revolt, but Hotspur was a vain, impetuous man and he carried the rest of his family with him. To make matters worse, the Percys were connected with Glendower by marriage. Glendower's daughter was married to Edmund Mortimer, uncle of Richard II's heir and brother of Hotspur's wife.

It was the most testing crisis of Henry's reign and he solved it with his usual speed and decision. He at once marched west to Shrewsbury, which was held by Prince Henry, and there brought Hotspur and his uncle, the Earl of Worcester, to battle before they could join the Earl of Northumberland. The savage battle fought near Shrewsbury on 21 July 1403 ended in a royal victory when Hotspur himself was slain. Worcester was executed two days later but Northumberland was spared after promising to surrender his castles and his office as Constable. Henry's restraint earned him little credit, for the Earl proved an implacable conspirator. Early in 1405 Thomas Mowbray, the Earl Marshal and son of the late Duke of Norfolk, was involved in a plot to spirit the Earl of March away from Windsor to Wales. The fugitives were caught by Henry himself at Cheltenham. The nineteen-year-old Earl of March was pardoned and promptly made off to join Northumberland in another armed rising. In the meantime Northumberland was said to have signed a compact with Glendower and Mortimer partitioning England between them. Richard Scrope, Archbishop of York, was also persuaded to join the plot, and posted on the church doors a manifesto accusing Henry of usurping the throne against his oath, murdering King Richard and levying taxes he had promised to abolish. The rebel army was dispersed and the Archbishop and the Earl Marshal captured by the Neville Earl of Westmorland before Henry arrived. This time there was to be no mercy. A great scandal ensued when not only Mowbray but also the Archbishop were executed, and the unidentified illness which partially paralysed Henry shortly afterwards was said to be God's punishment for this impiety. Northumberland fled to Scotland and was not finally called to account until February 1408 when he died in a skirmish with the Sheriff of Yorkshire's men on Bramham Moor.

After Northumberland's death Henry's throne was secure. The Scottish border had been relatively quiet since 1406, when the young King James I was captured on his way to France. Even the Welsh revolt gradually petered out when Harlech Castle was starved into submission in 1409. The French who had sent troops to Glendower's aid in 1405 were preoccupied with civil war between the rival factions of

Burgundy and Armagnac. But the King's health had been broken. From 1406 onwards he was frequently immobilised or bed-ridden by a mysterious disease which contemporaries called leprosy, and in the winter of 1408–9 there were fears for his life. A famous physician was summoned from Lucca, and Henry made his will. No doubt the campaigns of 1399 to 1405 had taken their toll. So too had the burdens which these campaigns imposed on his administrations. To wage war in Scotland and Wales was prodigiously expensive and lack of money proved a constant headache. No less than ten treasurers in thirteen years struggled to balance the books, but none succeeded. 'There is not enough money in your treasury to pay the messengers', wrote one of them in 1401. Almost annually between 1400 and 1407 Henry had to endure a running battle with his Commons over the granting of taxes and customs dues. Making capital of Henry's political weakness, the Commons aired all their grievances about the extravagance of his household, the membership of his Council, the grants made to his followers and the uses to which previous subsidies had been put, before assenting to taxation. The Commons did not hate Henry, as Adam of Usk implied, but they certainly treated him to more outspoken criticism than any other medieval king had to face. If Henry resented this, he seldom showed it. He met their demands with patient moderation, always careful to avoid a confrontation.

Adam of Usk's third point – that Henry was set aside and supplanted by his son – is an exaggeration, but it has a kernel of truth. Until 1407 the Prince had his hands full campaigning in Wales, and enjoyed his father's complete confidence. In the later years of the reign there were signs of tension, and sometimes even of opposition. As the King's health failed his eldest son expected to play a greater role in government. At first, however, Henry IV preferred to entrust his affairs to the veteran Archbishop Arundel, whom he appointed Chancellor. During this time the Prince emerged as the nucleus of an opposition within the Council.

In December 1409 the Chancellor was pressured into resignation and Prince Henry took over as the Council's president. For two years the Prince remained in control, but in November 1411 a serious quarrel with the King brought about the dismissal of his Council and Arundel's return. The causes of the quarrel are obscure, but it seems likely that Henry was goaded into action by the suggestion that he should abdicate in the Prince's favour. Polite formality was observed on both sides, but unhappily the matter was not allowed to rest there. In the following May there were rumours that the Prince was raising an army to depose his father, and he felt compelled to write a long letter from Coventry denying the charge. He then came before the King in London with a large following to demand the punishment of his slanderers.

Any further development of this sordid family quarrel was cut short before the year was out by the fact that Henry was obviously dying. By now his face as well as his body was badly disfigured. The end came on 20 March 1413 at Westminster Palace. The Prince was at his side and received his blessing.

So died the first of the Lancastrian kings; an old man at forty-seven, wasted by disease and worn out by the cares of state. The Crown so easily won in 1399 had brought him little joy since. For a king who strove so hard to do the right thing and a man whose strict piety in Church matters is well attested, his misfortune must have seemed a divine punishment for the sin of usurping Richard's throne. 'I Henry, sinful wretch,' he wrote in his will of 1408, '. . . ask my lords and true people forgiveness if I have misentreated them in any wise.' But his reign cannot be judged a failure. The fact remains that he founded a new dynasty and passed his kingdom intact to his heir. For a usurper this was a considerable feat, particularly in an age when legitimism lay at the heart of political theory and action. The rebel barons had been defeated, Scotland and France neutralised, and the Welsh restored to their allegiance. Even the Commons, for all their reluctance to pay taxes, never questioned Henry's title. Though he was seldom the master of events, he ruled with a mixture of decision, perseverance and tact which few kings could have matched in his place. This achievement goes a long way towards meeting the claim of at least one chronicler, Thomas Walsingham, that Henry IV 'for thirteen and a half years less five days reigned gloriously'.

HENRY V

r. 1413–22

HENRY IV SUCCEEDED, AGAINST the odds, in founding a royal dynasty; his son, against incalculably greater odds, conquered an empire. Two years from his father's death Henry V destroyed the chivalry of France at Agincourt. Within eight years he entered Paris as Regent of France. Within nine he was dead.

Henry V is a rare example of the men who shape history to their own design. The spectacular achievements of his reign are in a very real sense the achievements of one man. Well before he came to the throne in March 1413 his ability was proven beyond doubt. Created Prince of Wales at his father's coronation in 1399, shortly after his twelfth birthday, he was soon taking an active part in the administration of the principality. When Owen Glendower's reb- ellion signalled the beginning of a national Welsh uprising in 1400, the Prince's household was established at Chester with Henry Percy as his guardian. Hotspur, a seasoned campaigner in his late thirties, provided Henry's early lessons in the art of war. These stood him in good stead three years later, in 1403, when the fifteen-year-old Prince fought his first pitched battle, with Hotspur, now turned rebel, commanding the opposing army. The battle of Shrewsbury was a viciously contested action, lasting several hours. Henry commanded his father's right and showed his mettle by fighting the day out despite being wounded in the face by an arrow.

The royal victory at Shrewsbury ended Hotspur's career, but Glendower's revolt absorbed the Prince's energies for the next five years. Here he learned the value of a small mobile striking-force to harry his enemy and at the siege of Aberystwyth in 1407 he first experienced the tedium of starving an impregnable fortress into surrender. Constantly short of funds with which to pay his troops, he also learned the important of putting war on a proper financial footing.

The Prince did not spend all his time at war in the valleys. From 1406 onwards he was also making his presence felt at meetings of the Council, the body of advisers whom the King selected to run his administration. It was in this year that rumours first began to circulate about the Prince wanting his father to abdicate because of his ill-health. In the winter of 1408–9 Henry very nearly got his way when a particularly bad attack of illness almost killed Henry IV. The Prince had to wait and chafe until the spring of 1410 when he took over as the acknowledged leader of the Council in place of Archbishop Arundel. His father seems to have accepted this situation with some reluctance, and when there was more talk of abdication in the autumn of 1411 he reacted smartly by sacking his son and bringing the Archbishop back as Chancellor. However, the Prince had made a very good impression during his year and a half of office, and afterwards the Commons thanked him handsomely for his efforts.

The differences between the Prince's supporters and Archbishop Arundel's party owed more to temperament and personal loyalties than to political issues. The Archbishop and the Neville Earl of Westmorland represented the older generation, longtime associates of Henry IV, who probably found the

Opposite: *Thomas Hoccleve presenting his book,* Regement of Princes, *to the Prince of Wales, later Henry V.*

ye noble and myȝtti Prince excellent
My lord the Prince · o my lord gracious
The humble servant and obedient
Vn to youre estate hye and glorious
Of whyche I am ful tendre and ful zelous
Me recommande vnto youre worthynesse
With herte enter and spirit of meeknesse

Prince's impatience to rule as galling as did the ailing King. They were backed by most of the senior clerics who formed the backbone of any medieval administration. Among the Prince's councillors were two young Earls who shared his taste for military adventure – the Archbishop's own nephew Richard, Earl of Arundel, and Thomas Beauchamp, Earl of Warwick. But Prince Henry's chief support came from his Beaufort half-uncles, Henry and Thomas – John of Gaunt's sons by his third wife, Catherine Swynford. Thomas Beaufort acted as Chancellor while the Prince headed the Council, but his younger brother, Henry, Bishop of Winchester, was the abler of the two, a financial and administrative genius destined to play a leading role in the next two reigns. The Beauforts were shrewd enough to recognise that the future lay with the Prince and backed him accordingly. It was Bishop Henry who took it upon himself to suggest Henry IV's abdication.

There was, however, one political issue with broad implications for the future, on which Prince Henry took an opposite line to Arundel and his father. It concerned France. From the beginning of Henry IV's reign relations with France had been hostile. Charles IV of France, whose daughter had married Richard II, refused to recognise Henry IV as King, and when Henry sent the widowed Isabella back to France in 1400 he declined to part with her jewellery. The French renewed their claims to the Duchy of Aquitaine, raided Calais and sent help to Glendower in Wales. But these attacks were ill co-ordinated and half-hearted. Charles VI suffered from frequent bouts of insanity during which his brother, the Duke of Orleans, and his cousin, the Duke of Burgundy, fell to quarrelling. In 1407 the quarrel degenerated into civil war when the Duke of Orleans was assassinated at the instigation of his Burgundian rival, John the Fearless. For the English, hitherto paralysed by their own internal problems, this was a heaven-sent opportunity to divide and conquer. The only problem was which side England should choose as her ally against the other. Henry IV favoured the Orleans faction who called themselves the Armagnacs; his son preferred the Burgundian alliance.

In October 1411, while the Prince still controlled the Council, an English expedition commanded by the Earl of Arundel sailed to Burgundy's aid. But when the Prince was dismissed English policy went into reverse, and in 1412 his brother, Prince Thomas, crossed to Normandy at the head of a much larger army to help the Armagnacs. This second expedition was intimately bound up with the ill feeling between the Prince of Wales and the King. Prince Thomas, now created Duke of Clarence, had sided with his father and was thus chosen to command in his elder brother's place. Prince Henry refused to go and was accused of staying behind in order to stage a coup. His opponents at court also charged him with misappropriating funds intended for the defence of Calais. The Prince responded by sending a stream of messengers to important people explaining his case, and won from his father a promise to have the accusations against him examined in Parliament. In September 1412 he appeared in London with such 'a huge people' of retainers that fears of an armed take-over were again aroused.

Whatever we make of the poorly documented events of Henry IV's last year, it does seem that the King's final illness and death defused a potentially dangerous situation, with the royal family and the aristocracy splitting into factions, mutual accusations of disloyalty and malpractice, and retainers gathering to protect their lords. It also appears that Prince Henry behaved with an arrogance born out of the absolute conviction that he was in the right.

When the old King was finally dead and the Prince crowned Henry V, the atmosphere changed markedly for the better. Among the new King's first concerns was to extend the olive branch to those who had suffered under the previous reign. The Earl of March, whose father had been named as Richard II's heir, had his estates restored to him, the Earls of Huntingdon and Oxford were returned to favour, and the body of Richard II was reburied with pomp at Westminster. Perhaps Henry retained some affection for the murdered King who had taken him to Ireland in 1399 but declined to use the boy as a hostage when his father came to seize Richard's throne. But it was also a shrewd piece of propaganda, a call to bury old grievances and rally round to Henry's grand design – the conquest of France. The policy paid off, for two years later the only aristocratic conspiracy of Henry's reign was reported to the King by the Earl of March himself.

Clarence's expedition of 1412 had achieved nothing: as soon as he landed the Armagnacs changed their minds about seeking English help and bought him off. Henry still preferred the Burgundian alliance, but this time he was less eager to show his hand. He negotiated with the Armagnacs as well, forcing them to outbid their rivals for England's support or neutrality. Early in 1415 the Armagnacs offered him substantial territorial concessions in Aquitaine and the hand of Charles VI's daughter, Catherine, along with a dowry of 600,000 crowns. But Henry wanted much more than that. He told them he would settle for nothing less than the whole of the old Angevin Empire, lost in the reign of King John, including Normandy, Maine and Anjou. The extravagance of this claim, which no French government could possibly accept, suggests that the negotiations were just diplomatic window dressing. Henry had already made up his mind to go to war. By the time negotiations were broken off in June 1415 Parliament had already voted a double subsidy for the campaign, an army had been raised and the necessary transport requisitioned.

On 11 August Henry sailed from Southampton with an army of about 10,000 archers and men-at-arms. The army landed on the Norman coast and spent the first month of the campaign besieging Harfleur, which surrendered on 22 September. By now the season was too far gone for a march on Paris, and Henry settled for a cross-country march to Calais. Shortly after crossing the Somme he found his way blocked at Agincourt by a French army which outnumbered his own by three to one. On 25 October the two armies faced one another in a pitched battle, the French cavalry attacking the English archers in a massed charge on a narrow front. These disastrous tactics ended in a bloodbath for the chivalry of France, who lost perhaps 6,000 men dead and many more captured. Henry lost fewer than four hundred, including the Duke of York and the Earl of Suffolk.

The march to Calais had been a grave strategic risk, again the action of a man who never experienced an iota of self-doubt. The rewards were stupendous, not only in France where his bargaining position was immensely strengthened, but at home too where his people were now united to a man behind their victorious King. Agincourt achieved in a single day the goal which Henry IV had laboured for thirteen years to attain. For the next five years England's energies were harnessed exclusively to the completion of Henry's French conquests.

The task which confronted the King was still formidable. Pitched battles were rare in medieval warfare and after Agincourt the French were far too respectful of Henry's prowess to risk a second annihilation. The conquest of Normandy was to be a lengthy and tedious catalogue of sieges, of towns battered, starved or terrified into submission. This was a radical departure from the traditional forms of the Hundred Years' War – the large-scale mounted raids or *chevauchees* which devastated the countryside in search of plunder. From the very beginning Henry came in the guise of France's rightful King, determined to establish a permanent English presence in the country he subdued.

Before the second expedition sailed in 1417 the King achieved a notable diplomatic triumph. For four months in 1416 Henry entertained the Holy Roman Emperor, Sigismund, who arrived as a mediator and departed as an ally after putting his name to the Treaty of Canterbury. The treaty is proof of how well Henry argued his claim to the French Crown and dispelled the notion that he was a military adventurer taking advantage of the civil war distracting his neighbours. In October 1416 the two monarch conferred with Duke John of Burgundy at Calais.

On 1 August 1417 Henry set foot in Normandy again. Caen fell in September, followed by Verneuil

Following pages: The battle of Agincourt, in which Henry V destroyed the chivalry of France in a pitched battle which left some 6,000 French dead at a cost of 400 English lives. For the next five years Henry concentrated all his energies on completing his French conquests.

and Falaise before Christmas. John the Fearless fulfilled his part of the bargain struck at Calais by threatening Paris from the north. By August 1418 the English controlled the whole of Lower Normandy and Henry had invested the key target of Rouen. The Norman capital was too strong for an assault, but the city finally succumbed to starvation in January 1419. The remainder of the resistance throughout Normandy crumbled and by spring Henry was master of the whole Duchy.

At this point diplomacy again took precedence over military affairs. In July 1419 Henry's successes were seriously threatened by a reconciliation between the Burgundians and the Armagnacs (now known as the Dauphinists). But Henry's luck held. The murder of the Duke of Burgundy by the Dauphin's men on 10 September 1419 showed that the mutual hatred of the French factions was still more powerful than their fear of the English aggressor. The Burgundians were now ready to pay any price for Henry's alliance. By Christmas Philip, the new Duke of Burgundy, had given way to all Henry's demands: the mad Charles VI would retain the Crown during his lifetime but Henry would be recognised as his heir and would marry his daughter Catherine. In return Henry was pledged to avenge the Duke's murder and make war on the Dauphin, who still controlled most of France south of the Loire. These terms were embodied in the Treaty of Troyes in May 1420. On 2 June the King and Catherine were married at the altar of Troyes Cathedral, and on 1 December the royal couple entered Paris in triumph.

Henry had been absent from England for three and a half years when he returned in February 1421 for the Queen's coronation. A royal progress followed which took the couple through Bristol, the Welsh Marches and Leicester to the northern capital of York, then back to Westminster by way of Lincoln and Norwich. It was a brief and doubtless welcome respite, during which the Queen conceived the future Henry VI. But whatever pleasure it gave the King was cut short by the news of his brother Clarence's death on a raid in the Loire country – a bitter and timely reminder that his task in France was still only half done.

In June he returned to the wars, and the winter

In 1420 Henry married Catherine, the daughter of Charles VI of France, in Troyes Cathedral. Her dowry was 600,000 crowns.

months passed in the protracted siege of Meaux, one of the last Dauphinist strongpoints north of the Loire. The town's capitulation in May 1422 was to be Henry's last triumph. During the winter he contracted an illness – probably dysentery – which he could not shake off. In July he had to be carried in a litter to the siege of Cosne on the Loire. A few days later he had to turn back, and in the early morning of 31 August he died at Bois de Vincennes.

How can one assess the tremendous achievement of Henry V's nine short years as King? Certainly he owed a great deal to luck and circumstance. At Agincourt the blundering tactics of the French contributed as much to the English victory as did

Henry's generalship. His subsequent successes could not have been achieved without the internecine hatred of the two French factions. As one contemporary cynic noted, the English entered Paris through the hole in the Duke of Burgundy's skull.

But Henry was much more than a soldier with fortune on his side. He was a statesman with a range of exceptional talents which enabled him to bend fortune to his ends. Like Napoleon, Henry V was a glutton for hard work and no detail concerning the administration of his conquests was beneath his notice. The logistical effort of supplying the army of 1417 on foreign soil for more than three years was a feat in itself equal to the victory of Agincourt. During his campaigns in France he insisted even on dealing personally with all petitions forwarded from his Parliaments in England. Contemporaries, his enemies as much as his friends, were profoundly struck by Henry's sense of justice, which was linked with a strict adherence to the tenets of Catholic piety. As Prince of Wales he had personally presided over the funeral pyre of an unrepentant Lollard – one of those proto-Protestants who foreshadowed the Reformation of the succeeding century. On the way to Agincourt he had a man hanged for robbing a church. 'He was a Prince of Justice', wrote the Burgundian chronicler Chastellain, 'he gave support to none out of favour, nor did he suffer wrong to go unpunished out of regard for affinity'. Underlying all Henry's qualities was his ironclad will-power which not only drove him but also provided the inspiration for others. He gathered around him a team of outstanding military and administrative ability, most notably his Beaufort uncles and his brothers, Thomas the soldier and John, Duke of Bedford, who became Regent of France on Henry's death. No other fifteenth-century king was so ably or so devotedly served, and indeed most found more reason to fear their relatives than to favour them. Another Frenchman observed shrewdly that Henry did not look like a soldier at all, but rather possessed the gravity of a cleric. This view is confirmed by his portraits which reveal a lean, hatchet face dominated by sombre brown eyes, pursed lips and a long thin nose. The face contains more than a hint of the fanatic, so impatient to supplant his father and subordinate himself to the single obsession of conquering France. He certainly had little time to spare during his reign for any private life or domestic comforts. Even on his deathbed he was immersed in plans and provisions for his son's minority, without seeking or receiving a visit from the child's mother. There is a frightening quality about this all-conquering, all-competent zealot, which could account for the legends which sprang up after his death of his wild and boisterous youth as Prince of Wales. These tales lend to his character a posthumous humanity not apparent in life.

Perhaps Henry was lucky to die young and pass straight into legend. Even before his death there are signs that his heroic designs were parting company with his country's interests. The Commons were complaining of his long absences. From 1420 grants from Parliament to prosecute the wars were proving hard to come by. The Dauphin was still master of more than half of France and future success depended on the continuing split between his party and the Burgundians. It was a heavy inheritance to leave in the care of the nine-month-old infant, Henry VI.

HENRY VI

r. 1422–71

SOME FIFTY YEARS AFTER HENRY V was laid to rest, a lonely old man was quietly done to death in the Tower of London after he had lost his wits, his two kingdoms and his only son. Everything about the reign of Henry VI is in stark contrast to that of his father. But the first and most striking contrast is that whereas the father had to wait with ill-concealed impatience for his inheritance, the son had his thrust upon him before he was one year old.

From the earliest age Henry was frequently paraded at public ceremonies, either seated on his mother's lap or tottering on his own feet between his royal relatives. As he grew up he saw progressively less of the Queen, who had formed a liaison with a Welsh squire named Owen Tudor and was busy raising a second family. In 1428 he was placed in the care of Richard Beauchamp, Earl of Warwick, and one of his father's most trusted lieutenants. Warwick was instructed to 'teach him nurture, literature, language and the manner of cunning, to chastise him when he doth amiss and to remove persons not behoveful nor expedient from his presence'. Henry proved himself a precocious child. At the age of ten, so his governor reported, he was questioning whether he, a king, should be chastised for his misdemeanours and taking an interest in matters 'not behoveful'. The Council was called in to read the riot act.

At a tender age the boy King was introduced to the most intractable problems of his early reign – the deteriorating situation in France and the unedifying squabbles of those closest to the throne. The emergence of Joan of Arc and the crowning of the Dauphin as Charles VII at Rheims in 1429 heralded the Valois revival. Bedford, the English Regent in France, was sufficiently worried to call for his nephew's own coronation and to bring him over to France for a state visit. On 2 December 1431 Henry was crowned King of France at St Denis in Paris. However, the tide had turned against the English. Duke Philip of Burgundy knew it and was looking for a way out of his alliance. In 1435 he made his separate peace with Charles VII at Arras; in the same year the valiant Bedford, whose earlier successes had almost matched those of Henry V, breathed his last. From that point it was all downhill. When Henry heard of Burgundy's desertion he burst into tears.

At home the trouble was caused by Henry's other and infinitely less able uncle, Humphrey, Duke of Gloucester. Gloucester was a fine scholar but a poor statesman. Though he was nominated Regent of England in Henry V's will, his peers distrusted him sufficiently to insist that he govern with the advice of the Council, not as Regent but as Protector. He quarrelled incessantly with that other pillar of the Lancastrian establishment, the portly Bishop Beaufort, and twice, in 1425 and 1432, their animosity threatened an outbreak of violence. In 1434 Gloucester even picked a quarrel with his brother Bedford, accusing him of mismanaging the war. Henry, in an early display of well-meant but flat-footed conciliation, attempted to mediate between his uncles in person and declared both parties innocent of blame.

Despite their differences the Council did see Henry safely through his minority, which came to an end without a formal declaration to that effect in 1437. The story of the next thirteen years is such a

Opposite: A portrait, c. 1550, of Henry VI, who succeeded to the throne before he was a year old, and whose reign was to prove so tragically different to that of his illustrious father.

HENRICVS. VI.

Above: *Henry VI being crowned King of England in Westminster Abbey. His coronation as King of France took place at St Denis in Paris, making him the only sovereign to have been crowned both in England and France.*

dreary record of infighting at court, disorder in the shires and reverses in France that one is tempted to dwell instead on the anecdotes of Henry's Christian virtues compiled by his biographer and one-time confessor, John Blacman. It is true that he displayed qualities which would have done credit to a monk or a mendicant friar and that his two great foundations at Eton and King's College, Cambridge, in 1440 and 1441, still preserve his memory. He was chaste, pious and generous. He abhorred all forms of bloodshed, and intervened frequently to spare the lives of criminals and traitors. On one occasion, while riding through Cripplegate into London, 'he saw over the gate there the quarter of a man on a tall stake, and asked what it was. And when his lords made answer that it was the quarter of a traitor of his . . . he said, "Take it away. I will not have any Christian man so cruelly handled for my sake"'. This story, and others like it, have been much quoted by Henry's admirers, who see him as a man dragged down by the coarse spirit of his time.

But the truth is that even Blacman's eulogies sometimes cast Henry in a faintly ridiculous, if not downright foolish, light. He stormed out in a huff one Christmas when 'a certain great lord brought before him a dance or show of young ladies with bared bosoms'. He rebuked the scholars of Eton for visiting his own court over the Thames at Windsor 'bidding them not to do so again, lest his young lambs should come to relish the corrupt deeds and habits of his courtiers'. As a youth he spied on his servants 'through hidden windows of his chamber, lest any foolish impertinence of women coming into the house should . . . cause the fall of any of his household'. 'From his youth up he always wore round-toed shoes and boots like a farmer's . . . a long gown with a rolled hood like a townsman, and a full coat reaching below his knees, with shoes, boots and footgear wholly black, rejecting expressly all fashion of clothing.' On feast days, when custom demanded that he wear the crown, Henry atoned with a hair shirt next to his skin.

So it goes on. These were not the attributes of a king and the truth is that Henry had no real wish to act like one. His impatience with secular affairs emerges from another Blacman story: when 'a certain mighty duke' knocked at his door the King complained to his confessor, 'they do so interrupt me that by day or night I can hardly snatch a moment to be refreshed without disturbance'. There lay one half of the coming tragedy. The King was the linchpin of medieval government. It was not just a quaint custom that even during Henry's infancy official documents referred to him as King in fact as well as name. His job was to initiate, to unite, to inspire – the very things that made Henry V such a success. Henry VI proved himself incapable of all three.

There was, however, one regal function which Henry could not lay aside. A vast range of patronage – from the great offices of state to the smallest perks of feudal law – lay at his disposal and had to be disposed. This was the other half of the tragedy. Henry gave too freely and he often gave to the wrong people. The result was that after 1437 the executive power of the Crown fell into the hands of a narrow clique of men who had access to Henry. Two of these were William de la Pole, fourth Earl of Suffolk, and William Ayscough, Bishop of Salisbury. Both rose to eminence because of the key positions they occupied in the King's household. Suffolk, a veteran soldier

with fourteen years' continuous service in France to his credit, became Henry's Steward in 1435 and the Bishop was his confessor. Henry's great-uncle, Bishop Beaufort, also retained his influence until his retirement from political life in 1443 at the ripe old age of sixty-seven. These men were soon under attack for their excessive influence over the King, and resorted to some fairly shady manoeuvring in order to retain their monopoly. In 1439 Gloucester complained to the King that Beaufort and his friends had cut off 'me, your sole uncle, together with my cousin of York . . . and many other lords of your kin from having knowledge of any great matters that might touch your high estate and realm'. In the summer of 1441 the King's advisers replied with an accusation of sorcery against Gloucester's wife, Eleanor. The Duchess was forced to undergo public penance in the streets of London, and Gloucester, though not directly involved, was neatly discredited.

France was still the burning political issue of the day, with Henry's advisers favouring a peaceful accommodation while Gloucester followed a hawkish line which endeared him to the London mob. The doves of course prevailed and in 1444 Suffolk secured his ascendancy at court by arranging for Henry to marry Charles VII's niece, the fifteen-year-old Margaret of Anjou. The King gratefully added a marquisate to the long list of Suffolk's preferments. Unhappily the result of the marriage was not a lasting peace with France but the renewal of war which led speedily to the loss of all English territories in France save Calais. Margaret was carefully briefed before arrival to work on her future husband and persuade him to surrender the county of Maine. Henry duly promised to do so, but without telling anybody. When the news leaked out, it was greeted with a surge of patriotic outrage. The spring Parliament of 1447 had to meet in Bury rather than risk the fury of the Londoners, and Gloucester was arrested on arrival to be charged with planning an uprising. His death in confinement a week later quickly gave rise to rumours that Suffolk had ordered his murder. To retrieve his tarnished reputation at home, Suffolk suddenly turned hawk in France and launched a provocative attack on Charles VII's ally, the Duke of Brittany. Charles at once retaliated by invading Normandy.

Rouen fell in October 1449, Caen in the following July, and by September the whole Duchy was in French hands. In 1451 Charles turned on Gascony and took Bordeaux. Two years later a relieving force under the Earl of Talbot was cut to pieces at Castillon. The Duchy of Aquitaine, after nearly 300 years in England's possession, was lost for ever.

Not even Henry could save Suffolk from the repercussions of the loss of Normandy. In February 1450 the King's 'priviest and best trusted' adviser was impeached in Parliament, charged with every sort of mismanagement and embezzlement. Henry did his best to get him out of harm's way by banishing his favourite, but the ship carrying him to safety was intercepted in the Channel and Suffolk was executed on the spot. In truth he deserved little better, and not only because his bungling brought about the catastrophe in France. For years he had been feathering his nest while Henry's Exchequer plunged into debt. He had presided over a general slackening of control at the centre which in turn bred lawlessness, corruption and unrest throughout the kingdom. His most fitting memorial is the Kentish rising known as Cade's Rebellion which exploded shortly after his death in May 1450. The rebels' chief demand was for the punishment of 'the false progeny and affinity of the Duke of Suffolk'. 'His false council', they concluded, 'has lost his (the King's) law: his merchandise is lost: his common people are destroyed: France is lost. The King himself is so placed that he may not pay for his drink.' 'In this same time', wrote a later chronicler, 'the realm of England was out of all good governance, as it had been many days before, for the King was simple, and led by covetous counsel, and owed more than he was worth.'

It would be foolish to follow the polite fiction of the time and exonerate Henry of all blame for these events. Government was in the hands of the men he himself had chosen. There was no lack of critics to tell him what was wrong. Nor was he incapable of action: he would intervene readily enough when his favourites came under fire. The best that can be said of Henry is that he was quite exceptionally naive.

The disaster which overtook Suffolk did nothing to open the King's eyes. In August his defeated lieutenant in France, Edmund Beaufort, Duke of Somerset, returned to London and stepped into the vacant niche of court favourite. Somerset was a nephew of the departed Bishop and associate of Suffolk. It was bad enough that the new favourite should be tainted by failure in France and friendship with Suffolk's circle: but more serious in the long term was Somerset's long-standing personal feud with Richard, Duke of York, the greatest landowner in England after the King, who had long been at the losing end of a running fight with the Beauforts over the conduct of the war. As a supporter of the Duke of Gloucester he had been excluded from Henry's charmed circle, and in 1449 his opponents had him appointed Lieutenant of Ireland for ten years in order to get him out of the way. In 1450 he returned from his post without permission to take up the cudgels with his rival Duke.

Their rivalry was all the keener for the fact that both Dukes stood a good chance of inheriting the throne. Margaret had as yet borne no children. Somerset was descended from John of Gaunt and although the Beauforts had been barred from the succession by Parliament in Henry IV's reign, the Act was not immutable. York was descended from Gaunt's elder brother, Lionel, through his mother, Anne Mortimer, and from Gaunt's younger brother, Edmund, through his father, Richard, Earl of Cambridge. From the confrontation of these two men sprang the Wars of the Roses.

For the next three years (1450–53) the court party, headed by Somerset, successfully resisted all York's attempts to dislodge them. When the Member for Bristol suggested in the Commons that York should be recognised as Henry's heir, he was promptly sent to the Tower. In the spring of 1452 York actually marched on London with an army at his back. Somerset quickly assembled a larger force and the way at Dartford. On this occasion bloodshed was avoided by trickery. York agreed to dismiss his force on condition that Somerset should be arrested and called to account for his misdoings in Normandy. But when York allowed himself to be brought into Henry's tent, he found himself a prisoner. Somerset wisely refrained from putting his enemy on trial, for popular sympathy favoured York. The Duke was released after swearing never again to take up

Above: *A medal by Pietro da Milano depicting Margaret of Anjou, the niece of Charles VII of France, who was married to Henry when she was fifteen.*

arms against any of Henry's subjects.

In 1453 came several dramatic reversals of fortune. First, the Hundred Years' War came to an end with Talbot's annihilation at Castillon, and Henry's government was once more held to blame. In August the King suffered the first of those bouts of insanity which were to recur at intervals throughout the rest of his life. His illness reduced him to a state of paralytic melancholia, depriving him of memory, speech and reason. For this he had to thank the genes inherited from his mad grandfather, Charles VI of France. It is ironic that only two months later the House of Lancaster was blessed with the birth of a male heir. After eight barren years of marriage Queen Margaret presented her afflicted husband with a son. Prince Edward was shown to the King for his blessing at Windsor on New Year's Day 1454, 'but . . . in vain, for they departed thence without any answer or countenance, saving only that once he looked upon the Prince and cast down his eyes again, without any more'.

Henry and Margaret were in many respects a most ill-suited pair. In contrast to his ineffectual, otherworldly nature she was a tigress, quick-tempered, courageous and passionate in both her likes and dislikes. She cannot have found Henry a very attentive husband. In the early years of their marriage the rumour was that the King's confessor and councillor, Bishop Ayscough, was responsible for dissuading him from having 'his sport' with the Queen, advising Henry not to 'come nigh her'. Given Henry's prudish views on sex and nudity it is doubtful whether he needed much persuading. When he recovered from his first madness he himself expressed bewilderment at the birth of his son, who, he said, must have been conceived by the Holy Ghost.

Notwithstanding their incompatibility, the Queen was a powerful force in the world of politics. Henry was putty in her hands when she wanted something done, and she developed a fierce, almost partisan, loyalty to his chief ministers: first Suffolk, whom she treated as a father; then Somerset, who was accused of being her lover. Equally fierce was Margaret's dislike of York, whom she saw not as the self-styled victim of Somerset's wiles, but as an arrogant aggressor intent on destroying herself, her husband and her son. She was, as it happened, proved absolutely right, but it was her own implacable hostility towards York which converted him from the one to the other.

Ironically, York had his first taste of power soon after Prince Edward's birth knocked him out of the succession. With the King clearly unfit to rule there was nothing Margaret or Somerset could do to prevent York's appointment as Protector in March 1454. Somerset was arrested (in the Queen's apartments), impeached and committed to the Tower. Towards Christmas the King recovered, and in February 1455 York was dismissed, Somerset restored. Mutual hatred and suspicion were by now so deeply entrenched that a recourse to arms became inevitable. York's appeals to the King were suppressed by Henry's courtiers. On 22 May 1455 a Yorkist force confronted Somerset and the King at St Albans. Parleying broke down when Henry refused to surrender the Duke of Somerset. Within an hour the battle was lost, Somerset was dead, and the King, his neck grazed by an arrow, meekly allowed the victor to renew his oath of allegiance.

Above: *The Neville family at prayer from the Neville Book of Hours. The Nevilles were one of the most powerful families in the north of England, strong supporters of Richard, Duke of York.*

Despite the bloodshed a settlement should now have been possible. It would be wrong to think that the peerage was irrevocably split into two hostile factions, the Yorkists on one side, Lancastrians on the other. The men who backed York – including the powerful Richard Neville, Earl of Warwick – did so not because they wanted to make him King in Henry's place, but because of their various private grudges against members of the court circle. With Somerset out of the way most peers favoured conciliation, and Henry himself certainly had no wish to propagate a blood feud.

Queen Margaret unfortunately took a very different view, and it was she who prevailed. The heirs of the men who had fallen at St Albans readily supported her and soon the two leading northern families, the Nevilles and the Perceys, were at each other's throats again. In March 1458 Henry, on his own initiative, made a remarkable effort to forestall another explosion of violence. At a special ceremony of reconciliation all the chief protagonists, including Margaret and York, marched hand in hand to St Paul's behind the King.

This was all a charade. In the summer of 1459 Margaret raised another army and marched on York's stronghold of Ludlow in the Welsh Marches. This time the Yorkists were routed: the Duke fled to Ireland, the Earl of Salisbury, his son Warwick and York's heir Edward, Earl of March, to Calais. The Calais contingent reappeared in the summer of 1460 and in turn routed the royal army at the battle of Northampton. This time York was in no mood for further compromise. It was clear that while Margaret ruled the King any compromise would simply be undone the moment the court party felt strong enough to renege on it. Accordingly, in October, York submitted to Parliament his claim to the throne of England.

It looked as though a repeat performance of 1399 was about to be enacted. However, the Lords, including even the two Neville Earls, were not yet ready to sanction such a revolutionary move. It was agreed instead that Henry should remain King for life, but recognise York as his heir. Henry seems to have acquiesced in the disinheriting of his son. Not so Margaret who had eluded capture at Northampton and taken refuge with the Prince behind the battlements of Harlech Castle. In a fine display of martial courage she took ship for Berwick on the Scottish border and appeared in mid-December at the head of a new Lancastrian host. York and Salisbury hurried north with a small force to meet the threat and rashly committed themselves to battle without waiting for reinforcements. On 30 December 1460 York's army was crushed at Wakefield. The Duke himself died on the battlefield, and his head was later displayed on the gates of York wearing a paper crown.

In 1461, the final year of Henry's reign, events came thick and fast. As Margaret marched on London, St Albans was the scene of a second battle at which Warwick was defeated and the King restored to his wife. Nevertheless, London's gates remained closed, its citizens fearful of the looting which might ensure if Margaret's northerners gained admittance. Warwick managed to join his mauled troops with those of York's eldest son, Edward, who entered London in triumph, and was installed as King in Westminster Abbey on 4 March. Henry and Margaret withdrew towards Yorkshire, with Edward at their heels. On 29 March the two armies fought it out near Towton in a blizzard of wind and snow. It was a bloody engagement and ended in the massacre of Margaret's soldiers. The King and Queen took refuge over the border in Scotland.

Nine years were to pass before Henry regained his throne. The story is briefly told, for it is really an epilogue to his reign. For three years he hovered on the outskirts of his lost kingdom at Harlech and at the Northumberland fortress towns of Berwick and Bamburgh, while Margaret schemed to enlist the Scots and the French in his cause. Some minor successes were achieved in the north with the help of Piers de Breze, a renowned French captain on loan from Margaret's cousin Louis XI, but there was not enough money or manpower to pose a serious threat. By the summer of 1463 even Margaret was sufficiently discouraged to return to France with her French allies and her son, leaving Henry precariously ensconced at Bamburgh. Hopes flared again the following spring when the dwindling rump of Lancastrian leaders attempted a rising in Northumberland, but they were trounced at Hexham by Warwick's brother, Lord Montagu. The fall of Bamburgh in the summer deprived Henry of his last stronghold and he seems to have spent the best part of the next year as a wandering fugitive. He was finally picked up near Clitheroe, Lancashire, in July 1465, from where, in Blacman's words, 'he was brought as a traitor and criminal to London, and imprisoned in the Tower there; where, like a true follower of Christ, he patiently endured hunger, thirst, mockings, derisions, abuse and many other hardships'.

And so at last to the bizarre episode of Henry's restoration, the so-called Readeption of Henry VI. The background details belong more properly to the reign of Edward IV. Suffice it to say that on Wednesday, 3 October 1470 the astonished Henry – 'not

THE HOUSES OF LANCASTER AND YORK

Showing their descent from Edward III and the Tudor claim to the throne

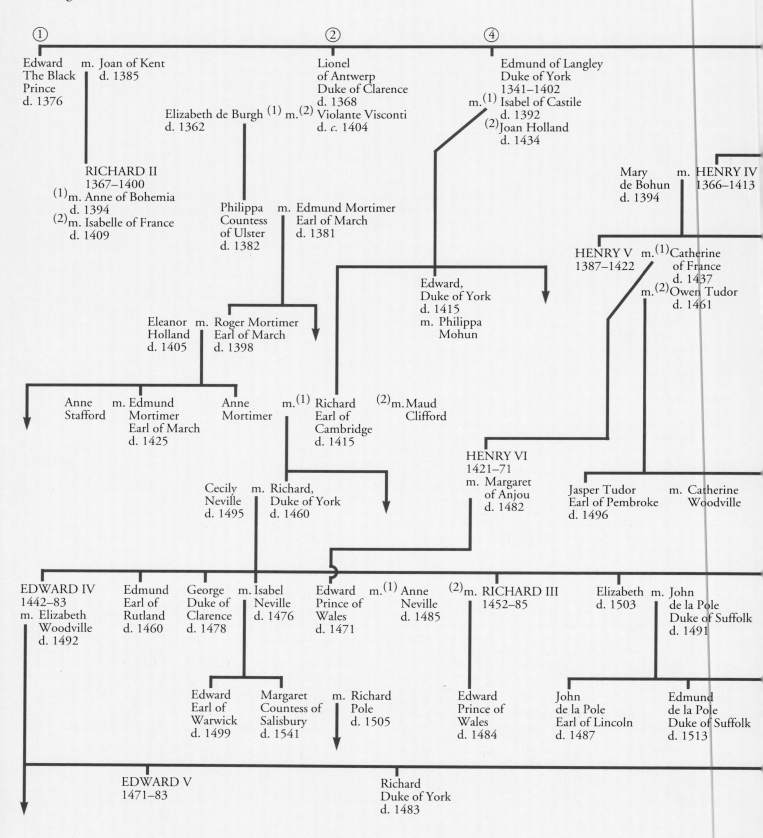

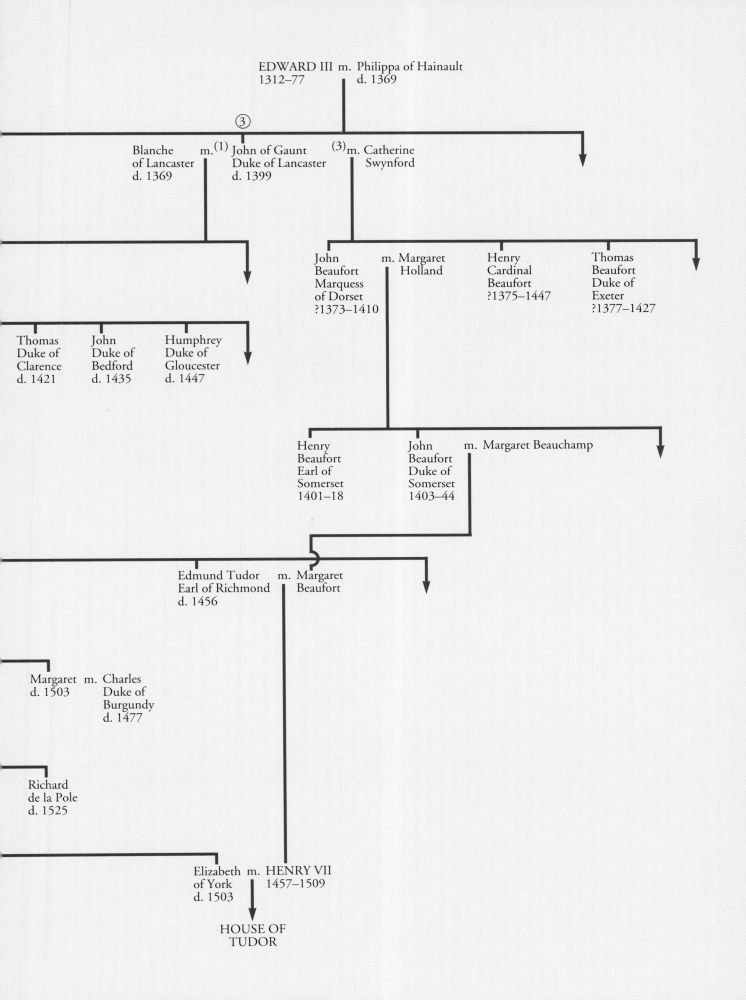

EDWARD III m. Philippa of Hainault
1312–77   d. 1369

③

Blanche   m.(1) John of Gaunt   (3)m. Catherine
of Lancaster   Duke of Lancaster   Swynford
d. 1369   d. 1399

John   m. Margaret   Henry   Thomas
Beaufort   Holland   Cardinal   Beaufort
Marquess   Beaufort   Duke of
of Dorset   ?1375–1447   Exeter
?1373–1410   ?1377–1427

Thomas   John   Humphrey
Duke of   Duke of   Duke of
Clarence   Bedford   Gloucester
d. 1421   d. 1435   d. 1447

Henry   John   m. Margaret Beauchamp
Beaufort   Beaufort
Earl of   Duke of
Somerset   Somerset
1401–18   1403–44

Edmund Tudor   m. Margaret
Earl of Richmond   Beaufort
d. 1456

Margaret m. Charles
d. 1503   Duke of
             Burgundy
             d. 1477

Richard
de la Pole
d. 1525

Elizabeth m. HENRY VII
of York   1457–1509
d. 1503

HOUSE OF
TUDOR

cleanly kept as should seem such a Prince' – was suddenly transferred to the luxuriously furnished apartments of Edward IV's Queen and addressed once again as King. Three days later his former adversary, the Earl of Warwick, knelt before him to ask forgiveness. Later Henry, dressed in a long blue gown, was conveyed to St Paul's to give thanks for his delivery. At his new quarters in the Bishop of London's palace in Fulham Henry learned from Warwick the details of the Earl's quarrel with Edward IV, of Edward's flight to Burgundy and of the Kingmaker's reconciliation with Queen Margaret at Angers Cathedral. In the following month Warwick's episcopal brother George opened Parliament with an address on the text, taken from the Book of Jeremiah, 'Return, O back-sliding children'. In December came news from France that Prince Edward had married Anne Neville, Warwick's fifteen-year-old daughter.

Throughout the Readeption Henry remained, as always, a puppet, while Warwick pulled the strings. In the words of one chronicler, 'the King was as mute as a crowned calf'. His one act was to send food and clothing to Edward IV's abandoned wife who was about to give birth in the Sanctuary of Westminster Abbey. He never saw his own family again. In March Edward IV landed in Yorkshire, and on 11 April, having outmanoeuvred Warwick, he re-entered London. Two days later Henry was compelled to join Edward's army on the road to Barnet, where on Easter Sunday, Warwick's army was put to flight and the Kingmaker slain. On the same day Queen Margaret landed too late in Weymouth, to be defeated in her turn some three weeks later at Tewkesbury. The seventeen-year-old Prince Edward was among the dead. Margaret was brought back to London and lodged in the Tower, though not in Henry's company.

Henry's captivity ended on the night of 21 May, the day Edward returned to the capital from his victory at Tewkesbury. The chronicler Henry Warkworth recorded that he 'was put to death . . . between eleven and twelve of the clock, being then at

the Tower . . . the Duke of Gloucester . . . and many other; and on the morrow he was chested and brought to St Paul's, and his face was open that every man might see him . . .'. Later he was buried in the Lady Chapel at Chertsey Abbey.

Henry was killed because the magic of his name could still inspire the respect and loyalty which men like Warwick needed as a cloak for their ambitions. His execution was an act of state designed to prevent further rebellion in his name. Even in those blood-soaked days it aroused a shiver of horror among contemporaries, who pointed to Henry's blameless conduct, his charity and his devotion to God. His burial-place soon became a shrine, and it was later said that Richard III moved the body to St George's, Windsor, to put a stop to the pilgrimages and the talk of miracles. Yet Henry must take his share of responsibility for the events which brought him down. The Wars of the Roses sprang from his failure to meet the enormous demands of medieval kingship. If the man was a saint, the King was a political simpleton, who would neither provide leadership nor delegate it to those who could.

A fitting epitaph is the poem Henry wrote himself:

Kingdoms are but cares,
State is devoid of stay,
Riches are ready snares,
And hasten to decay.

Pleasure is a privy prick
Which vice doth still provoke;
Pomp, imprompt; and fame, a flame;
Power, a smouldering smoke.

Who meanth to remove the rock
Owt of the slimy mud,
Shall mire himself, and hardly scape
The swelling of the flood.

Opposite: *An illustration from a law treatise of Henry VI's reign, showing the court of the King's bench at Westminster. At the top sit five presiding judges, and below them the King's attorney, the coroner and masters of the court. A prisoner stands at the bar, with six more in the foreground.*

This boke late translate here in sigh̃t
By Antony Erle   that vertuou̅s knyght
Please it to accepte to youre noble grace
And at youre comement leysou̅r and space

THE HOUSE OF YORK
1461–85

———❦———

EDWARD IV 1461–83

RICHARD III 1483–5

———❦———

Opposite: Edward IV with Elizabeth Woodville, the ill-fated
Prince Edward and his uncle Richard, Duke of Gloucester, later
Richard III, from *The Dictes and Sayenges of the Phylosophers*
(*c.* 1477), the first dated book to be printed in England.

EDWARD IV
r. 1461-83

'WORDS FAIL ME TO RELATE HOW well the commons love and adore him, as if he were their God. The entire kingdom keeps holiday for the event.' So wrote an Italian observer who witnessed the coronation of Edward IV on 28 June 1461.

The euphoria which greeted Edward is not difficult to understand. Over six feet tall and exceptionally good-looking, he had the physical presence of a king. At nineteen years of age he had already proved himself a brave and resourceful general. After the disaster of Wakefield which claimed the lives of his father, the Duke of York, his brother Edmund and his uncle, the Earl of Salisbury, he had defeated Jasper Tudor at Mortimer's Cross in Wales, saved London from Queen Margaret's northerners and won his crowning victory at Towton. With his prodigious feats on the battlefield he combined an instinctive grasp of political showmanship. He loved to be seen in public, dressed always in the latest fashions, and treated all his subjects, high and low, with the same easy familiarity. Among his many accomplishments was his reputation for being able to remember the names and fortunes of all his subjects of any importance throughout the kingdom.

He understood too the reasons why successive Parliaments under Henry IV and Henry VI had proved so stubborn in opposition to the sovereign. Edward won the approval of his Commons by adopting the policies once voiced in opposition. He saw it as his first priority to make the Crown solvent. The Crown lands were put in the hands of salaried officials rather than doled out at ludicrous rents to fortune-seeking courtiers and their clients. Many recipients of Lancastrian largesse found their lands confiscated or resumed by Act of Parliament. Detailed ordinances were set down for the control of the royal household expenses. The King also showed a keen interest in foreign trade and backed a number of successful commercial ventures as a merchant in his own right. Such measures testified not only to Edward's acumen but to the fact that the Yorkists owed a great deal of their support to the promise of better government and financial reform. Edward meant it when he told the Commons in 1467 that 'I purpose to live of mine own and not to charge my subjects but in great and urgent causes'.

However, these achievements really belong to the second part of Edward's reign. The first ten years were dominated by his relations with his power-hungry cousin, Richard Neville, Earl of Warwick. Although Edward wore the crown it was initially Warwick, fourteen years his senior, who called the tune. The Earl's pre-eminence was the supreme example of what inspired matchmaking could do for a family. Warwick's grandfather, Ralph Neville, had married Joan Beaufort, daughter of John of Gaunt. He could thus claim to be of royal blood as a great-great-grandson of Edward III. His father, also called Richard, acquired the earldom of Salisbury by marriage to the former Earl's daughter, Alice. This inheritance passed to Warwick when his father was captured and executed at Wakefield in 1460. Warwick himself married an even greater heiress, Anne Beauchamp, and through her acquired his earldom along with a vast inheritance in Wales and

Opposite: *A portrait of Edward IV, who was considered exceptionally good looking and, at over six feet tall, had a kingly bearing which he displayed to full effect in the latest fashions.*

ELIZABETH · VXOR
EDWARDVS · IIII

the West Midlands. His manors and castles spanned more than half the counties of England. Warwick's numerous brothers, sisters, uncles and aunts had also married well, none more so than his aunt Cicely Neville, a famed beauty who married the Duke of York and in April 1442 gave birth at Rouen to the future Edward IV.

Without the Neville connection the Yorkists could not have triumphed over the majority of the baronial houses who remained loyal to Henry VI. Warwick, a domineering, short-tempered and ambitious character, expected and received the rewards to match his services. He held office as Chamberlain of England, Captain of Calais and Warden of the Cinque Ports. The upbringing of Edward's youngest brother, Richard, was also entrusted to his care (at the ancestral Neville stronghold of Middleham in Yorkshire).

For the first four years of Edward's reign Warwick and his brother John continued their labours on the King's behalf. While they were mopping up the last pockets of Lancastrian resistance in the north, the King tasted the pleasures of court life at Westminster and Windsor. In 1464, after the decisive battle of Hexham, John Neville was rewarded with the hereditary Percy earldom of Northumberland and another brother, George Neville, became Archbishop of York.

But in the autumn of 1464 there arose the first signs of dissension between the great Earl and his royal cousin. Two issues – sex and diplomacy – lay at the root of the trouble. Edward was an insatiable womaniser with, it appears, a special taste for older ladies. According to the contemporary French historian Philippe de Commynes, Edward 'thought upon nothing but women and that more than reason would'. Another foreigner, Dominic Mancini, who visited England towards the end of Edward's reign records that 'he pursued with no discrimination the married and the unmarried, the noble and lowly: however he took none by force. He overcame all by money and promises, and having conquered them,

he dismissed them.' Early in the reign Edward apparently entered into a marriage contract with the widowed Lady Eleanor Butler, a daughter of old Talbot, 'the terror of the French', in order to coax her to his bed. In May 1464 another reluctant widow, Lady Elizabeth Woodville, refused to submit until Edward actually married her. With extraordinary lack of foresight the King agreed to her terms and the couple were secretly made man and wife, 'after which spousals ended, he went to bed and tarried there for four hours'.

At about the same time Warwick was negotiating with France's King Louis XI for a treaty of friendship which was to be sealed by the marriage of Edward IV to a French princess. These negotiations, which Warwick conducted off his own bat, meant a great deal to the Earl who was flattered by Louis's overtures and given to understand that he would receive French lands and titles as his reward. The revelation of Edward's secret marriage was therefore both a personal affront and a blow to Warwick's grandiose diplomatic ambitions. To rub salt in the wound the King's bride was the widow of a Lancastrian knight, and brought with her to court a swarm of relatives – two sons, five brothers and seven sisters – eager for advancement. Within two years of the marriage three of the sisters were in their turn married to the heirs of great baronial houses and one of her sons was married to the Duke of Exeter's daughter, previously pledged to a nephew of Warwick. The most notorious match was reserved for the Queen's brother, John: as one chronicler put it, 'Catherine, Duchess of Norfolk, a slip of a girl about eighty years old, was married to John Woodville, aged twenty years. A diabolical marriage.'

Over the next four years (1464–8) Edward made it abundantly clear that he no longer regarded himself as Warwick's protégé. The King favoured an alliance with Burgundy, England's traditional ally and trading partner, and backed the proposal that his sister, Margaret, should marry Charles of Burgundy.

Opposite: *The beautiful Lady Elizabeth Woodville, widow of a Lancastrian knight, withstood Edward's attentions until he married her, in secret, thereby spoiling the power-hungry Earl of Warwick's tactical negotiations for the King's marriage to a French princess.*

At the same time he did not feel strong enough to put a stop to Warwick's flirtation with Louis VI. England's diplomacy thus had two masters, each pursuing contradictory aims while interested spectators, like Sir John Paston, placed bets on the outcome. In the spring of 1468 Edward had his way and Margaret married the Duke of Burgundy. This match tipped Warwick from sullen opposition into undeclared rebellion. He had made one King; why not another? A new puppet was ready in the wings in the shape of Edward's own brother, George, Duke of Clarence. The foolish Clarence nursed exalted notions of his own importance which the King did not apparently share. He had already aligned himself with Warwick over the Burgundian alliance and in 1467 Edward had to scotch his proposed marriage to Warwick's elder daughter, Isabel Neville. The prospect of a crown made Clarence an easy prey to the Kingmaker's new conspiracy.

It started early in 1469 with a series of Neville-inspired risings in the north and Midlands. In July Warwick and Clarence slipped across the Channel to Calais, where Clarence was married to Isabel. In the meantime Edward was bottled up at Nottingham, where he confronted a rebel army easily outnumbering his own. On 26 July 1469 a relief force coming to the King's aid was cut to pieces near Banbury. With disaster staring him in the face, Edward now decided on a strategic capitulation. He dispersed his army and allowed himself to fall into Warwick's hands.

This was a crucial gamble and it paid off. Warwick, who had intended to depose Edward with the assent of a compliant Parliament, found himself beset by a breakdown of local order reminiscent of the worst years of Henry VI's reign. The conspirators lost their nerve and far from deposing Edward they were compelled to release him so that order could be restored in the shires by the King's authority. The rebels were formally reconciled with their King and in October 1469 Edward returned to his capital. It was a brilliant recovery whereby military disaster was transformed into a political victory. However, it was

abundantly clear that accounts would have to be settled. Edward could not contemplate a permanent truce with the man who had rebelled against him, executed the Queen's father and brother and turned his own brother against him. Warwick knew it too, and in the spring of 1470 rebellion broke out again in Wales and in Lincolnshire at the Kingmaker's instigation. This time Edward put the rebels to flight, and Warwick, with the wretched Clarence still in tow, had to flee to France.

For Europe's master spinner of diplomatic webs, the 'universal spider' Louis XI, this was a god-sent opportunity. The once-mighty Earl of Warwick, so assiduously courted over the years, was now sufficiently humbled for Louis to pull off his cherished ambition: the reconciliation of the Kingmaker with Margaret of Anjou. On 22 July 1470 Warwick made his submission to Henry VI's Queen at Angers Cathedral. In September he was in England again accompanied by two Lancastrian stalwarts, the Earl of Oxford and Henry VI's half-brother, Jasper Tudor. Their landing caught Edward ill prepared in York; marching south he was very nearly captured by Warwick's brother, John. The King, accompanied by his brother, Richard of Gloucester, Lord Hastings and a few retainers, dashed across country to Lynn and embarked for Burgundy. While Warwick brought Henry VI out of the Tower and put him back on the throne, Edward's future lay in the hands of the Duke of Burgundy. Charles was at first reluctant to embroil himself in his brother-in-law's problems, but he changed his mind when first Louis XI and then Warwick declared war on him. He finally agreed to lend his brother-in-law a fleet and some 1,500 Burgundian troops, and on 11 March 1471 Edward set sail for the reconquest of his kingdom.

One month later the Kingmaker fought his last battle at Barnet. Apart from his superior generalship Edward owed his victory to the lingering suspicions between the old-guard Lancastrians and their new-found ally. Margaret of Anjou did not land in England until the very day of Warwick's defeat and

Opposite: *From the memoirs of the contemporary French historian Philippe de Commynes, an illustration showing Edward IV landing at Calais in 1475 with an army of 10,000 men*

saison. Et au regard de luy il
auoit so armee si Kompute/
si mal en point et si poure q̃l
ne losoit mostrer deuãt eulx/
car il auoit perdu deuant
mez quatre mil hõmes pre
nans soulde/entre lesquelz
y mourut des meilleures gẽs
quil eust. Et ainsi verrez

de ce que son affaire requie
roit/ et contre ce quil sca
noit et entendoit mieulx q̃
nul autre dix ans auoit.

Cõment le koy Edouard
dangleterre passa en france
et descendit a Calaix pour
faire la guerre au koy/ et
de ce qui en aduint.

THE ROYAL ARMS IN
THE FIFTEENTH CENTURY

IT IS SAID THAT IN 1376 CHARLES V OF FRANCE formally altered the royal arms of France by reducing the number of fleurs-de-lys to three. Various theories have been put forward as to why he did this. The most romantic is that in 496 Queen Clothilde was given a holy cloth embroidered with three lilies, symbolising the Blessed Virgin, and that she gave this cloth to her husband King Clovis. It is suggested that Charles adopted the three fleurs-de-lys in order to give official sanction to this popular legend.

Whatever reason and at what exact moment it happened, from the end of the fourteenth century the French royal arms contained but three lilies and, when a new great seal was struck for Henry IV in 1405, he followed the French King's lead and reduced the number of lilies in the French quarterings in his arms to three.

Henry V, Henry VI, Edward IV, Edward V and Richard III used more or less the same arms. The only small difference occurred in the detail of the crest. Basically it remained the same but minor variations are to be found. For example, Edward IV at one time used an uncrowned lion standing within a crown on a chapeau, as illustrated, whilst in his third great seal the crown is shown with arches. Eventually, with Henry VIII, the chapeau and coronet gave way to an arched crown and the lion was similarly crowned. This is essentially the crest of England as borne by the Queen today.

Towards the close of the fifteenth century, representations of the royal arms are found, although not on the great seal, with supporters on either side of the shield. These supporters seem to have their origin in artistry. Seal engravers, sculptors and wood carvers took the liberty of adding favourite beasts or badges to representations of arms so as to obtain a more interesting artistic effect. This custom must have pleased the nobility and more and more of them began to affect these adornments to their arms. The Kings were no exception and there are examples of the arms of Henry VI, Edward IV and Richard III supported by a variety of beasts chosen from their family, rather than their royal, heraldry.

It was not long before the heralds began to take official notice of supporters and, as it were, admit them to the field of official heraldry, recording them, assigning them and making rules for their depiction and devolution.

RICHARD III

r. 1483–5

KING RICHARD REIGNED FOR only two years and two months before he went down fighting at Bosworth Field. Nevertheless his reign has acquired an importance out of all proportion to its length. Richard was the last of thirteen kings of the Plantagenet line, which had ruled England since 1154. He was the last English King to die in battle. His death in 1485 is said to mark the boundary between the medieval and the modern ages. And he is the chief suspect in the longest and most emotive murder investigation in English history – the problem of who murdered the Princes in the Tower.

Richard's career also exemplifies the pitfalls confronting the biographer of any medieval figure. The records preserve the facts, but not the motives. In Richard's case no court history, no personal correspondence, not even a contemporary portrait survives to illumine his personality or his appearance. His image has been blackened in caricatures compiled in the reign of his successful rival, Henry VII, and later adapted by Shakespeare to give birth to the monster portrayed in his play *Richard III*.

Before seeking to untangle motives, it is therefore best to start with the unembroidered facts. Richard, fourth and last surviving son of Richard, Duke of York, and Cecily Neville, was born at Fotheringhay Castle in Northamptonshire on 2 October 1452. His childhood was soon affected by all the vicissitudes of the Wars of the Roses. When York and the Nevilles were put to flight at Ludlow in 1459 he and his brother George were placed in the custody first of the Duchess of Buckingham and then of the

Archbishop of Canterbury. After York's death at Wakefield in December 1460 the Duchess of York took refuge with her two younger sons in the Burgundian Netherlands, where she remained until Edward's great victory at Towton made it safe to return. On the eve of Edward's coronation in June 1461 Richard, aged nine, became a Knight of the Garter and four months later the King created him Duke of Gloucester. For the best part of the next four years Richard's home was in the Yorkshire castle of Middleham, favourite residence of the Earl and Countess of Warwick. It was the custom among the nobility to farm out their children among families of equal rank, and, as the King's brother, Richard naturally rated the King's greatest subject. But when the great Earl's quarrel with Edward erupted into violence, Richard, unlike his brother George, remained steadfastly loyal to the King. In 1469 he was appointed Constable of England and charged with the suppression of a rising in Wales.

Richard's apprenticeship was now at an end: from 1469 till Edward's death Richard was to play a key role, both military and administrative, in the affairs of the kingdom. In 1470 he accompanied Edward in his flight to Burgundy, while the Warwick–Lancaster alliance restored Henry VI to his throne. At the battles of Barnet and Tewkesbury in 1471 Richard commanded with distinction a wing of the Yorkist army. There is no foundation for later stories that Richard was present at, or took part in, the death of Henry VI's son, Prince Edward. Contemporary accounts simply state that Edward was killed during

Opposite: *Richard III, whose character, and even his physical appearance, are so indissolubly linked in the public imagination to Shakespeare's demonic creation that it is hard to consider his reign objectively.*

RICARDVS III

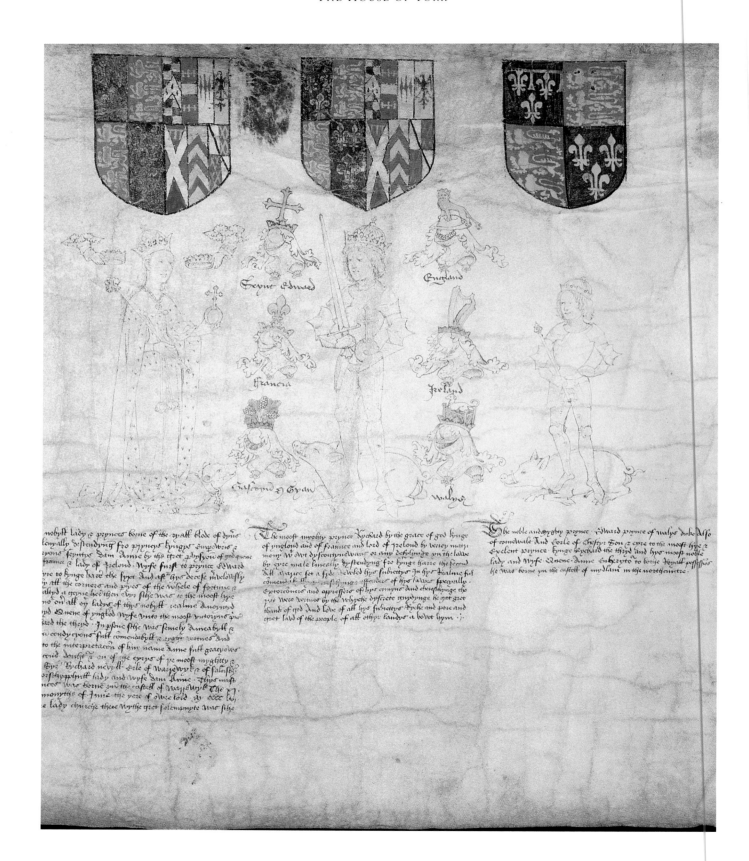

the battle. He was probably present at the Tower on the night Henry himself was put to death, but so were many other Yorkist leaders.

With the Yorkists safely restored to power, Richard was chosen to take up Warwick's former task of pacifying the lawless northern counties and sealing the border against Scottish incursions. This commission was to keep Richard occupied intermittently until 1475 and almost exclusively thereafter. In the autumn of 1471 Richard married Anne Neville, the sixteen-year-old widow of Prince Edward and younger daughter of the Kingmaker. As co-heiress of the Beauchamp estate, which Warwick had held in his wife's right, Anne brought her husband a valuable inheritance; but there is reason to suppose that Richard's intentions were not exclusively mercenary. He had grown up with Anne during his stay at Middleham, and subsequently treated her mother with kindness and generosity. This much cannot be said for George, Duke of Clarence, the husband of Warwick's other daughter, Isabel. George was in fact so keen to keep his hands on the whole of the Countess's estates that he put every obstacle in the way of Richard's marriage, including the attempted abduction of the intended bride. With Edward's mediation it was agreed that the marriage should go ahead, but that most of the Beauchamp estates would be reserved for Clarence. Early in 1473 Anne bore Richard a son, whom they christened Edward. Though he fathered at least two bastards before his marriage, he was faithful to her afterwards.

In 1475 Richard took part in the inglorious but profitable French campaign that ended with the Treaty of Picquigny. We are told that the Duke of Gloucester opposed this betrayal of the Agincourt spirit and so earned the distrust of France's King Louis XI.

The last act in Clarence's pitiful career provided the occasion for Richard's next visit to court in the autumn of 1477. Continually threatened by the disloyalty of Clarence, Edward at last had him tried for high treason. Despite the earlier rancour over the

Warwick–Beauchamp inheritance Richard was, according to one contemporary account, 'overcome with grief for his brother' when the death sentence was carried out. Three days after Clarence had been drowned in a wine butt the Duke of Gloucester procured a licence to set up two religious foundations to pray for his dead brother and other members of the royal family. Our source, the level-headed Italian cleric Dominic Mancini, goes on to say that 'thenceforth Richard came very rarely to court. He kept himself within his own lands and set out to acquire the loyalty of his people through favours and justice. The good reputation of his private life and public activities powerfully attracted the esteem of strangers . . . Such was his renown in warfare, that whenever a difficult and dangerous policy had to be undertaken, it would be entrusted to his discretion and generalship. By these arts Richard acquired the favour of the people, and avoided the jealousy of the Queen, from whom he lived far separated.'

Clearly there was no love lost between Richard and his sister-in-law, the Woodville Queen. Like many of the aristocracy he probably resented the favour shown to her innumerable relatives, and it is possible that he also held her responsible for Clarence's death. In any event he preferred a life of service in the north to the intrigues and luxury of Edward's court. Nor is there any doubt that his lieutenancy in the north merited Mancini's complimentary remarks. The records of the City of York contain many references to his activities – from suppressing illegal fish traps to commuting taxes in times of need – and record the gratitude of the city fathers: 'The Duke of Gloucester shall, for his great labour ... be presented ... with six swans and six pikes.' His legal commissions also toured the West Riding, Cumberland and Westmorland dispensing 'good and indifferent [i.e. impartial] justice to all who sought it, were they rich or poor, gentle or simple'.

As Warden of the West March Richard was also responsible for the defence of the border country,

Opposite: *The Rous Roll, showing the proper heraldic devices for Richard III, Anne Neville and their son Prince Edward, who died before his father's death at Bosworth Field in 1485.*

and from 1480 conducted several hard-fought campaigns against King Louis's ally, James III of Scotland. These culminated in 1482 with the recapture of Berwick and an unopposed entry into Edinburgh. Edward's gratitude for this victory and the ten solid years of service preceding it was expressed in 1483 when Parliament made the Duke of Gloucester's Wardenship of the West March a hereditary office and granted him all the royal manors and revenues in the county of Cumberland. This palatinate state within a state which Richard now controlled was a fitting reward for a brother who had more than fulfilled the promise of his adopted motto, *Loyaulté Me Lie*, loyalty binds me. Parliament approved the grant in February: two months later Edward IV died.

So passed the first thirty years of Richard's thirty-three years. Had he, rather than Edward, died in 1483 he would no doubt have earned a respectable footnote in history as an able soldier, a conscientious administrator and a self-effacingly loyal brother; a man whose old-fashioned sense of honour led him to disapprove of Picquigny-style diplomacy as much as the free-wheeling sexual mores of Edward's court; a blameless husband who remained faithful to his wife and shielded her relatives from the consequences of Warwick's fall. And yet, within six months of his brother's death he had bastardised Edward's children, executed Edward's closest friend, seized the Crown for himself and driven Edward's Queen into an improbable alliance with an obscure Lancastrian pretender named Henry Tudor.

Events came quickly to a head after Edward IV's death on 9 April 1483. The Woodville clan, led by the Queen, knew that they had many enemies including Richard of Gloucester whom Edward had named Protector in his will. They therefore opted for attack as the best means of defence. While Richard was still in the north they passed a resolution through the Council to replace Gloucester's protectorship with a regency council. They also arranged for the young Edward V to be brought from Ludlow to London as quickly as possible for his coronation. Once he was crowned the protectorship would lapse in any case. Clearly the Woodvilles were aware from the start that Richard might opt to grab the throne for himself. As Mancini says, 'they were afraid that if Richard took the crown, or even governed alone, they who bore the blame of Clarence's death would suffer death or at least be ejected from their high estate'.

Lord Hastings, an intimate friend of the late King, but no lover of the Queen's affinity, let slip these plans to Richard. With the help of another Woodville opponent, the powerful Duke of Buckingham, Richard promptly intercepted Edward V on the road to London and arrested his guardian, Anthony Woodville, Earl Rivers. When the news reached London on 1 May, the Queen immediately took sanctuary at Westminster with her younger son, Richard. The Dukes of Gloucester and Buckingham entered London unopposed on 4 May.

It is not strictly relevant to ask who was the aggressor in this situation, for the answer is that each party acted in self-defence for fear of the other. The situation itself was a legacy of Edward IV's marriage, which created the rift between the Woodvilles and the older aristocracy. Richard came out on top because the Woodvilles, without Edward's protection, were no match for their enemies. However, the Protector's position was still decidedly tricky. At the age of twelve his nephew was by contemporary standards nearly an adult, and his coronation could not be indefinitely postponed. Preparations were in fact going ahead for the coronation to take place on 24 June. Once deprived of his authority as Protector Richard could not expect Edward V to side with him against the boy's own mother and his former guardian. The logical conclusion was simple enough: to survive Richard must rule, and to rule he must be King.

By the second week of June Richard had decided to make his pitch for the throne. His faithful

Opposite: Richard III with his fool, from an illuminated manuscript of music made for the court. Jesters were a feature of court life until the seventeenth century.

en sm p̄ Benedictus

dixerunt. Omnes fines terre. P

...runt in iniquitatibz: non est

nr de celo pspexit sup filios

si est intelligens aut requirens

dimiserunt simul inutiles fa

faciat boni non est usk ad v

omnes qui operant iniquitate

Yorkshiremen were summoned to 'come unto us to London . . . with as many as ye can make defensibly arrayed, there to aid and assist us against the Queen, her bloody adherents and affinity'. On 16 June Prince Richard was removed from Westminster Sanctuary with threats of force and joined his elder brother in the Tower. All this was done under the pretext that the Queen's 'bloody adherents' were hatching a murderous plot, but in the meantime Richard was sounding out his principal supporters on the idea that he should be crowned in place of his nephew. Buckingham, a headstrong man with a special grudge against the Woodvilles, was willing enough; but some of the old guard from Edward IV's reign, notably Lord Hastings, would not stomach the disinheritance of Edward's children. Without hesitation Richard had him arrested at a Council meeting and beheaded on the spot. Two days later, on 22 June, the Lord Mayor's brother, Dr Ralph Shaw, preached a sermon at Paul's Cross on the text 'bastard slips shall not take deep root': his message was that Edward IV had made a marriage contract with Lady Eleanor Butler before his subsequent marriage to Elizabeth Woodville. Under canon law this would have invalidated the Woodville marriage and made bastards of their children. The true heir to the throne was therefore none other than the Duke of Gloucester. At the end of June Parliament met and assented to a document petitioning Richard to take the throne. The petition was brought to Richard at Baynard's Castle, where he graciously accepted after a show of reluctance. Richard's coronation on 6 July was attended by virtually the entire peerage, including Henry Tudor's mother, Margaret Beaufort.

Despite the exemplary speed and efficiency with which Richard carried out his *coup d'état*, he was soon prey to the same sort of troubles as the Lancastrian usurper Henry IV had encountered some eighty years earlier. He was on a royal progress at Lincoln in October 1483 when he learned that his chief accomplice, Buckingham, was now in arms against him, having come to terms both with the Woodvilles and with the exiled Henry Tudor. Buckingham's revolt seems as gratuitous as that of the Percys in 1403: according to Henry VII's historian, Polydore Vergil, Buckingham had encouraged

Richard's usurpation simply as the stepping stone to his own elevation. Whatever the motives behind it, the whole carefully co-ordinated rebellion ended in fiasco. After heavy rainstorms melted his army, the Duke was taken without a battle and executed on 2 November at Salisbury. Henry Tudor's little invasion fleet turned back to Brittany without attempting a landing and Richard's able lieutenant, the Duke of Norfolk, dispersed scattered risings in the south-east.

Richard had won the first round; but the revolt had crystallised the pattern of opposition to his rule and left little doubt that a second round would follow. Elizabeth Woodville, by now convinced that she would never see her sons alive again, had made an agreement with Henry Tudor that he would marry her eldest daughter, also named Elizabeth. Since Henry was the sole surviving heir to the Lancastrian claim and Elizabeth was the eldest daughter of Edward IV, this alliance was just as dangerous as the earlier *rapprochement* between Warwick and Margaret of Anjou. The Wars of the Roses created some strange bedfellows.

For Richard 1484 was a year of watching and waiting for the expected invasion. It was also witness to a personal tragedy and a diplomatic failure both of which seriously undermined his position. In April his only son, Prince Edward, died at Middleham. In the words of one chronicler, 'you might have seen his father and mother in a state almost bordering on madness by reason of their sudden grief'. Without a direct heir Richard was a far less likely prospect to the many who had tacitly supported his coup in the hope of avoiding a trouble-ridden minority. In the summer the King narrowly failed in his attempt to extradite Henry Tudor from Brittany. Henry escaped and found refuge at the court of a far more powerful friend, King Charles VIII of France. The year ended with only one success, a three-year truce with the Scots, which was sealed with great solemnity at Nottingham Castle in September. At Christmas the King learned from his agents in France that the invasion was definitely scheduled for the following summer.

The campaigning season of 1485 opened with a propaganda war. The death of Queen Anne in March – another blow to the beleaguered King – gave rise to rumours that he had poisoned her in order to marry Henry Tudor's intended bride, Elizabeth of York. It was not until 7 August that the Tudor made his landing at Milford Haven in South Wales. The final battle took place on Monday, 22 August a few miles west of Leicester, near the village of Market Bosworth. Anxious as ever to settle the affair by direct action, Richard led a cavalry charge directed at the person of his rival and was slain in the mêlée. The Earl of Northumberland, who led Richard's rear-guard, watched the proceedings as a spectator, while the Stanley brothers threw their levies into battle on Henry's side. When it was over Richard's naked body was strung over the back of a pack-horse and taken to Leicester for burial in the Grey Friars' chapel.

The country as a whole probably shared the Earl of Northumberland's view of the conflict. It mattered little who won at Bosworth because the issue at stake was simply a dynastic one. Even the dynastic issue was confused by the split within the Yorkist camp and the promised marriage of the Lancastrian Henry to Elizabeth of York. In the earlier stages of the Wars of the Roses, when the Yorkists promised good government in place of Lancastrian incompetence and corruption, there had been real issues to fight over. In 1485 it came to a choice between a childless usurper and a little-known Welshman who had spent most of his life in exile. Richard's only mourners were the knights and squires of his personal following – many of whom fell at his side – and those who remembered his administration in the north: 'King Richard, late mercifully reigning upon us, was . . . piteously slain and murdered, to the great heaviness of this city.' A brave tribute from the civic records of York.

Richard's career is too often judged on the issue of whether or not he had the Princes in the Tower murdered. The evidence is not conclusive, but it seems highly probable that he did. The Princes were not seen alive after the autumn of 1483 and Mancini feared they might already be dead when he left the country at the end of June. Had they still been living in 1484 or 1485 Richard would surely have produced them to scupper Henry Tudor's marriage plans. The murder of two innocent children was a horrible crime even by fifteenth-century standards, but it is difficult to see how Richard could have let them live without risking needless conspiracies in their names.

Richard's real failing as a king was his inability to win over the great magnates whose support was crucial to any medieval regime. For all his solid virtues as an administrator and his undoubted courage in battle, Richard lacked Edward IV's knack of making friends and he was a bad judge of character. He allowed Buckingham to lead him by the nose, and made an enemy of his erstwhile supporter, Lord Hastings. The Earl of Northumberland was his close associate in the north for ten years, but not, it seems, his friend. Lord Stanley was close at Richard's side for two years but turned his coat at the vital moment. Louis XI found him unsympathetic, and Sir Thomas More, admittedly a biased witness, described Richard's nature as 'close and secret'. Ill at ease with his peers, Richard preferred to put his trust in boyhood friends or able lieutenants who owed their positions to his favour. Three of these, William Catesby, Sir Richard Ratcliffe and Francis Lovell, are unflatteringly commemorated in the famous doggerel verse:

> *The Cat, the Rat*
> *And Lovell our Dog*
> *Rulen all England*
> *Under an Hog*

Yet it was a military rather than a political verdict which settled Richard's fate. Bosworth was the supreme test of his right to rule , just as Shrewsbury was for Henry IV, Towton for Henry VI, and Barnet and Tewkesbury for Edward IV. Richard failed and the crown, reputedly retrieved on the battlefield from under a gorse bush, was placed by Lord Stanley on the head of the first Tudor King.

THE TUDORS
1485–1603

HENRY VII 1485–1509

HENRY VIII 1509–47

EDWARD VI 1547–53

MARY I 1553–8

ELIZABETH I 1558–1603

Opposite: A coin struck to commemorate the marriage of Henry VII to Elizabeth of York in 1486. Their marriage was aimed at uniting the rival houses of York and Lancaster. The tall, golden-haired Elizabeth was a renowned beauty, and Henry was deeply affected when Elizabeth died in childbed in 1503.

HENRY VII

r. 1485–1509

THOUGH IT DID NOT SEEM SO at the time, 22 August 1485 remains a seminal date in the history of English monarchy, for it ushered in the House of Tudor and, ever since, the Crown of England has remained in the line of the heirs of Henry Tudor, the victor at Bosworth Field. A dynasty was born. Henry was head of the House of Lancaster through his remarkable mother, Margaret Beaufort, and he soon strengthened his claim to the throne of England by Parliamentary approval and by his marriage with Elizabeth of York who was destined to bear him three sons and four daughters, though only their second son, Henry, and their eldest and third daughters, Margaret and Mary respectively, were to survive their parents. Henry VIII was to become so desperate to beget a healthy male heir that he divorced his first wife to the consternation of Christendom and beheaded the second before embarking on four further marriages, the last three of them childless, and left, like his father, a son and two daughters. These all died without issue, yet their combined reigns lasted from 1547 to 1603, when James VI of Scotland, great-grandson of Henry VII's daughter Margaret, came south to inaugurate the rule of the House of Stuart. Such was a notable legacy of the first Tudor, who throughout his reign was haunted by the fear that an army no larger than the one which he had himself led against Richard III might overthrow him. His son too was threatened by Yorkist pretenders and his grandchildren troubled by rival claimants of 'the blood royal', yet they all died in their beds. The principle of legitimacy had triumphed.

The only son of Edmund Tudor, Earl of Richmond, and Lady Margaret Beaufort, the future Henry VII was very much a child of the civil wars of Lancaster and York, for his father had been taken by the Yorkists in the summer of 1456 and died a prisoner in Carmarthen Castle, leaving a widow of no more than thirteen years who pinned her hopes on giving birth to a son. Edmund's brother, Jasper Tudor, Earl of Pembroke, brought Margaret to his stronghold of Pembroke Castle, where Henry was born on 28 January 1457. In after years when he had achieved all her ambitions for him, she would write to him on his birthday, 'This day of St Agnes, that I did bring into this world my good and gracious prince'; but before then there were to be many tribulations. Henry was only four when, following Edward IV's seizure of the Crown in 1461, Pembroke fell to the Yorkists and mother and child were placed under the guardianship of William Herbert, the new owner, who was granted Jasper's earldom, while Jasper himself fled abroad. Henry was now parted from his mother, who married a Lancastrian knight, Sir Henry Stafford, but he received a sound schooling and was intended as a husband for Herbert's daughter.

When he was twelve his guardian was executed for alleged treason by Warwick, the Kingmaker, yet the following year, when Henry VI was restored to his throne, Jasper could return from exile and bring his nephew to the Lancastrian court. Henry VI, seeing the youth from Wales for the first time, greeted him, 'This truly, this is he unto whom both we and our adversaries much yield and give over the dominion.' Those were prophetic words, for within a year the King had died, his own line became extinct and the young Henry Tudor became the true heir of the House of Lancaster. Edward IV recovered the Crown at the battle of Barnet on Easter Day 1471, and as it was no longer safe for Henry and his uncle to remain even in wild Wales they found political asylum in north-west France, which then formed the

A sixteenth-century bust of Henry VII attributed to Pietro Torrigiano and made of painted gesso on wood.

independent Duchy of Brittany. Henry was destined to stay here for fourteen impressionable years. We know little about his exile, though by all accounts he was tall for a Welshman, and if his hair was dark he had a fair complexion; he was athletic and rode well.

What was the strength of Henry's claim to the throne? On his father's side it was weak. His grandfather, Owen Tudor, had secretly married Catherine of Valois, widow of Henry V, and when Henry VI came of age his step-father and his half-brothers, Edmund and Jasper Tudor, were high in favour, until civil war broke out in 1461. On his mother's side the

claim went much deeper, for her great-grandfather was John of Gaunt, who had a number of children by his mistress, Catherine Swynford, who were subsequently legitimised; they were known as Beauforts, after Beaufort Castle in France where they were brought up. The second boy, Henry Beaufort, became a cardinal and for a time ruler of England, but the elder boy was created Earl of Somerset, and his own son John, who came to the earldom, left at his death a daughter of three years, Margaret Beaufort, who ten years later gave birth to Henry Tudor. With the deaths of both Henry VI and his son Prince Edward in 1471, Henry Tudor became head of the House of Lancaster. As such, he was a potential threat to the Yorkist regime, and Edward IV made various attempts to lay hands on him.

Richard III's usurpation of the throne in June 1483 had antagonised many of the Yorkist nobility and subsequent rumours of the murders of Edward V and his brother brought Henry appreciably nearer the throne. Later that year the Duke of Buckingham had prematurely staged a rebellion in favour of Henry, which was easily suppressed, though the conspirators who escaped from England came to swell Henry's tiny court in exile. He took a solemn oath in Rennes Cathedral at Christmas 1483 that once he became King of England he would marry Princess Elizabeth, heiress of the House of York. His greatest asset was his Welsh blood and the bards fervently proclaimed his just cause, so that when he landed in Pembrokeshire in August 1485, he attracted a large following. His army marched north via Shrewsbury and thence to Stafford and Tamworth to face Richard III south-west of Market Bosworth in Leicestershire. Only nine peers had answered Richard's summons but they included Howard of Norfolk. It was Henry's good fortune to have the support of Oxford, a most experienced soldier, while Richard found himself deserted by Northumberland. As Richard rode down Ambien Hill with his household knights to charge at Henry's bodyguards, he was surrounded by Stanley's horsemen and toppled from his horse to death. In a brief engagement, Henry became master of the realm.

Henry's weak claim to the Crown was of small moment compared with the outcome of the day's fighting. He had accepted the invitation of Richard's rebellious subjects to put his claim to the test of trial by battle, and had slain the reigning King. Without doubt, he was *de facto* sovereign and on the last day of October was crowned in Westminster Abbey. Eight days later Parliament assembled to greet him as a second Joshua, sent to rescue his people from tyranny, and an Act was speedily passed declaring the inheritance of the Crown to have come as of right to Henry and the heirs of his body. Pope Innocent VIII subsequently threatened any who challenged his legitimate kingship with excommunication. Early in 1486 Henry married Elizabeth to unite the rival houses.

Elizabeth was eight years younger than her husband and a woman of considerable beauty. She was tall, of fair complexion with long golden tresses, and her funeral effigy indicates most graceful features. There was no role for her to play in politics beyond becoming Henry's Queen and the mother of his children. By contrast, her mother, the Queen Dowager Elizabeth Woodville, was a mischievous woman and Henry suspected her of being thick with the Yorkist conspirators in 1486, so he persuaded her to withdraw to Bermondsey Abbey, a religious house to which kings of England had the right to present their relatives. Her dower lands were settled on Elizabeth of York; she died in 1492 and was buried at Windsor beside Edward IV.

Henry's consort was gentle and devout in the tradition of the great ladies of medieval chivalric poetry, and brought out the best in her husband. After years of exile – almost his whole life until his accession – he had a settled home and a growing family. The moral laxity of continental courts was a byword, yet Henry remained faithful to Elizabeth. Theirs had been a political marriage, not a love match, but they grew together; he came to show her exceptional

Opposite: *The remarkable Lady Margaret Beaufort, mother of Henry VII and wife of Edmund Tudor, Earl of Richmond. In accordance with her will, St John's College, Cambridge, was founded in 1511.*

tenderness and consoled her in a most moving way when their eldest child tragically died in 1502. When, the following year, she died in childbed, Henry was stricken with grief and 'privily departed to a solitary place and would no man should resort unto him'. Thomas More wrote an elegy in which the dying Queen addresses her husband:

Adieu! Mine own dear spouse, my worthy lord!
The faithful love, that did us both continue
In marriage and peaceable concord,
Into your hands here I do resign,
To be bestowed on your children and mine;
Erst were ye father, now must ye supply
The mother's part also, for here I lie.

Until then, domestic happiness, with the future of the Tudor dynasty assured, had enabled Henry to weather the storms of internal disaffection and foreign intrigue.

In September 1486 Henry had chosen Winchester, the ancient capital of Saxon England, for Elizabeth's lying-in and here she was delivered of a son who was named Arthur 'in honour of the British race'. He was hailed as a prince who would inaugurate a golden age, this scion equally of Lancaster and York, and heir to a united England and a unified Wales. Whom he married was to be of fundamental importance. As early as 1489 Henry planned that Arthur should be betrothed to Catherine of Aragon, the daughter of Ferdinand and Isabella of Spain. It was recognition of England's new status that he should succeed in allying his family with those powerful sovereigns of Aragon and Castile and, despite the perils of diplomacy and mutual suspicion of the two Kings, a marriage treaty was ultimately signed so that Catherine left Spain for good and landed in Plymouth in October 1501. Anxious until he had set eyes on his son's bride, Henry was delighted with the graceful Princess and Arthur declared that 'no woman in the world could

be more agreeable'. They were married in St Paul's Cathedral and, after a month of court celebrations, set out for Ludlow; yet here in March the Prince of Wales and hope of England died of consumption in his sixteenth year.

Margaret had been born in 1489 and, two years later, another son, Henry, Duke of York, who was intended for the Church, but Margaret and Mary (born in 1495) were expected in that age of matrimonial diplomacy to marry into royal houses to strengthen England's alliances. Princess Margaret was to marry James IV of Scotland at Holyrood House in 1503, an event celebrated by William Dunbar in his poem, *The Thistle and the Rose*, which prophesied in a mysterious way the union of the Crowns of the two warring kingdoms which would come about exactly one hundred years later, when James VI travelled south to succeed Elizabeth I. The younger Princess, Mary, was to be the subject of a series of conflicting treaties of betrothal, but remained single until 1514.

To the end of his reign Henry was troubled by Yorkist claimants to the throne and by pretenders. Immediately after his victory at Bosworth he had sent to the Tower of London the ten-year-old Earl of Warwick (the son of Edward IV's brother, the Duke of Clarence) for he was the chief Yorkist competitor, yet King Henry could not feel secure until another claimant, John de la Pole, Earl of Lincoln, who had fled from the battlefield, was also in custody. In the autumn of 1486, not long after Arthur's birth, came disturbing news of a pretender, claiming to be the young Warwick, who, it was rumoured, had escaped from the Tower. Lambert Simnel, who had been carefully groomed for this impersonation, swiftly became the hope of the White Rose and even those, such as Lincoln, who were satisfied that Simnel was an imposter saw him as a useful puppet. With aid from Margaret of Burgundy, an implacable foe of Henry's, there seemed enough support for the Plantagenet cause 'to give the King's grace a breakfast'. Once the conspirators had toppled the throne, Simnel could be

Opposite: An English School portrait, c. 1499, of Arthur, Prince of Wales. Named 'in honour of the
English race' who carried on his young shoulders hopes for a golden age for the kingdom.
He died of consumption at the age of fifteen.

cast aside either for the real Warwick, if he were still alive, or for Lincoln himself. Lincoln and Francis Lovell were able to hire 2,000 German mercenaries as the nucleus of an army, which sailed to Ireland where Simnel was crowned 'Edward VI' on White Sunday 1487. (Long afterwards Henry mocked an Irish delegation by saying, 'My lords of Ireland, you will crown apes at last.') Yet in 1487 the threat seemed very real when the rebels landed in Lancashire and made their way towards the heart of England, for the King had no standing army and no mercenaries. But at the battle of Stoke the pretender's army was routed, Lincoln slain and Lovell drowned while attempting to escape. Simnel received unexpected clemency, for he was put to work as a turn-spit in the royal kitchen.

The White Rose did not, however, die at Stoke, for there was soon to be another impostor, Master Perkin Warbeck from Tournai, whom the men of Cork felt convinced was Richard of York, the younger of the Princes in the Tower. His cause was soon supported by the Kings of France and Scotland, by Margaret of Burgundy and by the Emperor Maximilian, all of them anxious to embarrass Henry Tudor. The King at first made derisory comments about 'this lad who calls himself Plantagenet', yet Perkin Warbeck was to trouble him for six years. After Lincoln's treachery, Henry felt he could trust no one and his minute inquiries established that Sir William Stanley and others in high places were prepared to throw in their lot with the pretender. Their execution took the heart out of the Yorkist disaffection and when Warbeck landed at Deal in Kent, he found no supporters, so he sailed on, first to Ireland, and then to Scotland, where he was fêted at court. The large-scale invasion of England planned by James IV degenerated into a border raid, yet Henry was bent on humbling the Scots and forcing the surrender of Warbeck, so he summoned Parliament to vote heavy war taxation.

The men of Cornwall resisted the collection of the subsidy and under Michael Joseph, a smith, and Thomas Flamank, a lawyer, raised an army, it was said, of 15,000 men to march on London and force Henry to dismiss his financial ministers, Archbishop Morton and Sir Reginald Bray, who had advised him 'to pill and poll the people'. Lord Audley agreed to lead the Cornish rebels who made their way across England to camp on Blackheath. On 17 June 1497 they were defeated by the royalist troops under Lord Daubeney. Joseph, Flamank and Audley were executed, but the rest were pardoned on condition they returned peaceably to Cornwall.

The problem of Perkin Warbeck remained. Henry sent an embassy to James IV to demand his surrender, but the pretender had already left by the west coast; instead of making straight for Cornwall he foolishly wasted precious weeks in Ireland and did not land in England until early September. For a time Henry looked like having to fight on two fronts, but when James crossed the border to begin the siege of Norham Castle he was repelled by a massive force under the Earl of Surrey and speedily agreed to a truce. In Bodmin, meanwhile, Warbeck had himself proclaimed 'Richard IV' and attracted a strong following. Exeter resisted the rebels, but they made for Taunton where the pretender learned that the King's army was only twenty miles off. In panic he tried to find a boat in Southampton Water, but the coast was too well guarded, so her threw himself on Henry's mercy. As with Simnel, Henry showed great clemency and only required Perkin to reside at court, but when he abused his freedom he was sent to the Tower. In 1499 there were rash plans to rescue his fellow prisoner, Warwick, and Henry decided he would take no further chances; both Warbeck and the Earl of Warwick were executed. It is hard to acquit the King of the charge of judicial murder over the latter's end, for Warwick had been a close prisoner since the accession and was guilty of no crime beyond his Yorkist blood.

Even with Warwick out of the way, Henry still felt uneasy, because Edmund de la Pole, Earl of Suffolk, the brother of Lincoln, had picked up the Yorkist gauntlet as the century closed and fled abroad to seek help from the Emperor Maximilian. Eventually in 1506 Henry succeeded in forcing the Archduke Philip to send him back to England and 'the White Rose of England' was confined in the Tower until seven years later he was summarily executed by Henry VIII.

Henry Tudor's dynastic success was exemplified by two buildings, Richmond Palace and his Chapel at Westminster Abbey. The small palace of Sheen in Surrey, by the River Thames, named after the Old

The gilt-bronze effigy of Elizabeth of York, which lies next to that of Henry VII on their black marble tomb in Westminster Abbey. This was created by the Florentine sculptor Pietro Torrigiano, who was brought to England to execute the detailed instructions of Henry's will. The tomb is the first Renaissance monument in England.

English word for a beauty spot, had been a favourite residence of Edward III and Henry found it a pleasant retreat from London. He planned to keep Christmas here in 1498, but a few days before the palace was seriously damaged by fire and, surveying the ruins, he decided to replace Sheen manor with a splendid residence in the Gothic style, built round a paved courtyard. Within two years the new building was ready for occupation. The privy lodging for the royal family was decorated with fourteen turrets and it boasted an exceptional number of windows, yet the main architectural feature was a great tower. To crown his achievement Henry gave the palace a new

name – Richmond – which perpetuated the title of the earldom and honour of Richmond in Yorkshire which had been his until he became King. Richmond Palace was to become a favourite residence of both Henry VIII and Elizabeth I.

Despite the union of the Red Rose with the White, depicted in the emblem of 'The Tudor Rose' worn by the Yeomen of the Guard which he had established, Henry was at pains to emphasise his own Lancastrian heritage by glorifying the name of the martyred King Henry VI who had predicted his own triumphant accession. Accordingly he decided to enlarge Westminster Abbey, pulling down the Lady

Chapel behind the high altar to make way for an impressive new chapel to house a shrine to Henry VI. Negotiations were opened with the Pope for a formal pronouncement on the claim for the King's canonisation, by submitting evidence about miracles performed at his tomb, though the affair had made little progress by 1509. There was also an unseemly dispute between the canons of St George's, Windsor, and the monks of Chertsey and of Westminster about the custody of the relics of Henry VI, for the offerings of pilgrims at important shrines added significantly to a monastery's income. In the end Henry's coffin remained at Windsor. Work on the memorial chapel at Westminster had been going steadily forward since 1503 and Henry had drawn up an elaborate series of foundation statutes for what had in effect become his own chapel. The stately proportions of the building owed much to Sir Reginald Bray's plans, but it was not to be completed until 1519 by the master mason Robert Vertue. In his will Henry charged his executors with the task of commissioning a sculptor to work on the tombs of his wife, his mother and himself and, as a result, the Florentine Pietro Torrigiano was invited to England to execute these tombs with their life-like effigies.

Overlooking Henry's tomb is a carving of the red dragon of Wales, which had been his personal standard in 1485. He had recognised the importance of paying due honour to his Welsh heritage in a way which would satisfy the ambitions of the men from the principality who had been swayed by the Anglophobia of the bards to rise for 'Richmond's cause'. Some of them later complained that after Bosworth Field there had been no vengeance meted out to the English foe and though minor posts were found at court for a number of Welshmen, and Rhys ap Thomas of Dynevor – affectionately called 'Father Rhys' by the King – was given the Garter, Henry had no wish to revive the troublesome Marcher lordships which had so weakened the Crown in the Wars of the Roses. The government of South Wales he left to his uncle Jasper and when he died without heirs, his extensive chain of lordships passed to the Crown. To give the Welsh people pride in the Tudor dynasty Henry created Arthur Prince of Wales and on his marriage he was sent to keep his court at Ludlow, where he received the homage of the Griffiths, Vaughans and Herberts, whose families were to provide the backbone of local government. Henry had become a thoroughly 'English' King and resisted all moves for Welsh vengeance across the Marches. Indeed he began a series of reforms which foreshadowed the Act of 1536 for incorporating Wales into the English administrative and legal system.

Henry VII was much less of an innovator than was once thought, for he built on the foundations of Yorkist experiments in autocratic, efficient government and there was much continuity in the servants of both regimes. But although he did not create the 'new monarchy' in England, he certainly strengthened the Crown's power and succeeded in taming the great landed aristocracy so that his writs ran throughout the realm. The Lancastrians had a reputation for financial incompetence, but Henry knew the importance of exploiting the Crown's revenues. He had set out to make himself solvent as the surest way of keeping his throne, and personally audited accounts. He took a keen interest in trade, especially with the Neth-erlands, where the great port of Antwerp was the unrivalled centre of European trade, and through his commercial treaties secured special privileges for the English Merchant Adventurers. He also financed the Cabots' voyages of exploration to Newfoundland. As he became fully aware of his strength he cowed the baronage by fines and bonds. Perhaps in re-establishing royal power and a strong administration he had pressed too hard, for once he was gone his key ministers, Empson and Dudley, were thrown to the wolves.

After Elizabeth's death Henry became almost a recluse and his court sombre. He seemed prematurely an old man, yet was reluctant to instruct Prince Henry in the science of government. To the end he was fearful that those foxy diplomatists the Emperor Maximilian and King Ferdinand of Spain might outwit him, and yet he seemed more of a pilgrim, seeking a crown of glory in the next world, in the tradition of the medieval Church, with his obsession for his new foundation at Westminster Abbey. Although he was never popular, when he died in April 1509, aged fifty-two, Henry Tudor had brought internal peace and prosperity to England and given her a reputation in Europe she had not enjoyed for a century.

HENRY VIII

r. 1509–47

AFTER THE PERVADING GLOOM OF Henry Tudor's last years, Henry VIII came to the throne on the crest of a wave of popularity, for this handsome, beardless youth of seventeen embodied a new age and seemed the antithesis of his father. He was tall and well proportioned, with a 'fine calf to his leg', had a fair complexion and auburn hair 'combed short and straight in the French fashion'; indeed he was 'altogether the handsomest potentate I have ever set eyes on', wrote an envoy not given to exaggeration, and there was no hint that this young man with the figure and features of a Greek god would one day swell into a gross Goliath. He was athletic, riding well, accurate in his marksmanship in the butts and determined to shine in jousts; but if he had led a sheltered life and was quite unprepared for the tasks of kingship, he had nonetheless received an enviable general education, understanding Latin easily, speaking French fluently, a boy with a profound interest in theological questions and in the problems of scholarship which worried his friend Erasmus, and possessing a flair for music-making of all kinds. He dressed superbly and by natural grace commanded the stage with easy authority. There was no question that here was a strong personality, who would leave an indelible mark on his country. 'Hitherto small mention has been made of King Henry', commented a Venetian in London, 'whereas for the future the whole world will talk of him', and that shrewd commentator Machiavelli (who never met him) described Henry by repute as 'rich, ferocious and greedy for glory'. Here was a Renaissance prince to his fingertips, who was determined to make his court a centre for the arts and humane studies. Unlike Henry VII the new King showed himself to his people everywhere, for he knew that showmanship was a most necessary branch of statesmanship.

On his deathbed his father had advised him to marry Catherine of Aragon, the widow of his ill-fated elder brother Prince Arthur, to whom he had been betrothed since his twelfth birthday, to preserve the Spanish alliance. She was now twenty-three, petite beside Henry, but dainty and graceful, with fine eyes, and since he was young enough to be in love with love, he became captivated by the Princess it was his duty to wed. They were married at Greenwich six weeks after the accession, to enable the coronation in Westminster Abbey on Michaelmas Day to be a double crowning. There was prolonged merry-making at court in those early weeks. Henry had inherited a full Treasury and was open-handed; there were lavish banquets, masques, dances and tournaments. 'Our time is spent in continual festival', wrote the Queen. Much more mature than her husband, Catherine's sense of dignity corrected his flamboyance and added a note of seriousness without dampening his high spirits.

Henry had been content to leave the direction of affairs to Archbishop Warham, who was Lord Chancellor, Bishop Foxe and Surrey, the Lord Treasurer, though he had sacrificed his father's hated ministers Empson and Dudley to popular demand. The death of his grandmother, the remarkable Lady Margaret Beaufort, Countess of Richmond, a devout woman and a great patroness of learning, snapped a link with the past and before long Henry would be playing a more independent role, especially in foreign affairs. Since he was anxious to earn a reputation as a military commander no less than to back a righteous cause, he joined the Holy League, formed by Pope Julius II with Venice and Spain against France, whose conquests in Italy had destroyed the balance of power, and in 1513 he himself led an expedition across the Channel, resuming the Hundred Years'

War. Even if he missed the battle of the Spurs, his presence at the sieges of Thérouanne and Tournai gave him a taste for campaigning he never lost; fighting an enemy was in quite a different category from jousting in Greenwich tiltyard, and even as an old man of 'chronic disease and great obesity' he insisted on taking the field again in 1544. While Henry was away in France, Surrey won a signal victory over the Scots at Flodden, leaving Henry's elder sister, Queen Margaret, Regent for the infant James v.

The preparations for the French campaign and the advantageous peace secured from Louis XII owed most to the King's almoner, Thomas Wolsey, who so impressed Henry by his ability that he was promoted Archbishop of York in 1514, a year later was appointed a Cardinal and soon afterwards succeeded Warham as Lord Chancellor. From 1515 to the summer of 1529 Wolsey's rule was undisputed. He had won the King's confidence and Henry delegated more and more to him, while he followed his own bent in field-sports and music. From time to time he would bestir himself to take greater interest in diplomacy and administration, yet for all his talents he was lazy, found paperwork distasteful and lacked powers of concentration, so that increasingly the partnership with the Cardinal became one-sided. Wolsey was the last English ecclesiastic to rule in the medieval tradition, and perhaps the greatest. He amassed benefices, holding in succession the richest bishoprics in addition to his archbishopric and was also Abbot of England's wealthiest religious house, St Alban's Abbey. With these enormous revenues he indulged in his passion for building at York Place in Whitehall and at Hampton Court, of which Henry grew envious, and lived in great pomp. Though granted special powers as a papal legate, the Cardinal took little interest in Church reform; he stood for the status quo and seriously underestimated people's dissatisfaction with clerical control, and while he was a skilled diplomatist he neglected domestic affairs. Men talked of him as if he were more powerful than the King himself, yet he was entirely dependent on Henry's favour and when he lost it he was finished.

Under the peace treaty with France in 1514 Henry's younger sister Mary, 'a nymph from heaven' of seventeen, was married off to the aged King Louis XII, still anxious to be father to a son, but he died soon afterwards and Mary impetuously made a runaway match with Charles Brandon, Duke of Suffolk, a boon companion of Henry's. They were pardoned, on being required to pay a crippling fine, and after long exile in the country Suffolk returned to court to become Wolsey's severest critic. From this marriage sprang the Suffolk line to the succession, for their elder daughter Frances married Henry Grey, to give birth to Lady Jane Grey and her sisters.

The old Europe was changing, and changing much faster than England. The rapid expansion of Spain's empire in the New World and Portugal's exploitation of the Eastern spice trade were to revolutionise the economies of the European nations. With these discoveries Europe was ceasing to be a Mediterranean continent, for there was a shift of balance to north-west Europe. Humanism, which embraced a fearless search for truth and beauty, questioned the purpose of man, and the search led inevitably to dispute with the authority of the Church. Yet England remained surprisingly orthodox. The contacts of John Colet and other scholars with Italy had made them anxious to reform the Church from within, much as Erasmus desired, but in England, if pockets of Lollardry remained and anticlericalism increased under Wolsey, there was no incident approaching the issue of Luther's theses at Wittenburg, which launched a specifically Protestant Reformation. England was regarded by popes as a most loyal member-state of Christendom and her King an apostle of orthodoxy. Indeed Henry felt it his mission to write a tract against Luther, the *Defence of the Seven Sacraments*, and though Thomas More and John Fisher helped him, the book was turned by his pen in 1521 into a most effective essay

Opposite: *A early seventeenth-century portrait of Anne Boleyn, by Frans Pourbus the younger, which shows off her best features – her eyes and her jet-black hair. Her marriage to Henry VIII lasted only three years, during which time she bore the future Elizabeth I and miscarried the male heir Henry so fervently wanted.*

in Catholic polemics. In later life he regretted some of his statements here about the indissolubility of marriage and about papal power: 'What serpent so venomously crept in as he who calls the most Holy See of Rome "Babylon" and the Pope's authority "Tyrannical"?' Dedicated to Leo x, that all might see Henry 'was ready to defend the church not only with his armies, but with the resources of his mind', the book caused a great stir and became a best-seller on the continent; not until Queen Victoria's *Leaves from the Journal of Our Life in the Highlands* would an English royal author be so successful.

In recognition of his championship of the church Henry was given the title *Fidei Defensor*, which was confirmed by the golden bull of 1524, and though this did not make the title hereditary, its use by subsequent kings and queens of England was to be warranted by an Act of Parliament in 1544.

In France the dashing Francis I had replaced Louis XII, while in Spain Charles of Ghent had succeeded the foxy Ferdinand. The Emperor Maximilian, who had transformed the Habsburg monarchy and strengthened its hold on the Netherlands, was approaching his end. He had recently contemplated resigning the headship of the Holy Roman Empire to Henry VIII and when Maximilian died in January 1519, Henry, no less than Francis, decided to stand for election, for he was captivated by the mystique of the Empire and wanted to be recognised as the leader of Christendom; he was the most experienced of the contestants, and the senior, being six years older than Francis and nine older than Charles. But the seven imperial electors wanted only a Habsburg to rule the confederation of German states and Charles V became the victor. Personal rivalry between the three sovereigns, each of whom regarded himself as the embodiment of Renaissance chivalry, dominated European politics for another thirty years. Habsburg–Valois disputes in

The family of Sir Thomas More, from a miniature by Rowland Lockey. Despite his position as Henry VIII's Lord Chancellor, Sir Thomas would not go against his conscience in swearing an oath to the Succession. For his challenge to Henry's wishes he was tried for treason and executed.

Italy, Flanders and the Rhine Valley made each turn to England for support, and despite Wolsey's aim to preserve neutrality as a method of holding the balance of power, Henry found it hard to overcome his own animosity towards Francis I and his inherited conviction that France was the traditional enemy.

Wolsey's finest hour was the glittering gathering of the Field of Cloth of Gold which he devised for Henry to meet Francis, near Guisnes. This was intended as a summit meeting to guarantee the peace of Europe. The two Kings were supported by the greatest in their realms who spent four weeks from midsummer 1520 in banquets, jousts and other contests to celebrate the rebirth of chivalry, but the burial of old animosities never succeeded. Both before and after the Field of Cloth of Gold, Henry had private meetings with Charles V at Dover and then at Gravelines, but there was no duplicity on his part. Under Wolsey's guidance he hoped to extend the entente to the Empire, but Valois–Habsburg rivalry proved too strong.

Another opportunity for Henry to become 'arbiter of Europe' came with Pope Leo X's death, and he was anxious that Wolsey should be elected, for only once before had there been an English pope – Nicholas Brakespeare in the twelfth century. Despite much diplomatic activity and fair promises from both Charles and Francis, he failed and the Emperor's tutor, Adrian of Utrecht, became Pope. His pontificate was brief and Henry again pushed forward Wolsey's candidature with no better success.

Dynastic problems soon became enmeshed in the trammels of international politics. Henry had been overjoyed on New Year's Day 1511 when Catherine had presented him with a son, but the Prince Henry survived for no more than six weeks to their intense grief. Thereafter there was an unhappy series of miscarriages and still-births, but in 1516 the Queen gave birth to the Princess Mary, who seemed a healthy enough infant. 'The Queen and I are both young', Henry told the Venetian ambassador, 'and if it is a girl this time, by God's grace boys will follow.' Alas, the Almighty withheld his blessing and with the passing of the years it became painfully clear that no further children would be born to Catherine. Until

marriage Henry had been shy with women, but Catherine had given him confidence and now he cast a roving eye at the beauties at court. In 1519 his mistress Bessie Blount, who 'excelled all other damsels in singing, dancing and goodly practices', gave him a son, Henry Fitzroy, who was subsequently created Duke of Richmond and groomed for the succession, but a natural son was a poor substitute for a prince born in the purple. The Duke died in 1536, after marrying the Duke of Norfolk's daughter.

Henry began to think that his marriage to Catherine was unfruitful because it was against God's law, despite ample papal dispensations, for he had disobeyed Holy Writ by marrying his deceased brother's wife and the more he dwelt on the matter the clearer it seemed to him that under canon law he was a bachelor who had been living in sin. No word of consolation, not even from the Pope himself, would satisfy him; Catherine was not, had never been, his lawful wife. He desperately wanted a son born in wedlock who could ultimately succeed to his throne unchallenged. Dynastic need and the burden on his conscience had become unsupportable by the beginning of 1527 and he prayed for the church to give him the relief which was his due, requiring Wolsey to use his influence with Rome to declare unequivocally that his marriage with Catherine had been invalid so that he could marry again. Dissatisfaction with Catherine as a wife preceded his infatuation with Anne Boleyn, who was not content like her elder sister Mary to be a royal mistress, but wanted to be a queen consort, while Henry wanted a legitimate heir. Thus developed the 'King's Great Matter'.

Anne, the younger daughter of Sir Thomas Boleyn and Lady Elizabeth Howard, had been brought up in France in the household of Queen Claude and perhaps Henry first set eyes on both Boleyn girls at the Field of Cloth of Gold, when Anne was thirteen. She did not develop as a dazzling beauty, as Bessie Blount had been, yet she came to exercise an unprecedented fascination over the King. Her strongest points were her almond-shaped eyes and her raven hair, but she also possessed remarkable vivacity and acquired in France a flair for fashion which made Catherine seem downright dowdy. Her

of frendshepe· Alas ser, what hawe I offended yow, or what occasion of displea=
sure have I showed you, intending thus to put me from you after this sorte
I take God to my iudge. I haue bene to you a trwe and an humble wyfe,
evar confirmable to youre will and pleasure, that never contraried or
gaine saide anye thynge there of, and being alwayes contented withe
all thinges wheare in you had anye delight or daliaunce, whether
it were litle or miche, withoute grudge or countenaunce of discon=
tention or displeasure. I lowed for youre sake, all them whome ye loved,
withar I had cause or no cawse, or whether they weare my frendes
or enemies. I have bene yore wyfe these ·20· yeres & moare, and ye
haue had by me diuers children, and when ye had me at the firste
I take God too my Judge, that I was a very maide, and whither
it be trwe or no, I put it to your conscience. Yf there be anie iust
cause y ye can alledge againste me, eithar of dishonestie, or matter
lawfull to put me from you, I am content to departe to my shame
and rebuke. & if theire be none, then I praye you to let me have
Justice at youre handes: the kinge yo ffather was in his tyme
of suche an excellent wilt, that he was accompted amouge allmen
for his wisdom, to be a second Solomon, And the kinge of Spaine
my father ferdinando, who was recouned to be onne of the wisest
Princes, y raigned in Spayne, many yeres before, who were bothe
wyse men and noble Kinges: it is not therefore to be dowbted, but
that they had gathered as wyze counsaylors vnto them of euery
realme as to there wysdomes they thowght mete. And as me semeth

Above: *A copy of part of the letter Catherine of Aragon wrote to Henry when she learned
that he was going to divorce her.*

enemies remarked on the rudimentary sixth finger on her left hand – a sure sign, they said, of a sorceress. Before Henry had tired of her sister Mary, four years her senior, Anne had charmed Sir Thomas Wyatt, the poet, who lived near her parents' home of Hever Castle; and then came a more serious suitor, Sir Henry Percy, Northumberland's son, who was a ward of Wolsey's, but the Cardinal, sensing the King'sinterest in her, asked the Earl of Northumberland to call home his son. Sensual love letters survive from 1527 in which Henry assures Anne of his undying devotion: 'I would you were in mine arms or I in yours for I think it is a long time since we kissed.' He somehow saw himself as a chivalrous knight, protecting that same 'virtue' which she so vigorously defended. It was marriage or nothing. In February 1528 he told her that with the negotiations Wolsey

had in hand 'shortly you and I shall have our desired end'. Neither foresaw the difficulties ahead in his achieving a separation from Catherine, but each setback over the next five years made him long more fervently for Anne as his true wife.

The sack of Rome by imperialist troops in 1527 made Pope Clement VII a puppet of Charles V, who would never consent to his aunt Catherine being cast aside, and despite great activity Wolsey failed to secure a satisfactory verdict from Rome. The most Clement would do was to issue a commission jointly to Cardinals Campeggio and Wolsey to hold a court in London which could hear the parties but make no judgement. Queen Catherine refused to acknowledge the authority of the court, but in a moving speech appealed to her husband: 'This twenty years I have been your true wife . . . And when ye had me at the first I take God to be my judge, I was a true maid without taint of man.' At the end of the law-term Campeggio adjourned the court, to procrastinate further before the suit was removed to Rome, and this signalled Wolsey's fall. Parliament was summoned for the autumn, when the cry was 'Down with the Church', and after a period of ineffectual shadow-boxing with the papacy, Henry hearkened to the advice of Thomas Cromwell that England must break away from papal allegiance as the necessary preliminary for him to be legally rid of his wife. Wolsey was spared an attainder and allowed to retain his archbishopric. He had never visited his province and on the eve of his enthronement in York Minster in November 1530 he was arrested on suspicion of treason, but died on his journey south to face his accusers. As Cardinal legate and Lord Chancellor he had combined the reins of government in both church and state and now, under Cromwell's astute guidance, the Reformation Parliament made Henry Pope, as well as King, in his own dominions. He became Supreme Head of the Church of England, a national Church which retained its medieval organisation but lacked a firm confession of faith.

Henry secretly married Anne in January 1533 and, following Archbishop Cranmer's judgement at Dunstable that Henry's marriage to Catherine had been null and void since its beginning, she was crowned Queen in Westminster Abbey at Whitsun, the folds of her robes concealing her pregnancy. She was imperious and unpopular, for there was great sympathy for Catherine of Aragon, who now reverted to her former title of Princess of Wales and lived out her remaining days at Ampthill and Kimbolton manors with a tiny household, whose wages were always in arrears. She was heartbroken, but remained firm in her Catholic faith and died in January 1536. Henry celebrated her death by dressing from head to foot in yellow.

The King had confiscated the Cardinal's residences and made extensive alterations to them. York Place, with which Anne was enchanted, was transformed into Whitehall Palace and it soon covered twenty-four acres, the largest palace in the Western world, symbolising, no less effectively than Holbein's portraits, the power of the new monarchy. At the same time he took over the neighbouring site of the Hospital of St James, where he built St James's Palace; the royal initials 'H.S.' are still depicted in the brickwork of the Clock Tower. Before long, out of the spoils of the monasteries, Henry embarked on the Palace of Nonsuch in Surrey, a fantastic pleasure dome, with its strange turrets and pinnacles and the intricate carving and plasterwork of the inner court dominated by a massive statue of the King.

It was Greenwich which Anne had chosen for her lying-in and here she gave birth in September 1533 to Princess Elizabeth. Henry treated mother and child coldly; it was not for another daughter that he had broken with Rome and made Anne his Queen, but the child was healthy and precocious and he hoped a son would follow. To distract himself he took immense personal interest in the legislation Cromwell was devising to make him supreme in his own domain and to make government more efficient; there was brought about an administrative revolution to modernise the workings of the old medieval departments of state even while the Reformation Parliament was still in session. The King was adamant that his decisions over Anne and the church, ratified by Parliament, should be unreservedly supported by all his subjects, through the taking of an oath to the succession. Sir Thomas More, who had been close to Henry and had succeeded Wolsey as Lord Chancellor, would only swear if the oath could be so framed that it did not imply his own sanction to the repudiation of the Pope's authority or the invalidity of Henry's first marriage. Neither More nor Bishop Fisher of Rochester, the two men whose support Henry wanted most, would go against their conscience; they were tried for treason and executed, yet the King feared their stand on principle would be interpreted abroad as a powerful witness against his rule.

The month in which Catherine died, Henry had

(continues on page 183)

Opposite: *A page from the English-language Great Bible of 1539, based on the work of Miles Coverdale and William Tyndale, which had to be placed in all churches following Henry's split from Rome.*

The Byble in
Englyshe, that is to saye the con=
tent of all the holy scrypture, bothe
of ye olde and newe testament, truly
translated after the veryte of the
Hebrue and Greke textes, by ye dy=
lygent studye of dyuerse excellent
learned men, expert in the forsayde
tonges.

Prynted by Rychard Grafton &
Edward Whitchurch.

Cum priuilegio ad imprimen=
dum solum.
1539.

THE ARMS OF HENRY VII
AND HENRY VIII

THE FIRST KING SERIOUSLY AND CONSISTENTLY to use supporters was Henry VII. He favoured the dragon and greyhound. The dragon was traditionally associated with Cadwalader, the last native ruler of Britain, from whom Henry claimed descent. Certainly it was a favourite beast of the first Tudor King, who used it freely as a badge and motif in decoration and even created a new pursuivant (a junior herald) and named him Rouge Dragon.

The greyhound appears to have been a badge or beast associated with the House of Lancaster, from which line came Henry VII's drop of royal blood, his mother being a great-granddaughter of John of Gaunt, Duke of Lancaster. It was later associated with the earldom of Richmond and Henry VII's father, Edmund Tudor, used it as a supporter after being created Earl of Richmond. Although there are examples of early mottoes, Henry VII was the first king to use the motto *Dieu et mon droit* (God and my right) more or less consistently. For this reason it has been shown in the illustration. The archaic spelling of *droict* has been used below.

In the illustration of Henry's arms it will be seen that the shield is the fluted and scalloped tilting shield. There is no significance in this except that it was fashionable at the time. Arms may be shown on any shape of shield, just as the mantling may be drawn in any way the artist pleases. In heraldry only the actual objects (called charges), their disposition and colour remain unalterable.

The other coat illustrated is that of Henry VIII. He sometimes used a greyhound supporter but preferred the crowned lion of England for it must not be forgotten that the Lancastrians and the Beauforts would have had less significance for the son of the heiress of the House of York, for Henry's mother Elizabeth was Edward IV's eldest daughter.

Henry VIII was the first monarch consistently to use a crown of crosses formy and fleurs-de-lys with arches. There are some representations of his father's arms ensigned with such a crown but Henry and succeeding sovereigns always used it.

They also encircled their arms with the insignia of the Order of the Garter; a blue garter garnished with gold and embroidered with the motto of the Order *Honi soit qui mal y pense* (Evil to him who evil thinks).

a serious accident while riding in the lists and his life seemed in danger. Norfolk brought the news to his royal niece and, according to her, the shock was so great that it brought on the miscarriage of a male child. Henry was so angered that nothing could save her; he talked about being 'seduced by witchcraft' when he married her, and others said the Queen must have a defective constitution. Already Jane Seymour was waiting in the wings. There was enough circumstantial evidence that Anne had behaved indiscreetly and in the highly-charged atmosphere at court, chivalrous attention could be transformed by a gesture into passionate devotion. First Mark Smeaton, a lutanist, confessed on the rack to adultery with the Queen; then Henry Norris was implicated, two other Gentlemen of the Chamber and finally her own brother, Lord Rochford. Henry was convinced of the guilt of all five men and his own profligacy assured him that Anne's own behaviour had been utterly libidinous – an English Messalina. She was tried after her alleged lovers had all been found guilty and was executed on Tower Green on 19 May 1536. The same day Cranmer issued a dispensation allowing Henry to marry Jane Seymour.

Jane was the daughter of Sir John Seymour, a Wiltshire knight who had served with Henry in France in 1513, while her mother, a Wentworth, was descended from Edward III. She was now twenty-five, fair, of medium height, rather pale-faced, and with a reputation for modesty and an inclination towards the Reformed faith. She was married to Henry in the Queen's Chapel, Whitehall, on 30 May, but her coronation, arranged for the autumn, never took place because of the plague. She chose as her motto 'Bound to obey and serve' and realised her essential role was as mother of England's heir, but first she acted as peacemaker between Henry and Princess Mary. On Trinity Sunday 1537 a *Te Deum* was sung 'for joy of the Queen's quickening of child' – an unprecedented step in the development of the liturgy – and on 12 October in Hampton Court she bore a son in a difficult confinement which cost her her own life. In dynastic terms Jane had achieved all that had been expected of her and, alone of Henry's Queens, she was buried in St George's Chapel, Windsor. When ten years later he was called to his Maker he ordered that his coffin should be laid beside hers, for Jane had given him, after twenty-eight years of ruling, the Prince he had wanted, Edward, Prince of Wales.

Cromwell had enriched Henry beyond his wildest imaginings through dissolving first the smaller religious houses and then the greater monasteries, provoking the one serious threat of the entire reign, the Pilgrimage of Grace. The insurgents were suppressed as ruthlessly as the abbots who refused to surrender their houses. At the same time an authoritative English Bible based on the work of Coverdale and Tyndale was required to be placed in all churches and Cromwell and Cranmer began doctrinal discussions with the German Lutherans. Isolated in Europe Henry cast about for an ally, for when Francis I and Charles V signed a ten-year truce Henry feared they would join forces to invade England to put into practice the papal bull deposing him. This search for an alliance with Protestant states became caught up in Henry's search for a further wife and as a result he married Anne of Cleves, whose portrait by Holbein had been so flattering, in January 1540. Fearful of the consequences of the Cleves alliance if he were not to proceed with the marriage he went through with the ceremony, but found his bride from the Rhenish principality impossible; she spoke no English, had no accomplishments and, worst of all, was the antithesis of beauty. Their marriage was never consummated and once more he turned to Cromwell, the minister who had arranged the match, to secure a divorce.

While the Cleves marriage negotiation had been in progress, a Catholic reaction had begun in England, through the initiative of Stephen Gardiner, Bishop of Winchester, and Treasurer Norfolk. They had the King's ear and Henry himself came down to the Lords for the debate on the Act of Six Articles;

Opposite: A portrait of Henry VIII from the school of Hans Holbein, showing the King as no longer the lithe, well-proportioned youth who succeeded to the throne in 1509.

persecutions of Anabaptists followed, though Cromwell endeavoured to mitigate the operation of the law. Henry had barely created him Earl of Essex, when he was arrested at the Council table as a result of a well-planned conspiracy of Norfolk and Gardiner. He had not attempted to procure a royal divorce because he knew that once free from Anne of Cleves Henry would marry the beautiful and ortho-dox Catherine Howard, niece of his enemy Norfolk. He was condemned for treasonable heresy and for the moment even the King believed he was a sacramen-tary and had been too close to the Lutherans. With the Habsburg–Valois struggle renewed his policy was out-dated.

Norfolk might have profited from Cromwell's fall had the young Catherine Howard not proved such a liability. She had, like Anne Boleyn, been schooled for court and the royal bed but then it came out that she continued adulterous relations with Francis Dereham, an old flame, and with Thomas Culpeper. Henry vowed he would cut off her head with his own sword, and then self-pity overcame rage and he 'regretted his ill luck in meeting with such ill-conditioned wives'. She was executed on 13 February 1542.

After such experiences few imagined Henry would embark on a sixth marriage, yet the next year he married Catherine Parr, who had already buried two husbands, Sir Edward Burrough and Lord Latymer. She was a blue-stocking of thirty-three, who though childless had successfully brought up three step-children. She was amazed at Henry's proposal, but loyally responded it was 'the greatest joy and comfort' to look after him and his children. By now lonely, and much troubled by his ulcerous leg which had devel-oped from his fall in 1536, Henry wanted an intellectual companion who could make a home for his family. She succeeded in meeting his expectations as nurse and step-mother, though he disapproved of her friendship with the Cambridge Reformers. Edward, Mary and Elizabeth were all brought to court and she took the closest interest in their education. Catherine also encouraged Henry's foundation of Trinity College, Cambridge, and his transformation of the rump of Wolsey's Cardinal College, Oxford, into Christ Church.

In those last few years of the reign Gardiner fought for Catholic dogma, while Henry supported Cranmer in a much more broadly-based church. At the political level there was a struggle for the regency when Edward should succeed, in which the main con-testants were Norfolk and the Prince's uncle Edward Seymour, Earl of Hertford. It was Hertford who won the final laurels of the French war, while Norfolk was compromised by his son Surrey's treason. Here, as in the doctrinal dispute, Henry aimed at a consensus. By his will no single minister would direct affairs after he had gone, but a balanced Council of Regents. The Colossus who had founded the modern English nation state died in the early hours of 28 January 1547 in Whitehall, with Thomas Cranmer at his side, but his wife and children were deliberately kept away. He wanted no farewells.

EDWARD VI

r. 1547–53

'GOD'S IMP', HENRY VIII'S SON by his third wife, Jane Seymour, was born at Hampton Court on 12 October 1537 as a result of a Caesarean section. As Bishop Latimer remarked, 'We all hungered after a prince so long that there was as much rejoicing as at the birth of John the Baptist.' His mother never recovered from the ordeal of childbirth, but died 'through the fault of them that were about her, who suffered her to take great cold and to eat things that her fantasy in sickness called for'. Yet the fact that the boy had lived and seemed healthy enough quite put his mother's death in the shade.

Elaborate precautions were taken to safeguard Prince Edward's health to protect him from the slightest risk of infection and no less elaborate rules were drawn up for his education and his spiritual development, so that in the fullness of time he would be fully prepared to succeed his father as King and Supreme Head of the Church of England. In March 1538 the Prince was assigned a separate establishment at Hunsdon in Hertfordshire in which the key figure was Lady Bryan, a woman of long experience of royal nurseries. His father remained torn between having Edward at court to lavish affection on him and show him off as a proud parent who, after twenty-eight years as King, had at last solved the intractable problem of the succession, or leaving the child safely at a manor house in country air. The motherless boy's relations with his father before Henry's final marriage to Catherine Parr were non-existent; as he later wrote in his personal chronicle, until he was six years he was 'brought up among the women' – including his half-sisters Elizabeth, four years his senior, and for some of the time, Mary, a grown woman of twenty-one. Catherine Parr, however, felt it would be in the Prince's best interests to spend longer periods at court, since his whole education was being framed to

help him in his future responsibilities. At last she had her way and this extraordinary family became reunited.

On Catherine Parr's recommendation Richard Cox, a Cambridge humanist, was given formal charge of Edward's studies while John Cheke, professor of Greek in the same university, was appointed his regular tutor. Cox told King Henry that his six-year-old charge 'undertaketh and can frame pretty Latins . . . and is now ready to enter into some proper and profitable fables of Aesop and other wholesome and godly lessons'. Cox and Cheke were both scholars in the Erasmian tradition – humanists concerned with learning, not ministers preaching a gospel – and neither would have dared to indoctrinate the Prince with the advanced views of some of the Cambridge Reformers during the years of Catholic reaction which came with Cromwell's fall. Little Edward heard Mass daily, for 'every day in the mass time he readeth a portion of Solomon's proverbs', learning from them 'to fear God's commandments, to beware of strange and wanton women, to be obedient to father and mother and to be thankful to him that telleth him of his faults'. The precocious child was schooled in conscientious duty, 'in part to satisfy the good expectations of the King's Majesty' – as he himself put it; *in part* because he could never hope to be wholly satisfactory to his father, nor to God, and the Almighty must have seemed to him as a heavenly version of his earthly father.

His was an unbending curriculum which, as he described it himself, included 'learning of tongues, of the Scriptures, of philosophy and the liberal sciences'. Perhaps it is fitting that Edward's name is chiefly remembered today as the nominal founder of a score of grammar schools, such as Birmingham and

Opposite: *Henry's delicate and short-lived heir Edward VI, painted in the manner of William Scrots.*
Above: *Thomas Cranmer, Archbishop of Canterbury to Henry VIII, Edward VI and Mary I, who perished at the stake in the fires of Smithfield.*

Southampton, when a small proportion of chantry and other ecclesiastical revenues were diverted to educational purposes during his reign. If he appears as rather a prig, it is worth remembering that on occasion Dr Cox beat him for failing in his lessons and also that the life of the schoolroom was leavened by riding, archery and music-making. Nor was Edward alone, for Catherine brought in boys of much the same age to share his lessons and sports, including Henry Brandon, Duke of Suffolk, Lord Thomas Howard and Barnaby Fitzpatrick, son of an Irish peer, who was Edward's closest friend, and one girl, Jane Dormer, with whom he would dance.

Edward was not yet ten years old when his father died on 28 January 1547, leaving as he believed careful constitutional arrangements for the government of the realm during his minority. However, the new King's uncle, Edward Seymour, Earl of Hertford, seized power, overturning the Council of Regents to establish himself as Protector of the realm and sole guardian of the boy King, who soon created him Duke of Somerset. Edward became puppet of a

faction for under Somerset's rule England became established unequivocally as a Protestant state. The Catholic Act of Six Articles of 1539 was repealed, the chantries were abolished and an English Prayer Book was issued in 1549 which owed most to the genius of Thomas Cranmer. This new Reformation was enforced by an Act of Uniformity for public worship

and it was to take an even more radical turn with the preparation of a Second Prayer Book in 1552, in which the central doctrine of the service of Holy Communion was declared to be no more than a commemorative rite. Gone were the veneration of saints and remembrance of the departed; in churches there was widespread iconoclasm, for monuments

The coronation procession of Edward VI painted in watercolour by Grimm from a wall painting in Cowdray House, destroyed by fire. The route marches from the Tower of London along East Cheap, past Bow Church into Cheapside, past the spire of old St Paul's and down the Strand to the Embankment and Westminster

THE ARMS OF PHILIP
AND ELIZABETH I

EDWARD VI AND MARY I, UNTIL HER MARRIAGE TO Philip of Spain, used the same arms as their father. After Mary's marriage half of Philip's complex quartered coat was placed side by side with the quartered royal arms on a single shield supported by Philip's black eagle crowned with a golden crown and a lion of England, for it must be remembered that Philip was King of England although he had to demit his regal powers when Mary died childless.

As the illustration shows, Philip's arms were divided into four grand quarters so that when just the two on the left-hand side were shown conjoined to Mary's arms no symbolism was lost. The first and last grand quarters are the castle of Castile and lion of Leon quartered and repeated. Side by side in the other quarters are the coats of Aragon and Sicily. In the second and third grand quarters are four coats, namely Austria (the white band on red), Burgundy modern (the French royal arms with a border), Burgundy ancient and the lion of Brabant. Over all is a shield on which the lion of Flanders is shown   side by side with the eagle of Tyrol. The pomegranate in the point in base symbolises Granada.

Elizabeth I, whose arms are shown beneath Philip's, added an extra touch of splendour to the royal arms. She adopted a gold barred helmet facing outward and substituted a gold for a red mantling. From her reign onwards this helm and mantling have been a coveted privilege of royalty. Queen Elizabeth also affected her own motto *Semper eadem* – always the same.

I have, in passing, mentioned badges. Badges, unlike arms, were usually simple devices employed to mark retainers and property. They also appeared on the long rallying flag, the standard. In the Middle Ages the badge was more often associated with a place than a person or family. The royal family, having vast possessions, have used a multiplicity of badges. The Tudor rose, crowned thistle, white boar and gold portcullis are among the best known.

The badges illustrated are the falcon badge, which was a favourite badge of Elizabeth and had been previously used by her mother Anne Boleyn, and the crowned Tudor rose. This famous badge symbolised the coming together of the Houses of York and Lancaster in the Tudor dynasty. It was used by all the Tudors and, uncrowned, has remained a popular heraldic symbol.

ANNO
ÆTATIS

DOMINI 155
SVÆ 57

Opposite: *A portrait of Cardinal Reginald Pole, Mary's leading minister, who became deeply unpopular for his part in the burnings of the martyrs. He was later to reconcile England with the Church of Rome.*
Above: *The two faces of the medal struck to commemorate the marriage of Mary Tudor and Philip of Spain in 1554.*

Wales (as Arthur had been by Henry VII, though for very different reasons) and was agonisingly deprived of her mother's company. Inevitably she took her mother's side in the King's Great Matter and Anne Boleyn hated her for it. Once Anne, as Queen, had produced a rival princess, she demanded that Mary's ears be boxed 'for the cursed bastard she is' and at Hatfield the seventeen-year-old girl was now assigned the pokiest room in the house, deprived of her personal maids and made to serve as lady-in-waiting to her baby half-sister. The animosity between Catherine and Anne was understandably to be continued in the next generation by their respective daughters. Mary was heartbroken at her mother's death. In her last hours Catherine had written to Henry, pleading with him to be a good father to Mary and to preserve her rights to the succession.

With Anne Boleyn's fall, there was a chance of *rapprochement*, for Jane Seymour desperately wanted to reconcile Henry with Mary. She was now twenty, with a mind of her own, and persistently refused to recognise her father as Supreme Head of the Church, for such contradicted all she had learned about religion from her earliest years. The Duke of Norfolk told her if she had been *his* daughter he would have knocked her head 'against the wall until it was as soft as baked apple'. At last Cromwell, with the help of Chapuys, the imperial ambassador, succeeded in bringing home to Mary the peril in which she lay. He sent her a draft letter in grovelling terms which he told her to copy out verbatim and sign, making her submission to Henry. This she did, making mental reservations about the Pope's authority, and when summoned to court to acknowledge her faults personally before her father, 'most humbly laying at his feet', the worst of their estrangement was over. Above all Mary wanted to be taken back within his family circle: 'I would rather be a chamberer, having the fruitions of Your Highness' presence than an empress away from it.' Henry was overjoyed that his 'chiefest jewel' was again living with him, though Mary was still under the slur of bastardy. Prince Edward's birth brought the two sisters together, for both must now give way to a brother; yet there were seventeen years between them. At Hunsdon Mary taught Elizabeth to play cards for stakes and encouraged her fool to amuse her with his antics.

King Henry's final marriage meant much to Mary, for she was now more regularly at court than at any time since 1530 and she regarded Queen Catherine Parr as more of a sister than yet another step-mother. Catherine showed her many kindnesses and for the first time the Princess had an adequate allowance for clothes. The Queen suggested Mary should undertake a translation of Erasmus's paraphrases of the New Testament, which she began and Nicholas Udall completed when her ill-health made serious study impossible. Mary suffered much illness throughout the 1540s.

On Edward VI's succession the Protector's brother Admiral Seymour attempted to make a bid for Mary's hand before turning his attentions to the Queen Dowager, when he implored the Princess to use her influence with Catherine Parr to accept him. Mary wisely refrained – 'I being a maid am nothing cunning' in love affairs. Such circumspection did not desert her throughout the reign, when the revolution in religion was anathema to her. No one, not even her royal half-brother, knew how they might 'turn her opinions'. She resided quietly, outside London, waiting for sickly Edward's demise, but praying for him fervently. When Northumberland had Lady Jane Grey proclaimed Queen in London, Mary was in Suffolk and the country rallied to her, content to allow the succession to take its proper course, even if the sovereign were a woman, single and at heart a Catholic.

The key question was whom should Mary, England's first Queen Regnant since Matilda challenged Stephen's accession in 1135, marry? She secretly sought the advice of Simon Renard,

Charles V's ambassador, telling him she had 'never felt that which is called love, nor harboured thoughts of voluptuousness'. His list of eight possible bridegrooms was rapidly reduced to a single name, Philip II of Spain, now a widower, and reports of his religious orthodoxy delighted her no less than his portrait. In her private oratory, accompanied by Renard and a lady-in-waiting, Mary led the saying of the *Veni Creator* and then solemnly declared she would marry Philip and 'love him perfectly'. A marriage treaty was signed in November. By then Parliament had begun to dismantle the Edwardian Reformation settlement and the Roman Mass was again celebrated. In due course Cardinal Reginal Pole would return to England to absolve Mary's subjects from their sin of heresy and reconcile them with the Church of Rome.

The Spanish marriage proposal alarmed many Englishmen and there were widespread plans for a rising to force Mary to abandon her betrothal to Philip, but they were mishandled and only Kent rose, under Sir Thomas Wyatt in January 1554. Wyatt, with a following, succeeded in crossing Kingston Bridge to march on London, but he was routed, while the Queen stayed impassively at St James's Palace. Mary was convinced that her sister was in league with Wyatt and sent her to the Tower, but no evidence could be found to incriminate her so she was moved to Woodstock Palace to be out of the way when Philip arrived, for Elizabeth was the obvious focus for opponents to Mary's regime.

Philip and Mary were married in Winchester Cathedral in July 1554 and proceeded to Hampton Court for their honeymoon. It was to Hampton that she returned the following May, convinced she was pregnant. Midwives were engaged and announcements of the happy event were prepared, ready signed, with blanks left for the sex and the date, to send to foreign courts. The weeks passed, yet no child was delivered, for Mary had mistaken the symptoms of dropsy for signs of pregnancy. So desperately did she want a child, for its own sake quite apart from the need to maintain the Catholic succession, that next year there was a plot at court to pass off a supposititious prince, though it never reached her own ears.

Mary Tudor felt deserted by Philip, whose sole interest in marrying her had been to secure England's support for his continental designs. Besides Spain, he now had the government of the Netherlands, Milan and Naples assigned to him by his father, Charles V, who was abdicating, and there was the growing problem of the Spanish Empire in the New World. Philip could not believe it when Parliament refused to have him crowned 'King of England'. His Queen was sure the ill-success of their marriage was due to divine vengeance – a punishment for the heresies still practised in England, and so the fires of Smithfield began. Hooper, the deprived Bishop of Gloucester, was burnt at the stake in February 1555 and later in the year Archbishop Cranmer and Bishops Ridley and Latimer followed him. Many clergy and lay folk who would not be turned from their Protestantism escaped to Geneva or Zurich to await safer, saner times, but the militants who remained faced persecution and risked death. Their heroism is enshrined in John Foxe's 'Book of Martyrs' as his *Acts and Monuments* soon became familiarly termed. The burnings provoked utter disillusionment with Mary's regime and her leading minister Cardinal Pole.

England had entered the war with France as Spain's ally and despite an early success at St Quentin, there came in January 1558 the great national disaster of the loss of Calais, England's last possession in France to which it had hung tenaciously since the end of the Hundred Years' War. Mary bore the brunt of the blame and she knew that instead of raising the stature of England by her marriage to Philip, she had brought national prestige to the lowest point in memory.

Mary's illness became progressively worse and Philip's absence caused her to turn to her step-sister and achieve in her final months some measure of reconciliation. Elizabeth was at Hatfield when Mary died at St James's on 17 November 1558. It was in the Chapel Royal at St James's that Mary's heart and bowels were buried, though her corpse was laid to rest at Westminster Abbey. Perhaps this symbolises her torn interests. Half-Spanish by birth and married to a Spaniard, she never understood her native people.

ELIZABETH I

r. 1558–1603

THE DAUGHTER OF HENRY VIII and Anne Boleyn came into her inheritance on 17 November 1558, a day to be marked by celebrations even after the close of her long reign some forty-four years later. The 'crown imperial' was hers of right, and for this she had never known a mother's love, had carried the stigma of bastardy, had faced the terrors of suspicion when Somerset and Northumberland ruled for her young brother Edward and had endured the peril of the Tower and the ignominy of exile at Woodstock in her sister Mary's reign. Elizabeth had triumphed over endless difficulties and at the age of twenty-five learned at Hatfield that her reign had begun: 'This is the Lord's doing; it is marvellous in our eyes', she quoted from the Psalms. Throughout the land there was rejoicing; bonfires were lit in thankfulness that the burnings at Smithfield were over, tables were brought into the streets of London for folk to 'eat and drink and make merry for the new Queen', and in York when the accession proclamation was read, her name was greeted as a true sovereign 'of no mingled blood of Spaniard, or stranger, but born mere English here among us'. She saw it as her mission to unite a divided people and she came to embody a truly national consciousness with such success that she gave her name to an age.

Her early years had been spent chiefly at Hunsdon and Hatfield manors under the care of Lady Bryan, but when she was four Catherine Champernowne was appointed her governess and quickly won her confidence. Catherine gave her a remarkable grasp of languages and classical scholarship; by the time she was six one courtier reckoned that if her formal education ceased forthwith 'she will prove of no less honour and womanhood than shall be seen her father's daughter'. Though she saw little of him Elizabeth was devoted to King Henry and later on would revere his memory for what he had achieved in Church and state. At last, after he married Catherine Parr in 1543, the three royal children were brought to court for long periods, so with a room at Whitehall Palace next door to the Queen's she felt she had a settled home. Catherine encouraged her studies so she now had Greek lessons from John Cheke, learned Italian from Battisti Castiglioni and, to her father's delight, made excellent progress on the virginals. Godly learning in the Erasmian tradition was varied by riding, archery and dancing in all of which Elizabeth excelled. There was much practical relevance in the curriculum for a future ruler, though at the time no one expected the Princess to become more than the consort of a foreign sovereign.

The earliest portrait shows a pale-faced girl of thirteen, with auburn hair and innocent eyes, regal and confident in her bearing, seriously reflecting on the book she is holding. Those final years of Henry's reign were perhaps the most peaceful of times. He had been the one constant factor in her life and once he died there would be endless difficulties for her. The Act of Succession had settled the Crown in turn on Edward, Mary and Elizabeth and although Henry had confirmed this in his will, he went on to provide for the remote possibility of all three of his children

Right: Queen Elizabeth I, painted by Marcus Gheeraerts (c. 1561–1635). This is unusual among surviving portraits of the queen as it shows the ravages of age – it was painted in 1595, when Elizabeth was sixty-two years old.

Opposite: *Robert Dudley, Earl of Leicester, by an unknown artist. He was one of Elizabeth I's most passionate admirers, known to her affectionately as 'sweet Robin', and he remained devoted to her until his death a month after the victory against the Armada in 1588.*
Above: *An illustration portraying Richard Tarleton, Elizabeth's favourite clown.*

dying childless, in which case the Crown should descend to the heirs of his younger sister Mary (the Suffolk line) instead of the heirs of his elder sister Margaret, who had married James IV of Scotland in 1503 (the Stuart line). In the event Elizabeth was to override his preference, just as Edward Seymour, Earl of Hertford, immediately abrogated the dying King's plans for a Council of Regents by seizing power himself.

Elizabeth stayed with her step-mother in Chelsea but soon the Protector's brother, Lord Admiral Seymour, had intruded on their household to marry the Queen Dowager and then to flirt with the four-teen-year-old Princess. He would barge into her bedroom to tickle her and snatch kisses, but for all his charm he became repulsive to her and she was

relieved when Catherine sent her to stay at Cheshunt, where she had the company of 'Kat' Ashley (her governess had married John Ashley, the friend of Roger Ascham). Soon Ascham himself became her tutor, extending her scholarship by his method of 'double translation'. Later in life Ascham remarked on her industry, her prodigious memory and her modesty. She was not entirely free from Thomas Seymour, for when Catherine Parr died in childbed he was indeed free to marry her; rumours were rife, but the Princess dismissed the topic – 'it was but a London news'. The Admiral's plans to over-turn his brother were tumbled and he was sent to the Tower. In the investigations both Mistress Ashley and Thomas Parry, the Princess's cofferer, were themselves examined in the Tower to wring from them any

Above: *Sir Christopher Hatton was another of Elizabeth's favourites, author of ardent love letters and rewarded for his loyalty with the Bishop of Ely's house in Holborn and the post of Lord Chancellor.*

incriminating evidence, while Elizabeth was cross-questioned by Sir Robert Tyrwhit who was amazed at her circumspect answers. For a time she was denied Kat Ashley's service but made such a fuss that the Council relented. The list of treasons alleged against Seymour, which sent him to the block, included craftily attempting to marry Elizabeth; long afterwards she spoke of him as 'a man of much wit and very little judgement'. She survived by steering clear of pol-itics under Northumberland and, despite her Protestantism, was relieved at the failure of the attempt to place Lady Jane Grey on the throne, for the establishment of the Suffolk line would have ruled out her own right to succeed, and with Mary's accession she became heir apparent.

With Mary's re-establishment of Catholicism and betrothal to Philip of Spain, the real test began for Elizabeth. Opposition to Mary naturally focused on her sister, who was popular, and she had to be on her guard to avoid entanglement in the plots woven about her. Suspected of complicity in Wyatt's revolt, she was summoned from Ashridge to court and, as she was ill, was brought in a litter by easy stages to Whitehall Palace where Mary refused to see her. After a month she was taken by barge to the Tower in terror of being quietly put out of the way, but she bravely told her warders she was no traitor 'but as true a woman to the Queen's Majesty as any'. Mary suspected much and could not believe Elizabeth was being frank when she swore that though Wyatt might have written to her, 'on my faith I never received any from him'. Yet since the Queen had no evidence to send her for trial she had no justification for confining her, even though the political situation required her to be under close surveillance. At last after eight weeks in the Tower she was moved to Woodstock in Oxfordshire in the custody of a stiff-necked Norfolk squire, Sir Henry Bedingfield. Here Elizabeth remained for ten months, to all intents a prisoner, while Mary married Philip and Cardinal Pole reconciled England with the Church of Rome.

At Woodstock there were pin-pricking restrictions about her books, about letter-writing and about her devotions. When she was ill, Mary refused her request for a royal physician to attend her and said an Oxford doctor would do just as well. This brought a characteristic outburst – 'I am not minded to make any stranger privy to the state of my body, but commit it to God.' The Queen gave way and sent Dr Owen to her, and his treatment reduced the swellings in her face and arms. She kept up her spirits by her duel of wits with Bedingfield and remained ambivalent about her conversion to Catholicism; some said she only heard Mass daily 'to give the impression that she had changed her religion. However she is too clever to get herself caught.' At last in April 1555 she was allowed to return to court and though she stubbornly denied there had been any fault in her behaviour, which angered Mary as it made plain that Elizabeth felt she had been wrongfully punished, there came a reconciliation between the half-sisters when the Princess unreservedly professed her undying loyalty. For the rest of the reign she remained chiefly at Hatfield, with Sir Thomas Pope, who proved a much more cultivated and endearing guardian than Bedingfield. Proposals for her hand had come thick and fast, from Habsburg Princes, from the Duke of Savoy and from the King of Sweden's son, but Elizabeth said 'she had

no wish to marry'. In the summer of 1557 Queen and Princess kept midsummer together at Richmond and later in the year Mary paid a state visit to Hatfield. In her last illness Mary agreed with the Spanish ambassador and her Council that only Elizabeth could succeed her and sent word imploring her to maintain the old faith.

As Queen, indeed, the most urgent problem was the religious settlement. From the beginning Elizabeth was determined to avoid the extremes of both her brother's and her sister's reigns, so that her people could live together in unity and concord and she strove hard to establish a Church which was broadly based with a doctrine sufficiently elastic to satisfy the vast majority of her subjects. This middle way naturally antagonised the Protestant exiles returning from Geneva and Zurich who had greeted Elizabeth as Deborah, the restorer of Israel, and hoped that the doctrine embodied in the 1552 Prayer Book would be reintroduced, but episcopacy abolished, for they had drunk deeply at the wells of Calvinism. Such partisan views were anathema to the Queen and, despite the pressure of Protestants in Parliament, the *via media* was to be pursued. She would not, she said 'open windows in men's souls'. Outward conformity by attendance at church of a Sunday was enough; if men chose also to hear the Roman Mass privately or to attend a sectarian meeting there would be no harm done. Alas, because she was both Queen and Supreme Governor of the Church of England, 'nonconformity' would come to be interpreted as 'disloyalty' to the regime and after 1570, when the Pope had the effrontery to issue a bull deposing her and absolving her subjects from their allegiance, practising Catholics were turned into potential traitors. In a similar way the Puritan wing of Protestantism came to undermine royal authority. Under the pressure of political events Elizabeth's ideal of a golden mean could not be achieved, but there is no denying her abhorrence of persecution and her fundamental dislike of extremes.

From the first Elizabeth placed exceptional trust in William Cecil, who had helped to administer her properties as Princess, and he was destined to serve her devotedly until his death in 1598, first as Principal Secretary, then as Lord Treasurer – a remarkable partnership. Matthew Parker, whom she selected as Archbishop of Canterbury, fulfilled all her expectations of him in moulding the Church of England, though she never approved of his having a wife. These two men were links with the past, for Cecil's grandfather had fought for her grandfather at Bosworth, while Parker had connections with the Boleyns.

At the outset of the reign de Feria, the Spanish ambassador, had noted that Elizabeth was 'much attached to the people and is very confident that they take her part'. Her popularity was indeed most obvious during the festivities accompanying the coronation on 15 January 1559, a date which the astrologer John Dee had helped her to select. The post of Lord High Steward of England at the coronation went to Henry, Earl of Arundel, a widower who fancied his chances of becoming consort. Another English candidate was Sir William Pickering, a diplomat whose swagger upset everyone, but there was no shortage of foreign princes offering their hands – Philip of Spain himself, the Duke of Holstein, Eric of Sweden and two Habsburg Archdukes. It was taken for granted in England and abroad that Elizabeth would marry and that marriage would solve the problem of the succession; her marriage and the succession were the twin topics on which Parliament continued to press her, to her extreme annoyance – they would never have dared to treat her father thus, she growled.

The problem of the succession was the more acute since, immediately on Mary's death, her cousin Mary Queen of Scots, wife of the Dauphin of France, had claimed to be rightful Queen of England in Elizabeth's place, and when the Dauphin succeeded to the throne as Francis II in July 1559, England looked most vulnerable; never had the 'auld alliance' between Scotland and France been so menacing, for both were controlled by the Guise faction. That winter the English fought over the border as allies of the Protestant Lords of the Congregation to expel the French and, by the Treaty of Edinburgh which followed, the Scots fully recognised Elizabeth's right to her throne and undertook that their own Queen, still in France, should relinquish her claim. The sudden death of Francis II in December 1560 increased Elizabeth's difficulties, since Mary would now reside in Scotland. Mary consistently refused to ratify the Treaty of Edinburgh, unless Elizabeth would name her as her successor, and Mary's search for another husband, in England and on the continent, further aggravated the matter. The two Queens, enemies to the end, would never meet each other.

Elizabeth caught smallpox in 1562, and seemed near to death. Ministers discussed who might succeed her, which was no longer an academic question, especially as there were 'nearly as many different opinions as there were councillors present'. When the Queen recovered she said that in case of a like emergency, Lord Robert Dudley should be made Protector of the realm. Dudley, Northumberland's fifth son, had been appointed Master of the Horse and had come to high favour by April 1559; he was so much with the Queen that men said that had he not already a wife Elizabeth would have married him and exaggerated tales of their relationship were related in foreign courts. Then Dudley's wife, Amy Robsart, died in suspicious circumstances and though the coroner's inquest cleared Lord Robert – he was with the Queen at Windsor at the time – the tragedy at Cumnor made all the difference to the question of marriage. Dudley was in any case too controversial a figure in personality and politics for her to take him as a husband without dividing her court and people, though she remained emotionally tied to 'sweet Robin' till his death. The request that he might become Protector if anything happened to her indicates the strength of their special relationship. 'The Queen would like everyone to be in love with her', commented a shrewd ambassador, 'but I doubt whether she will ever be in love with anyone enough to marry him.' Though there were to be other suitors from abroad, notably the Archduke Charles and then

Opposite: The dramatic rise in favour of the dashing and handsome Walter Raleigh, shown here in an anonymous portrait, deeply annoyed the triumvirate of Elizabeth's closest confidants, Dudley, Hatton and Heneage.

the French Duke of Alençon, Dudley long cherished the hope of marrying the Queen, nor was he the only Englishman with this ambition.

Christopher Hatton, who had caught her eye at a masque by his fine dancing, became one of the corps of Gentlemen Pensioners, her personal bodyguard of which in 1572 he became Captain. While she nicknamed Robert Dudley 'Eyes', Hatton became 'Lids' and wrote her passionate love letters: 'To serve you is heaven, but to lack you is more than hell's torment.' He wept when she spurned him and vowed to stay celibate for her sake, dreaming of the idyll which might have been, and she loved him for it. She forced the Bishop of Ely to give him his house in Holborn, while the favourite built Holdenby House in his native Lincolnshire as a 'shrine' for her. He was to become Lord Chancellor. There developed a curious bond between Dudley, Hatton and also Heneage through their rival devotion to the Queen, but none of them could stand the outsider, Walter Raleigh, who made his début at court in 1581.

Though the society in which she lived at court was essentially masculine, Elizabeth succeeded in dominating it, evoking a genuine emotional response from courtiers in general because she was a woman as well as a queen. She charmed those about her into participating in the sophisticated allegorical fantasy of the Virgin Queen, contriving to live out a mystical romance on a public stage. The musicians and poets praised her as Fair Oriana or as the immortal shepherdess of a pastoral and the older she grew the more she delighted in the cult. Her household resembled a large family, often on the move between residences, and as a family it had its feuds, when factions formed around strong personalities. It was not out of malice that Elizabeth opposed her maids of honour's plans to marry, but because marriages broke up her own family circle. Like her father Elizabeth wanted her court to become a great cultural centre, an academy where scholars, musicians and artists could find fellowship and patronage, although she was not prepared to spend as freely as Henry VIII. Musicians such as William Byrd fared much better than the poets, and Edmund Spenser failed to find a post at court even when he had dedicated *The Faerie Queene* to his sovereign.

To solve the problem of Mary of Scotland, Elizabeth had suggested that Mary might marry her own Dudley, whom she created Earl of Leicester. Mary, however, had set her heart on Lord Darnley, descended from Queen Margaret's second marriage with the Earl of Angus. The fact that Darnley was an English subject made him even more unsuitable in Elizabeth's eyes, yet in July 1565 their marriage took place. 'King Darnley' fathered the future James I and VI, but soon showed himself a worthless sot and he was murdered at Kirk o'-Field, probably on the Earl of Bothwell's order. Next month Mary married Bothwell, provoking the Lords of the Covenant to arms; they defeated Bothwell at Carberry Hill and forced Mary to abdicate. In May 1568, however, she escaped from Lochleven Castle, to throw herself on Elizabeth's mercy, but the Queen decided she had no alternative but to keep her in close custody. Unwillingly she found herself acting as arbiter between Mary and her subjects and while she could never forgive a claimant to her throne, she would not lightly sacrifice an anointed queen to rebellious subjects.

Mary's presence in England provoked the Northern Rebellion of 1569 in which the Earls of Northumberland and Westmorland aimed to restore Catholicism and place Mary on the throne. The rebels were defeated by Hunsdon, the Queen's cousin, but another cousin, Thomas Howard, fourth Duke of Norfolk, was found to be deeply implicated in the rising and in 1572 was executed for his share in the Ridolfi conspiracy. Elizabeth would have preferred to pardon him, but Cecil pointed out to her the inexorable logic of statecraft. Thereafter a further series of conspiracies were planned by Catholics to carry out the papal bull deposing Elizabeth; all

Above: *Portrait of Sir Francis Drake made in about 1580. The globe in the background commemorates the circumnavigation of the world that Drake had undertaken between 1577 and 1580.*

Habes Lector candide, fortiß, ac inuictiß Ducis Draeck ad Viuum Imaginem qui toto terrarum orbe, duorum annorum, et mensium decem spatio, Zephiris fauentibus circumducto, Angliam sedes proprias, 4. Cal. Octobr. anno à partu Virginis 1580 reuisit cum antea portu soluißet sd. Decem: anni 1577.

HONI SOIT QVI MALY PENSE

The most noble ROBERT
Earle of Eſſex and Ewe, Earle
Marſhall of England, Vicount Hereford and Bourgcher, Lord Ferres
of Chartley, L. Bourgcher and
Louayn, and her Maieſties
lieutenant, and Gouernour generall
of the Kingdome of Irland. 1601.

HIC TVVS ILLE COMES GENEROSA ESSEXIA NOSTRIS
QVEM QVAM GAVDEMVS REBVS ADESSE DVCEM.

hinged on foreign aid and saw the Queen's death as a preliminary to Mary Stuart's accession. In this atmosphere of plot and counterplot Elizabeth showed remarkable courage and forbearance, trying hard to reduce the severity of the Draconian laws against her Catholic subjects. Francis Walsingham, now Secretary of State, longed for her to take a positive role in opposing the forces of the Counter Reformation in Europe by supporting the Dutch Protestants against Philip of Spain and intervening on the side of the Huguenots in the French religious wars, but she was anxious to be at peace with her neighbours, hating the waste and inhumanity of war, even if she profited by the marauding of Hawkins and Drake against Spanish possessions in the New World. In 1572, however, England at last found an ally in France and to preserve this alliance Elizabeth undertook a protracted courtship of the Duke of Alençon, throwing herself into the role of lover with gay abandon.

Francois Alençon was half her age and diminutive beside her, yet he had remarkable charm and she fell for his flattery. During 1579 it seemed as if she would really marry him, but there was a Puritan outcry against the Duke's 'unprince-like, French kind of wooing'. The discovery that Leicester had secretly married the beautiful Lettice Knollys, while still protesting his undying love for Elizabeth, would almost have driven her into Alençon's arms, had it not been for Protestant fervour; the match eventually failed, as the Habsburg marriage negotiations had also foundered in 1567, because the potential bridegroom was a Catholic. Her head overcame her heart and she let Alencon go, but by now she was in her late forties and knew that it was her last chance of marriage and children.

Her depression was saved by the arrival of Walter Raleigh, a west countryman of singular wit and gallantry, who praised her in verse. Leicester's nose was soon out of joint and Hatton in utter despair, for his rise to favour was meteoric. She was truly fascinated by Raleigh and fed on his adoration; only Raleigh

would have tried to plant a colony in North America and name it Virginia, after his Queen. Yet eventually, when he realised that she would never marry him and found happiness with Bess Throckmorton, the Queen was furious and banished them both from court.

War with Spain loomed nearer as Walsingham's agents pieced together plans for Philip II's enterprise against England, and then Mary Queen of Scots was found to be personally committed in the Babington Plot against the Queen's life. Elizabeth hesitated long over sending Mary to her execution at Fotheringhay and then blamed it on her officials. Burghley (as Cecil had become) was in disgrace and for a time feared the Tower. Already, following the murder of William the Silent, she had been persuaded to send an army under Leicester to fight against the Spanish in the Netherlands, though she refused to accept the sovereignty of the Dutch people. Drake and the seadogs, flushed with their successes in the Caribbean, urged open war with Spain, but still Elizabeth held back, preferring negotiation to fighting. Drake's raid on Cadiz postponed the sailing of the Armada for a year, but at last in August 1588 the great Spanish fleet was in the Channel, endeavouring to gain command of the Straits of Dover to launch a full-scale invasion.

In this moment of crisis Elizabeth was superb. Against her councillors' wishes she went down to Tilbury Camp to exhort the troops under Leicester at the very moment when it was feared an invasion would be attempted. 'Let tyrants fear. I have always so behaved myself that, under God, I have placed my chiefest strength and goodwill in the loyal hearts and goodwill of my subjects . . . I know I have but the body of a weak and feeble woman, but I have the heart and stomach of a King.' She spoke for England. The Armada, scattered from Calais Roads by the fireships, was driven into the North Sea, to find its way home by the north of Scotland and Ireland. The Spanish defeat did not bring Philip II to his knees, but it put fresh heart into the cause of Protantism

Opposite: An engraving by Boissard of Robert, Earl of Essex, who relied too heavily on Elizabeth's indulgence and patronage, eventually to be executed for treason after an unsuccessful attempt to seize the throne.

The Fleete of Portugall consisting of 12 Vessells, in wch were 3330 Souldiers, 1233 Marriners, 200 Canons

The Spanish Fleete weighing Ancor from the River Tagus, the 20th of May 1588.

The twelve Spanish Shipps Caled the 12 Apostles

The Spanish Armada consisting of 130 Shipps where of 72 were Galleasses and Galeons in wch were 19290 Souldiers, 8350 Marriners, 2060 Gally slaves & 2630 great Ordinance. ye Navy was 3 whole yeares span̄g

The Pope Consulting with his Cardinalls & Contributing a Million of Gold towards the Charge of the Armada —

The Army of 1000 horse, and 22000 Foot, which ye Earle of Leicester comanded when hee Pitched his Tents att Tilbury

in Europe, especially in Holland. Through divine intervention, men said, the Colossus of Spain had at last been stayed and Elizabeth was the heroine of the hour. None then predicted that the war would outlast the Queen's reign.

Leicester's death the following month soured the fruits of victory. She locked herself in her room and would see no one, so that her councillors ordered her door to be broken down, fearing for her safety. The intensity of her feeling for Leicester was revealed only after her own death when in a little casket by her bed was found among her treasured keepsakes the letter he had written to her from Rycote the night before he died, with her own inscription in a shaky hand 'His last letter'.

Old age brought its harsh losses. Soon she was being called to the bedside of Christopher Hatton at Ely Place to feed him 'with cordial broths' as he lay dying, then Walsingham went and finally old Burghley, who had triumphed by bringing in his second son Robert Cecil to share his power. The series of 'Armada portraits' and the splendid painting of Elizabeth standing on the map of England (1592) concealed the ravages time had made on her face and figure. Marvellous in jewels and ruff, Gloriana was almost sixty, and had resorted to an auburn wig to hide her thinning hair, and a liberal use of cosmetics. Still the masquerade went on and the final act was dominated by Leicester's step-son, Robert, Earl of Essex, a handsome youth who fancied himself as a general and looked to the Queen to retrieve him from financial ruin. Robert Cecil outwitted him in Council, yet Essex banked all on success against the Irish rebels. He came home in defiance of the Queen's orders and gambled on saving himself by his charm, but she had decided to teach him a long-overdue lesson and she refused to underwrite his vast debts. In 1601 he drifted into conspiracy, aiming at the throne himself, but his revolt was easily suppressed and Essex was executed for treason. Elizabeth reckoned he had as little judgement as Thomas Seymour, two generations back.

That year she addressed her last Parliament and her touch was as sure as ever. She had always taken great care with her speeches from the days of her first Parliaments, but now she delivered what posterity

Den VIII februarij werde onthalst Maria
Stuart Schots Coninginne's tervende Roomsch Catho-
lijck Hebbende gesocht veel onrusten aen te richten Haer selven
mee ter te maecken van Engelant, doordich Haer vanden Rael
ofte parlement Volcomelijck svende vertoont, Anno 1587.
☞ Metreu XIII sol XIII en XIIII. ☜

Opposite: *Six engraved Armada playing cards from the late seventeenth century, demonstrating strong anti-Catholic feeling.*
Above: *An illustration of the execution of Mary Queen of Scots at Fotheringhay Castle, following the discovery of her involvement in the Babington Plot against her cousin Elizabeth's life.*

called her 'golden speech', because it epitomised the relationship of sovereign and people in a golden age of monarchy which effectively ended with her death. Being Queen, she told them, was a glorious thing, but it was her people's loyalty and love that mattered: 'There will never Queen sit in my seat with more zeal to my country . . . And though you have had, and may have, many Princes more mighty and wise, sitting in this state, yet you never had, or shall have, any that will be more careful and loving.'

She had never named her successor and even at the last would not do so, for she knew that the careful Cecil was discreetly planning for James VI of Scotland, the son of Mary Stuart and Darnley, to enter upon the seat of kings on her demise. After Christmas 1602 she began to feel most frail and six weeks later fell ill at Richmond. Insomnia was far worse to bear than sickness and it increased her melancholy. Her work of 'having brought up, even under her wing, a nation that was almost begotten and born under her' (as Thomas Dekker put it) was over. She died on 24 March 1603, the last of the Tudors and the greatest of queens.

THE STUARTS
1603–1714

—————⊰●⊱—————

JAMES I 1603–25

CHARLES I 1625–49

CHARLES II 1660–85

JAMES II 1685–8

WILLIAM III 1688–1702

AND MARY II 1688–94

ANNE 1702–14

—————⊰●⊱—————

Opposite: King Charles I on horseback, with Monsieur Saint Antoine, by Sir Anthony van Dyck (1599–1641). Charles I was a connoisseur as well as a shrewd observer of the power of the arts to increase the dignity and stature of rulers: he and Van Dyck made a speciality of equestrian portraits modelled on those of antiquity and the Renaissance.

THE TUDORS AND STUARTS

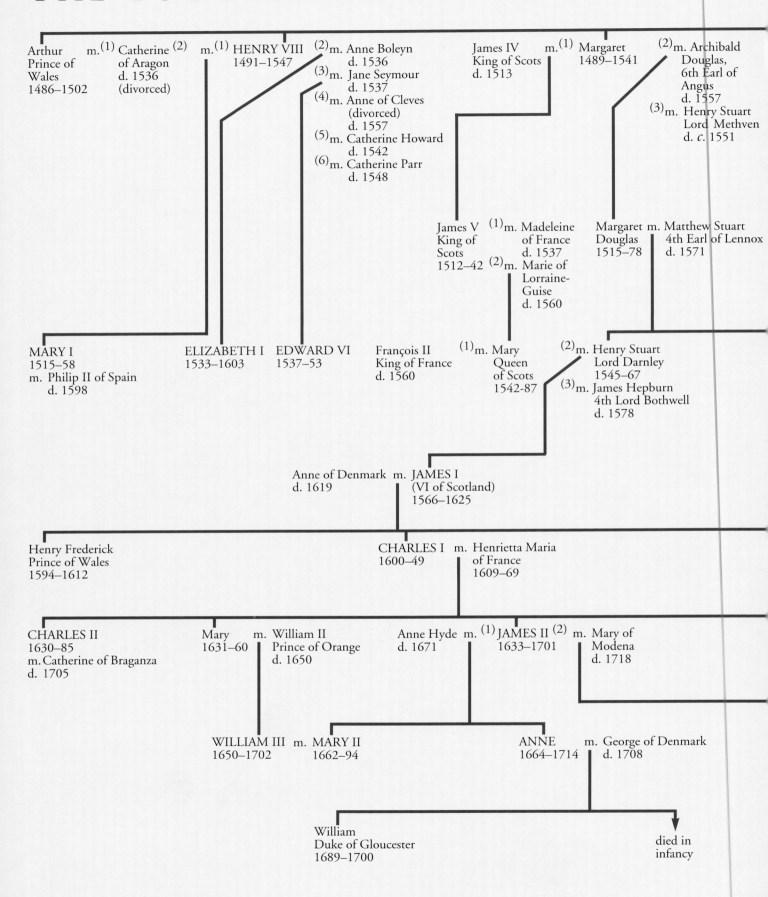

Arthur
Prince of
Wales
1486–1502

m.(1) Catherine (2) m.(1) HENRY VIII (2)m. Anne Boleyn
of Aragon   1491–1547   d. 1536
d. 1536   (3)m. Jane Seymour
(divorced)   d. 1537
                                  (4)m. Anne of Cleves
                                      (divorced)
                                      d. 1557
                                  (5)m. Catherine Howard
                                      d. 1542
                                  (6)m. Catherine Parr
                                      d. 1548

James IV   m.(1) Margaret   (2)m. Archibald
King of Scots   1489–1541   Douglas,
d. 1513   6th Earl of
                                    Angus
                                    d. 1557
                               (3)m. Henry Stuart
                                    Lord Methven
                                    d. c. 1551

James V   (1)m. Madeleine   Margaret m. Matthew Stuart
King of   of France   Douglas   4th Earl of Lennox
Scots   d. 1537   1515–78   d. 1571
1512–42   (2)m. Marie of
                Lorraine-
                Guise
                d. 1560

MARY I   ELIZABETH I   EDWARD VI   François II   (1)m. Mary   (2)m. Henry Stuart
1515–58   1533–1603   1537–53   King of France   Queen   Lord Darnley
m. Philip II of Spain   d. 1560   of Scots   1545–67
d. 1598   1542-87   (3)m. James Hepburn
                                                                                         4th Lord Bothwell
                                                                                         d. 1578

Anne of Denmark m. JAMES I
d. 1619   (VI of Scotland)
                    1566–1625

Henry Frederick   CHARLES I m. Henrietta Maria
Prince of Wales   1600–49   of France
1594–1612   1609–69

CHARLES II   Mary   m. William II   Anne Hyde m.(1) JAMES II (2) m. Mary of
1630–85   1631–60   Prince of Orange   d. 1671   1633–1701   Modena
m. Catherine of Braganza   d. 1650   d. 1718
d. 1705

WILLIAM III m. MARY II   ANNE   m. George of Denmark
1650–1702   1662–94   1664–1714   d. 1708

William   died in
Duke of Gloucester   infancy
1689–1700

HENRY VII m. Elizabeth of York
1455–1509   d. 1503

Louis XII m.(1) Mary (2) m. Charles Brandon
King of   1498–1533   Duke of Suffolk
France   d. 1545
d. 1515

Henry Brandon   Henry Grey   m.(1) Frances (2) m. Adrian   Eleanor
Earl of Lincoln   Marquis of Dorset   Brandon   Stokes   d. 1547
1516–34   Duke of Suffolk   1517–79   d. c. 1581 m. Henry Clifford,
                      d. 1554   Earl of Cumberland
                                                                                         d. 1570

Charles Stuart m. Elizabeth Cavendish
6th Earl of
Lennox

                                              Jane Grey m. Guildford Dudley
                                              d. 1554   d. 1554

Arabella Stuart m. William Seymour
d. 1615   Duke of Somerset

                                                          Elizabeth m. Frederick V
                                                          1596–1662   Elector Palatine
                                                                          of the Rhine
                                                                          d. 1632

Elizabeth   Henry   Henrietta m. Philip   Sophia   m. Ernest Augustus   Rupert
1635–80   Duke of Gloucester   1644–70   Duke of   1630–1714   Elector of Hanover   of the
                 1640–60   Orleans   Duke of Brunswick-   Rhine
                                                         d. 1701   Luneborg   1619–82
                                                                                   d. 1698

James Francis Edward m. Maria   Louisa   GEORGE I m. Sophia Dorothea
'The Old Pretender'   Clementina   d. 1712   1660–1727   of Celle
1688–1766   Sobieska   1666–1726
                          d. 1735

Charles Edward   m. Louisa of   Henry Benedict   HOUSE OF
'The Young Pretender'   Stolberg-Gedern   Cardinal York   HANOVER
1720–88   d. 1824   1725–1807

JAMES I
r. 1603–25

WHEN ON 24 MARCH 1603 James Stuart ascended the English throne, he was, as he himself boasted, an experienced king. His ancestors had ruled or at any rate reigned in Scotland since the fourteenth century and James was crowned King of the Scots when he was only thirteen months old in 1567. His father, Lord Darnley, had been mysteriously murdered and his mother, Mary Queen of Scots, had first abdicated, then reclaimed the throne and finally, defeated in battle, fled to England where she was kept a prisoner in honourable captivity until her execution for treason in 1587. A regent, the fourth Earl of Morton, governed Scotland for fourteen years during James's minority.

Although James grew up in an atmosphere of civil strife he had a sound Presbyterian and classical education. When he became an adolescent, homosexual feelings were first aroused in him by a sophisticated French nobleman, D'Aubigny Lennox. In 1581 Lennox helped engineer the execution of the Regent but his power angered some of the nobility; James was kidnapped by the Earl of Gowrie and Lennox was banished. However, James was soon rescued by his supporters and in 1583, at seventeen, assumed the reins of government. When he was twenty he concluded a treaty with Queen Elizabeth 1 of England, a year before his mother's death. As Elizabeth was childless and his mother, who claimed to be her successor, was dead, the likelihood of James inheriting the English throne was enhanced. He devoted all his attention to remaining on friendly terms with the Queen of England, although he made

formal protests about his mother's execution. In his anxiety to obtain the throne of England he even cultivated the Pope and the English Roman Catholics. In 1600 he survived a plot on his life by the Gowrie family. After entering into friendly correspondence with Sir Robert Cecil his efforts were finally crowned with success. On the death of Elizabeth 1, being the direct descendant of King Henry VII, James VI King of the Scots was acknowledged as the ruler of England and went happily to London.

The conditions of monarchy in England were very different from those in Scotland. There the King was little more than the first among equals. He had twice been kidnapped and held prisoner by his own subjects and though eventually he succeeded in imposing bishops upon the Kirk, the power of the General Assembly of the Scottish Church was great. In England, on the other hand, the King was the chief executive, the Supreme Governor of the Church, the possessor of hereditary wealth, the leader of his subjects in war and peace. But his authority was constitutionally limited by tradition. The English Parliament was more independent than that of Scotland. To wage war or to meet extraordinary expenses the House of Commons had to be asked to vote money for their sovereign.

Three immediate problems presented themselves to James when he reached London. The first was a growing Puritan movement which wished to sweep all Roman Catholic rites from the church services and to revert to what were claimed to be primitive usages which laid stress on preaching and prayer

Opposite: A formal portrait of the young James VI of Scotland attributed to Adrian Vanson, from 1595. The young king received a good and varied education and as King of England he engaged on a level footing with the leading philosophers and theologians of his time.

IACOBVS · 6 · D · G ·
SCOTORVM
ÆTA · 29 ·
1595 ·

Opposite: *James I, the son of Mary Queen of Scots, had already ruled as James VI of Scotland for thirty-six years before being crowned King of England after Elizabeth's death.*
Above: *The Gunpowder Plotters, who in an act of Roman Catholic rebellion attempted t o blow up the Houses of Parliament on 5 November 1605. The illustration also shows the bloody end to which they came, their heads displayed on stakes for all to see.*

rather than ceremonial and sacraments. Secondly, Parliament had waxed stronger under the Tudors and the rich gentry, who provided most of the members of the Commons, were seeking to play a larger part in state as well as church affairs. Lastly, England was still at war with Spain, a war which had continued for some fifteen years. With the last problem James coped expeditiously: he concluded peace without betraying the Dutch who were still fighting for their independence from the Spanish Habsburgs in Madrid. James refused even to sanction privateering, a profitable form of licensed piracy, in which the Elizabethan seafaring heroes from Drake to Raleigh had enthusiastically engaged.

With the Puritans James initially had some sympathy, for he himself had been brought up as a Calvinist. After receiving a petition from a group of representative Puritans, James summoned a conference at Hampton Court Palace between the bishops and leading Puritans, over which he presided in

S pes patris et patria caboeum Hee thath ALIFE of this FACE eury saw Or elfein FEARE that HEE would WAR Asonefore
lege carentus The MILDNES in it nothing, and the AVE Concluded with him HEE should Live with
Ante diem, lachrimas et inana Will iudgeth PEACE did either in for LOVE To both His agines fluculue afaires ;
vota relinquo So soone aduance him to hir STATE aboue In eurie SOLDIER s greise SCHOLLEES knres

Above: Henry, Prince of Wales, heir to James I until his death aged eighteen in 1616.

Opposite: Anne of Denmark painted in 1617 by Paul van Somer. She married James when he was King of the Scots and bore six children, but he tired of her, preferring the company of his male favourites.

person. Although he was ready to offer some concessions to the Puritans, he was provoked by the suggestion that the episcopacy should be abolished and uttered the famous dictum: 'No bishop, no king.' He ordered the preparation of a new translation of the Bible which became known as the Authorised Version or King James's Bible. On the whole, his attitude to religion was fairly tolerant and eclectic. But when the famous Gunpowder Plot by Roman Catholics to blow up the Houses of Parliament on 5 November 1605 was discovered, James became less kind to practising Catholics;

having waived the penalties against them for not attending English church services, he reimposed them.

As a result of the Gunpowder Plot James remained for some time on friendly terms with his first Parliament, which had met in March 1604; but he had an irritating way of making exaggerated claims for the rights of the monarchy. In a book which he wrote before he left Scotland called *Basilikon Doron*, printed in 1603, he stressed the patriarchal nature of kingship and compared monarchs to gods; he was fond of addressing Parliament in lofty terms extolling the supremacy of kings. Nevertheless he was a shrewd politician and actually repudiated the argument put forward by a Cambridge professor that he was above the law.

James set himself two constructive tasks: the first was to effect a complete union between the kingdoms of Scotland and England whose crowns he wore; the second was to arrange a financial deal with the House of Commons which would guarantee him a regular and permanent income. His chief minister, Sir Robert Cecil, whom James raised to be Earl of Salisbury, attempted to carry out his master's wishes. Promoted Lord Treasurer in 1608, Salisbury took advantage of a test case to levy additional Customs – known as 'impositions' – to increase the royal revenue. Parliament would not assent to either scheme. Though James assumed the title of King of Great Britain, the Commons were not prepared to concede equal rights to the Scots; nor would they accept a plan put forward by the King's government – the Great Contract – by which, in return for a regular revenue, the King promised to give up all feudal dues belonging to the Crown and not to levy new impositions without the consent of the Commons. Faced by this opposition, James dissolved his first Parliament in February 1611.

In May 1612 Salisbury died, worn out in the King's service, for though James was willing enough to take decisions, he spent most of his daylight hours hunting stags and falling off horses in the process, while Salisbury had done all the hard work. After Salisbury's death, power came into the hands of royal favourites. James had married Princess Anne of Denmark in 1589 while he was the King of the Scots;

*A study of George Villiers, Duke of Buckingham, by Peter Paul Rubens. As one of James I's
favoured circle, he came to have a great influence on policy-making and encouraged
the King into war with Spain.*

he had romantically braved the perils of the Baltic in order to meet his wife at Oslo on her way to Scotland. They had six children, two sons, Henry and Charles, and four daughters, two of whom died very young. But basically James was homosexual and grew bored with the frivolity and stupidity of his Queen. His first favourite in England was a Scotsman, Robert Carr, who rose to power in 1610 and in 1613 was married with James's connivance to Frances Howard, daughter of the Earl of Suffolk, after her marriage to the third Earl of Essex was annulled. (Her father was to succeed Salisbury as Lord Treasurer.) But in 1616 Carr, who had been created Earl of Somerset and was made Lord Chamberlain, and his wife were accused of poisoning a former secretary of Somerset while he was imprisoned in the Tower of London. Though both were found guilty neither was severely punished, but

Somerset's influence at court came to an abrupt end. James's next favourite was George Villiers who rose rapidly in the King's esteem and in 1623 was created Duke of Buckingham. During the last years of the reign Buckingham's influence on policy, particularly foreign policy, was decisive.

Although it was James's avowed intention to be a prince of peace, much of the remainder of the reign was absorbed in foreign affairs. In February 1613 his eldest daughter, Elizabeth, was married to Frederick the Elector Palatine who was a Calvinist and prominent among the German Protestant Princes. James himself entered into an alliance with the German Protestant Union and regarded himself as a Protestant champion. But at the same time he was anxious for an agreement with Spain, a country then regarded as the strongest in Europe. He aimed to reach an understanding by marrying his son Charles to the Spanish Infanta, sister of King Philip IV of Spain. He also put an end to his alliance with the Dutch, soon to renew their war against Spain, by selling back to them the towns acquired by Queen Elizabeth I.

In 1619 his son-in-law the Elector Palatine accepted the throne of Bohemia offered him by the Bohemian Protestant leaders. This led to war against the Holy Roman Emperor who himself claimed to be the rightful holder of the Bohemian throne. Thus James became reluctantly and at first indirectly involved in what was to be known as 'The Thirty Years' War' in Germany, in which the Spaniards engaged on the side of the Emperor against the Elector Palatine who lost his hereditary throne. So James's foreign policy fell to pieces. Nevertheless he hoped that if the Spanish marriage alliance could be achieved he might persuade the Spanish government to use its influence with the Holy Roman Emperor to conclude a peaceable settlement with his son-in-law. But this elaborate manoeuvre was doomed to failure and on Buckingham's instigation James was forced into a war with Spain and into hiring a mercenary army to fight against the Emperor.

Even before this James had grave financial difficulties. For he was grossly extravagant, spending, for example, a small fortune on his daughter's wedding,

besides being lavish to his male favourites. When his second Parliament had met in 1614 he had vainly tried to persuade the Commons to vote him money, but the Members expressed many grievances, especially over James's Scottish favourites, so that he was obliged to dissolve Parliament after two months. His third Parliament, which met in 1621, though avid for a war against Spain, thought that such a war should pay for itself and again demanded to discuss grievances before voting supplies. James said that foreign policy and religion were his business; when the Commons entered a protestation in its journal James tore the protestation out of the book and gave the order for the arrest of three or four of its leading Members.

James employed various expedients other than impositions to raise money. Lionel Cranfield, the Earl of Middlesex, was appointed Lord Treasurer and reorganised the royal finances; Sir Walter Raleigh, one of Queen Elizabeth's favourites, was allowed to seek a mythical gold mine in Guiana; James granted commercial 'monopolies' from which Buckingham and his relatives largely profited; and he still hoped to procure money through his son's marriage. But he allowed his ablest servants to be dismissed and punished. His talented Lord Chancellor, Francis Bacon, was deprived of all his offices for taking bribes; Raleigh was put to death for conspiracy; and Middlesex was impeached by the Commons after Buckingham was convinced that the Lord Treasurer had failed him. So James's reign ended in confusion and disaster both at home and abroad.

Though James's mental capacities declined towards the end of his life, he was a highly intelligent ruler who did not provoke his leading subjects too far and was ready to withdraw unpopular policies. He was a learned theologian and after an original belief in witchcraft was persuaded finally of its falsity. But he was vain, lazy and too fond of his own voice. He allowed himself to be increasingly imposed upon by men favourites while 'he piqued himself on his great contempt for women'. Before he died on 27 March 1625 he recognised the growing influence of the House of Commons and vainly warned his heir of the dangers which awaited him.

CHARLES I
r. 1625–49

THE SECOND SON OF JAMES I and Anne of Denmark was born in Dunfermline Palace, twelve miles from Edinburgh, on 19 November 1600. Charles was a weak and backward child and needed the permission of the royal doctors to be brought south in a curtained litter after his father settled in England. Like his father he was educated by a Scottish Presbyterian tutor, mastered Latin and Greek and showed an aptitude for modern languages. His brother Henry, who was six years his elder and whom Charles admired, died in 1612 when he was eighteen. In the following year Charles's sister Elizabeth departed with her husband for Heidelberg. Thus the shy and reserved boy – he never overcame a stammer – was created Prince of Wales in 1616, becoming important but lonely. In 1619 his mother died, but he struck up a friendship with the Marquis of Buckingham, his father's favourite, while James himself proved a conscientious and loving father. By 1624, going with Buckingham on an incognito mission to Madrid in search of a Spanish wife, Charles was described as having 'grown into a fine gentleman'. He was five feet four inches tall. The flattering portraits of him by Van Dyck and Bower made him appear more dignified than he really was. In fact he was a small man who in due course enjoyed asserting himself.

On 27 March 1625 Charles succeeded to the throne and within two months was married to Henrietta Maria, the sister of King Louis XIII of France. When in Madrid Charles had been attracted by the languorous Spanish Princess, who shrank from him as a heretic; at first he thought his French wife disappointing and took a dislike to her train of priests and women she brought over with her from Paris, some of whom he sent packing. For the first years of his reign he was under the influence of Buckingham and found himself at war with both Spain and France. The expeditions against these countries organised and on occasion led by Buckingham were complete failures. Because of their distrust of Buckingham the House of Commons refused to grant Charles the supplies he needed to wage wars, while even the Customs duties (known then as tonnage and poundage) were voted for his use only for a single year. So Charles was driven to a number of financial expedients; he cashed his wife's dowry; he exacted forced loans from his wealthier subjects, imprisoning five knights who refused to pay; he billeted soldiers without paying for them; and he collected tonnage and poundage without Parliamentary sanction. Both the Parliaments of 1625 and 1626 showed their distrust of the King and Buckingham.

When Charles's third Parliament met in 1628, after the failure of the campaigns against Spain, the leading Members of the Commons were extremely critical of the government. Not only did they resent the royal financial methods but they complained about the mismanagement of the war against the Spaniards and on behalf of the French Protestants, and also objected to the King's attitude to the Church of England. For although Charles had been tutored by a Scottish Calvinist, he was a man of

(continues on page 229)

Opposite: *The young Duke of York, later Charles I, painted by Robert Peake. He was a sickly child, yet it was his brother Henry, six years his senior, who died prematurely, leaving Charles as heir to their father's throne.*

The Arms
of the Stuarts

WHEN JAMES VI OF SCOTLAND INHERITED the English throne a change in the royal arms was necessary in order to include James's other kingdom. The resultant arms are here illustrated. The shield has been divided into four grand quarters. The old French and English quartered arms, as used for about two hundred years, were put in the first and fourth quarters. The Scottish lion within its *double tressure flory counterflory* was assigned the second quarter, whilst the harp of Ireland made its début in the royal coat in the third quarter.

Although Ireland had been raised from a lordship to a kingdom by Henry VIII and although the badge of a harp had been associated with Ireland, no proper arms of dominion existed. This was put right in the new version of the royal arms.

The supporters of the Scottish royal arms were two unicorns and so the Tudor dragon supporter was replaced by one of the Scottish unicorns. As King of Scotland, James and his successors used the arms in a different manner. The Scottish lion changed places with the English and French coats; the Scottish crest and motto replaced the English and the supporters changed sides and were depicted in a slightly different manner.

When William III and Mary II became joint sovereigns William as Prince of Orange could have added a complex quartered coat but opted for a little shield (illustrated below the arms of the Stuarts) of the arms of Nassau, which he placed in the centre of the Stuart coat. These arms are today the royal arms of Holland.

After William's death without issue the Crown passed to Mary's sister Anne but, as she did not succeed her brother-in-law as a hereditary Statholder in the Netherlands, she dropped the arms of Nassau and reverted to the Stuart royal arms until, in 1707, the two kingdoms of England and Scotland were united to form 'one Kingdom by the Name of Great Britain'. As the Act for the Union with Scotland provided that the arms of the United Kingdom shall be 'as Her Majesty shall appoint', they were duly altered.

The Highe and Mightie Prince FREDERICK the fift by the grace of God Counte Palatine of Rhyne, Duke of Bauier, Elector, and Arch-Sewer, of the Sacred Romane Empire and in vacance of the same Vicar therof And Knight of the most noble order of the Garter. Born 1596.

The most excelent Prinsces ELIZABETH th'only Daughter to our Soueraigne Lord Iames King of Great Brittaine. France. and Ireland &c: Borne the 19 of August 1596. Maried the 14 of Februarie. 1612.

Opposite: *Cornelius Johnson's portrait of Henrietta Maria, the sister of King Louis XIII of France who married Charles I in the year of his coronation. His initial indifference turned to love after the death of the Duke of Buckingham, under whose powerful influence he, like his father, found himself.*
Above: *Prince Frederick, Elector Palatine, and Elizabeth, Queen of Bohemia. Elizabeth was the eldest daughter of James I and her marriage to the German Protestant prince was part of James's scheme of championing the Protestant cause in Europe.*

fastidious tastes who disliked the kind of church services of which the Puritans most approved. He was accused of promoting so-called 'Arminians' or high churchmen who believed in free will rather than predestination to achieve salvation and of appointing clergy who preferred the retention of Catholic ritual and rites in services to long sermons and extempore prayer.

The Commons showed themselves extremely restless; a Petition of Rights was drawn up with the concurrence of the House of Lords in which forced loans, the billeting of soldiers, the imprisonment of subjects without cause shown, and other grievances were condemned. Charles accepted the petition with reluctance, but scarcely abided by it. When the Commons went on to condemn the King's favourite divines and to threaten the impeachment of his friend Buckingham, Charles felt obliged to adjourn

An engraving from 1651 of the symbolic Royal Oak Tree being destroyed in the Civil War under the guidance of Oliver Cromwell, showing not only the royal arms, the crown and the royal sword but also Magna Carta, the Statutes of Parliament and the Bible itself.

Parliament without obtaining the money he needed from it.

The assassination of Buckingham by a fanatic in August 1628 failed to reconcile Charles with his Parliament. Before he again adjourned it in March 1629 the Speaker of the Commons was held down in his chair while resolutions were unanimously passed condemning 'innovations' in religion and the illegal levying of tonnage and poundage. For the next eleven years Charles governed without Parliament and saved money by bringing the wars to an end. In 1633, however, he appointed a leading 'Arminian', William Laud, as Archbishop of Canterbury and with his aid set out to impose a service book drawn up in London on the Scottish Church or Kirk so that the religious practices of his two kingdoms should become uniform. Provoked by this action the Scottish lowlanders turned against their King and swore to uphold a National Covenant embodying loyalty to the Kirk, as exemplified in the public rejection of the new service book. Infuriated by this rebelliousness, Charles raised an army to enforce his wishes on Scotland. He was humiliatingly rebuffed in what was known as the first Bishops' War. To pay for a second campaign he was compelled to summon a new Parliament at Westminster.

This Parliament insisted on discussing their pent-up grievances before voting the King money. So Charles dissolved it after a few weeks, which gave it the sobriquet of 'the Short Parliament'. For a second time Charles sent an army against his Scottish subjects; this time he was conclusively beaten. The King was thus obliged to pay the Covenanter army while it was encamped on English soil in Northumberland and Durham and again threw himself on the mercy of an English Parliament, which met in November

1640 and was to be called the Long Parliament.

During the long interval before the Short and Long Parliaments met, the King's government had employed a number of dubious methods of raising money. 'Ship money', a tax which had been used in Tudor times, was imposed on inland towns as well as ports to pay for the upkeep of the navy. Tonnage and poundage continued to be levied illegally. Various irritating medieval imposts, such as fines upon gentry who refused to accept knighthoods, were collected. Thus the whole of the House of Commons, consisting of country gentlemen, lawyers and merchants, were alienated from the King's government which they considered to be acting unconstitutionally. Fears grew that the English army in the north and the garrison of Ireland were going to be employed to enforce the King's absolute will on Parliament. In fact Charles had no intention of doing anything of the sort, but his ablest minister, the Earl of Strafford, Lord Lieutenant of Ireland, whom he had summoned to organise the second Bishops' War, was selected by the Commons as a scapegoat. They reckoned him with Archbishop Laud as the chief of the King's 'evil counsellors' and it was decided to impeach Strafford for treason before the House of Lords.

Charles understood what the Commons had in mind. But he hoped that if Strafford defended himself successfully before his fellow peers the whole absolutist system of government, called by its opponents 'the eleven years' tyranny', would be vindicated. However, when the trial for treason faltered, Charles was asked to sign a Bill of Attainder by which Strafford could be put to death without any legal judgement. The King was subjected to heavy pressures; the House of Lords was menaced by city mobs; the King believed that his Roman Catholic Queen, with whom he had fallen in love since the death of Buckingham, was in peril. Reluctantly he signed the Bill. Afterwards he gave way over ship money and agreed that this Long Parliament should not be dissolved without its own consent.

Only on two questions did Charles refuse to yield to the pressure of the leaders of Parliament. The first was over the reform of the Church of England, which they held was being catholicised by the King's High Church bishops; the second was over the control of the militia, the only permanent armed force in the kingdom apart from the King's own guards. In the summer of 1641 Charles visited Scotland in the hope that by offering concessions to his subjects there he could rally them to the defence of the throne. When he returned empty-handed from Scotland, he found that about half the Members of the Commons were now veering towards his side. A 'Grand Remonstrance', which set out all the grievances against his government, was only carried by a few votes in November. Egged on by his Queen, the King now attempted to arrest five leading Members of the Commons, including his chief critic, John Pym. But when he entered the House in January 1642 he discovered that 'the birds had flown'. He then left London and both sides – the Royalists and the Parliamentarians – prepared for civil war.

During the next seven months negotiations went on between the two parties for a peace treaty. But they broke down on the two principal questions over which the King was willing to compromise but not to yield. Parliament also demanded the right to nominate all his ministers and military officers, even to supervise the upbringing of his children. Gradually hopes of a peaceful settlement faded; and the first civil war began when Charles raised his standard at Nottingham on 22 August 1642.

Charles had many fine qualities. He was temperate and grave, a devoted husband and father, and a sincere Christian. He was an aesthete who spent money on beautiful things. Inigo Jones, to be famous as an architect, and Ben Jonson, the playwright, designed masques for the court; Rubens was brought over to England to paint the ceiling of the banqueting house in Whitehall Palace in memory of Charles's father. Van Dyck did portraits of the royal family, and other artists, such as William Dobson, an outstanding native portrait painter, enjoyed the King's patronage. But Charles also had serious defects. He was lazy and lacked any sense of humour. Moreover he thought any means were justified to win the war and regain his absolute authority. Consequently he made all sorts of contradictory promises to Scottish Presbyterians, English Anglicans, Irish Roman Catholics and the Puritan leaders of the Parliamentary army, which he had no intention of keeping.

Above: *The costumes designed for King Charles and Queen Henrietta Maria by Inigo Jones to be worn in the masque* Salmacida Spolia *in 1640. In such masques the court presented itself in an idealised way, offering images of the king and queen that bore little relation to political situation.*
Opposite: *A contemporary German print depicting the public execution of King Charles I on 30 January 1649.*

Gradually he forfeited all trust.

As commander-in-chief of the army which he raised with difficulty from among his loyal subjects to fight Parliament, he was by no means negligible as a tact-ician. He distinguished himself at the battle of Edgehill in 1642, at Cropredy Bridge and Lostwithiel in 1644 and at the relief of Hereford in 1645. But as a strategist he constantly vacillated. He refused to march on London after Edgehill or when his fortunes were high in 1643. He failed to impose his will on his generals. Towards the end he could not decide whether to fight in England or to join his supporters in Scotland. Eventually, after major defeats, he resolved to leave his headquarters at Oxford in disguise and make for the camp of the Scottish Covenanter army which had allied itself with the English Parliamentarians and conquered the north-east of England. As he refused to promise to introduce the full Presbyterian system of Church government in England, the Covenanters handed him over to the English Parliament, but in 1647 he fell into the hands of the victorious Roundhead army led by Thomas Fairfax and Oliver Cromwell.

Both Fairfax and Cromwell were anxious to come to terms with the King on the basis of a written constitution, in which the King's authority could be harmonised with the wishes of his leading subjects. A scheme drawn up by the army commanders known as the 'Heads of the Proposals' was considered by some of Charles's advisers to be a cheap way of regaining authority after his defeat.

But rather than come to an agreed settlement Charles preferred trying to play off his enemies against each other. He escaped from honourable captivity in Hampton Court and fled to the Isle of Wight; thence he bargained both with the Parliamentarians, among whom there was a substantial peace party, and with his Scottish subjects, who did not care for the imprisonment of a Stuart king by the English and were ready to engage themselves in his service in return for mainly religious concessions.

Charles accepted this 'engagement'; the Scottish 'Engagers' invaded England in 1648 while earlier in the same year many Royalists, tired of Puritan restraints and exactions, took up arms again. The second civil war was quickly over. Cromwell defeated the Scots and left a garrison in Edinburgh; Fairfax overcame the Royalist revolt in south-eastern England. Though part of the navy deserted the Parliamentarians for the King, it did not even attempt to rescue him from imprisonment in the Isle of Wight.

The army leaders determined that the King should be put on trial for waging war on his own people. The House of Commons was purged of the peace party which had vainly negotiated with Charles in the Isle of Wight. A high court of justice was erected and the King brought to Westminster Hall in January 1649 to face his trial. The King conducted himself with dignity, refusing to recognise the legality of the court and thus making no real defence. The court condemned him to death. On 30 January 1649 he was publicly executed outside Whitehall Palace and his body was secretly buried in Windsor Castle.

CHARLES II
r. 1660–85

THE ELDEST SURVIVING SON OF Charles I and Henrietta Maria was born on 29 May 1630 and sealed his father's and mother's newly-found married happiness. He was brought up as a child in that idealistic atmosphere which was pictured by Van Dyck and described by the Earl of Clarendon in his celebrated *History*, before the clouds which heralded the civil wars began to gather. His first governor was the wealthy and cultivated magnifico, the second Earl of Newcastle, who told him that he would learn more from men than books. He was only twelve when the civil war began and was present at the first big battle, Edgehill. Two years later he accompanied his father on his victorious campaign in Cornwall, and in March 1645 Charles I sent him, when only fourteen, to be nominal commander-in-chief in western England with his headquarters at Bristol.

After being driven for a year from pillar to post by the conquering Parliamentarians, he was forced to leave England together with his Council (which included some able men) first for the Scillies, then Jersey, and finally, on his father's orders, he joined his mother in Paris. In 1648 he took command of the warships which had mutinied against Parliament during the second civil war, but was obliged to return to his base in Holland where at the beginning of 1649 he learned of his father's execution. The next eleven years he devoted to trying to gain the thrones of England and Scotland.

Charles arrived in Scotland in 1650 where he was humiliatingly treated by the bigoted Covenanters. However, after Cromwell's victory at Dunbar, his stock rose; he was crowned King of the Scots and allowed to take command of a united Scottish army. In the summer of 1651 he led this army into England only to be conclusively defeated by Cromwell at the battle of Worcester, where he fought extremely bravely. He escaped from the field of battle and after many exciting adventures managed to return safely to France. Next year the first war between England and the Dutch Republic broke out. Charles vainly offered his services to the Dutch and later when Spain was at war with England he succeeded in concluding a treaty of alliance in Brussels which promised that if the Royalists could lay hold of a port in England he would be provided with an expeditionary army. Nothing came of his plans. It was not until after the death of Oliver Cromwell, which was followed by anarchic struggles between Oliver's would-be successors, that Charles was by general acclamation welcomed back to England. He arrived in London on his thirtieth birthday.

Charles had been extremely skilful in the way in which he seized this opportunity. In his Declaration of Breda (4 April 1660) he did not commit himself to any specific undertakings about a constitutional settlement except that he promised 'liberty of conscience' to all Christians and demanded the punishment of his father's murderers. In fact he was relatively merciful, and made earnest efforts to achieve an agreement between the enthusiastic supporters of the old Church of England and the Presbyterians who had helped to procure his restoration. However, negotiations broke down. A new prayer book was drawn up; an Act of Uniformity was passed; and some 2,000 clergy left their parishes.

Opposite: A bust-length portrait of King Charles II wearing the robes of the Order of the Garter, by an artist from the circle of Sir Peter Lely.

Charles 2nd.

Above: *Charles II's widely welcomed entry into London in 1660 after his eleven-year quest to restore the throne to the House of Stuart.*
Opposite: *A pamphlet printed for Langley Curtis. The scene on the left shows two kings kneeling before the Pope, with London burning in the background, the poisoning of Charles II, the body of a loyal courtier lying in a field and the martyrdom by burning of English bishops. The right-hand scene shows Charles II with the church at his feet (symbolised by a woman with a church on her head) and the executions of traitors in the background.*

Moreover Charles's second Parliament, elected in May 1661, refused to accept a Declaration of Indulgence which he issued and for a time showed itself to be more rigidly Anglican than the King.

Charles had been crowned on 23 April 1661 and a year later he was married to Catherine of Braganza, the daughter of the King of Portugal. His ministers were chiefly the old Royalists who had served him during his long exile from England together with General George Monck, the man chiefly responsible for the Restoration, who was created Duke of Albemarle. In 1665 the House of Commons pressurised Charles into a war with the Dutch over which he was not at all keen and the causes of which were largely naval and commercial rivalries. Though the King had inherited a big navy from the Cromwellian period, the Dutch more than held their own. The reason for their success was not that Charles lacked good admirals but that the kingdom was distracted first by the Great Plague and then by the Great Fire in London. Furthermore naval warfare was expensive and the Commons did not vote enough money to wage a long war. In July 1667 a peace was concluded which left the position much as it was before the war. Nevertheless the leading subjects of the King were disappointed and to appease them Charles dismissed his chief minister, Edward Hyde, Earl of Clarendon. A group of five men now became the King's closest advisers: Lord Clifford, Lord Arlington, the Duke of Buckingham, Lord Ashley and Lord Lauderdale, known as 'the Cabal', the word formed by the first letters of their names.

The next few years were dominated by questions of foreign policy. Charles decided that he must have his revenge on the Dutch. Though for a time he entered upon a Protestant alliance with the Dutch and the Swedes, he was resolved to become the ally of the French monarchy which had become the strongest single power in Europe. After complicated negotiations in which Charles's youngest sister, Henrietta, played an important part, a secret treaty was signed at Dover in May 1670. By this treaty Charles undertook to wage war against the Dutch together with the French, while by a secret clause he promised to declare himself at an appropriate time to be Roman Catholic. The French undertook to pay him financial subsidies and, when the war had been won, to award him Dutch ports. The treaty was concealed from Charles's dedicated Protestant ministers of state such as Anthony Ashley Cooper, Earl of Shaftesbury. One of his Catholic ministers, Lord Clifford, offered by hook or by crook to raise the money necessary to fight the war even if the House of Commons refused. To keep his promise to the French King about helping the English Catholics, Charles published a second Declaration of Indulgence; then without Parliament being informed the war began.

Although the French army overran much of the Dutch Republic the English navy was kept away from the Dutch coasts where the intention had been to land an expeditionary force to aid the French. The House of Commons showed itself to be increasingly anti-French and anti-Catholic. Charles was asked to withdraw his Declaration of Indulgence and to agree to a Test Act excluding Roman Catholics from all offices. Though the King did so, he was refused the money he needed to continue the war and so he was compelled to make a separate peace. The next five years were concerned mainly with foreign affairs. Charles tried to act as a mediator between the Dutch and the French, though he was still drawing subsidies from the French King, while the Commons vigorously demanded that he should go to war with France. In the end he was driven to agree to a marriage between Prince William III of Orange, the Dutch Captain-General, and his niece Mary, and to threaten war against France. But his actions had small influence upon the Peace of Nymegen which ended the war in 1678.

In the course of these years Charles had managed to raise a small army; Parliament became afraid that he was aiming at absolutism, though that was not his intention at this stage of his reign. Domestic affairs

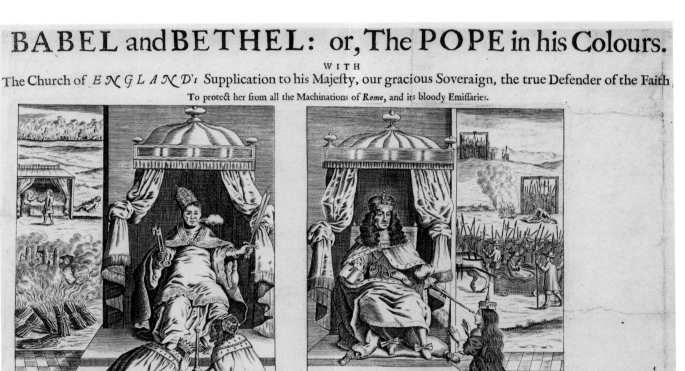

BABEL and BETHEL: or, The POPE in his Colours.

WITH

The Church of *E N G L A N D's* Supplication to his Majefty, our gracious Soveraign, the true Defender of the Faith,
To protect her from all the Machinations of *Rome*, and its bloody Emiffaries.

*Rome's Scarlet whore doth here in Tryumph Ride,
And Spurns off Soveraign Crowns in Height of Pride
Poor Chriftians and brave Citties too fhee Burns
And Stabbs and Poifons daily ferve her Turns.*

*Behold our Church (like Efther here doth tender
Her Supplication to the Faiths Defender:
In vain Rome Plots, whilfe Charles's Scepter Sway'd
May Sled and Gibbet end all Traitors Days.*

S Carce had *bright Truth*, with an enliv'ning Ray,
Chac'd the *black Mifts* of Ignorance away,
Reftor'd the *Gofpel*, and our Souls fet free

Two Swords are brandifht in his bloody hand,
Boafting both *Souls* and *Bodies* to Command;
The double *Engines* of his fatal Ills;

"Let not *Zerviah's brood* too ftrong become,
"But fcatter all th'Intrigues of *bloody R O M E*.
This faid ———

became difficult for him as an anti-Catholic agitation boiled up. His brother James, Duke of York, was now known to be a Roman Catholic convert because he had resigned all his offices after the passing of the first Test Act; he then married a Roman Catholic Italian princess as his second wife; the Queen was also a Roman Catholic, as was Charles's principal mistress, the French Duchess of Portsmouth; and suspicions arose over what Charles had promised the French by treaty. In the summer of 1678 a 'Popish Plot' was revealed to the government by perjured informers. Charles insisted that the whole plot was 'a contrivance'. But when the Duchess of York's secretary, named Coleman, was arrested and incriminating letters found outlining Roman Catholic aspirations, Charles was unable to keep the general frenzy under control. Coleman and a number of Jesuits were put to death. The Earl of Danby, who became Lord Treasurer and the King's chief minister when the Cabal broke up in 1674, was threatened with impeachment and the Commons were angered by revelations about Charles's pro-French policy for which in fact Danby had not been responsible. In January 1679 Charles dissolved the former Cavalier Parliament which had sat for eighteen years. Before its dissolution a second Test Act was passed excluding Roman Catholics from sitting in either House of Parliament.

When a new Parliament met in the spring a Bill to exclude the Duke of York from succession to the throne was introduced. Charles, now virtually his own first minister, was determined to prevent its enactment. For two years a contest took place between the King's supporters, the Tories, and their opponents, the Whigs, who were led by the unscrupulous Shaftesbury. Charles stopped the passage of an Exclusion Bill by bringing his own influence to bear on the House of Lords. In 1680 the fourth Parliament of the reign met and again the Commons voted for exclusion. Charles dissolved it. In 1681 he summoned a fifth Parliament to meet in Oxford where he exerted military pressure upon the

Whigs. He and his brother were now genuinely afraid of civil war, but the King kept his head. He came to a secret understanding with the French King that he would be given support in the event of a rebellion. A Tory reaction slowly set in, aided by the revelation of what was called 'the Rye House plot', an alleged conspiracy to murder the King on his way from the Newcastle races, engineered by the Whigs. By using his influence to obtain friendly officials in key posts both in the government and in the counties, the King succeeded in crushing the Whig movement and its leaders fled abroad. Shaftesbury died in Holland. The last four years of Charles's reign were peaceable. He had enough money to live on because of the expansion of the receipts from the Customs and Excise, and he had an army on which he could rely. His Roman Catholic brother in effect resumed his post as Lord High Admiral.

Charles thus proved himself an extremely shrewd politician as well as a ready liar. Though like his father and grandfather he was rather lazy, he could exert himself effectively at times of crisis. With the exception of the two Test Acts he made few concessions to Parliament. Like his father he refused to give up control over the armed forces of the kingdom; unlike him, he saved his leading ministers from execution for treason. Charles had charm and a vast sense of humour which caused him to be much loved by ordinary people. The 'Merry Monarch' did not eat or drink to excess but he had a large sexual appetite, enjoying a succession of mistresses – Nell Gwynne is the best remembered – whom he rewarded generously but did not love. He refused to divorce the Queen, though she could bear him no children. His main interest was the navy, but he also enjoyed horse races and fishing. He was very human and, from the point of view of his dynasty, a successful king. Before he died on 6 February 1685 he was received into the Roman Catholic Church, but there is good evidence that since before his restoration he had been a Catholic at heart. He was buried in Westminster Abbey.

Opposite: *Nell Gwynne's portrait from the studio of Sir Peter Lely. She rose from selling oranges on the street to become a leading actress of the day and the most famous of Charles II's mistresses.*

JAMES II

r. 1685–8

THE SECOND SON OF CHARLES I, James, Duke of York, was only twelve (he was born on 14 October 1633) when the City of Oxford, in which he had been raised, surrendered to the Parliamentarians and the Prince himself was taken as a prisoner to St James's Palace in London. In April 1648 he managed to escape dressed as a girl and found his way to his sister Mary in Holland. After his father's execution he was appointed Lord High Admiral by his brother, but Charles II refused to let him sail with the fleet. Instead James was commissioned as an officer in the French army. By the time he was twenty-one he had been promoted to lieutenant-general. He distinguished himself as a soldier, and his conduct was commended by the famous French marshal Turenne. But when the French government came to terms with the Cromwellian Protectorate James reluctantly resigned his commission. Instead he served with the Spaniards, who were fighting the French and the English republicans in 1658. That June in the battle of the Dunes James again fought courageously and thus by the time that his brother was restored to the English throne James had earned a high reputation as a soldier.

Two occurrences, which were kept secret before the Restoration, were that James had been attracted to the Roman Catholic Church and that he had signed a contract of marriage with Anne Hyde, the daughter of the future Earl of Clarendon who had been the Chancellor of Charles II's Exchequer and was afterwards Lord Chancellor. Charles II insisted that his brother should publicly acknowledge the marriage. James took an active part in Charles's counsels and when the first Anglo-Dutch war of the new reign broke out he commanded the navy in person, inflicting a defeat on the Dutch at the battle of Lowestoft in June 1665. But the King refused to let him go to sea again until the second war of the reign. Then he was in the thick of the battle of Solebay fought in May 1672, but, though assisted by a French squadron, failed to defeat the Dutch who were determined to prevent enemy troops landing from the sea.

James's conversion to the Roman Church took place in 1668, but he continued to attend Anglican services for another eight years. When the first Test Act was carried he felt constrained to resign his post as Lord High Admiral, but consoled himself by his second marriage, to the young Mary of Modena. As the anti-Catholic agitation, which culminated in the disclosure of the 'Popish Plot', was intensified, he became the target of the Whigs' wrath. They aimed to exclude him from succession to the throne and Charles sent James into exile first in Brussels and then in Edinburgh to allow tempers to cool. It was not until the Tory reaction set in that the King allowed his brother to return to Whitehall. This was in 1682 when the Duke brought an action for libel against Titus Oates, the fountain-head of the Popish Plot. During the last three years of Charles II's reign James served in the Privy Council and on the Committee for Foreign Affairs and in effect resumed his position as Lord High Admiral. Sir John Reresby noted in January 1682 that 'the Duke of York did chiefly manage affairs, but with great haughtiness'.

When Charles II died in February 1685 James succeeded to the throne unexpectedly peacefully (continues on page 245)

Opposite: *James II succeeded his brother Charles surprisingly peacefully given his open allegiance to Roman Catholicism, but his reign was to be a brief one.*

THE ROYAL ARMS
1707–1837

THE ALTERATION MADE IN THE ROYAL ARMS to reflect the union of England and Scotland was as illustrated. The arms of the two countries were placed side by side in the first and last quarters, France was assigned the second quarter and Ireland stayed put. No alteration was made to crest nor supporters; these have remained unchanged from 1603 until the present day. It will be noticed that the *double tressure* which surrounds the Scottish lion is discontinued where the coat is joined to that of England. This is an old heraldic convention which affects all forms of border when arms are shown side by side, that is *impaled*.

This new version of the arms was short-lived as Anne died in 1714 and, under the terms of the Act of Settlement of 1701, George, Elector of Hanover, Duke of Brunswick and Luneburg and Arch Treasurer of the Holy Roman Empire, succeeded to the throne. Another reshuffle was called for in order to make reference to his German dominions. This was easily effected by removing the last quartering, which was only a repetition of the first, and substituting a coat divided into three, containing the two lions of Brunswick, the lion and hearts of Luneburg and the white horse of Hanover. The little shield in the centre, which will be seen in the illustration of this coat, has on it a representation of the crown of Charlemagne. This was the badge of office of the Arch Treasurer of the Empire; other members of the royal family never showed this shield.

In 1801 the royal arms were altered yet again in order to reflect better the new kingdom of Great Britain and Ireland created by the Act of Union with Ireland in 1800. The opportunity was taken to remove the French arms, an excision which some might think several hundred years overdue. The three kingdoms were each given a quartering, the arms of England being repeated in the last quarter in the cause of symmetry. The German arms were placed in the centre, thus enabling the Electoral Bonnet, which by right should have ensigned them, to be shown. This shield is illustrated whilst next to it is the same shield ensigned by the crown which replaced the bonnet in 1816. Under the terms of the Congress of Vienna the electorate, which had disappeared when Napoleon overthrew the Empire, was erected into a kingdom.

Princess Mary of Mode[na]
Married to King James the
of Scotland & II. of Engla[nd]

considering the attempts that the Commons had made to exclude him because he was an avowed Roman Catholic. He at once openly attended Mass, but informed the Privy Council and a new Parliament which met in May 1685 that he would protect the Church of England 'whose members have shown themselves so eminently loyal in the worst of times'. The House of Commons consisted for the most part of members who were strongly Royalist and Anglican; it was determined to give James a fair trial as ruler and voted him a generous revenue. Nevertheless the King treated it superciliously and he was annoyed when a resolution was passed asking him to publish a proclamation to put in force the laws against 'all dissenters whatsoever from the Church of England'. For James's intention was precisely the opposite. He was determined to place both Roman Catholics and Protestant dissenters in a position of civic equality with his Anglican subjects.

In June 1685 Scotland was invaded by a rebel force directed by the Marquis of Argyll, while Charles 11's eldest illegitimate son, the Duke of Monmouth, landed in the south-west of England. The two rebel leaders had assumed that their countries would refuse to obey a Roman Catholic king but the invasions were defeated without undue difficulty. Parliament showed its loyalty to James and during the summer harmony reigned. Yet by the autumn James's decision to allow Roman Catholic officers to serve in the army in spite of the first Test Act and his insistence on the suspension of the penal laws against nonconformists provoked the Commons to protest. They did not at all care for the idea of a standing army, recently victorious over Monmouth and officered by Catholics, being at the King's disposal. So this Parliament, initially entirely loyal, became so restive that James prorogued it on 20 November 1685, though he did not dissolve it until July 1687. Thus he lost some of his promised revenue, but was able to exploit his royal prerogatives of suspending or dispensing with laws to pursue his policy of introducing complete religious equality.

The first thing he did was to appoint an ecclesiastical commission which was intended to prevent Anglican clergy from attacking the tenets of the Roman Catholic religion from their pulpits, which James called 'indiscreet preaching'. This commission proceeded to suspend the Bishop of London from his office because he disobeyed the King's orders. Next a test case was brought before the high court which decided (after the judges had been purged) that it was legal for James to dispense with the law in individual cases. This verdict enabled him to admit Roman Catholics into the Privy Council, freely to employ Roman Catholics as military and naval officers, and even to choose Catholics for positions in Oxford colleges. On 4 April 1687 he issued a Declaration of Indulgence aiming at complete religious toleration; a second Declaration was published a year later. The Anglican clergy were instructed to read it from their pulpits on the following Sundays. Finally James dismissed from office his two brothers-in-law, sons of Clarendon, who as Protestants did not altogether approve of his policies. The unscrupulous Earl of Sunderland then became Lord President of the Council as well as Secretary of State.

The summer of 1688 was the turning point in James's reign. The Archbishop of Canterbury and six other bishops petitioned the King to withdraw his orders about the second Declaration of Indulgence on the grounds that Parliaments of Charles 11's reign had insisted that the King had no right to dispense with the penal code. James was furious and ordered that the seven bishops should be put on trial before the King's Bench for seditious libel. They were acquitted by a jury and the verdict was celebrated not only in the streets of London but even in the army camp at Hounslow. On 10 June the Queen gave birth to a son – to be known as the Old Pretender. Thus it seemed as if a Roman Catholic dynasty would become permanent. On the same day that the bishops were acquitted the Bishop of London and six laymen – to be called the Immortal Seven – secretly invited James's nephew and son-in-law, William of

A portrait of Mary of Modena, who was James's second wife and became Queen. He had previously signed a marriage contract with Anne Hyde, who bore him two daughters, Queen Mary II and Queen Anne.

THE PORTRAICTVRE OF THE MOST ILLVSTRIOVS &
Noble, William of Nassau Prince of Orange, &c borne 1627
& maried 23. May, 1641.
Are to be sold, by Tho: Ienner at the old Exhange.

Above: *William of Orange, who upon his arrival in England told the crowd:*
'I come to do you goot; I am here for all your goots.'
Opposite: *A portrait of Queen Mary II from the studio of Sir Godfrey Kneller. Mary was fifteen*
when she married the Calvinist William.
Following pages: *Contemporary oil painting of William, showing his customary flair for fighting, at*
the battle of the Boyne, which ended James II's reign.

Charles II, who withdrew in a humiliated way from the war in 1674, was anxious to gain prestige as an intermediary between the French and the Dutch. At first he aimed to please his nephew by carving a little kingdom for him out of the dismembered republic, but William was not to be bribed. Then Charles wanted William to use his influence with the Dutch States-General to accept a mediated peace. William refused to discuss the latter proposal until he had concluded his dynastic marriage with Princess Mary, which would draw together, at least symbolically, the English and Dutch peoples in resisting French ambitions. There is no doubt that this marriage impressed and annoyed Louis XIV. A mediated peace came next

year. As the elder daughter of James, Duke of York, Mary was after her father the heir presumptive to the English and Scottish thrones. William soon found himself in an extremely awkward situation because his father-in-law was an avowed Roman Catholic and the great majority of the English House of Commons (from which Roman Catholics were excluded by a Test Act of 1678) were determined that James should be stopped from succeeding. It was even believed that the Popish Plot had been concocted to murder Charles II and to replace him by his Catholic brother. There was no such plot; but the Whigs or Exclusionists were committed to preventing James from coming to the throne and to replacing him either by his daughter Mary, William's wife, or by the Duke of Monmouth.

In 1681 William again visited England, Charles II hoping that he would assuage the anxieties of the Exclusionists. William was naturally cautious. He did not want to jeopardise his wife's hereditary rights, but on the other hand he did not wish the English monarchy to be so weakened by internal squabbles that it became a dependant of France. Charles for his part would not accept exclusion at any price and he did in fact count as a last resort on French protection to shield him from rebellion at home. In the end he skilfully defeated the Exclusionist movement, thus enabling William's father-in-law to succeed peacefully to the throne.

William viewed the whole political situation in England not so much from the point of view of religious controversy or personal ambition as in the context of Europe as a whole. By the 1680s the French had overrun much of Western Europe and therefore, above all, William wanted to preserve a close friendship with England as a counterweight to Louis XIV's undimmed aims for glorious expansion. Although an Anglo-Dutch treaty was renewed in 1685, the danger was that his father-in-law would alienate his subjects by granting too many concessions to his fellow religionists and thus provoke a rebellion which would paralyse English influence on the continental mainland. His relations with James II were thus ambivalent. James was willing to be friendly only if both William and Mary would give their open support to the repeal of the anti-Catholic

Penal and Test Acts. Both refused to do so since they were afraid that the predominance of Roman Catholic ministers and advisers in England would carry the kingdom over into the French camp even if this did not cause an insurrection. That was why ultimately William felt compelled to intervene actively in England in 1688 at the time when Louis XIV was launching large armies into Germany.

The Revolution of 1688, as it was called, though actually it was a Dutch invasion welcomed by English Protestants, was a bloodless success. To William's relief, since his father-in-law had left the kingdom it could be argued that he had 'abdicated' or 'deserted' his throne. It was not until early February in 1689 that a 'convention' or Parliament met which invited William and Mary to become King and Queen with the executive authority in William's hands. Thus it could be asserted that their reign did not begin until 1689; but in fact William had exercised administrative authority since Christmas 1688. Before they were offered the Crown William and Mary were asked to agree to a Declaration of Rights (subsequently converted into a Bill) which condemned the way in which James II had used his prerogative, particularly by dispensing with the laws. They agreed to this in general terms so that in effect a limited monarchy was established. Mary, who came to England in mid-February and put a cheerful face on things (for which she was censured by some as having usurped the throne of her father) ,had made it clear from the beginning that she had no intention of seeking a superior or even an equal position to her husband. She was content to love and obey him, but was willing to preside over the government during his absences abroad.

In fact substantial constitutional changes took place in the course of William's reign. An Act of Indulgence permitted Christian nonconformists (but not Roman Catholics) to worship freely subject to specific conditions; a Triennial Act required a new Parliament to be summoned every three years; a Mutiny Act prevented the employment of a standing army in times of peace without the consent of the Commons; a Civil List Act gave the Commons control over the King's expenditure, and indeed when he attempted to appropriate money from forfeitures of land in Ireland there was a rumpus. Finally in 1701 an Act of Settlement was passed which, among other things, not only provided for the Protestant succession, but required future monarchs specifically to be members of the Church of England, and forbade them to leave the kingdom without Parliamentary permission. Judges were not to be dismissed without the approval of Parliament. (William did not in fact try to do so.) Other clauses, which would have hampered the evolution of Cabinet government, did not become effective. But possibly the most important event to take place in the reign of William and Mary was the establishment of the Bank of England, which, by enabling the government to borrow money in a sensible way, was to simplify foreign and colonial problems.

William's main concern was the war which broke out in Europe even before he had become King. Though the Holy Roman Emperor and the Dutch Republic had agreed to ally themselves in May 1680 so as to prevent the French mastery of Europe, it was not until September that William was able to induce the English people to accede to what became known as the first Grand Alliance. Then he had to campaign in Ireland before himself engaging upon fighting the French in Flanders. He proved himself a fairly capable general, his chief success being the capture in September 1694 of the heavily fortified town of Namur against a French covering army. The peace of Ryswick, concluded in 1697, reduced French power. Afterwards William devoted his efforts to averting another major European war by negotiating two treaties defining the partition of the Spanish Empire

when its childless ruler died. Unfortunately neither of them worked and the English Parliament blamed him for his secret diplomacy.

Queen Mary, whose influence had considerable effect on the moral climate of the court and country, died of smallpox in December 1694 at the age of thirty-three. William wrote to a friend just before her death: 'You can imagine what a state I am in, loving her as I do. You know what it is to have a good wife.' Though he was pressed to do so, he did not marry again. William was never a congenial king and indeed his popularity diminished after his wife's death and as memories of the causes of the revolution of 1688 faded. His original attempt to govern by employing more or less non-party men as his ministers did not really succeed, although he had a gift for discovering capable (but not always loyal) administrators. His difficulty was that whereas he could not be called a 'Tory king', he disliked the Whigs because their aim was to limit monarchical authority. Furthermore the Tories were 'Little Englanders' while the Whigs were more anti-French, which better suited his taste. He was able, however, to provide for the succession by reconciling himself with Princess Anne, Mary's younger sister, who had quarrelled with her, and by appointing Anne's friend, John Churchill, Earl of Marlborough, to be commander-in-chief and the architect of a second Grand Alliance against France when the danger of another war over the partition of the Spanish Empire loomed up. Before William died on 8 March 1702 his only regret was that he could not live to witness the final defeat of Louis XIV's France.

ANNE

r. 1702–14

THE SECOND DAUGHTER OF THE future James II by his first wife, Anne Hyde, was born on 6 February 1665. As her likelihood of succeeding to the throne appeared to be remote she was uneducated and untrained for the profession of monarchy, while her husband, Prince George of Denmark, whom she married in 1683 and loved dearly, was an amiable nonentity, who preferred being in the background. On the whole, Anne led an unhappy life. Though she had seventeen children, not one of them survived for long; her son William, Duke of Gloucester, was hydrocephalic and lived for only eleven years.

When Anne became Queen she was in permanent pain. Modern doctors are not in agreement about her precise maladies, but contemporaries called it gout. Being stout and unwieldy she often had to be moved on chairs or by pulleys. Her chief amusements were playing cards, drinking tea and admiring gardens; but she disliked fresh air. Her passionate affection for Sarah Churchill, the future Duchess of Marlborough, which began before she was married was to give her much pleasure and later much pain. Sarah's voluminous writings have been largely relied upon by Anne's biographers as a basis for assessing her character, but it has to be remembered that what Sarah recorded was chiefly written after they had quarrelled. The fact was that Anne was an extremely conscientious Queen – though she had her personal prejudices – and was also a stout pillar of the Church of England. The bounty which she established out of her private resources for the benefit of the poorer clergy kept her name respected among churchmen long after she was dead.

When William III invaded England in 1688 it had evidently been arranged between Anne's friends, Bishop Compton and John and Sarah Churchill, that they would all desert her father in favour of her sister Mary's husband. For both Mary and Anne were devout Protestants and genuinely believed that James II had been using autocratic methods to catholicise England. The two sisters were also convinced that the son born to James by his second wife in June 1688 was suppositious. The letters that they wrote to each other sustaining this view are rather revolting. In any case it was a blow to James when both his daughters deserted him. After he went into exile Anne acquiesced in the decision made by Parliament that William should rule England during his lifetime, thus postponing her own right to succeed to the throne until after his death on the assumption, which proved correct, that William and Mary had no children. She rejoiced in an income of £50,000 a year voted her by Parliament and she moved into her own palace known as the Cockpit, on the site of the present Downing Street.

Unfortunately she was to be on bad terms for nearly five years with her sister, Queen Mary. The reason for this was that John Churchill, who had been created Earl of Marlborough by William and who had served him brilliantly during the Irish campaign, did not consider that he had been adequately rewarded for his services at the Revolution and therefore engaged in political intrigue against the King

Opposite: A portrait of Queen Anne by Edmund Lilly, painted a year after she succeeded to the throne. Although untrained for the role of monarch she was a diligent and hard-working queen. She is wearing the necklace of the order of the Garter, with its emblem of the dragon-slaying St George.

Sir Godfrey Kneller's painting of Sarah Marlborough playing cards with Lady Fitzharding.
Anne had a deep affection for Sarah, although she was later to alienate her when Sarah's attitude
became condescending and she took to staying away from court.

while Sarah remained Anne's closest friend. How far it was Churchill's intention to make use of the Jacobites (the followers of James II) in these intrigues is not clear. But Anne herself was conscious of guilty feelings over the way in which she had treated her father and even appears to have written him a contrite letter. William was fully aware of these intrigues in which not only Marlborough but some of his ministers engaged, but he was magnanimous enough to ignore them. For a short time Marlborough was deprived of his offices and put in the Tower of London. Mary naturally enough sided with her husband, thinking it was monstrous that Anne should keep Marlborough's wife so close to her. When Anne refused to dismiss Sarah from her service, she was obliged to leave Whitehall and sever relations with the King and Queen. It was not until after Mary's death that a reconciliation was effected with her brother-in-law. Then William restored Anne and John Churchill to his favour. Meanwhile Sarah had given birth to four healthy daughters which made her feel very superior to Anne, whom she treated with some condescension. Her eldest daughter, Henrietta, was married to Francis, only child of Sidney Godolphin, one of King William's ablest ministers. Thus Anne, the Churchills and Godolphin became a closely-knit group. When after William's death in March 1702 Anne became Queen, she wrote to Sarah, whom she appointed her Mistress of the Robes: 'We four must never part until death mows us down with his impartial hand.'

Anne, like William, tried at first to govern with a Cabinet of non-party or all-party ministers. Marlborough, who took command of the English and Dutch armies when war with France began in May 1702, and Godolphin, whom at his suggestion Anne appointed Lord Treasurer, were really non-party men, though they were often described as Tories. But Anne tended to favour the Tories, first because they were enthusiastic supporters of the established Church and second because they upheld the royal prerogatives. For most of the reign England was involved in the war of the Grand Alliance against France, in which Marlborough won three notable victories as well as planning successful campaigns. The extreme Tories, however, became critical of Marlborough because they favoured naval warfare rather than the expensive commitment of the kingdom to continental campaigns on land.

Anne was upset by this and showed it. For she at once raised Marlborough to a dukedom, asked that he should be voted a generous income in perpetuity and poured offices and money into Sarah Marlborough's lap. After his great victory at Blenheim in 1704 she presented him with one of the royal estates at Woodstock in Oxfordshire and in the

following year dismissed his chief Tory critic, her uncle the Earl of Rochester, while another Tory leader, the Earl of Nottingham, resigned from his post of Secretary of State and was replaced by Robert Harley who was also Speaker of the Commons. Godolphin, Marlborough and Harley became known as 'the Triumvirate' which concentrated on winning the war. After the general election of 1705 the Queen dismissed three more leading Tories and under pressure from Sarah Marlborough appointed another of her sons-in-law, the third Earl of Sunderland, to the important ambassadorship in Vienna.

Anne, though she had her own principles – for example she was a patriot and spoke of 'her English heart' – was strongly influenced by personal likes and dislikes. She could not abide Sunderland, an extreme Whig; she took to Harley, a moderate Tory. Thus she resented it when after Whig compulsion in the House of Commons she was obliged to accept Sunderland as one of her Secretaries of State. Marlborough, Sunderland's father-in-law, and Godolphin became increasingly sure that the war against France could only be won if the support given it by the Whigs in Parliament was reinforced by the presence of all the leading Whigs in the government. Harley, on the other hand, who had proved himself an able statesman and contributed markedly to the formation of the union with Scotland, of which the Queen approved and which was celebrated in May 1707, professed still to believe in the virtues of a central coalition government. Gradually, partly through the help of Abigail Masham, one of the Queen's ladies-in-waiting, Harley came to exert so much influence over the Queen, visiting her up the backstairs, that Godolphin and Marlborough were perturbed. A keen rivalry between Harley and Godolphin eventually culminated in the dismissal of Harley, mainly because Anne was still dependent on Marlborough's military genius to win the war.

At a general election in May 1708 the Whigs won a majority in the Commons and the Queen was compelled to admit all the members of what was called 'the Whig junto' into her Cabinet. Thus in spite of another victory achieved by Marlborough at Oudenarde, 1708 was a sad year for Anne. In October her beloved husband died. She ceased to trust any members of her government, while her alienation from Sarah Marlborough, which had begun not long after her accession owing to Sarah's haughty attitude towards her as Queen, was increased by the fact that Sarah absented herself from her duties at court for long periods and devoted herself to pro-Whig propaganda.

But in 1709 the party tide turned. The kingdom was growing tired of the long and costly war, while Anne herself reflected these feelings. Also, she was half persuaded that her Church was 'in danger' especially since she was not allowed to appoint the bishops she herself preferred, who were usually High Churchmen. When in February 1710 a clergyman named Henry Sacheverell, who had delivered an outspoken attack on the Whig settlement after the Revolution of 1688, was impeached in Westminster Hall, Anne showed sufficient interest to follow the proceedings in person. Despite being condemned Sacheverell was punished extremely lightly, and a political reaction set in. Harley got in secret touch with the Queen, offering to relieve her from the thraldom of the extreme Whigs. Thereupon she plucked up sufficient courage to dismiss her faithful servant Godolphin almost as cavalierly as Charles II got rid of Clarendon or James II of Sunderland. Afterwards she was to regret having done so. Furthermore, as the French had gallantly resisted the threat of invasion in the previous year, heavy losses being inflicted upon Marlborough at the battle of Malplaquet, the war looked as if it were going on for ever.

Thus pro-Anglican emotions and anti-war sentiments were expressed in the general election of 1710, which resulted in an overwhelming Tory victory. At the beginning of 1711 Anne dismissed Sarah from all her offices after some painful scenes, and at the end of the year Marlborough was also dismissed. Harley took office and another extremely able and highly ambitious Tory, Henry St John, Viscount Bolingbroke, assiduously if unscrupulously devoted himself to securing a separate peace with France. To make certain that both Houses of Parliament approved the peace, Anne agreed to create twelve additional Tory peers at one time. When she opened Parliament in 1713 she was able to give news of the Treaty of Utrecht, which was by no means unfavourable to British interests; it was followed by another general election when once again the Tories won a victory.

But Harley's powers were failing fast and Anne dismissed him from office in July 1713. She distrusted Bolingbroke and preferred, even though her sufferings were culminating in a last and fatal illness, to hand the office of Lord Treasurer, virtually prime minister, to her old and trusted friend the Whiggish Earl of Shrewsbury; she also had a woman friend in the red-headed Duchess of Somerset, another moderate Whig. On 1 August 1714, still perplexed by the exigencies of party politics, the Queen died; her doctor said, 'I believe sleep was never more welcome to a weary traveller than death was to her.'

Anne's was a notable reign in British history because it saw not only the Union with Scotland but also the acquisition of territorial gains and economic privileges which led to the foundation of the first British Empire. What the Queen's personal contribution was is hard to measure but recently it has been contended that her reign was the first in which Parliamentary elections and party contests were genuinely significant. In her support first of a coalition government then of a moderate Whig government, then her reluctant acquiescence in a purely Whig government, and finally her approval of a peacemaking Tory government, it is reasonable to argue that she exemplified the feelings of the majority of her subjects, doing her duty, sometimes reluctantly, sometimes harshly, as she understood it.

Opposite: Sir Godfrey Kneller's 1688 painting of Queen Anne presenting the plans of Blenheim Palace to Military Merit. The Queen presented the royal estate at Woodstock, Oxfordshire, to the Duke of Marlborough after his victory at Blenheim in 1704.

THE HOUSE OF HANOVER
1714–1901

GEORGE I 1714–27

GEORGE II 1727–60

GEORGE III 1760–1820

GEORGE IV 1820–30

WILLIAM IV 1830–37

VICTORIA 1837–1901

Opposite: The German composer Handel with his patron King George I in a barge on the River Thames. George's patronage, which was so to enrich English music, began in Hanover where Handel was *Kappelmeister* at the Herrenhausen, George's country home.

THE HOUSE OF HANOVER

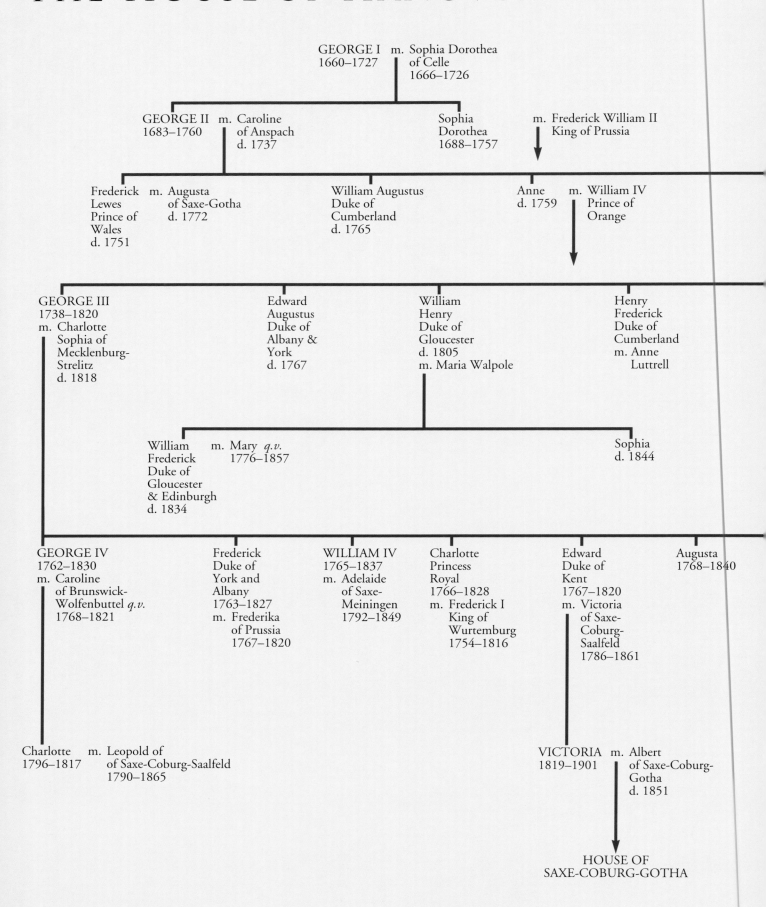

GEORGE I
1660–1727
m. Sophia Dorothea
of Celle
1666–1726

GEORGE II
1683–1760
m. Caroline
of Anspach
d. 1737

Sophia
Dorothea
1688–1757
m. Frederick William II
King of Prussia

Frederick
Lewes
Prince of
Wales
d. 1751
m. Augusta
of Saxe-Gotha
d. 1772

William Augustus
Duke of
Cumberland
d. 1765

Anne
d. 1759
m. William IV
Prince of
Orange

GEORGE III
1738–1820
m. Charlotte
Sophia of
Mecklenburg-
Strelitz
d. 1818

Edward
Augustus
Duke of
Albany &
York
d. 1767

William
Henry
Duke of
Gloucester
d. 1805
m. Maria Walpole

Henry
Frederick
Duke of
Cumberland
m. Anne
Luttrell

William
Frederick
Duke of
Gloucester
& Edinburgh
d. 1834
m. Mary *q.v.*
1776–1857

Sophia
d. 1844

GEORGE IV
1762–1830
m. Caroline
of Brunswick-
Wolfenbuttel *q.v.*
1768–1821

Frederick
Duke of
York and
Albany
1763–1827
m. Frederika
of Prussia
1767–1820

WILLIAM IV
1765–1837
m. Adelaide
of Saxe-
Meiningen
1792–1849

Charlotte
Princess
Royal
1766–1828
m. Frederick I
King of
Wurtemburg
1754–1816

Edward
Duke of
Kent
1767–1820
m. Victoria
of Saxe-
Coburg-
Saalfeld
1786–1861

Augusta
1768–1840

Charlotte
1796–1817
m. Leopold of
of Saxe-Coburg-Saalfeld
1790–1865

VICTORIA
1819–1901
m. Albert
of Saxe-Coburg-
Gotha
d. 1851

HOUSE OF
SAXE-COBURG-GOTHA

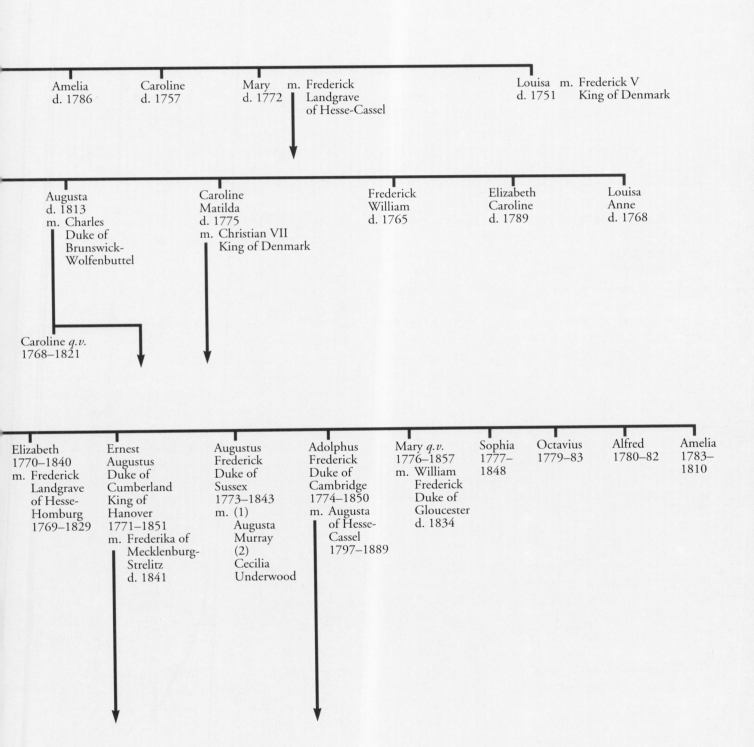

Amelia
d. 1786

Caroline
d. 1757

Mary   m. Frederick
d. 1772   Landgrave
            of Hesse-Cassel

Louisa   m. Frederick V
d. 1751   King of Denmark

Augusta
d. 1813
m. Charles
   Duke of
   Brunswick-
   Wolfenbuttel

Caroline *q.v.*
1768–1821

Caroline
Matilda
d. 1775
m. Christian VII
   King of Denmark

Frederick
William
d. 1765

Elizabeth
Caroline
d. 1789

Louisa
Anne
d. 1768

Elizabeth
1770–1840
m. Frederick
   Landgrave
   of Hesse-
   Homburg
   1769–1829

Ernest
Augustus
Duke of
Cumberland
King of
Hanover
1771–1851
m. Frederika of
   Mecklenburg-
   Strelitz
   d. 1841

Augustus
Frederick
Duke of
Sussex
1773–1843
m. (1)
   Augusta
   Murray
   (2)
   Cecilia
   Underwood

Adolphus
Frederick
Duke of
Cambridge
1774–1850
m. Augusta
   of Hesse-
   Cassel
   1797–1889

Mary *q.v.*
1776–1857
m. William
   Frederick
   Duke of
   Gloucester
   d. 1834

Sophia
1777–
1848

Octavius
1779–83

Alfred
1780–82

Amelia
1783–
1810

GEORGE I
r. 1714–27

IN 1701 THE ACT OF SETTLEMENT declared that, after Princess Anne, 'the most excellent Princess Sophia, Electress and Dowager Duchess of Hanover, daughter of Elizabeth, late Queen of Bohemia, daughter of James 1, shall be next in succession to the Crown'. It was Sophia's son, George Lewis, born in 1660, who became King when Anne died on the morning of 1 August 1714. George had had his agent, Baron von Bothmar, in London since 1710, but it was not until the dying Anne made the Whig Duke of Shrewsbury her chief minister that the Elector could be sure of the Crown. The change of dynasty was surprisingly peaceful – 'not a mouse stirred against him in England, in Ireland or in Scotland'. George took his time in coming to England, stopping for festivities and congratulations at several towns in Holland. It was not until 30 September that the King's barge arrived at the steps at Greenwich. Candles and flares scarcely pierced the swirling fog as courtiers and politicians jostled to ingratiate themselves with their new master.

George was not altogether delighted with his good fortune. He loved the flat north German landscape between the Weser and the Aller; he loved his fine country house, the Herrenhausen, his very own miniature Versailles. George's territory might be small, but his people were obedient and prepared to let him rule as he wished. In Hanover, the Elector decided everything; all expenditure over £13 had to receive his personal sanction whilst the army was regarded as his private property. England, on the other hand, was the most fractious, constitution-ridden country in Europe. George might remember that English ingratitude had often made William 111 wish that he had stayed in Holland. Like William 111, George became King of England for European reasons. The new dignity would enormously enhance

his prestige amongst the other Electors of the Holy Roman Empire and England's resources would be of incalculable help in resisting any power which might seek to destroy the independence of the German Princes.

The new King was welcomed with ecstatic verses:

Hail mighty George! auspicious smiles they Reign,
Thee long we wish'd. Thee at last we gain.

The true feeling of the nation was less enthusiastic. Of course, there was a party – well represented in the Church of England, amongst the country gentry and above all in Scotland – which felt that this 'wee, wee German lairdie' had no right to the Crown. George's prospects would have been bleak if the rightful king 'James 111' had had the sense to take Henry St John's advice and become a Protestant. In an age when royal power was still enormously strong, the personal abilities of the sovereign were of paramount importance. George may have been an improvement on Anne but no one could pretend that he was a remarkable man. In many ways, the King closely resembled his father, Ernest Augustus. George was of medium height and build with the usual Guelph features of bulbous eyes and fair complexion. His main interests in life appeared to be food, horses and women. England's new King was a shy, suspicious and unimaginative man who said little and at least gave the impression of being a good listener. Certainly there were good qualities; his bravery was unquestioned and he had fought with great distinction at the siege of Vienna in 1683. Unfortunately, even to an uncensorious age, there was one aspect of George's private life which was discreditable in the extreme.

George's wife, the beautiful but empty-headed Sophia Dorothea of Celle, had soon grown bored

Detail from Sir Godfrey Kneller's portrait of George I, who somewhat reluctantly left his beloved native Germany to take up his succession to the English throne.

with her husband and had become involved with a Swedish Colonel of Dragoons, Philip von Königsmark. On 1 July 1694, Königsmark disappeared and was never seen again; it was rumoured throughout Europe that George had ordered his wife's lover to be hacked to pieces and that his mutilated body had been buried under the floorboards at the Herrenhausen. What really shocked people was George's inhuman treatment of his wife. Sophia Dorothea was divorced, forbidden to see her children again and then imprisoned in the Castle of Ahlden for the rest of her life. Sophia was twenty-eight at the time and was to live for another thirty-two years; perhaps von Königsmark's fate had been kinder.

Above: *James Thornhill's study for the Painted Hall of George 1 landing at the steps of Greenwich, after his leisurely eight-week journey from Hanover to become King of England.*
Opposite: *George's beautiful but doomed wife, Sophia Dorothea of Celle. Her indiscreet affair with Count Königsmark, a Swedish officer, led to his disappearance (and rumoured murder) and her own imprisonment for the remaining thirty-two years of her life.*

But what interested people in 1714 was who was going to benefit from the new regime. The extreme Tories under St John had worked for a Jacobite succession and would be lucky to escape impeachment, heavy fines and disgrace. Those who had supported George in and out of season demanded their reward; power and patronage were soon in the hands of a Whig 'junta' of Halifax, Sunderland, Stanhope, Townshend and a rising young man called Robert Walpole. It was not only English friends who expected their reward; George had to consider 'all his

German ministers and playfellows, male and female'. Public opinion was easily roused against foreign favourites. The King certainly took a good deal of notice of the loyal Bothmar, of the prime minister of Hanover, Baron von Bernstorff and of William III's old friend, the Huguenot, Jean de Robethon. Robethon was very unpopular – 'a prying, impertinent, venomous creature, for ever crawling in some slimy intrigue'.

As soon as the King had settled down after his coronation, the English took stock of the situation

S. Harding del.

A. Birrell sculp.

and started to laugh. George just did not know how to behave like a king; the new monarch never dined in state but had his meals served in his apartments – a set of two rooms. In the early days of his reign the King made many *faux pas*. He issued his guards with new uniforms to celebrate his birthday but the soldiers refused to wear their new tunics on the grounds that the cloth was too coarse. With the best will in the world, George expressed interest in the new craze for agricultural improvements. How much would it cost, he asked, to close St James's Park to the public and plant it with turnips? His Secretary of State replied laconically, 'Only three crowns, sire.'

George's shyness made it hard for him to make new friends. He was determined to surround himself with people who had become part of his routine, people who would not make clever jokes about their master behind his back. The result was a very motley court. George's two Turkish servants, Mustapha and Mahomet, were regarded as distinctly odd, but the King's taste for ugly women provoked the greatest ribaldry. One German mistress was very fat and the other German mistress was very thin. The skinny Ehrengard Melusina von Schulenberg, later Duchess of Kendal, was nearing sixty. George's passion for her had cooled but he spent most of his evenings with her, cutting out paper patterns with a pair of scissors. The fat Charlotte Sophia Kelmanns (who may have been George's half-sister) was more vivacious, even though her vast uncorseted bulk terrified Horace Walpole as a little boy. Both women grew rich taking bribes from those who wanted a favour from the King. They certainly made more like this than they would have done from what was regarded as their real profession – 'old, ugly trulls, such as would not find entertainment in the most hospitable hundreds of old Drury'. The Duchess of Kendal was soon christened 'The Maypole' whilst Charlotte Kelmanns became 'Elephant and Castle'.

George's circle was not the most cultivated in Europe. The King's first language was German but he spoke French tolerably well. With his habitual dislike of clever women, he always described his daughter-in-law, Caroline of Anspach, as 'Cette diablesse Madame la Princesse'. Despite Walpole's story that his father had to 'brush up his Latin' in order to communicate with the King, it is not quite correct to say that George knew no English. The King certainly had unorthodox ideas about grammar and pronunciation; on one occasion he declared roundly, 'I hate all boets and bainters.' But if George had none of his mother's linguistic ability or artistic interests, he did have a deep and genuine love of music. George Frideric Handel had been *Kappellmeister* at the Herrenhausen. As soon as his old master became King of England, Handel was able to present concerts at St James's Palace and begin to make his enormous contribution to English music. By the beginning of 1715 then, George was beginning to adjust to his new position, putting down a few tentative roots, finding new reasons to quarrel with his son, acquiring a more presentable English mistress, going to the opera incognito and making up a card-playing circle. Perhaps George was beginning to hope that he could enjoy a quiet life as King of England; any illusions were soon to be destroyed.

George's reign witnessed two major crises – the Jacobite rebellion and the South Sea Bubble. The Jacobite rising began on 6 September 1715 when the Earl of Mar proclaimed 'James III' at Braemar. Although Edinburgh remained loyal, most of the other towns in Scotland welcomed the rebels. From France, Henry St John was directing a superb propaganda campaign against 'the flight of hungry Hanoverian vultures' with their 'cacophonous, outlandish, German names'. Perhaps George should have trembled – there were indeed riots in many English towns – but there is no evidence that the King ever considered packing his bags and returning to his beloved Hanover. The only indication of the King's feelings was in his behaviour after the rebellion had been defeated. Six Scottish noblemen were

Opposite: Sir Joseph Banks, one of the leading figures in the South Sea Company, caricatured by James Gillray. The financial scandal of the South Sea Company in 1720 could have brought down the House of Hanover but for Robert Walpole's skilful handling of the crisis.

Pub. July 4th 1795. by H. Humphrey Nº 37.
New Bond Street

J.s Gy. del et fecit

The great South Sea Caterpillar, transform'd into a Bath Butterfly.

Description of the New Bath Butterfly — taken from the Philosophical Transactions for 1795. — "This Insect first crawl'd into notice from among the Weeds & Mud on the Banks of the South Sea: & being afterwards placed in a Warm Situation by the Royal Society, was changed by the heat of the Sun into its present form — it is noticed & Valued Solely on account of the beautiful Red which encircles its Body, & the Shining Spot on its Breast: a Distinction which never fails to render Caterpillars valuable. —

GEORGE II
r. 1727–60

KING GEORGE II WAS A TALL AND well-built man, with prominent blue eyes, a ruddy complexion and a nose which was perhaps a shade too large. The new King was interested in history and genealogy; he had a good grounding in the classics and could speak French, Italian and English tolerably well. George Augustus had a very German passion for detail, uniforms, the pleasures of the battlefield and the minutiae of court etiquette. His was not an inquiring mind; in matters of religion he 'jogged on quietly in that which he had been bred without scruples, zeal or inquiry'. Hatred of his father had long dominated the life of George Augustus, Prince of Wales. As a boy he is alleged to have tried to swim the moat surrounding the castle at Ahlden in a vain attempt to see his mother. In Hanover, the Elector had steadfastly refused to entrust his son with even the most minor responsibility and constantly denigrated his considerable achievements at the battle of Oudenarde. Such treatment did nothing to improve George's quick temper; within his own circle he made up for his lack of power by behaviour arrogant in the extreme – 'looking upon all men and women he saw as creatures he might kick or kiss for his diversion'.

In 1714 George Augustus was thirty years old and had been married for eight years to Caroline of Anspach. Caroline, an extremely intelligent and lively woman, was a great asset to her husband. She was large, blonde, blatantly sensual and earthy. A tremendous flirt, Caroline knew precisely what she was doing in charming men to advance her own political influence. George was genuinely attracted to his wife who, despite her artful and somewhat bawdy ways, was probably never unfaithful to her husband. Caroline discreetly dominated George Augustus and was far too intelligent to make a fuss over his occasional lapses with her ladies' maids. She had readily accepted the situation when Henrietta Howard became her husband's chief mistress in 1710; as the Dowager Duchess Sophia pointed out, Mrs Howard would at least improve George's English.

George Augustus and Caroline soon established a rival 'court' where life was much more fun than in the stupefying boredom at St James's. At any rate Caroline was able to provide a veneer of culture; she collected Van Dycks and as a girl she had had a learned conversation with the philosopher Leibniz. The stakes at the card tables were higher than at the King's court and there was even dancing – 'the Princess danced in slippers very well and the Prince better than any'. Above all, the Prince and Princess went out of their way to cultivate the English. Caroline's Ladies of the Bedchamber were all English, although George Augustus was probably rather overdoing it when he declared, 'I have not one drop of blood in my veins dat is not English.' The best jokes against George I tended to come from the Prince's circle; the young Lord Chesterfield told a delighted audience: 'The standard of His Majesty's taste, as exemplified in his mistress, makes all ladies who aspire to his favour, and who are near the suitable age, strain and swell themselves, like the frogs in the fable, to rival the bulk and dignity of the ox.

Opposite: *George II in a portrait by Robert Edge Pine. During his father's reign, George, Prince of Wales, was given no responsibility or training for his future role and even suspected a practical joke when told that he was King upon his father's death.*

Some succeed, and others – burst.'

But it was not all fun and games. For years the only time when the Prince of Wales met his father was at the christenings of his children; on these occasions there were fearful scenes and after one of them the King ordered that his son should be arrested for threatening to murder the Duke of Newcastle. George I firmly refused to allow the Prince to assume the title of Regent during the King's long absences in Hanover and would only grudgingly permit 'Guardian of the Realm' – with virtually no powers attached. Even in death, George Augustus would not trust his father. The Prince of Wales merely suspected a trick when told that he was now King. When Walpole gave him the news on the evening of 14 June 1727 he is said to have replied, 'Dat is one big lie.'

Unlike his father, George II had gained considerable experience of English politics by the time he came to the throne. The new King was forty-four and was to live for another thirty-three years. He had the time and the opportunity to arrange things to suit himself; most people expected that he would reverse everything his father had done. As Prince of Wales, George had been resentful at Walpole's 'betrayal' in rejoining the government in 1720. Few expected 'Robin' Walpole to survive long.

Unhappy, me amongst the Birds of Prey
Once I'd a comfort, now he's turned to clay.

Opposition Whigs like Pultenay and even the now forgiven St John believed their day had come. George II did indeed ask his friend Sir Spencer Compton to take over the government but Compton only burst into tears and declared that he was not up to the job. Although George had recently described Walpole's favourite brother Horatio as 'a scoundrel and a dirty buffoon', in the end the old gang remained in power. Walpole's triumph should not be seen as the victory of Parliament over the Crown. The prime minister owed his survival to the influence of Queen Caroline. Despite constant rumours of an affair, Caroline found the twenty-stone Walpole physically repulsive, but his tolerant, worldly and cynical outlook coincided precisely with her own. Whilst the opposition courted George's mistresses, Walpole remained on good terms

with Caroline. The ministry was safe when the Queen told George that Walpole was the only man who could get large increases in the Civil List through Parliament. Walpole always appreciated Caroline's ultimate hegemony over her husband; he remarked crudely but perceptively, 'I have the right sow by the ear.'

As soon as George I was dead, George Augustus seemed to grow more and more like his father. The court was not very exciting; most of Caroline's bright young friends, 'the Virgin Band', had gone off and married disreputable husbands. The new King's concern for the strictest observance of court etiquette and absolute punctuality was fast becoming a mania. Parties like those before 1720 were now very rare; George had decided that economy should be his watchword. In the long boring evenings at court the King reminisced *ad nauseam* about his exploits at the battle of Oudenarde. To some extent things were enlivened by the malice of the strange Lord Hervey, but Hervey scarcely enjoyed his life at court. 'No mill horse ever went on a more constant track or a more unchanging circle.'

The most striking similarity with the previous reign was the deplorable relationship between the new Prince of Wales and his parents. 'Poor Fred', who was born in Hanover in 1706, did not even look like a Guelph. He had a yellowish complexion and a curved, rather semitic nose. There were stories that he was a changeling but these seem highly improbable. What is certain is that Frederick's father – and even more his mother – hated him from the moment of his birth. George I had wanted his eldest grandson to marry Princess Wilhelmina of Prussia, a match which Frederick appeared to welcome. As soon as George II ascended his throne he broke off the marriage negotiations with the comment, 'I did not think that ingrafting my half-witted coxcomb upon a mad woman would improve the breed'. Later the King exclaimed, 'Our first-born is the greatest ass, the greatest liar, the greatest canaille and the greatest beast in the whole world and we heartily wish he was out of it.' Even George I would not have said that about his son.

In some ways Frederick was rather a foolish young man but he was not really vicious. A little extravagance, a little gallantry with the ladies can hardly justify or even explain this intense hatred. Kings certainly do not like being reminded that they too are mortal and that a successor is waiting in the wings. It is probable, however, that the main reason for George's hostility to his son came from the knowledge that Frederick was bound to be the focus of opposition to the royal government. Even as a young man, it was said of George II: 'Whenever he meets with any opposition to his designs, he thinks the opposers insolent rebels to the will of God.'

The King did his best to reduce Frederick's social influence by keeping his allowance down to £24,000 per annum; as Prince of Wales, George II had received £100,000. Queen Caroline suggested that Frederick was reduced to offering Lord Hervey a half share in his mistress in order to raise cash. In the eighteenth century, however, so long as there was an heir to the throne, there would always be a 'Leicester House Set'. Even with his limited resources, Frederick could patronise the Italian opera of Buononcini and sneer at his parents' loyalty to Handel. George II told Frederick sourly that no persons of quality would demean themselves by setting up 'factions of fiddlers'.

The fashionable world thought otherwise, and disappointed politicians, wits and dramatists began to find the Prince's company far more agreeable than that of his parents. Walpole's power appeared to be crumbling with the introduction of the unpopular Excise Scheme, whilst his policy of non-involvement in European affairs was threatened by the outbreak of the war of the Polish succession. George faced the nightmare that Frederick would use the political influence of the Duchy of Cornwall to eject the present ministers and install his own friends – a group derisively described by Walpole as 'The Patriot Boys'.

For the moment, Walpole survived but his power was weakened; the King was compelled to allow Frederick to marry, a step which would entail a separate establishment and a larger income. The King and Queen chose the seventeen-year-old Princess Augusta of Saxe-Gotha as a suitable bride for their son; the future Princess of Wales arrived at Greenwich clutching her doll. George and his wife immediately added their new daughter-in-law to their list of enemies. Ambassadors were forbidden to call on Augusta; the House of Lords, the armed forces and officers of the court were told that a visit to the Prince of Wales would incur royal displeasure. Primed by Henry St John, Frederick was making the appropriate noises about the Crown being in bondage and exploited by a parasite gang of Whigs. George II had limited his own political freedom because, at the back of his mind, he believed that all Tories were secret Jacobites; his son had no such qualms. Frederick's popularity grew and grew: 'My God,' said the King, 'popularity always makes me sick, but Fretz's popularity makes me vomit.'

Eighteenth-century Princes of Wales usually tried to persuade society that their fathers were simply rather unpleasant and disagreeable old men. George II had said it about his father; now he was subjected to the same treatment. Frederick described the King as 'an obstinate self-indulgent miserly martinet with an insatiable sexual appetite'. This observation was sadly close to the truth. When George was fifty-two he had gone over to Hanover to acquire a new mistress. Madame von Walmoden caught his eye and immediately he wrote to the Queen, 'You must love the Walmoden, for she loves me.' Under Walmoden's influence, the King became more German-orientated, a trait which the English had always deplored in their Hanoverian monarchs. George became increasingly rude to his courtiers; those who had had the honour of having the King's back suddenly turned on them formed themselves into a Rumpsteak Club. Nothing English would suit now: 'I am sick to death of all this foolish stuff and wish with all my heart that the devil may take all your bishops, and the devil take your Minister, and the devil take your Parliament and the devil take the whole island, provided I can get out of it and go to Hanover.'

Perhaps George had reason to be in a bad mood. The same mocking laughter which had made George I so absurd was beginning to attach itself to him. During one of George's foreign tours, a broken-down old horse was turned loose in the streets of London; the animal bore a placard saying: 'Let nobody stop me – I am the King's Hanover equipage going to fetch His Majesty and his whore to England.' When the government tried to reduce the consumption of gin, mobs stormed round the royal coach screaming, 'No Gin! No King!' But there were much more serious blows. Queen Caroline died a lingering and painful

FRANCFORT

Offenbach

HANAW

Dettingen

eligenstadt

french Battery

Gens d'armes

french Battery

Gens d'Armes

B

Battery

2 Bridges of boats

Aschaffenberg

Cronbach

N.B. the shaded lines thus — that are coloured r
the allied Army. The unshaded lines thus — t
lour'd green shew the French Army

FRA...
Stein-
heim
Hochst
Seligenstadt
Bobenhausen
Darmstat
Aschaffenberg
Somm
Milten

A

Hanoverian Battery

E

the King

D E

Previous pages: *The victorious battle of Dettingen against France, at which George II was the last British sovereign to fight alongside his troops.*
Above: *A portrait of George II's favourite son, William, Duke of Cumberland, on his grey charger. He is pictured at the scene of the battle of Culloden in which he vanquished Bonnie Prince Charlie.*

death in November 1737. George, who hated illness, was a mixture of irritation and remorse. One moment he asked Caroline how the devil she could expect to sleep when she would not lie still; the next, he was in tears at the prospect of losing his beloved wife. When Caroline died, George was genuinely heartbroken; he had known many woman yet 'I never saw one fit to buckle her shoe'.

Caroline's death had serious political implications. Women certainly had a great power over the King; it had been Caroline who had kept royal influence behind Robert Walpole. Which politician would benefit from the new situation? The Duke of Newcastle suggested that the greatest influence in George's life now was likely to be his favourite daughter; the prime minister would do well to cultivate Princess Caroline. Walpole knew what really influ-

enced the King – 'Will she go to bed with her father? If not, I am for Madame Walmoden, I'll bring her over; Lady Deloraine will do as a stop gap.' Disagreement soon appeared between George and the man who was almost deputy king. Walpole's success was not just a matter of exploiting the greed of his opponents with large doses of 'Doctor King's Golden Soporific'. Not enough funds were available to bribe everybody and some did not care to be bribed. Walpole's policy was one of Whig men and Tory measures; low taxation and peace kept the squires contented. Walpole clung to peace but George II wanted war and a chance to relive the military triumphs of his youth.

The war which broke out on 26 September 1739 – first against Spain and then against France too – delighted the King but it was the beginning of the end for Walpole. It had been the opposition and Prince Frederick which had really wanted war. Walpole resigned on 1 February 1742 but even then Frederick was denied his triumph. George was able to reconstruct the government by retaining some of the existing ministers and filling the other places with men who claimed to be the Prince's friends. The trouble with the Reversionary Interest was that no one knew how long it would take to mature; faced with the temptation of immediate power many of 'Poor Fred's' erstwhile friends deserted Leicester House for St James's Palace as fast as their legs could carry them. The fortunes of war, too, looked more encouraging. At the age of sixty George was again on the battlefield. At Dettingen, on 15 June 1743, the King led a joint army of British, Hanoverians, Hessians, Austrians and Dutch to victory over the French. George was often under heavy fire. 'Don't tell me of danger,' he cried, 'I'll be even with them. Now boys! Now for the honour of England! Fire and behave brave, and the French will run.' They did. Whatever one may say against George 11, he was the last British sovereign to risk his life fighting alongside his soldiers. The King's popularity, at a low ebb for years, received a tremendous boost.

The popularity was badly needed when, in the summer of 1745, the Young Pretender, so much more dashing than his father, launched another invasion of Britain. The threat was more serious than in 1715; this time Edinburgh fell, then Carlisle, then Derby. Some of the King's ministers thought they would be lucky to spend the rest of their lives in exile – living in miserable attics in Hanover. George remained calm and the rebellion was defeated by his favourite son, the Duke of Cumberland. War at home and abroad meant increasing taxation which in turn meant increasing the power of Parliament. George might rail against the 'republican' features of the British Constitution but he never had the nerve to try to get rid of a government he was not keen on. The events of the mid-1740s consolidated the position of the Duke of Newcastle and his relations, the Pelham family. The Pelhams were to remain in control for the remainder of George 11's reign.

The King constantly complained that he was 'in toils' to his nominal servants but in fact ministers still needed royal support. After a protracted royal visit to Hanover, the Duke of Newcastle went to Germany to beg his master to return to England and show his approval of the administration. A modern sovereign would be bound to accept such a request; George 11 not only refused but 'said a great many things I will not repeat'. There were other consolations; although no woman ever took Caroline's place, the King was fond enough of Madame von Walmoden to make her Lady Yarmouth. George also had the satisfaction of outliving the hated 'Fretz'. 'Poor Fred' had spent his life talking about what he would do when his father expired but it was the son who died first – in March 1751. George put on a show of the sorrowing father but many people did not find the performance convincing; at any rate he adamantly refused to pay his late son's debts.

George did not care for the Pelhams and he liked their occasional ally, William Pitt, even less. George's own miscalculations were partly responsible for getting England involved in the Seven Years' War. England's traditional ally on the Continent was Austria; George had substituted Prussia and seriously underestimated the expansionist plans of his nephew Frederick the Great. George may have been at fault, but Pitt, who had begun his career as a 'Patriot Boy', was the man to lead the country in war. Another round with France was probably inevitable after the inconclusive peace of 1748. The King, 'the good old King' – tactless and short-tempered as ever – took his time before accepting Pitt. He swallowed his pride at the end of 1756 and after that, despite reverses in Hanover, most things seemed to go right. The year of 1759 saw England's greatest military triumphs – complete command of the sea, conquests in Canada, India and the Caribbean. At seventy-seven the King was beginning to fail, he had always wanted military glory and now it was his. No reign has ended on a grander note.

But somehow George 11 never quite made greatness; there was about him a hint of the ridiculous which dogged all the Hanoverians. The King's death was mercifully sudden but it was not dignified. For years, George had suffered from constipation; on the morning of 25 October 1760 his exertions to overcome his difficulty were too much for him and brought on a fatal heart attack. Poor King George 11 died sitting on the lavatory.

GEORGE III

r. 1760–1820

GEORGE WILLIAM FREDERICK, eldest son of Frederick, Prince of Wales, and Augusta of Saxe-Gotha, was only twelve when his father died. Even the circumstances of the future George III's birth illustrate the bitterness between George II and 'Poor Fred'. George was born in lodgings in St James's Square because the King had evicted Frederick and Augusta from their apartments in the nearby palace. George's schoolwork was poor, and he was thought young for his years. From earliest childhood, however, he was made conscious of his royal rank. One of his few playmates was the future Lord North, but North's parents told him: 'Bow to the Prince, my son, address him as Your Royal Highness, if you play a game with him, he must win; never, never, raise your hand to him and, who knows, my son, if you play your part well, you may in time get a sinecure post and your father exchange his barony for an earldom.' Under the circumstances, it is astonishing that George had such a pleasant character; he was described as 'silent, modest and easily abashed'.

The main influences in George's life were his rather possessive mother and her close friend, the Earl of Bute. Bute was very much a father figure to George who constantly sought the Earl's approval. In 1759, when it was clear that he would soon be King, George fell in love with Lady Sarah Lennox, a descendant of Charles II and Louise de Kerouaille. The young man wrote to Bute: 'I don't deny having often flattered myself with the hopes that one day or other you would consent to my raising her to the throne.' It was Bute who persuaded George that he must give up the idea of marrying one of his own subjects and should send for accounts of eligible princesses in Germany. Bute and Augusta were largely responsible for George's views on politics. Ideas that the Prince was deliberately indoctrinated with notions of absolutism can be dismissed – the history dispensed by Bute was impeccably Whiggish – but George was taught that his grandfather was a despicable cipher in the power of corrupt ministers. Bute was a scholarly, cultivated and ambitious man who hoped to follow the example of Cardinal Fleury, Louis XV's tutor who had become first minister of France. George readily supported his friend's plans but neither appreciated that the Earl's lack of experience in practical politics would be an enormous obstacle to the realisation of this project.

George III was proclaimed King immediately after his grandfather's death. The twenty-two-year-old monarch seemed to have many advantages. Horace Walpole said, 'His person is tall and full of dignity, his countenance florid and obliging.' George inherited the family features of prominent eyes and fair colouring. Although not remarkably handsome, the young King was generally regarded as good-looking in a rather Germanic way. Unlike his two predecessors, George had been born and educated in England. He was entirely English in sympathy, never visited Hanover and was the first sovereign since Queen Anne to speak his subjects' language without a foreign accent. Such things mattered with the xenophobic English.

George might not be outstanding in book learning but he was intensely hard working; he would

Opposite: Queen Charlotte, who had been Princess Charlotte of Mecklenberg-Strelitz before her marriage to George III, painted by Thomas Gainsborough. She and the king had fifteen children, doing their duty in providing for the succession.

AFFABILITY.

"Well, Friend, where a'you going. Hey?—what's your Name, hey?—where d'ye Live, hey?—hey?"

Above: *The King was very interested in farming and agricultural improvement, and showed a level of enthusiasm for rural matters here lampooned in a contemporary satirical illustration. He was also inclined to add 'hey, hey' to the end of sentences.*

Right: *The King and Napleon playing chess, showing Napoleon's early flair in the eponymous wars. However, George's choice of Pitt the Younger was crucial in securing Napoleon's eventual defeat.*

spare no efforts to do the job of king properly. Few monarchs have been more acutely conscious of their duty to God and to their people. The King was a deeply religious young man; unlike George II's half-hearted formal religion, George III's faith was very real. Throughout his life George spent long hours in private prayer; perhaps this enabled the King to remain calm in moments of crisis – like the terrible Gordon Riots of 1780 – when his ministers com-

pletely lost their heads. One of George's first priorities was to clean up the disreputable moral tone of his grandfather's court; within a month of his accession, he had issued a royal proclamation for the encouragement of piety and virtue. It is true that, when nervous, the King tended to speak too fast – a common enough failing – and to fill gaps in his conversation with meaningless patter; it is a gross slander, however, to use this fact to support the contention that the King was already showing signs of mental instability. Compared to George I and George II, George III may seem a little dull and a little priggish. He made his mistakes but, even then, his actions have been subject to greater distortion than those of any other British monarch. The plain fact is that George III was the only Hanoverian who could be called a genuinely decent and good man.

After selecting and marrying an appropriate German princess, Charlotte of Mecklenberg-Strelitz, George III set about destroying the power of the Whig clique which had dominated the government since 1714. George II had indeed chosen his own ministers but he had done so from within the limits of a narrowly defined caste of professional politicians.

In refusing to accept this constraint, George was not acting unconstitutionally; he was not planning to establish an enlightened despotism on continental lines but was attempting something no British monarch had done for the last fifty years. Language difficulties, long absences in Hanover and a desire for a quiet life had meant that power had slipped away from the Crown almost imperceptibly. George III was going to stop the rot. The young King eased Pitt out of office, then Newcastle, began peace negotiations with France and installed Bute in power.

Bute was not one of the Whig grandees; he had had Jacobite relations and he came from Scotland, a country still regarded by Englishmen as both foreign and savage. George had a difficult first decade; he

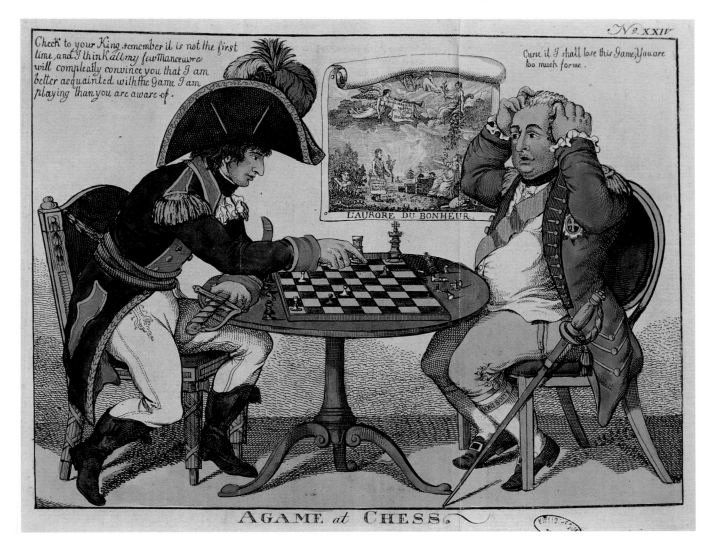

had to learn several lessons before he could succeed in politics. He had wanted to abolish corruption, yet in order to keep Bute in power he had to resort to the very tactics he deplored in others. Sadly he concluded, 'We must call in bad men to govern bad men.' Bute managed to get the peace with France through Parliament and then resigned rather than face an all-out attack. Prime ministers followed in rapid succession – George Grenville, Lord Rockingham, William Pitt and the Duke of Grafton. Ministers claimed that political instability was caused by George's failure to give his official advisers proper support; ignoring his constitutional duty to consult them in all things, he 'went behind the curtain' to seek advice from Bute. Grenville had some cause for complaint but, instead of trying to win the King's confidence, he indulged in long lectures upbraiding George for ingratitude. The King declared, 'When he has wearied me for two hours, he looks at his watch to see if he may not tire me for an hour more.' All the time, George was subjected to crude abuse from the gutter press, whilst the irresponsible libertine John Wilkes stirred the London mob to riot and sedition.

George had shown that governments which did not enjoy the monarch's full confidence tended to have a short life but, equally, prime ministers could stay in office only if they had the respect and votes of Parliament. Patronage might help but it was not enough on its own; was there anyone in politics who was genuinely acceptable to both King and Parliament? In 1770 George thought he had found his man – Lord Frederick North, 'the man who lost America' and allegedly the worst prime minister in British history. George's selection of North seems proof of the King's stupidity – 'a fool chosen by a fool'. Yet one cannot so dismiss a man who retained a working majority in Parliament for ten years. Within the context of British politics George's judgement was sound. The 'green boy' of 1760 had become a shrewd politician; North was a good Parliament man, an able speaker and would have been an excellent peacetime premier. Claims that George wanted to enslave his colonial subjects are absurd. The King certainly supported his prime minister's attempts to suppress the American rebels; perhaps George III

might have shown more imagination but then the same charge can be made against almost all of the political establishment. Those who became advocates of American Independence were converted only very late in the day when the war was virtually lost. Kings are expected to be consistent.

The loss of America was a terrible blow. Catherine the Great of Russia said, 'Rather than have granted America her Independence as my brother monarch, King George, has done, I would have fired a pistol at my own head.' The political problems created by the collapse of North's ministry were enormous. Charles James Fox described the King as an arbitrary despot who had squandered his subjects' blood and treasure in his mad lust for revenge. After North, Lord Rockingham took office with a programme of reducing royal influence in politics, but even this was not enough. The country was soon confronted with the astonishing spectacle of Fox joining up with the now discredited North to impose even greater restrictions and humiliations. 'The King's closet had been stormed' by men George had reason to hate. It must have seemed absurd to suggest that anyone short of a political genius could ever recapture for the King the right of choosing his own ministers. To the astonishment of everyone, this is what George proceeded to do.

On 18 December 1783 the House of Lords rejected the government's East India Bill – at 1 a.m. the King sent out notices of dismissal to all members of the Fox–North coalition George had chosen his moment carefully; the country would not permit an illegitimate extension of royal power or of ministerial power against the Crown. Influential people felt that Fox was going too far and swung around to support the King. The next prime minister, William Pitt the Younger, was only twenty-four. Pitt was very much George's personal choice; for several months the new government was constantly defeated in Parliament, yet the King refused to think of accepting its resignation. When Pitt felt that the time had come for a general election, George put all the resources of the Crown behind his protégé. The result was a tremendous defeat for Fox. The King's choice of Pitt is probably the best proof of royal sagacity. Pitt was to remain in power for twenty-one years and was to lead

An engraving published in November 1788 showing the Prince of Wales and some of his drinking friends, including the author Sheridan, bursting in upon George III. This cartoon was published at the time that the king's health had become a matter for serious concern.

England in the terrible struggle with Revolutionary France. In such perilous times it was better that Pitt, rather than the wild Charles James Fox, should be running the country.

The mid-1780s were probably the best years of George's reign. Under Pitt's guidance, Britain was fast recovering her prosperity and self-confidence. George III was in vigorous middle age, his figure kept trim and youthful by a spartan diet and plenty of exercise. Apart from one illness in 1765 the King had enjoyed excellent health throughout his reign. George was a good and faithful husband; although not the most exciting of women, Queen Charlotte was at least contented with her lot. She declared that since her marriage she had never known a real moment of sorrow. There had been no less than fifteen children to the marriage; no one could say that George had not secured the succession. The atmosphere at court was more relaxed. The King was less prudish than in the early years of the reign and laughed heartily at Cibber's play *She Would and She Would Not*. Absence of political pressure meant that George was able to develop his knowledge of botany and write pamphlets on agricultural improvements under the pen name of Ralph Robinson. Intellectually the King had been a slow starter but he had caught up; in the 1780s he compared favourably with most European monarchs, certainly with Louis XVI.

The one black spot was the growing antagonism between George III and his eldest son, the future Prince Regent. The same conflicts which had soured the relationship between George I and George Augustus and between George II and 'Poor Fred' were appearing yet again. There were faults on both sides; George III's great failing was that he was over-protective. He genuinely loved his son but he wanted the Prince of Wales to remain a child for ever. The 'cotton wool' atmosphere of Kew Palace was far too restrictive for the high-spirited young Prince and the desire to rebel against it led him into all kinds of wickedness. But the King's reaction to his son's follies was more of sorrow than anger; the Prince of Wales really had far less to complain about than 'Poor Fred' had done.

Such was the state of the country and the royal family when George III 'went mad'. The King had not been well in the summer of 1788; he had an alarming attack of convulsions after riding in the rain on 16 October. George's manner was thought odd and he seemed never to stop talking. It was about this time that the famous Oak Tree incident is alleged to have occurred with the King talking to a tree as if it were the King of Prussia. This story was put about by a page who had been dismissed from the royal service so its veracity must be questionable. On 5 November 1788, however, there were obvious signs of derangement. At dinner in Windsor Castle the King attacked the Prince of Wales and tried to smash his head against the wall. George was talking non-stop gibberish, foam was coming from his mouth and his eyes were so bloodshot that they looked like currant jelly.

When it was clear that the King would survive although he might never recover his reason, he was removed from Windsor and taken to Kew. George's doctors may have thought they were doing the right thing, but there can be no doubt that their treatment was abominably cruel and only served to delay the patient's recovery. George's chief doctor at Kew was Dr Francis Willis, the proprietor of a private lunatic asylum in Lincoln. Lectures, threats and the strait-jacket played a large part in Willis's treatment. If the King refused food or was restless, his legs were tied to the bed and a band strapped across his chest. Later, Willis introduced a special iron chair to restrain his patient; with bitter irony George called this terrible contraption his 'coronation chair'. As the real thing had brought him respect and honour so this travesty brought only humiliation. Willis was not the only tormentor; Dr Warren insisted on putting poultices of Spanish fly and mustard all over the King's body; the idea was that the painful blisters which resulted would draw out the 'evil humours'. Despite the efforts of his doctors, George III gradually regained his reason and was well enough to attend a service of thanksgiving for his recovery in St Paul's Cathedral on 23 April 1789.

Ever since that time, doctors and historians have argued about the nature of George III's madness. One school believes that the King's illness is best explained in psychological terms, the other thinks that George was suffering from a rare physical illness. If the second explanation is correct then, in the strict sense, George III was never 'mad' at all. It has been variously claimed that George III had an Oedipus complex about his mother, that he suffered from sexual repression by remaining faithful to an ugly queen, or even that he was burdened with the guilt of a secret marriage in 1757 to 'the Fair Quakeress' Hannah Lightfoot. Others believe that the strains of kingship were too much for George and see the trau-matic loss of America as the crucial factor. George III, it seems, might have been an excellent country squire but he was just not up to being King. More recently, attention has been focused on the physical symptoms which accompanied George's illness – rapid pulse, an angry rash, yellow or bloodshot eyes, swollen feet and red-coloured urine. From this, it is possible to argue that George III was suffering from porphyria, an unusual disease which was not prop-erly understood until the 1930s. Porphyria is the name given to a disturbance of the porphyrin metab-olism, the process which creates red pigment in the blood. If too much of this pigment is produced, the urine becomes discoloured and the whole nervous system, including the brain, is poisoned. The por-phyria explanation may sound too exotic but it does fit the known facts very well. Above all, it has the advantage of demolishing theories that George III was rather unbalanced throughout his life.

George's illness showed how much the people of his country loved and respected him. In November 1788 there was panic on the Stock Exchange when it was thought that the King would die and be succeeded by the Prince of Wales. Most people were delighted that George recovered in time to prevent the implementation of the provisions of the Regency Bill. The royal tour of the south of England in the summer of 1789 was a tremendous success, crowds and triumphal arches in every village and a local band wading into the sea to play 'God Save the King' when George went bathing at Weymouth.

George III was less outraged by the French Revolution than some other European monarchs. He felt that the Revolution was Divine Punishment of the House of Bourbon for its unnatural support of the rebels in the Thirteen Colonies. Of course, the outbreak of the war with France in 1793 brought serious strains and republican ideas were formed in some circles. The King was the object of a number of assassination attempts. On 15 May 1800 George was standing in the royal box of the Drury Lane Theatre when a man in the pit stood on a box and fired two pistol shots at the King. The bullets missed by inches and embedded themselves in the panelling of the box. George ordered the performance to continue and was so calm that he went to sleep in the interval.

The King had two brief relapses into his old complaint in 1801 and 1804 but it is far from true that the King was unimportant by the first decade of the new century. George's main concern now was to prevent the passage of 'Catholic Emancipation', a measure which would allow Roman Catholics to sit in Parliament. The King believed that if he agreed to such a measure he would be guilty of breaking the solemn coronation oath to defend the Protestant religion. Such a view may seem incredibly benighted but it was certainly the opinion of the vast majority of George's subjects. In his determination to stop Catholic Emancipation George forced Pitt out of office in 1801 and summarily ejected the Grenville ministry in 1807. To the end of his active life, therefore, the King maintained the vital principle that the choice of ministers remained with the Crown.

Until he was over seventy, George III had been 'mad' for less than six months. It was only in 1810 that permanent insanity descended upon him. The last decade of George's life was very sad. He was a blind old man with a long white beard, wearing a violet dressing gown and shambling around an isolated set of rooms in Windsor Castle. Only the Star of the Order of the Garter which he kept pinned to his chest was a reminder that this wreck of a man was King of England. George found release on 29 January 1820; he was nearly eighty-two. The Lear-like figure of the last years was still revered by his people. They knew that 'Farmer George' had been a good man and a good king. Many books have been written to explain why the monarchy fell in France and survived in England; historians would do well to consider whether the personal integrity of King George III did not have a lot to do with it.

GEORGE IV

r. 1820–30

GEORGE IV WAS KING FOR ONLY ten years, from 1820 to 1830, but, as Prince Regent from 1812 to 1820, he exercised all the powers of sovereign for a total of eighteen years. There can be no doubt that George wasted his great gifts and abilities. As a young man the Prince was outstandingly handsome and charming. He was tall and dignified in his bearing and Mrs 'Perdita' Robinson was only one of the many women who found it impossible to forget 'the grace of his person, the irresistible sweetness of his smile, the tenderness of his melodious yet manly voice'. A taste for gargantuan meals and heavy drinking soon changed that. By the time he had reached his late thirties, George had become very like the repellent creature depicted in Gillray's cartoon 'A Voluptuary under the horrors of Digestion'. This shows George recovering from an enormous meal at Carlton House, his huge belly bursting from his breeches and his florid face on the verge of apoplexy. He is surrounded by empty wine bottles, unpaid bills for which an overflowing chamber-pot acts as paperweight, and various patent medicines including famous cures for venereal disease. There is certainly some justification for Leigh Hunt's damning comments on George's fiftieth birthday in 1812: 'A libertine over head and ears in debt and disgrace, a despiser of domestic ties, the companion of demi-reps, a man who has just closed half a century without a single claim on the gratitude of his country or the respect of posterity.'

More than anyone else, the Prince was responsible for the cruel slander that George III spent most of his life insane. When George III was desperately ill in November 1788, his eldest son was going round the London clubs giving intimate details of the King's condition, mimicking his ravings and even speculating on a *coup d'état* to take over full royal power. The Prince's behaviour to women was no better. His affair with Perdita Robinson ended with a curt note saying that they must meet no more. In 1784, after a brief affair with Lady Melbourne – who exploited her position to get for her husband the appropriate job of Gentleman of the Bedchamber – George met a rather strait-laced Roman Catholic widow. Maria Fitzherbert was five years older than the Prince; although attracted to the young man, she resolutely refused to become his mistress. In the end, the only way to overcome her scruples was to go through a form of marriage. The Reverend Robert Butt, then confined to the debtors' prison, agreed to perform the ceremony on condition that he was given a bishopric when George became King. Although canonically valid, the marriage was null and void from the beginning un der the terms of the 1772 Royal Marriages Act and was to prove a great embarrassment for George's Whig friends who tried to deny its existence in Parliament.

George was genuinely in love with Mrs Fitzherbert – for a while – but it was not long before he left her for Lady Jersey, who was already a grandmother. George's extravagance frequently got him into difficulties; as early as 1783, George III denounced plans to increase his son's allowance as 'a shameful squandering of public money to gratify the passions of an ill-advised young man'. But George's

Opposite: *A portrait of George IV by Sir Thomas Laurence. Unlike his philistine Hanoverian predecessors, George had a distinct personal style and taste which found expression in the palaces he built, particularly in the fabulous Brighton Pavilion.*

A

BILL

To deprive Her MAJESTY Caroline Amelia Elizabeth of the Title, Prerogatives, Rights, Privileges, and Pretensions of Queen Consort of this Realm, and to dissolve the Marriage between His MAJESTY and the said Queen.

Note.—The first column contains a Copy of the Bill—The second column contains the CLAUSES THAT DROPT OUT, *and which are now proposed to be restored.*

WHEREAS in the year one thousand eight hundred and fourteen, Her MAJESTY, *Caroline Amelia Elizabeth,* then Princess of *Wales,* and now Queen Consort of this Realm, being at *Milan,* in *Italy,* engaged in her service in a menial situation, one *Bartolomo Pergami,* otherwise *Bartolomo Bergami,* a foreigner of low station, who had before served in a similar capacity : AND WHEREAS, after the said *Bartolomo Pergami,* otherwise *Bartolomo Bergami,* had so entered the service of her Royal Highness the said Princess of *Wales,* a most unbecoming and degrading intimacy commenced between Her Royal Highness and the said *Bartolomo Pergami,* otherwise *Bartolomo Bergami :* AND WHEREAS her Royal Highness not only advanced the said *Bartolomo Pergami,* otherwise *Bartolomo Bergami,* to a high situation in her Royal Highness's household, and received into her service many of his near relations, some of them in

WHEREAS on the eighth day of *April,* one thousand seven hundred and ninety-five, your MAJESTY, then being Prince of *Wales* and Heir apparent to the throne of these Realms, intermarried with the Princess *Caroline Amelia Elizabeth* of *Brunswick,* by whom, on the seventh day of *January,* one thousand seven hundred and ninety-six, you had issue the late Princess *Charlotte* of happy memory.

AND WHEREAS on the thirtieth day of *April,* in the said year one thousand seven hundred and ninety-six, your Majesty was graciously pleased to write to Her said Majesty, in and by a letter of that date, as follows ;—" *Our inclinations* " *are not in our power, nor should* " *either of us be held answerable to* " *the other* ; because nature has not " made us suitable to each other ;" and in which said letter your Majesty defined to Her Majesty, the terms whereon you proposed from thenceforth to live wholly and entirely

greatest disaster came in 1795 when he agreed to marry his cousin, Caroline of Brunswick, in order to persuade Parliament to write off his debts. George was appalled when he met his bride to be; his first words were 'I am not well, pray get me a glass of brandy'. In turn, Caroline found George 'very stout and by no means as handsome as his portrait'. The Prince was helplessly drunk at the wedding.

Caroline was scarcely an ideal Princess of Wales; she was fat, coarse, vulgar and unwashed. After the birth of a daughter, Princess Charlotte, on 7 January 1796, the couple lived apart. In ten years, Caroline spent much of her time in Italy and, according to her accusers, lived 'in a most unbecoming and disgusting intimacy' with Bartolomo Pergami, the handsome Chamberlain of the Queen's Household. In 1820 Caroline returned to England to claim her rights as Queen and quickly became a focus of popular discontent against George and his government. Slogans appeared all over London – 'The Queen for ever! The King in the River!' George forced the government to bring in a Bill which deprived 'Her Majesty Caroline Amelia Elizabeth of the title of Queen' and declared her marriage to the King 'for ever wholly dissolved, annulled and made void'. A great deal of titillating but not altogether trustworthy evidence was produced and the Bill was eventually dropped. Caroline appeared at George's coronation only to be turned away from the doors of Westminster Abbey. Fortunately for the King's peace of mind, his unsuitable Queen died suddenly on 7 August 1821.

George's critics overplayed their strong hand. A great deal of the animosity against the Prince came from political reasons and it was in this spirit that *The Times* could dismiss him as 'a hard-drinking, swearing man who at all times would prefer a girl and a bottle to politics and a sermon'. But there was more to George than that. When he was moderately sober, his conversation was fascinating and full of amusing anecdote. He had a good memory and was an excellent mimic. George (Beau) Brummell said that he could have been the best comic actor in Europe. He was by far the most intelligent of the Hanoverians and could hold his own in the Sublime Society of Beefsteaks, to which he was elected in 1784.

But George's greatest claim to fame was as a man of style, a man of taste. Before George, the Hanoverians had been decidedly philistine. Almost as if they expected to be sent back to Germany at any moment they had virtually camped in the rambling and uncomfortable buildings left by the Stuarts. George was determined to create palaces which would rival any in Europe. Styles varied from the 'Gothick' restoration of Windsor Castle, the 'rustick' of the Royal Lodge to the extraordinary 'Oriental' of the Brighton Pavilion. Of course it was easy to make

Gent .　　　　　No Gent .　　　　& Re gent !!

Opposite: *The Bill George tried to force through Parliament to dissolve his empty marriage to Queen Caroline and deny her right to a title.*
Above: *Cruikshank's cartoon satirising George's physical and moral deterioration from being a handsome, regal Prince of Wales to a bloated, debauched Prince Regent.*

fun of the Brighton Pavilion; William Cobbett wrote: 'Take a square box, take a large Norfolk turnip and put the turnip on the top of the box. Then take four turnips of half the size and put them on the corners of the box. Then take a considerable number of bulbs of the crown-imperial and put them pretty promiscuously about the top of the box. Then stand off. There! That's a Kremlin.'

Despite Cobbett's jibe, there can be no doubt that the Brighton Pavilion was a success. The mixture of domes and minarets, the Chinese furniture and the lotus and dragon chandeliers could have pro-

duced a palace of quite hideous vulgarity. But the Pavilion's exuberance always stops short of vulgarity and it was the personal sensitivity of George IV which prevented this outcome. George did not follow fashions, he set them. One of his most important discoveries was of the seaside resort and the life-style which went with it. The style evolved; in the early days Brighton was a byword for almost every kind of wildness but later the Prince enjoyed a quiet, almost domestic, existence there. Perhaps the change was symbolised by the abandonment of multi-coloured 'peacock' fashions in favour of the smart black,

A WELLINGTON BOOT
Or the Head of the Armye

'A Wellington Boot, or, the Head of the Army'. A contemporary cartoon of the Duke of Wellington in the boot to which he gave his name. Wellington not only orchestrated the defeat of Napoleon's armies, he also became a leading politician – and was frustrated by the vacillations of George IV.

sombre dress pioneered by George and Brummell in the 1790s. In 1800 Mrs Fitzherbert returned to live with the man whom she regarded as her lawful husband, cut down his drinking and nursed him back to health when he was stricken with inflammation of the stomach.

Politically, George was not to be trusted. As a young man one of his closest companions was Charles James Fox; George had even applauded when

Fox had strutted in the uniform of the American rebels. But George's Whiggism was really a means of annoying his father. He supported Fox because Fox was an enemy of William Pitt and Pitt was his father's choice as premier. Politics was a game which became deadly earnest after 1793. The Prince came to the conclusion that the type of Whiggery dispensed by Fox could lead to anarchy and revolution. George had made countless promises to the Whigs but as soon as he gained any real power he told them that they could expect nothing from him and that he intended to keep his father's Tory ministers in office. As King, George came to share his father's views that the concession of the right of Roman Catholics to sit in Parliament would involve a violation of the sacred coronation oath. By the late 1820s, the Whig of the 1780s had become an ultra-Tory.

Whigs like Lord Grey never forgave this 'betrayal' of their cause, yet George was not a vicious man. Perhaps he was too worn out even by the time he became Regent for one to expect determined stands. George was a weak and vacillating ruler. He was untrustworthy because he did not like scenes, because he was lazy and because he always took the easy way out. In 1829 he appeared to accept Wellington's decision that the government must grant Catholic Emancipation and then, under pressure from the Duke of Cumberland, denied that he had ever given his consent. Even in his worst moments there was still a streak of kindness in George IV. He might be ferocious in his general pronouncements but it was a different matter when it came to individual cases. When Robert Peel became Home Secretary he was amazed to find himself being woken up at 2 a.m. with messages from the King urging him to reprieve criminals due to be executed the next morning.

George was forty-eight when he became Prince Regent. He put on great spectacles to celebrate his new power; later there were banquets and triumphal arches to celebrate the Allied victory over Napoleon and entertainments for visiting sovereigns. When it came to planning things like this, George forgot his ailments, overcame his laziness and mastered every detail. His coronation was probably the most elaborate of all time, the ultimate in regal splendour, with the new King looking like 'some gorgeous bird of paradise'. In the following year George made enormously successful state visits to Dublin and Edinburgh where he paraded up Princes Street wearing the Stuart tartan. The visit to Ireland, the most rebellious part of the United Kingdom, was a particularly bold step. There must have been something a little special about a man whose presence could make an old Irishman declare, 'I was a rebel to Old King George in '98 but, by God I would die a thousand deaths for his son.'

George was at his best on such occasions. He could behave with superb royal dignity and at least temporarily remove the bad impression his other actions created. In the days of the Regency, *The Morning Post* could still describe George as 'an Adonis of Loveliness' but the picture depended on cosmetics and corsets. The hectic style of the first two years of the reign did not last. George was an old man well before he was sixty. He did not sleep well and his remaining energy was sapped by the large doses of laudanum he took with his brandy. George became a very expensive recluse living at Windsor Castle, his mind filled with fanciful building projects rather than the affairs of state. In his declining years, the King was surrounded by a group of elderly former mistresses and dominated by his sinister doctor and confidant, Sir William Knighton. Visitors from London found the scene pathetic or just plain boring. Occasionally the King pretended that he had played a prominent part in the battle of Waterloo; no one could tell if it was a joke to annoy the Duke of Wellington or whether George IV, like his father, was going mad. It was a world of fantasy, of 'might have been'; in a way George had been a great man but the sad thing was that his last years were haunted by the realisation that he might have been – indeed should have been – very much greater.

WILLIAM IV

r. 1830–7

IT WAS NOT UNTIL AFTER THE DEATHS of Princess Charlotte in 1818 and the Duke of York in 1827 that people began to pay much attention to William Henry, Duke of Clarence. As third son of George III and Queen Charlotte, it seemed so unlikely that he would ever be King that no one attempted to teach him to behave in a regal way. Unlike George IV, William had been given a job to do. At the age of thirteen he became a midshipman in the navy. William enjoyed his life at sea and soon became a competent if rather severe officer. His tastes were those of a sailor, his language strong and his opinions forthright. William was certainly an honest man but no one could call him sophisticated. He followed his eldest brother in rebelling against their father and actually tried to become a Member of Parliament in the opposition interest. Unlike the Prince of Wales, William was not the man to wound his father by some brilliant epigram nor could he put the same intensity of bitterness into the quarrel. William was liked by most members of the royal family but the general opinion was that he was rather a fool – 'Silly Billy' was the inevitable nickname.

From 1791 to 1811 William lived in irregular but very domestic bliss with Mrs Jordan, a famous London actress. The Prince's mistress was thirty, stout and was to be the mother of a large family of Fitzclarences. Perhaps William was genuinely happy in these years but he was certainly angry that no one thought of asking him to take command of a fleet, or even a ship, throughout the long struggle against Revolutionary France. The Duke's tactlessness was frequently revealed in his speeches in the House of Lords. During a discussion on the Slave Trade he asserted: 'The promoters of abolition are either fanatics or hypocrites and in one of these classes I rank Mr Wilberforce.' The rest of the speech was drowned by cries of 'Withdraw'.

In the royal scramble to marry and produce an heir to the throne after the death of Princess Charlotte in 1818, William's prize was Adelaide of Saxe-Coburg-Meiningen, an excellent wife but plain, evangelical and much concerned with 'the end'. She must have been dull after Mrs Jordan and, unlike that prolific lady, none of her children lived more than a few hours. As he grew older, William became increasingly eccentric. In 1827 he was appointed High Admiral of England, an entirely honorific post, and caused great scandal by hoisting his standard at Plymouth and taking a squadron to sea in defiance of orders from the Admiralty. Despite his views on slavery, William was more progressive than George IV and after 1827 he was assiduously courted by the Whigs and the more liberal Tories. He was a strong supporter of Catholic Emancipation and intervened in a debate in the House of Lords to deliver a very bitter attack on the Protestant champion, Ernest, Duke of Cumberland. Opinions differed about William. Charles Grenville dismissed him as 'a mountebank bidding fair to be a maniac', but for most people in June 1830 he was an unknown quantity.

William IV heard that he was King on the morning of 26 June 1830 when Sir Henry Halford, physician to George IV, rode out to Bushey to

Opposite: A portrait of William IV by John Simpson. Apprenticed to the Royal Navy at the age of thirteen, the Duke of Clarence, nicknamed 'Silly Billy' by the royal family, had never expected to rule.

announce his master's death. William had taken care to live to this day – gargling two gallons of water every morning and wearing huge galoshes to guard against chills. The new King could scarcely contain his glee. William was an excitable man and, in the first few days, behaved extremely wildly. On the first day of his reign, this bluff, hearty-looking man of sixty-four was seen racing through London in an open carriage, grinning all over his face, frequently removing his hat to reveal his bullet-head and bowing low to any of his new subjects who appeared interested. He allowed himself to be kissed by street-walkers and was liable to stop his carriage and ask anyone who looked moderately respectable if they wanted a lift. It must have been a hideous experience for courtiers who had modelled themselves on the aloof and remote George IV. William's habit of spit-ting – frequently and copiously – when in public was considered as indicating a lack of gentility.

William's delight in his new position was summed up when he asked, 'Who is Silly Billy now?' as the Privy Council lined up to kneel before their new master. The King had been practising his new signature 'William R' for several months. There was a backlog of literally thousands of documents from the previous reign. The new monarch kept on signing 'William R' far into the night – with a basin of warm water to ease the pain of chalk stones in his hands. But William soon showed himself to be more than an amiable old fool. To the horror of his court, he insisted on the simplest of coronations. He would not hear of the new robes and vast banquets indulged in by George IV. William was adamant that his coronation would cost only a tenth of the expense incurred in 1821. When some old-fashioned peers threatened a boycott, the King replied, 'I anticipate from that greater convenience of room and less heat.' Royal economy was popular with hard-pressed tax-payers and even the King's detractors had to admit that he was received with great acclamation.

Queen Adelaide was in constant dread of revolu-tion and prayed that she would behave as well as Marie Antoinette when taken to the guillotine. William, on the other hand, looked at the future with greater confidence. A Whig government com-mitted to sweeping changes came to power in November 1830. Wellington warned the King that Lord Grey was an 'ill-tempered violent man' but William got on well with his new premier. He assured Grey that he had 'complete confidence in your integrity, judgement, decision and experience'. In April 1831 Grey asked the King to dissolve Parliament so that the Whigs could secure a larger majority to carry their proposals for Parliamentary reform. As there had been an election less than a year earlier, William could have refused and the Reform Bill of 1832 would have been postponed – perhaps very dangerously.

But William accepted Grey's request. Court offi-cials told the King that he could not go to Westminster at short notice. There would be no time for the guards to line the streets or for the royal grooms to plait the manes of the horses for the state

La Promenade en Famille. — a Sketch from Life.

Opposite: *A playbill advertising a performance starring Mrs Dora Jordan. She was an immensely successful actress.*
Above: *A Gillray cartoon from 1797 called 'La Promenade en Famille', lampooning the private life of William, Duke of Clarence. For twenty years he lived with Mrs Jordan, and she bore him several children.*

coach. William turned to Grey and said, 'My Lord, I'll go if I go in a hackney coach.' The King walked into the House of Lords, his crown on crooked, and read the speech of dissolution. He returned to the Palace through cheering crowds. 'Well done, old boy,' they cried, 'served 'em right.'

William did not long remain the hero of progressives and was soon to be accused of tricking Grey and going back on his promise to create peers to get the Reform Bill through the Lords. After his initial enthusiasm, William was finding the pace of reform rather too hot. In November 1834 he abruptly dismissed the

Whigs from office and persuaded Peel to become prime minister. The experiment failed and by the following spring he had to submit to the humiliation of asking the Whigs to return. The two politicians William most loathed were Brougham and Lord John Russell. He said of Russell, 'If you will answer for his death, I will answer for his damnation.'

The pleasures of kingship which William had so eagerly embraced were further embittered by quarrels within the royal family. The heir to the throne was the King's niece Victoria, daughter of Edward, Duke of Kent. The Duke had died in 1820 and between

*Whig supporters of Lord Grey's Reform Bill, designed to reform Parliament, attack the
Rotten Boroughs tree. William IV watches from a safe distance.*

the Duchess and the King there was much bad feeling. Victoria was not allowed to come to court because her mother said it was a hot-bed of vice. Although the King was not a man to mince his words, even in the presence of young girls, the charge was absurd. The King responded by circulating crude stories about the Duchess of Kent's relationship with Sir John Conroy, the Controller of her household. In 1836 the Duchess took over a large suite of rooms in Kensington Palace without the King's permission.

William was furious. If he died now, Victoria would be too young to rule without her mother as Regent. At a public dinner, attended by over a hundred guests, William said that he hoped his life would be spared long enough to prevent such a calamity. His wish was granted; he lived for a month after Victoria's eighteenth birthday. William IV died on 20 June 1837, muttering 'The Church, the Church' — a remark utterly out of keeping with the rest of his life.

VICTORIA

r. 1837–1901

QUEEN VICTORIA WAS BORN AT Kensington Palace in London on 24 May 1819, the daughter of Edward, Duke of Kent, and Princess Victoire, the widow of the Prince of Leiningen. The Duke of Kent was the fourth son of the reigning monarch, George III. Princess Victoire was the daughter of the Duke of Saxe-Coburg, and the sister of Leopold of Saxe-Coburg, who afterwards became King Leopold I of Belgium – Queen Victoria's uncle, to whom she turned so frequently for advice on political and other matters until his death in 1865. The Duke and Duchess of Kent wished to name their baby Victoria, but the Prince Regent – the future George IV – insisted that she be named Alexandrina after her godfather, Tsar Alexander I of Russia, and she was therefore christened Alexandrina Victoria. Her father died when she was eight months old. His three elder brothers had no surviving children, and when, on the death of George IV in 1830, the Duke of Clarence succeeded him as King William IV, Princess Victoria, at the age of eleven, became heir presumptive to the throne.

After her father's death, her mother, the Duchess of Kent, had fallen under the influence of the Controller of her household, Sir John Conroy, who was an ambitious Irish officer. Conroy was generally thought to be the Duchess's lover, and as he took complete control of her household and of Princess Victoria, it was rumoured that he was planning to become the power behind the throne in the event of William IV dying before Princess Victoria was eighteen and the Duchess of Kent becoming Regent. Conroy organised a number of 'journeys' on which the Duchess of Kent took Princess Victoria travelling in semi-regal pomp through the West Midlands and the north of England. William IV was annoyed at these tours, and took steps to curtail the honours which were to be paid to the Duchess and to Princess Victoria.

But Conroy's hopes of exercising power during a regency were disappointed. Princess Victoria reached the age of eighteen in May 1837, twenty-seven days before William IV died on 20 June; and as she disliked Conroy, and resented his control, her first act as Queen was to free herself from his influence and from her mother's. Conroy was excluded from court, to the great distress of the Duchess.

During her first years on the throne, Queen Victoria's closest confidants were her governess, the German Baroness von Lehzen, and the prime minister, Lord Melbourne. Melbourne, who was aged fifty-eight in 1837, was a Whig of the old school, whose attitude to the great campaigns for the reform of the political and social systems was summed up in the phrase which he used whenever any reform was suggested: 'Why not leave it alone?' He showed no concern over the sufferings of the poor in the mines, factories and workhouses which were causing great social unrest. A symptom of this unrest was the attempt to assassinate, or at least to assault, the Queen when she was driving in her carriage in London in 1840. Two similar attempts were made in 1842, and other attempts in 1849, 1850, 1872 and 1882.

Melbourne's charm, his perfect manners and his gallantry to the ladies had made him the centre of London society, and he developed a respectful and avuncular intimacy with the Queen. He delighted in the company and friendship of his young female sovereign; and her attitude to him is shown by such diary entries as 'Lord Melbourne rode near me the whole time', 'Lord Melbourne sat near me the whole evening', 'I am so fond of Lord Melbourne'. She accepted his opinion on all matters from politics to the comparative merits of Shakespeare's plays.

This led to a political crisis in 1839, when Melbourne resigned after a defeat in Parliament, and Queen Victoria invited Sir Robert Peel, the Conservative leader, to form a government. Peel insisted that the Queen's Whig Ladies of the Bedchamber should be replaced, in accordance with the usual practice, by Tory ladies; and when the Queen refused to agree, Peel refused to form a government, and Melbourne and the Whigs returned to office for another two years. Queen Victoria's victory was only temporary, because never again did she challenge the principle that the officers of the royal household should change with the government.

In the same year, the Queen became very unpopular as a result of the case of Lady Flora Hastings. Lady Flora, one of the Queen's ladies-in-waiting, suffered from a cancerous growth on the liver which made her appear to be pregnant, and as she was unmarried this gave rise to scandal. The Queen was very ready to believe the worst, because on one occasion Lady Flora had been seen alone in a carriage with Sir John Conroy. Lady Flora was virtually compelled, against her protests, to submit to a medical examination, which proved that she was a virgin, and a few months later she died of the cancer. Public opinion strongly condemned the conduct of the Queen and court in the affair, and Queen Victoria was hissed on the racecourse at Ascot, and greeted with shouts of 'Mrs Melbourne'.

As soon as the festivities of the coronation of June 1838 were over, the Queen's advisers considered the question of her marriage. When one of the candidates, her cousin Prince Albert of Saxe-Coburg-Gotha, visited London in 1839, the Queen fell in love with him. Prince Albert was three months younger than Queen Victoria. His father was Duke of a German state which was about the size of Worcestershire. When Prince Albert was seven years old, his father divorced his mother on a charge of adultery with an officer at his court, and she was sent to live in Switzerland on a pension and forbidden to see her children. This subsequent accusation of adultery against his mother appears to be the only real ground for the rumour which arose many years later that Prince Albert's father was not the Duke, but another officer – a Jew – with whom his mother was alleged to have had an affair. Prince Albert always remembered his mother with great affection. He did not immediately reciprocate Queen Victoria's feelings for him – perhaps he was never as deeply in love with her as she was with him – but a strong affection for her, as well as a sense of mission, made him willingly agree to marry her. The wedding took place in London in February 1840, when both bride and bridegroom were aged twenty. It was very unpopular in certain quarters. To Queen Victoria's great indignation, Parliament made difficulties about voting a suitable allowance for Prince Albert and about granting him precedence over the Queen's surviving uncles; and Radical journalists and ballad-writers jeered at the 'pauper Prince' who had come begging to England, and instead of being sent to the workhouse, like other beggars, had been given the hand of England's Queen.

The marriage was very happy. Now that the royal archives are open to inspection it is known – which no one suspected at the time – that Queen Victoria and Prince Albert sometimes quarrelled about such matters as the upbringing of the children and the influence which Baroness von Lehzen still held over the Queen. But these were unimportant incidents in a very happy relationship. They had nine children – in 1840, Victoria, the Princess Royal, who married the future Emperor of Germany, Frederick III; in 1841, Edward, Prince of Wales, the future King Edward VII; and three boys and four girls followed.

Opposite: *The coronation of the eighteen-year-old Queen Victoria in Westminster Abbey in 1838, painted by John Martin.*
Following pages: *Sir David Wilkie's 1838 painting of Queen Victoria's first Crown Council session, in Kensington Palace. Seated in front of the Victoria is Prime Minister Lord Melbourne, while the Duke of Wellington stands by the column. Victoria relied heavily upon Lord Melbourne and found it hard when his government fell in 1841.*

Prince Albert was considered to be very handsome, and his arrival had caused considerable excitement among the ladies of the court; but he showed no interest in them. His attitude had repercussions far beyond the family circle. At the beginning of the nineteenth century a great moral revival had been launched by Wilberforce and his Society for the Suppression of Vice, as part of the campaign to inculcate religion and discipline among the working classes as an antidote to the Radical and free-thinking propaganda which followed the French Revolution. At first the gambling, heavy drinking and sexual licence common in aristocratic society,continued unabated; and although the aristocracy made every attempt to present a moral face in public while they sinned in private, their vices, and those of the royal Dukes, were well known, and featured prominently in Radical propaganda. Under Queen Victoria and Prince Albert the royal family became moral, and set an example which was followed, at least to some extent, in society as well as among the middle classes. Both Queen Victoria and Prince Albert strongly disapproved of any sexual misconduct, especially if practised by their sons or ministers, though they reacted differently. Queen Victoria sadly resigned herself to the fact that men have love affairs; but Prince Albert reacted with almost hysterical indignation when he heard that his son the Prince of Wales had had an affair with an actress, or that the Foreign Secretary, Lord Palmerston, had tried to enter the bedroom of one of the ladies-in-waiting in the middle of the night at Windsor Castle.

Albert also influenced Victoria's attitude towards social problems. Her first mentor, the Whig Lord Melbourne, had advised her not to read Charles Dickens's *Oliver Twist* because it dealt with paupers, criminals and other unpleasant subjects with which she should not be troubled; but Albert invited Lord Ashley – later Lord Shaftesbury – to the palace and told him how moved he and the Queen had been at Ashley's revelations in Parliament about the sufferings of the children who worked in the mines. Ashley invited Prince Albert to preside at meetings of the committee of the Labourer's Friend Society; and when, despite all the apprehensions of the government and court, Prince Albert attended the meeting and delighted the other members of the committee by his interest, Ashley noted that this was the way to defeat the Chartists and the socialists. As well as showing interest in plans for model workers' houses and the relief of poverty, Prince Albert interested himself in projects for the encouragement of trade and industry. His most ambitious venture in this field was the Great International Exhibition of 1851, for which he was chiefly responsible. It encountered considerable opposition, both from those who objected to the felling of the trees in Hyde Park and the interference with the riding in Rotten Row, and from patriots who resented the influx of foreigners into Britain; but it was a great success.

The fall of Melbourne's government in 1841 brought the Tories to power. The Queen was very distressed to lose Melbourne, and said so frankly to her new prime minister, Peel; but she soon abandoned her practice of writing to Melbourne about state affairs, and partly thanks to Prince Albert's influence she came to have a high regard for Peel. She supported the policy of Peel's Foreign Secretary, Lord Aberdeen, of a diplomatic *rapprochement* with France, and played her part in it when she visited the French King, Louis Philippe, at the Château d'Eu at Tréport in 1843, this being the first time that a reigning English sovereign had met a foreign sovereign since the reign of Henry VIII. In the following year King Louis Philippe paid a return visit to England. In the next decade Queen Victoria similarly exchanged state visits with the French Emperor, Napoleon III.

When the Whigs returned to power in 1846, with Lord John Russell as prime minister and Palmerston as Foreign Secretary, the Queen and Prince Albert

Opposite: *The handsome and morally upstanding Prince Albert, Victoria's beloved Prince Consort, in a portrait from the studio of Franz Xavier Winterhalter. Their marriage was a long and happy one, and Victoria never really recovered from his death.*

soon came into conflict with Palmerston. The first clash came in connection with the civil war in Portugal in 1846–7. and more serious disagreements arose during and after the revolutions which broke out in so many countries of Europe in 1848. Palmerston, who had begun his political career as a junior minister in a Tory government, had not basically changed his political opinions at the age of sixty; he was still profoundly conservative, anti-revolutionary and anti-democratic. But he was convinced of the superiority of the British system of constitutional monarchy over the absolutist monarchies of the continent; he was eager to embarrass and weaken foreign governments in order to improve the relative position of Britain; and he was playing for Radical support in British home politics. He therefore gave moral support to revolutionary Liberal, and even Radical, movements throughout Europe. Queen Victoria and Prince Albert, on the other hand, believed in solidarity with the sovereigns of Europe, many of whom were their friends and relations, and favoured a policy of preserving peace and avoiding revolution by international co-operation between rulers. They were too logical, broad-minded and cosmopolitan to share the attitude of Whigs like Russell and Palmerston, who, on hearing that the Austrian military authorities had flogged rebellious patriots in Italy and Hungary, could exclaim in all sincerity, 'The Austrians are really the greatest brutes that ever called themselves by the undeserved name of civilised men', almost on the same day on which they themselves authorised the wholesale flogging of peasants who had risen in revolt against British rule in the Ionian Isles. Queen Victoria and Prince Albert could not see what right the British government had to protest against the suppression of revolution in the territories of foreign kings who had never protested to Britain against the suppression of revolution in Ireland or the sentences passed on Chartist rioters. They did not share the enthusiasm of nearly the whole of the British people for Garibaldi; and when Garibaldi visited England in 1864, Queen Victoria was indignant that aristocrats and society hostesses should acclaim and fall in love with a revolutionary Radical. 'Brave and honest though he is,' she logically commented, 'he has ever been a revolutionist leader.'

The Queen, with Prince Albert acting as her private secretary, insisted on her constitutional right to have all Palmerston's despatches to foreign governments submitted to her before they were sent off. She and Prince Albert often altered Palmerston's text, in order to delete or soften the most provocative passages. Palmerston therefore sometimes sent off despatches without submitting them to the Queen. In the summer of 1850 Queen Victoria and Prince Albert asked Lord John Russell to dismiss Palmerston from the Foreign Office. Russell told them that this was impossible because of Palmerston's great popularity in the House of Commons and in the country; but the Queen and Prince bided their time. In December 1851 Palmerston for once made a move which was unpopular with the majority of Englishmen, especially his Radical supporters, by congratulating Louis Napoleon Bonaparte – the future Emperor Napoleon III – on his *coup d'état* in France. Queen Victoria and Prince Albert seized their chance, and persuaded Russell to dismiss Palmerston from the Foreign Office. Within six weeks Palmerston had brought down Russell's government in the House of Commons, and a year after he left the Foreign Office he returned to office as Home Secretary in Lord Aberdeen's coalition government.

In 1854 the Crimean War broke out – the first major European war for forty years – when Britain and France declared war on Russia in support of Turkey. For nearly a year before the declaration of war, the prime minister, Lord Aberdeen, tried to avoid war by pursuing a conciliatory policy; Palmerston, in the Cabinet, urged a tougher policy which he believed was the only way of deterring the Russians from attacking Turkey. Prince Albert

Opposite: *The Great International Exhibition, which took place in Hyde Park in 1851, was one of Prince Albert's most ambitious and most successful projects. The Prince Consort was deeply interested in the arts, manufacture and commerce as well as in social issues.*

been inevitable, but that as despatches took a month to travel between London and Washington, there was time for passions to cool. At the height of the crisis the Prince Consort, though seriously ill, rose from his bed to alter the wording of a draft despatch from the British government to the United States so as to make it less provocative, and to make it easier for the US government to accept the British demands. The US gave way and released the two envoys, and thus avoided a war between Britain and the United States which might have altered the future course of history.

Queen Victoria was prostrated by Prince Albert's death. It was an accepted convention at the time that widows should display their grief and show signs of mourning in a way which would seem morbid today; but the Queen's reaction seemed excessive even by the standards of 1861. She withdrew into complete seclusion, and refused all her ministers' requests that she should open Parliament in person and show herself at least occasionally to her subjects, though throughout this period, from the very first days after Prince Albert's death, she insisted on reading all the diplomatic despatches and on carrying out her constitutional duties in the privacy of her closet. She spent much time in the Scottish Highlands at her house at Balmoral, which she and Prince Albert had acquired in 1847 and where they had spent happy times together.

It was during the decade after Prince Albert's death that Queen Victoria came under the influence of John Brown, a Scottish servant. Brown's blunt manner and kindly concern pleased the Queen, who did not resent it when he addressed her as 'woman' as he put a scarf around her shoulders to keep her warm or bullied her into taking care of her health. Queen Victoria believed, as Prince Albert had done, that the working class, who showed their loyalty to the throne without observing the accepted conventions of court etiquette, were far more worthy than the arrogant and often immoral aristocracy with whom, to her regret, her son the Prince of Wales associated. Her ideal of government was a benevolent sovereign ruling constitutionally over a contented and loyal people; and she thought that this ideal was thwarted both by a selfish, pleasure-loving aristocracy and by Radical agitators with their belief in democracy.

The Queen's friendship with Brown caused resentment among her family and courtiers, and stories spread in society, and were published in foreign newspapers, that the Queen had secretly married Brown. References to 'Mrs Brown', meaning the Queen, were common at society dinner tables in London. The Queen's isolation was resented. Radical spokesmen publicly stated that she was not earning the money that the state paid her, and some of them, especially the prominent Liberal politician Sir Charles Dilke, spoke in favour of abolishing the monarchy and replacing it with a republic. The campaign for a republic caused some stir in 1871, but soon died out.

The last thirty-five years of Queen Victoria's reign were a period of struggle between the new Liberal Party and the Conservatives. The forces of Liberalism were led by William Ewart Gladstone, who had begun his political life as a Tory, but at the age of fifty, when he was Chancellor of the Exchequer in Palmerston's government, had developed Liberal and almost Radical ideas which aroused his prime minister's opposition and alarm. Queen Victoria's relations with Gladstone were worse than with any of her other prime ministers. His sincere devotion to the throne and to the Queen as a woman was expressed in a pompous and impersonal way, and although he was very eager to win her approval, he failed completely to do so. As in the case of her hostility to Palmerston in earlier years, her personal dislike of Gladstone was not as important a factor as her political opposition to the cause which he represented. On the great issues which dominated British politics in the last quarter of the nineteenth century – the extension of the Parliamentary franchise, the limitation of the power of the House of Lords, social reform, home rule for Ireland, and the new, aggressive

Opposite: *Victoria accompanied by Benjamin Disraeli, her favourite prime minister.*
As a result of his influence, Parliament voted to grant the Queen the title of Empress of India, which
pleased her greatly.

Opposite: *Victoria, photographed in 1880 with her youngest child, Princess Beatrice,*
aged twenty-three. Before the birth of Prince Andrew in 1960 Beatrice was the last child born to a
reigning British monarch.
Above: *Celebrations in Bombay to mark Victoria's Golden Jubilee in 1887. A triumphal arch was*
raised, together with a statue of the Empress. Victoria was genuinely popular in India and took her
responsibilities to her Indian subjects seriously.

Conservative imperialist policy abroad – Queen Victoria strongly sympathised with the Conservatives and disapproved of Gladstone and the Liberals.

In 1868 Benjamin Disraeli became prime minister, and though he held office for only nine months, he established a very close relationship with the Queen which became more intimate after he returned to office in 1874 for his second term as premier, which lasted for six years. He told a friend:

'Everyone likes flattery, and when you come to royalty, you should lay it on with a trowel.' He spoke and wrote to the Queen in the most exaggerated and fulsome language; but it was not too exaggerated or fulsome for Queen Victoria's liking. She became genuinely attached to Disraeli, paid him the signal honour of visiting him in his private house in the country, and was deeply unhappy when he fell from power in 1880. When he died in the next year, she wrote to his private secretary: 'Dear Lord Rowton, I cannot write in the third person at this terrible moment when I can scarcely see for my fast falling tears.'

Disraeli gratified the Queen in 1876 by persuading Parliament to agree to grant her the title of Empress of India. Queen Victoria relished the title, and showed great interest in her Indian Empire. At the time of the Indian Mutiny in 1857 she had been one of the very few people in Britain who did not join in the clamour for indiscriminate slaughter of Indians in revenge for the murder of British women and children at Cawnpore and elsewhere; and she and Prince Albert supported the Governor-General of India, Lord Canning, when he aroused a storm of indignation in Britain and among the British residents in   India by his proclamation in which he urged the commanders in the field to show some restraint in the number of executions. The Queen was very conscious of her duties to her Indian subjects, and here, as in Britain, she believed in her ideal of paternalistic government. She always expressed her indignation when she encountered signs of racial prejudice by British officials in India. In the last years of her life she angered her courtiers by her intimate friendship with an Indian servant; and her disapproval of the attitude of the Boers towards the blacks in South Africa was another reason for her patriotic and belligerent attitude during the Boer War.

It was during Disraeli's second term of office that the Queen developed her deep dislike of Gladstone, with whom she had been on reasonably good terms during Gladstone's first premiership in 1868–74. She strongly approved of Disraeli's imperialist foreign policy and his support of Turkey against Russia during the Russo-Turkish war of 1876–7, and she applauded his success at the Congress of Berlin in 1878, when he thwarted Russia's plan to liberate the Balkan provinces of Turkey. This policy, which involved supporting the Sultan's oppressive regime in the Balkans against the Christians in Bulgaria and Herzegovina who were fighting for their freedom, outraged the feelings of Gladstone and the 'Nonconformist conscience' of his Liberal supporters. Gladstone and the Liberals proclaimed that England, in her foreign policy, must never support a cause which was morally wrong; Disraeli proudly

claimed that his foreign policy was 'as selfish as patriotism'. The Queen thought Gladstone and his followers were not merely misguided, but traitors to their country.

During Gladstone's last three terms as premier – in 1880–85, 1886 and 1892–4 – his relations with the Queen, to his great regret, were very strained. On most occasions her conduct was correct and courteous, but there were occasions when she administered personal slights and incivilities, and she privately passed on confidential documents of Gladstone's government to the Conservative Leader of the Opposition, Lord Salisbury. In 1885 she administered a public rebuke to Gladstone when she sent him an uncoded telegram – which was delivered to him by a local station-master, and became public knowledge – in which she condemned his government for not acting sufficiently promptly and energetically to relieve General Gordon at Khartoum, after she and the great majority of her subjects had been shocked by the news of Gordon's death at the hands of the Mahdi's nationalist rebels in the Sudan.

The Queen's Conservative and imperialist views coincided with those of a substantial proportion – at most times a majority – of the British people and a Conservative government under Lord Salisbury was in power during twelve of the last fifteen years of her reign. Her former unpopularity disappeared, and she was revered and almost worshipped by the public. Her Jubilee on the fiftieth anniversary of her accession in 1887 was the occasion for great national celebrations. On 23 September 1896 she noted in her diary that she had reigned one day longer than George III or any previous English sovereign; and on 20 June 1897 her Diamond Jubilee was celebrated amid scenes of enthusiasm which completely eclipsed those of ten years earlier, and which culminated in the Queen's visit to St Paul's Cathedral in London on 22 June, when she was cheered by a vast crowd. 'I was much moved and gratified', wrote the Queen.

During her remaining years, Britain engaged in the last of the many wars of the Victorian era. General Kitchener's success in destroying the Mahdi's successor and avenging Gordon in the Sudan in 1898, and his diplomatic triumph over the French at Fashoda, had delighted the Queen; and she

Contemporary collage of Victoria with the two succeding queens: Alexandra (Edward VII), and Mary (George V).

enthusiastically supported the Boer War in 1899. Although dis-tressed by the British defeats in South Africa in the opening stages of the war, she refused to permit any defeatist talk at court. 'In this house', she declared, 'we are not interested in the possibilities of defeat; they do not exist.' Before her death, the tide had definitely turned in favour of Britain in South Africa, after the relief of Mafeking and Ladysmith in the summer of 1900.

Queen Victoria died at her house at Osborne in the Isle of Wight, after a short illness, on 22 January 1901, at the age of eighty-one. None of the court officials had any personal experience of the measures which were to be taken at the death of a sovereign and the accession of a new king, and her death caused consternation among nearly all her subjects, as no one under the age of seventy could remember living under another monarch.

THE HOUSE OF SAXE-COBURG-GOTHA

1901–10

EDWARD VII 1901–10

Opposite: Four generations of the monarchy. From left to right:
Prince George, Duke of York (later George V), Queen Victoria,
Prince Edward, Duke of Windsor (later Edward VIII) and
Edward, Prince of Wales (later Edward VII).

EDWARD VII
r. 1901–10

PRINCE ALBERT EDWARD, the future King Edward VII, was born at St James's Palace in London on 9 November 1841, the second child and eldest son of Queen Victoria and Prince Albert. The title of Prince of Wales was conferred on him when he was twenty-five days old. His father had clear ideas as to the education and training which were necessary for a future king; above all, he wished to prevent him from reverting to the pleasure-loving and immoral life of George IV and Queen Victoria's other uncles. He provided him with a number of suitable tutors, and gave them precise instructions as to how they should perform their duties. The tutors themselves considered that the regimen was too strict, and that the child was likely to go to the bad under the pressure to which he was subjected; and the constant moral exhortation was combined with a lack of parental affection, because the Queen and Prince Albert were convinced that their eldest son 'Bertie' had no intelligence or gifts of application.

It was perhaps because of this pressure and this lack of affection that the Prince of Wales, as a child, often indulged in outbursts of rage which alarmed his tutors as well as his parents. As a boy he showed a lack of consideration, and even signs of cruelty, which gave some cause for alarm. Prince Albert, although he impressed upon him that a gentleman should show consideration for the feelings of his inferiors and servants, was distressed to find that at the age of seventeen he tormented his valet by pouring wax over his new livery, water on his clean linen, and

by rapping him on the nose. The Prince of Wales soon abandoned behaviour of this kind, and in later life showed a warm-hearted loyalty to his friends and consideration for his servants. His natural assertiveness manifested itself in such harmless ways as blaming his partner when he lost at bridge or ordering the replanning of a golf course when he did badly at the game, and sometimes in making caustic remarks about his friends' style of dress.

The Prince of Wales performed his first important public duty at the age of eighteen, when the Queen and her government agreed, with some misgivings, to send him on a state visit to Canada and the United States in 1860. The idea of sending a member of the British royal family to the United States was indeed a novelty, because the United States was generally regarded in Britain as a land of dangerous republicans and democrats. But the Prince's visit was a great success. He endeared himself to the American people by visiting George Washington's grave in Virginia, and by his charm at the balls and receptions in Washington, where it was noticed that he showed a great interest in pretty girls.

This interest involved him in an unfortunate incident soon after his return to Britain. When he was nineteen, in 1861, he was sent on manoeuvres with the army at the Curragh in Ireland. Some of his brother-officers arranged for an actress to be smuggled into his tent one night. In due course the news of the incident reached his mother and father. Prince Albert reacted violently, though he respected the Prince of Wales for his refusal to name the officers

Opposite: A king in waiting: Edward, Prince of Wales, looks particularly dashing in the astrakhan fur trim and frogging of his dragoon uniform. He was renowned for his easy manners, love of society and sense of style.

Above: Alexandra, wife of Edward VII, in her coronation robes with her six pages, pictured on the day of the coronation itself – 9 August 1902.
Opposite: Lily Langtry, the actress, was perhaps the best known of Edward's many British and European mistresses.

responsible. Prince Albert died a few weeks later. Queen Victoria believed that his grief at 'Bertie's' misconduct at the Curragh had shortened his life, and she declared that she would never be able to look at 'that boy' without a shudder.

In 1863 the Prince of Wales married Princess Alexandra of Denmark. Queen Victoria was charmed by Princess Alexandra's beauty and her respectful affection; but the marriage led to political differences between the Queen and the Prince of Wales. When Prussia and Austria went to war with Denmark in 1864 over Schleswig-Holstein, Queen Victoria's sympathies were with the German states; but the Prince of Wales supported his wife's nation, as did Palmerston and Russell, the prime minister and

Foreign Secretary, and most of the British people. The Prince of Wales gave further offence to his mother in the same year by visiting Garibaldi when the Italian revolutionary general came to England, and, to the Queen's indignation, was enthusiastically welcomed in London by the people and by society alike. Queen Victoria sternly reprimanded the Prince of Wales, who defended his conduct and insisted on taking the responsibility on himself when Queen Victoria blamed his Controller, General Knollys, for having arranged the interview with Garibaldi.

For the remaining thirty-seven years of Queen Victoria's reign, the Prince of Wales played his part in public life. The Queen refused to agree to the suggestion made by several of her ministers that he should be permitted to see the state papers; nor would she accept the offers he made from time to time to visit some foreign sovereign or statesman in an attempt to help reach a settlement of an international crisis. But he increasingly performed the duties of opening bridges and public buildings, which now for the first time in history became one of the functions of the royal family. He also paid many state visits to European countries, including Russia; and in 1875–6 he spent four months in India. His chief interest, however, was the pursuit of pleasure. His life was a round of visits to large country houses, with shooting, gambling and attendance at race-meetings, followed by weeks in London with parties and banquets, and frequent visits abroad to Paris, the French Riviera and Marienbad in Bohemia. He did not indulge in heavy drinking, but ate five large meals every day, eating ten or more courses at some of them; and he smoked twelve large cigars and twenty cigarettes a day. By the time he was middle-aged he was fat, being forty-eight inches round the waist.

His way of life did not please the Queen. She tried unsuccessfully to convince him that a pleasure-loving and immoral aristocracy provoked the loyal working classes into adopting Radical and democratic ideas. The Prince of Wales replied that the landed aristocracy was an essential bulwark of society, and that as long as they performed their public duties – for example, by acting as Lord Lieutenants of the counties – they should not be denied their pleasures. But the Prince's friends were not all members of the landed aristocracy; they included Jewish bankers and other businessmen – in fact, almost anyone who was rich enough to entertain on the scale which the Prince demanded at the house-parties which he attended and to provide the large quantity of game which was needed for a big shoot. His interest in people and his charm of manner led him to seek and obtain the friendship of outstanding individuals of all types and classes. He met the Labour leader, Joseph Arch, the founder of the National Agricultural Labourers' Union, and invited the working-class MP Henry Broadhurst to stay at his country house at Sandringham in Norfolk, though as Broadhurst did not possess evening dress, dinner was served to him in his private room in order to save

him embarrassment. In Paris, the Prince of Wales became very friendly with General the Marquis de Gallifet, who had aroused the hatred of the French left wing by his wholesale executions during the suppression of the Paris Commune of 1871, as well as with the Radical politician, Gambetta; and he accomplished the seemingly impossible task of persuading Gallifet and Gambetta to meet each other when they lunched with him at the Café Anglais. He loved company, and could not bear to be alone. It was said of him that he liked men better than books, and women better than either.

His love of the company of beautiful women was a great contrast to the attitude of his father, and caused both his mother and many of her subjects to fear that the future sovereign was reverting to the habits of the Regency. He was on terms of intimate friendship with a number of beautiful British and continental women – actresses like Lillie Langtry in London and Hortense Schneider in Paris, and French and English society beauties like the Princesse de

THE HOUSES OF SAXE-COBURG-GOTHA AND WINDSOR

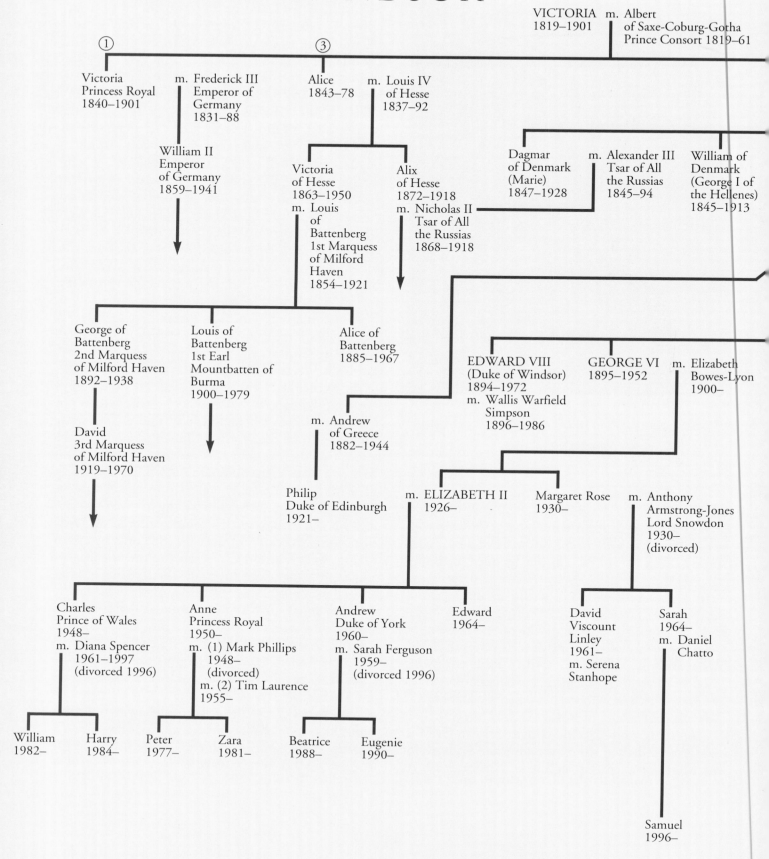

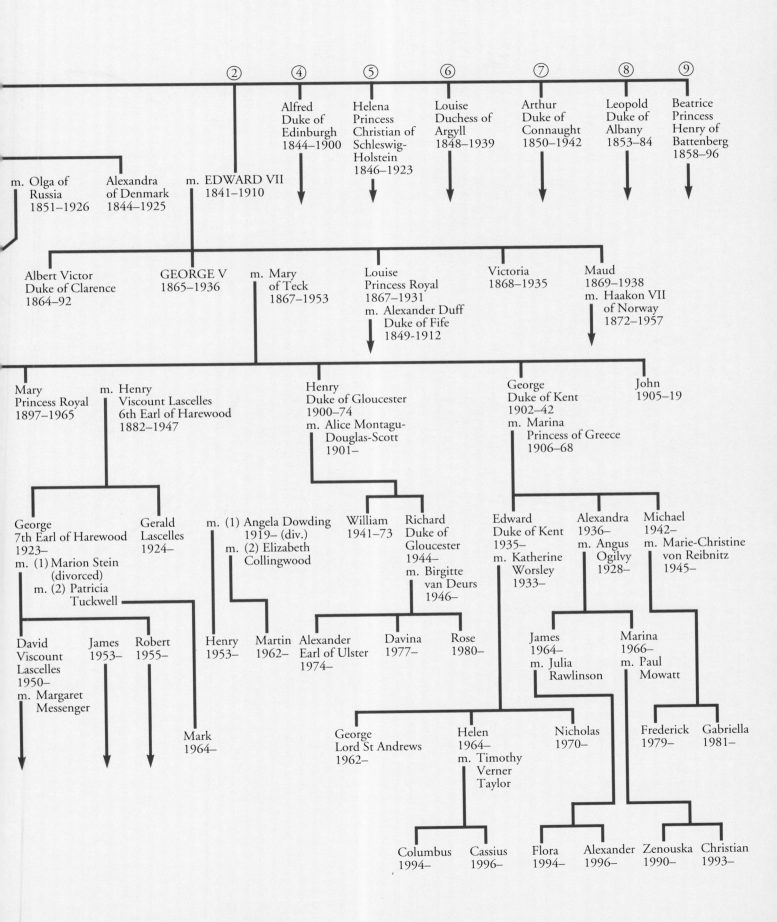

Victoria Mary

George

*In Commemoration of the Visit
of Their Royal Highnesses the Prince and Princess of Wales to India. 1905-1906.*

*Dedicated by Special Permission to H.R.H. the Prince of Wales
by His Royal Highness' most obedient Servants*

Raphael Tuck & Sons

THE HOUSE OF WINDSOR
1910–

GEORGE V 1910–36

EDWARD VIII 1936

GEORGE VI 1936–52

ELIZABETH II 1952–

Opposite: A card commemorating the visit of George,
Prince of Wales, to India in 1905–6.

GEORGE V

r. 1910–36

ON 17 JULY 1917, THE Privy Council proclaimed that henceforth the royal family would be called the House of Windsor, having divested itself of its previous surname, as well as 'all other German degrees, styles, titles, dignatories, honours and appelations'. After a number of alternatives were considered – including Plantagenet, York, England, Lancaster, D'Este and Fitzroy – George v's Private Secretary Lord Stamfordham's suggestion of Windsor was adopted, after a minor title once held by Edward III.

This anti-German gesture, made at a critical juncture of the First World War, produced one of Kaiser William II's few jokes, when he remarked with heavy Teutonic humour that he looked forward to attending a performance of 'The Merry Wives of Saxe-Coburg-Gotha'. A more serious and altogether grander criticism came from the Bavarian Count Albrecht von Montgelas, who observed that 'the true royal tradition died on that day in 1917 when, for a mere war, King George v changed his name'. In fact the College of Arms could not even determine whether the royal surname had originally been Guelph, Wettin or Saxe-Coburg-Gotha in the first place.

The effect in Britain was instantaneous and overwhelmingly positive. With the whole family swapping Germanic-sounding for overtly British names – the Teck family became the Cambridges and took the earldom of Athlone, the Battenbergs were transformed into Mountbattens with the marquisate of Milford Haven – the royal family proclaimed itself thoroughly British, to national applause. Despite the whispering campaign against some members of his family that they were pro-German, King George v had always been quintessentially British, finding German 'a rotten language'. When H. G. Wells criticised 'an alien and uninspiring court', the King retorted, 'I may be uninspiring, but I'll be damned if I'm an alien.'

Born at Marlborough House on 3 June 1865, Prince George Frederick Ernest Albert was not expected to succeed to the throne, and had a happier, less pressured childhood as a result. His elder brother, Prince Albert Victor, Duke of Clarence – known as 'Eddy' – was a dissolute youth, who took after their father the future Edward VII in flouting the social and sexual mores of the day, in a way which the conscientious, dutiful and genuinely Christian young Prince George never did. In a dynasty long plagued by bad parent–child relationships, however, Prince George's love of and utter devotion to his father – which was fully reciprocated – was a refreshing exception to the rule.

The greatest influence on the Prince's personality was not, however, his uniformly happy childhood, so much as his fifteen years of hardy service in the Royal Navy. Joining HMS *Britannia* as a naval cadet in 1877, Prince George soon showed genuine accomplishments in a profession which was watching closely for the smallest sign of nepotism. He became Britain's most widely-travelled king, serving in the West Indies, South America, Australia, Japan, South Africa and China in various vessels, sometimes experiencing serious danger.

This period aboard ship gave him a disciplined,

Opposite: *King George V and Queen Mary in the summer 1914 edition of the* Illustrated London News. *Their marriage of mutual affection was one of the most successful modern royal unions.*

ultra-conservative outlook, a bluff manner, a certain saltiness of language, a commonsensical attitude and a profound belief in the ideals of the British Empire, all of which were to stay with him throughout his life. In 1885, by then promoted to First Lieutenant after a period on the North America Station in the corvette HMS *Canada*, Prince George won a first class in seamanship, gunnery and torpedos from the Royal Naval College at Greenwich, a justifiable source of pride to him. Afterwards he served for three years on the Mediterranean Station before acquiring his own command, of the gunboat HMS *Thrush* in 1890.

It was whilst as a commander, on illness furlough, that he heard of the death from pneumonia of his elder brother on 14 January 1892. This meant a complete alteration of every aspect of his existence, from being a well-connected officer destined for future well-earned naval commands, to being heir apparent to the heir apparent to the throne of the largest empire the world had ever seen. His nautical career over, he was created Duke of York and given residences in York House in St James's Palace as well as York Cottage near Sandringham House.

A few weeks before his very premature death at twenty-six, his brother had got engaged to Princess Victoria Mary of Teck, known in the family as May. Rather than allow this demure, sensible and bright girl out of the family, Queen Victoria acted decisively to arrange that the Duke of York carry on the suit. Thus a country which was at that time obsessed with the proprieties of men marrying their deceased wife's sister, on 6 July 1893 enthusiastically celebrated the Duke of York's marriage to his deceased brother's fiancée.

The wedding took place in St James's Chapel, and was attended by the crowned and soon-to-be crowned heads of Europe, including Queen Victoria, the King of Denmark and the Tsarevich of Russia, the future Nicholas 11. It turned out to be one of the most successful royal marriages of modern times, a genuine love match in which Princess, later Queen, Mary's qualities complemented her husband's and provided him with a source of sound advice distinct from that proffered by politicians and courtiers. Queen Mary proved the personification of royal rectitude, an impossibly grand, even terrifying figure

who yet also provided genuine domestic tranquillity for her husband, and thus rescued the popular conception of royal family life from its louche Edwardian image.

Children followed with impressive rapidity and regularity. Prince Edward (later King Edward VIII) was born in 1894, Prince Albert (later King George VI) in 1895, Princess Mary in 1897, Prince Henry (later Duke of Gloucester) in 1900, Prince George (later Duke of Kent) in 1902 and Prince John (an epileptic who died aged only thirteen) in 1905. Although in his memoirs the Duke of Windsor was keen to present his parents as stern, somewhat heartless disciplinarians – a myth which has endured to this day and has been greatly exaggerated in the retelling – the King and Queen should be judged by the exacting standards of the Victorian upper classes rather than by today's more indulgent child-rearing mores. The problems they had with the wayward Prince Edward were largely his own fault, and his accusations of parental harshness can usually be traced back to the Duke of Windsor's attempts to excuse his subsequent behaviour.

On the death of Queen Victoria on 22 January 1901, and the accession of his father as Edward VII, the Duke of York became Duke of Cornwall as well, and took a major step towards the throne of the King–Emperor. He got closer to the King in a physical sense also, as his desk was moved beside his father's at Buckingham Palace so they could work side by side whenever they were in London. Unlike his mother Queen Victoria, who had deliberately kept her heir starved of official papers, Edward VII ensured that his son saw all important state documents. To help him with them, the Duke – who in November 1901 became Prince of Wales – inherited Sir Arthur Bigge, later Lord Stamfordham, as his Private Secretary from Queen Victoria. This counsellor, suffused in wisdom and experience, was also to become a trusted friend until his death, still in the job, in 1931.

In the nine years of the Edwardian era, the Prince of Wales enjoyed himself to the full, but was always heavily conscious of the burden which would eventually fall on him. Although a competition-standard golfer and tennis player, it was in yachting and

George V rides behind the body of his father at the King's funeral in 1910. He is flanked by, on the left, his cousin Kaiser Wilhelm of Germany and, on the right, his uncle the Duke of Connaught.

shooting that he really excelled. One of the finest half-dozen shots in the country, he and six other guns once bagged 10,000 birds in four days at Sandringham. A keen yachtsman, he won racing cups at Cowes and established his right to be nicknamed 'the Sailor King' alongside William IV. More sedentary was his passion for stamp-collecting, where he built up the world's greatest collection – over 250,000 specimens housed in 325 big volumes. In his near-obsessional interest in uniforms and decorations he followed the family tradition, but he could also be sartorially innovative – the creases in his trousers were found at the sides, for example, and he pulled his tie through a ring rather than knotting it.

The most important aspect of his time as Prince of Wales and his father's understudy, during which he dutifully attended many House of Lords debates, was his commitment to the Empire; he believed in it implicitly as the foremost global agency for promoting peace and human progress. On their 231-day tour of Australia, New Zealand and Canada in 1901, he and the Princess travelled 45,000 miles, received 544 addresses, laid a score of foundation stones and shook hands with no less than 24,855 people. On his return he delivered a widely reported speech at the Guildhall on 5 December 1901, in which he said that 'the Old Country must wake up if she intends to maintain her old position of pre-eminence in her Colonial trade against foreign competitors'.

'At 11.45 beloved Papa passed peacefully away', the new King-Emperor George V wrote in his diary on 6 May 1910, 'and I have lost my best friend and

H.M. THE KING AS A YACHTSMAN

the best of fathers.' The moment he had been both dreading and preparing for over the seventeen years since his brother's death had come. The mantle of imperial responsibility had fallen upon a Norfolk squire of nearly forty-five, with deeply conservative views, few intellectual or artistic interests, little oratorical ability, but a passionate desire to do his duty.

The pre-Great War era, now often seen as a tranquil, even lazy period of cucumber sandwiches and croquet on well-cut lawns, was in fact an extremely uncertain and worrying time for those concerned with defending the social order. Forces such as organised labour, Irish republicanism, Indian nationalism, foreign protectionism, militant suffragettes and anarchist revolutionaries – let alone the High Seas Fleet of the Imperial German Navy – now seemed to threaten British policy-makers in a way their nineteenth-century parents and grandparents hardly contemplated. The period between George v's accession in May 1910 and the outbreak of the Great War in August four years later saw a succession of crises which the King generally tried to avert by conciliation and appeasement.

The reign started off on this note when on 16 November 1910 the Liberal prime minister Herbert Asquith and his Leader of the House of Lords the Marquis of Crewe extracted a secret 'hypothetical understanding' from George v that in the event of the Liberals winning the forthcoming general election – the second that year – the King would sanction the creation of possibly hundreds of new Liberal peers, enough to defeat dogged Unionist resistance and pass a Parliament Bill restricting the powers of the House of Lords. The Parliamentary guerrilla warfare had been going on since the Unionist peers had flung out Lloyd George's 'People's' Budget the previous year. The ultra-Tory Stamfordham advised resistance to Asquith's demands; this would have placed the King in the highly invidious position of appearing to support the Unionists in an election, but his master cleaved

instead to the view of his other private secretary, his father's former adviser the more Liberal-minded Lord Knollys, who counselled surrender to the duly constituted government's demands.

By making public, in a debate on 10 August 1911, the agreement which the King had regarded as secret, the Liberal government managed to browbeat the Unionists into surrender. It took the King a long time to forgive Asquith; even twenty-one years later he told Lord Crewe that he regarded 'forcing my hand' as sheer bullying of a fledgling monarch, 'the dirtiest thing ever done . . . a dirty, low-down trick'. It was the implication in asking for a formal promise that he could not be trusted to do the right thing should the constitutional moment arise which the King most resented, and it served to confirm his generally low view of politicians.

Politics took a back seat in the great coronation celebrations of 22 June 1911. These were accompanied by the magnificent Spithead Review, in which the King proudly sailed around the greatest fleet ever assembled in human history. He then travelled to Delhi where at a huge Durbar he presented himself as King-Emperor to the teeming millions in the newly-declared capital of the greatest of his dominions and took the oaths of allegiance from all the Indian princes.

On his return he found a smouldering situation in Ireland, where the Ulster Unionists were resolving to repudiate the Irish Home Rule Bill, by force if necessary. After the Bill was thrown out by the House of Lords, and Ulstermen began armed drilling in public, the King made serious behind-the-scenes efforts to resolve the situation peacefully. The senior figures on all sides were invited to a Round Table Conference at Buckingham Palace in July 1914, where they failed to agree, and anyhow soon found that events on the continent were overshadowing their deliberations.

For on 4 August 1914 the First World War broke out, and the King faced the greatest challenge of any

Opposite: George V, 'the Sailor King', is featured on a magazine cover at the helm of his famous yacht Britannia. His abiding love of the sea dated from his time in the Royal Navy as a young man.

Above: *At the Second Army Headquarters in Blendecques, George V awards Second
Lieutenant Knox with the Victoria Cross on 5 August 1918.*
Opposite: *The King encourages a young war worker in Sunderland, during one of his many tours
to boost morale during the war.*

monarch since George III had presided over the Seven Years' War a century and a half previously. 'I cannot share your hardships,' the King told the troops in the trenches, 'but my heart is with you every hour of the day.' In the course of the conflict the King made numerous morale-boosting visits to the Fleet and Army, field hospitals, factories and almost every other part of the war effort. He distributed over 58,000 decorations. He supported Earl Haig against Lloyd George, on the grounds that the soldier on the spot probably understood the situation better than the man in Whitehall, with results which

are still subject to historical debate today, albeit one which increasingly seems to be going Haig and George V's way. In October 1915 he broke his pelvis falling from a horse whilst on an inspection of the Royal Flying Corps on the Western Front, which, once misdiagnosed, gave him great pain.

The King and Queen Mary abjured alcohol for the duration of the war, in a largely vain attempt to set an example to the munition workers. It was Lloyd George's idea, and one the King was understandably reluctant about and found 'a great bore'. Nevertheless it helped to dispel the unpleasant but persistent

rumour that he was an alcoholic. (Similarly a myth that he was a bigamist who had contracted a marriage with an admiral's daughter whilst on service in Malta had been scotched in 1911 when a newspaper editor, E. F. Mylius, was imprisoned for twelve months for criminal libel.)

Only on one occasion during the war did the royal nerve break, when as a result of a ludicrously overblown fear of domestic republicanism – at a time when millions were under arms fighting for King and Country – George v countermanded Lloyd George's March 1917 attempt to give his deposed cousin Tsar Nicholas 11 political asylum in Britain. Fearing that it might inflame a socialist and republican outcry amongst the industrial working classes should he send a British battleship to bring over the Tsar, the King effectively condemned 'cousin Nicky' to remain in Russia, with consequences few could have foreseen at the time, months before the Bolshevik revolution.

Rarely smiling – 'Sailors on duty don't smile' – but giving an admired national lead, the King never attempted to grab the limelight from politicians during the war, still less from the Services. The British people seemed to sense this, and when the day of victory finally came on 11 November 1918 – 'the greatest in the history of the country', wrote the King in his diary – it was to Buckingham Palace that they flocked to celebrate all night, the royal family waving from the balcony of the façade which he had had refaced in 1912. With peace came an end to his love of travel. In the eighteen years left of his reign he only went abroad for eight weeks, of which five were spent convalescing on a Mediterranean cruise.

The collapse of the Russian, Austrian, German and Ottoman empires left the British monarchy looking exposed as an institution, and all the King's political efforts were henceforth devoted to appeasing those dangerous new forces which he perceived might threaten the British constitutional settlement in the future. In his dealings, therefore, with the Labour Party, trade unions, Mahatma Gandhi, Irish republicans and eventually even the continental fascist movements, his first instinct was to try to conciliate and find some common, middle ground. In 1921 he played an important role in encouraging the Lloyd George coalition government to be as generous as possible to Eamon de Valera during the foundation of the Irish Free State. He wanted every possible effort made to ensure that the new self-governing southern Irish state should be born with as little bitterness as possible.

In 1923, advised and abetted by Lord Stamfordham, he chose the relatively junior Stanley Baldwin to succeed Bonar Law as prime minister, instead of the vastly better qualified former Viceroy and Foreign Secretary Lord Curzon. They felt that it would be insulting to the Labour Party not to have a prime minister in the House of Commons, able to answer questions there. When Labour came to power the following January, the King, for all his private distrust of socialism, observed minutely all the constitutional niceties and gradually came to admire the first Labour prime minister, Ramsay MacDonald. 'Today twenty-three years ago Grandmama died,' he wrote in his diary the day before MacDonald formed the first Labour government, 'I wonder what she would have thought.' It is not hard to guess, considering that Queen Victoria even regarded the Gladstonian Liberals as dangerous radicals.

When the General Strike broke out in 1926, the King called for an end to bitterness. This sort of well-meaning message to the nation reached far further when in 1932 the King made the first of his Christmas broadcasts to the Empire. These simple, homely, Christian if somewhat saccharine addresses, through the powerful new medium of radio, helped connect the monarchy with the people more personally than had ever been previously possible.

By then the King's personal authority was unassailable, his reign universally considered a success; indeed the institution of monarchy in Britain saw something of a golden age between 1918 and the King's death in 1936. For all his distaste of 'advertisement' he did have a fine sense of what today is called public relations. When the world economic crisis known as the Great Depression threatened sterling in 1931 he voluntarily surrendered a significant part of his Civil List to the Exchequer, and called a conference of party leaders which eventually led to the formation of a National Government by Ramsay MacDonald and Stanley Baldwin. 'You have kept up the dignity of the office,' he admiringly wrote to an ill MacDonald who was considering retirement in June 1934, 'without using it to give you dignity.' The resignation of Sir Samuel Hoare in December 1935, over the notorious Hoare–Laval Pact which had been negotiated in Paris, produced a classically George v joke, when he said to the departing minister: 'You know what they're all saying, no more coals to Newcastle, no more Hoares to Paris.' He later complained to Hoare's successor Anthony Eden, 'The fellow didn't even laugh.'

The Silver Jubilee celebrations in 1935 saw a huge national outpouring of thanks and affection to the King and Queen, although typically the King thought of the church service that there had been 'too many damned parsons getting in the way'. Through twenty-five years of international and domestic upheavals the King had, to use a nautical metaphor he might have appreciated, steered a steady course. The fact that his natural reaction to crises was always to call a conference and hope the goodwill of the participants would help find agreement cannot be held against a monarch who saw his political task largely in terms of effecting conciliation.

The last great worry for the King, the personification of that generation of Britons who, in John Betjeman's words, were 'old men who never cheated, never doubted', was over the conduct of his eldest son Edward, the Prince of Wales. This intensely self-disciplined, blue-eyed churchman, a stickler for form who read the Bible daily, was disgusted to hear of his heir carrying on with an American divorcee, two of whose husbands were still living. He predicted disaster for the coming reign, when his own loud voice,

common sense and explosive temper could no longer affect his son's activities. 'After I am dead', he predicted dolefully, 'the boy will ruin himself in twelve months'. In fact it took only eleven.

Another disaster he foresaw was the Second World War. His experience of its predecessor made him almost a pacifist when contemplating the possibility of another Anglo-German conflict. 'I will not have another war,' he told Lloyd George in May 1935, 'I will not. The last one was none of my doing and if there is another one and we are threatened with being brought into it, I will go to Trafalgar Square myself and wave a red flag myself rather than allow this country to be brought in.'

On 20 January 1936 one of the greatest British monarchs died, after a short illness. His reputation for salty, down-to-earth language created a myth that his last words were 'Bugger Bognor', after a doctor had ingratiatingly suggested that he might recuperate in the same seaside resort as he had after a serious illness in 1929. In fact the story probably dates from the King's response to the town's request to be styled Bognor Regis for its part in the royal recovery, which Stamfordham took as approval. In 1936 though, the King's actual last words were far more characteristic of him. A Privy Council had somewhat officiously been forced upon him as he lay on his deathbed, in order to organize arrangements should he become incapacitated. 'Gentlemen,' he told them when he felt capable of speaking, 'I am so sorry for keeping you waiting like that. I am unable to concentrate.' So he died as he had lived, bravely and modestly doing to his duty without undue regard for self.

EDWARD VIII

r. 1936

'AT LONG LAST I AM ABLE TO SAY a few words of my own' said Edward VIII in a radio broadcast the day after his abdication in 1936. 'You must believe me when I tell you that I have found it impossible to carry the heavy burden of responsibility and to discharge my duties as King as I would wish to do without the help and support of the woman I love.'

At the time the Abdication seemed almost a defining moment, but in the light of international events three years later it has been relegated to a footnote of the history of the 1930s, albeit a fascinating one. The short reign of the charismatic but incurably vain and lightweight King still has the capacity to divide opinion between those who consider old-fashioned values and duty to be the paramount considerations for monarchy, and those who believe love and being true to the dictates of the heart matter more.

Prince Edward Albert Christian George Andrew Patrick was born on 23 June 1894, the eldest son of the Duke of York (later King George V) and Princess (later Queen) Mary. In the confusing Windsor tradition of rarely calling people by their real names he was nicknamed 'David'. Queen Victoria doted on him; it was the first time in history that four generations of monarchy lived contemporaneously.

Although he later attempted to convince himself and others otherwise, he had a relatively happy childhood, and there is a mass of evidence, not least his own correspondence, testifying to the varied activities and contented nature of his upbringing. Like his father and younger brother Bertie (later George VI)

he entered the navy young, joining the Royal Naval College, Dartmouth, in May 1909. His disastrous showing in the exams there might have been the fault of his tutor teaching the wrong syllabus, but even when years later he went up to Oxford the head of his college began a report with the words: 'Bookish he will never be'.

In May 1910 his grandfather Edward VII died and Prince Edward became heir to the throne. The blond young Prince made a tremendous impression in 1911 at the coronation service, when in his Garter robes he vowed allegiance to his father. Similarly, everyone admired the way in which at his investiture as Prince of Wales at Caernarvon Castle later that year he recited the few words of Welsh which Lloyd George had taught him.

But already he was beginning to speak his own mind, a course of action which was to lead to ever more severe clashes with his father. Complaining about the 'preposterous rig' he had to wear at the investiture, he gave notice to the court of a temperament which was over the following quarter-century to irritate and finally infuriate his parents and long-suffering courtiers.

In 1912 he went to France for four months to brush up on his French, but it was after that in Germany that he found a country he could fully admire, eventually becoming fluent in German while staying with royal cousins such as the King of Württemberg. He then passed his eight terms at Magdalen College, Oxford, in learning how to hunt, shoot, give and attend parties, drink and womanise, indeed enjoying all the traditional pursuits of the

Opposite: *Sir Edward Munnings's portrait of Edward, Prince of Wales. The handsome and charming Prince was everywhere adulated, and many looked forward to his reign as an era of youth and optimism.*

The investiture of Edward, Prince of Wales, at Caernavon Castle in July 1911. He took the trouble to learn a few words of Welsh from Lloyd George to recite at the ceremony.

undergraduate barring the intellectual. Those he found 'a dreadful chore'.

In June 1914 he left Oxford for attachment to the Grenadier Guards, and when in August the Great War broke out he believed that at last he would have an opportunity to prove to his contemporaries that he had martial qualities. Writing to the Secretary of State for War Lord Kitchener, he explained how much he wished to go to the front line and serve in his regiment, and that because he had four brothers it hardly mattered drastically if he were killed there. Kitchener laconically answered, saying that his death would indeed cause few problems, but his capture might and that he was therefore to be relegated to a staff post behind the lines. Not so far behind as to be entirely out of danger, however, as on one visit to the

Front he left his car only minutes before a shell landed on it and killed his driver.

These vicarious threats to his safety were not enough to satisfy his sense of honour, and it was with acute disgust that he learned he had been awarded the Military Cross, knowing how others of his generation had had to distinguish themselves in action for it. It is not too fanciful to suggest that for the whole of the rest of his life he despised himself for not having undergone the hardships of his contemporaries in the trenches. This gnawing guilt was a common enough affliction in the post-war period, suffered even by people who had served but somehow survived. Prince Edward had a better excuse than most, as every attempt he made to go on active service had been blocked by the authorities, which ultimately meant his father.

After the war, George v unconsciously did everything possible to accentuate his son's feeling of inadequacy, even forbidding him to steeplechase after he sustained a particularly bad fall. Instead his good looks, sense of informality, supposed social conscience and undeniable charisma – part matinée idol, part international 'celebrity' of a royal type not really seen again until Diana, Princess of Wales – was harnessed to the cause of Empire. Long, well-organised and sensationally successful tours of Canada, America, New Zealand and Australia in 1919 and 1920 established the Prince's status as one of the world's great crowd-pleasers, and only Gandhi's political boycott partially spoiled what would have been another success in India. Ticker-tape welcomes in America, his courage during a railway accident in Australia, boyish high jinks on board ship with Lord Louis Mountbatten – all served to add to his reputation as an iconic royal figure with the common touch. He also tried to identify himself with the cause of ex-servicemen and the unemployed in the 1920s, which added greatly to his popularity at relatively little effort.

Clashes with the King multiplied as the stories of his exasperating and absurd whims, for which he would change long-standing arrangements and alter tight schedules at the last minute, percolated back to court. The tinder over which these rows could ignite might be as trivial as the Prince's trouser turnups, or a particularly informal photograph in a magazine. But the underlying concern was over his lack of a stable love-life, something the King and Queen worried about as he approached his fortieth year with only mistresses and no suitable consort in sight. The King, in contrast to the trust he had enjoyed from his own father, excluded the Prince of Wales from any real role of responsibility, which was almost an invitation to the Prince to behave irresponsibly instead.

Part of the reason why secret information was not generally included in the Prince's briefings was the Foreign Office's fear that he was a Nazi sympathiser – a situation which continued throughout his reign. His pro-German sentiments merged with a growing contempt for Parliamentary government and old-fashioned constitutional methods and gradually led

him further than any other British royal in the direction of admiration for the fascist regimes in Germany and Italy. The sporty, unintelligent, fashionable, 'fast' set into which he moved in the early 1930s was peculiarly vulnerable to pro-fascist sentiment, and at least two of his close friends were 'ardent Hitlerites'.

By June 1933 Kaiser Wilhelm II's grandson Prince Louis Frederick was reporting that the Prince of Wales was 'quite pro-Hitler, and said it was no business of ours to interfere in Germany's internal affairs either re Jews or anything else and we might want one in England before long'. Two years later, in June 1935, the Prince had to be rebuked by his father for the warmth of his public declaration of friendship with Germany in a speech to ex-servicemen.

It was, however, sexual shenanigans, not political extremism, which worried the Palace most, just at the time when George v's failing health meant that they could do little about either. After enjoying the favours of Freda Dudley Ward, the wife of a Liberal MP, for nearly twenty years, he fell in love with a married American divorcee, Mrs Ernest Simpson (née Warfield), in 1934. Unlike earlier encounters with married, separated or divorced women – including Lady Furness with whom he went on safari, along with Lord Furness – this turned out to be more than merely sexual, but a genuine love affair. It was, as a marriage, to last for thirty-six years, longer indeed than most modern royal marriages. There is still speculation about the exact physical nature of the relationship, but it is certain that the Duchess was incapable of having children, a fact crucially not known to the royal family at the time.

Becoming King Edward VIII on 20 January 1936, his first act was to order that the Sandringham clocks which ran half an hour fast for reasons connected with his father's shooting passion, should be returned to the correct time. It was ironic that a moderniser should begin by turning the clocks back, and his two other modernising acts – substituting morning dress for court frock coats and occasionally walking short distances in public rather than always using a car – were equally easy and insubstantial.

Living at Fort Belvedere, a mock castle he had bought near Sunningdale in Berkshire in 1929, he continued his carefree Prince of Wales existence, failing to deal with his red boxes efficiently or punctually and sacking his father's retainers with the minimum of thanks and compensation for lifetimes of service. Far from the refreshing post-Victorian unstuffiness hailed by much of society, the new reign in fact heralded an undisciplined, excitable, lackadaisical future, for those who were close enough to know the truth about the King's real nature.

His only significant, and to the government potentially embarrassing act as King was taken on 18 November 1936 when, in greatcoat and bowler hat, the King toured the derelict Dowlais iron and steel works and met people who had been laid off there. 'These works brought all these people here', he declared. 'Something should be done to get them at work again.' It is a measure of his irresponsibility that he raised hopes in the hearts of the unemployed of South Wales only two days after he had intimated to Stanley Baldwin that he would abdicate sooner than lose Mrs Simpson. He knew perfectly well when he was raising the issue that he would probably not himself be around to see it through, but that Baldwin's National Government would have to deal with the heightened but doomed expectations he left behind.

For on 16 November 1936 he calmly informed Baldwin that he was 'prepared to go'. The negotiations had gone on since 20 October 1936, when he had refused Baldwin's request to ask Mrs Simpson to withdraw the divorce petition which she had instituted. The following week a decree nisi was granted on the grounds that her husband, an American businessman and former Coldstream Guards Officer, had committed adultery, albeit in a pro forma way known in those days as 'hotel' adultery, a charade organised entirely for legal reasons. The decree was due to be made absolute in April 1937.

Rumours had been circulating in society ever since the King met Mrs Simpson in 1934, but especially since they went on a cruise down the Dalmatian coast together in the summer of 1936 on the yacht *Nahlin*. A self-denying ordinance on the part of the British press meant that the public were largely kept ignorant of what was happening, although rumours and foreign newspapers and magazines tended to filter through. As early as February 1936, the Labour politician J. H. Thomas told Harold Nicolson that the British people "ate 'aving no family life at court' and as a result 'it won't do, 'arold, I tell you that straight'. He was soon proved right.

On 1 December 1936 the Bishop of Bradford, the ideally named Dr Blunt, speaking at his diocesan conference about the forthcoming coronation, said of His Majesty's sense of duty that 'Some of us wish that he gave more positive signs of his awareness'. First the provincial press and then *The Times* used this outburst – to the Bishop's professed surprise – as the excuse to break their long, embarrassing, self-imposed restraint. But by the time the public en masse discovered what had been happening, the general outlines of the Abdication settlement had been laid. It is hard in those pre-opinion polling days to be certain of the public response to the news, but the responses to Conservative MPs from their constituency association chairmen convinced Baldwin that most respectable people rebelled at the thought of a twice-divorced American adventuress sitting on the British throne.

On 25 November the King brought up the possibility of marrying Mrs Simpson morganatically, a continental practice whereby she would be his legal wife, but not his official consort. After Baldwin had consulted the Cabinet – whose deliberations on the subject are still kept secret sixty-two years later – as well as the Labour Opposition and the prime ministers of the major dominions, he informed the King on 2 December that it was impracticable. Had the King attempted to stir up political trouble for the government – fascists and communists were declaring their support for him, and both Lord Beaverbrook and Winston Churchill saw it as an opportunity for discomfiting Baldwin – he might have at least partially succeeded, but instead he soberly and responsibly decided to go quietly. Mrs Simpson, too, acted well during the crisis – offering to leave him if it would help him put his duty to the country before his love for her.

On 10 December 1936, the day after the Cabinet pleaded with him in vain to reconsider, King Edward VIII signed the Instrument of Abdication in the presence of his brothers at Fort Belvedere. The next day Parliament passed the Bill of Abdication which, when

INSTRUMENT OF ABDICATION

      I, Edward the Eighth, of Great
Britain, Ireland, and the British Dominions
beyond the Seas, King, Emperor of India, do
hereby declare My irrevocable determination
to renounce the Throne for Myself and for
My descendants, and My desire that effect
should be given to this Instrument of
Abdication immediately.

      In token whereof I have hereunto set
My hand this tenth day of December, nineteen
hundred and thirty six, in the presence of
the witnesses whose signatures are subscribed.

SIGNED AT
FORT BELVEDERE
IN THE PRESENCE
OF

The Instrument of Abdication, photographed at 10 Downing Street, with which Edward VIII relinquished the throne. It bears the signatures of Edward and his three brothers, Albert (later George VI, Henry, Duke of Gloucester, and George, Duke of Kent.

at 1.52 a.m. it received Royal Assent, ended his reign. That evening he broadcast to the people a message partly penned by Churchill, in which he stated that 'if at any time in the future I can be found of service to His Majesty in a private station I shall not fail'. But the Palace had other ideas, and fearful of his continuing popularity, far greater until the war than his younger brother the King's, they determined ruthlessly to sideline the ex-King for the rest of his life.

The Prince left for Austria in the early hours of 12 December 1936, to stay with Baron Eugene de Rothschild at Schloss Enzesfeld. He could not see Wallis Simpson, who was staying in the South of France, until her decree nisi had been made absolute. Soon after leaving England, the slights, rows and disagreements between the Duke of Windsor – as he was gazetted in March 1937 – and the British establishment began, which embittered relations for the rest of his life. As in any family row, all the blame cannot be attributed to one side or the other, but if the Windsors did react over-sensitively to events, that was because their wounds were kept deliberately raw.

First the new King, Edward's younger brother George VI, told Walter Monckton, the Duke's confidant and lawyer, that he no longer wished to receive the ex-King's telephone calls. Then the financial settlement, which had been arranged at a long formal meeting on the day of the signing of the Abdication, was reduced and reneged upon in tangible and humiliating ways, including the demand that in order to receive it the Duke had to undertake never to live in the United Kingdom. Then, after Mrs Simpson's divorce became absolute in April 1937 and the couple were reunited at Château de Condé in May, the news arrived that none of the royal family would attend the wedding. The fact that Lord Louis Mountbatten, who had been so keen to befriend the Duke all his life and who had agreed to be his best man just as he had been 'Dickie's', also declined the invitation drew the couple's lifelong ire.

The deepest cut came at the time of the wedding itself, on 3 June 1937, when the Duke received from Monckton a communication from the King, saying that although he could style himself 'His Royal Highness' neither his wife nor any descendants of theirs would be permitted to do so. The fear that the marriage might not last, or that any future children of theirs might seem to those ignorant of the Constitution to have a better claim to the throne than Princess Elizabeth, added to the loathing felt for an adventuress whom no one trusted, combined to create an act almost calculated to incite lifelong bitterness. All British precedent and law was against the act of separating the style and status of the husband from the wife; indeed it was precisely because it had been impossible to do this that the Duke had abdicated in the first place.

What had been genuinely tragic about the former King's life swiftly degenerated into the farcical. Suddenly he had nothing, or at least nothing worthwhile, to do. In October 1937, keen to have the Duchess accorded full state honours by a Great Power, the couple made a fantastically ill-judged visit to Germany, ostensibly 'for the purpose of studying housing and working conditions'. The authorities in London were furious. 'A bombshell and a bad one,' the King wrote to Monckton, who could nevertheless do nothing to prevent the trip taking place.

The Nazi high command, which believed that the King had been forced to abdicate for his pro-German views, laid out the red carpet, and the delighted couple took tea with Hitler himself at Berchtesgaden. This inevitably fuelled rumours about his willingness to consider returning to the British throne under German dictation in the event of a German victory over Britain, doubts which persist to this day. Whether he would, doubtless encouraged by his genuinely pro-German wife, have ever really made such a Faustian compact must of course be a matter for speculation rather than history.

September 1939 found the couple in their French Riviera home La Cröe in Cap d'Antibes. The destroyer HMS *Kelly*, commanded by Mountbatten, brought him back to Portsmouth, where there were

Opposite: The Duke of Windsor with his wife, the former Wallis Simpson, the American divorcee for whom he gave up the throne to live a life in exile.

no family or state representatives to meet him at the quayside. Instead, after a brief and cool interview with his brother at Buckingham Palace, to which the Duchess was pointedly not invited, it was arranged that he should be attached, with the rank of Major-General, to the British Military Mission in France. Further limitations and humiliating restrictions were regularly placed upon him once out there, despite his best intentions to help the war effort. When France fell in May and June 1940 he behaved characteristically selfishly in leaving his friend, long-time equerry and best man Major Edward 'Fruity' Metcalfe badly in the lurch and escaping first to La Cröe and then to neutral Madrid and Portugal.

A daring German plot was hatched to kidnap the Duke and take him first to Franco's Spain and eventually to Germany, presumably for use as a future puppet king of an occupied Britain. The British government, now led by his old friend and former supporter Winston Churchill, was demanding his return to Britain, and the prime minister even threatened a formal court-martial if he continued to refuse. Meanwhile the Duke was tactlessly dining with German agents and predicting military disaster for Britain, whilst attempting to make conditions to the British Government for his return.

These began with demands that he be allowed to serve in a significant capacity, and that his wife should have equal ranking to royal duchesses, but eventually wound down to a request that the court circular be allowed to state that the King and Queen had invited the Duke and Duchess to Buckingham Palace, if only for a quarter of an hour. As his obituary in *The Times* was to put it: 'Although his pride was touched, England's "darkest hour" was an unfortunate moment at which to make an issue of this matter.' The Duke also requested the German authorities to put a guard on his houses in Paris and the Riviera for the duration of the war, which they obligingly did.

With the pressure mounting on him, and the royal family entirely refusing to grant even the shortest formal interview to the couple in order to prove they were not in disgrace, the Duke reluctantly accepted the Governorship of the Bahamas, one of the Empire's least significant colonies, and sailed from Lisbon on 1 August 1940, to general relief in Whitehall. When they arrived they found the authorities had been specifically instructed by the Palace to let it be known that no one should on any account curtsey to the Duchess. For the rest of the war they stayed in the Bahamas, with occasional shopping trips to America, but in general carrying out his Abdication speech promise to serve George VI, albeit in a relatively menial capacity. He did the job well, but was not accorded the customary gubernatorial interview with the King when he retired in 1945.

Returning to France, where the City of Paris had generously provided him with a beautiful house in the Bois de Boulogne, and the French government had even more generously exempted him altogether from income tax, he lived out the next twenty-seven years in an unrewarding round of golf, gardening, dinner parties, gardening and more golf. Ghost writers helped him produce occasional best-selling books, *A King's Story*, which unfairly blamed everything on his father, in 1951, *The Crown and the People*, a saccharine history of the monarchy from Edward VII's coronation to Queen Elizabeth II's in 1953 and *Family Album* in 1960.

The royalties from these books, his original but reduced stipend from his late brother, and some large and totally illegal currency transactions managed to keep the couple afloat financially. The Duchess's glamorous entertaining made invitations to the house in the Bois de Boulogne sought after in Parisian society, although Prince Charles's diary recollections from a visit made in 1971, eight months before the Duke's death from lung cancer on 28 May 1972, show how much of their lives were led in a penumbra of make-believe: 'I found footmen and pages wearing identical scarlet and black uniforms to the ones ours wear at home. It was rather pathetic seeing that. The eye then wandered to a table in the hall on which lay a red box with "The King" on it . . . While we were talking the Duchess kept flitting to and fro like a strange bat . . . The whole thing seemed so tragic – the existence, the people and the atmosphere – that I was relieved to escape it after 45 minutes and drive round Paris by night.'

GEORGE VI

r. 1936–52

'GEORGE VI'S REIGN WILL GO down in history', wrote a waspish Evelyn Waugh to a friend, 'as the most disastrous my country has known since Matilda and Stephen'. As his time on the throne spanned the Nazi annexation of Austria, the Munich crisis, the Second World War, Stalin's domination of Eastern Europe, the independence of India, post-war Austerity and the end of Britain's Great Power status, Waugh might well have been right, but the blame certainly cannot be laid at the door of the intensely well-meaning King.

He exhibited many of the qualities of his father, and indeed his father's reign stood as the model on which George VI himself sought to act. Both ex-naval second sons not expected to succeed to the throne, even their handwriting was similar. They both took Britain through a world war soon after their accessions and, fortified by strong wives and simple religious faith, both eventually won the admiration and even love of the people. But where George V had presided over the first shock to the imperial system, his son had to face the start of its complete unravelling, whilst still fervently believing in its capacity to do good.

Born at York Cottage on the Sandringham estate on 14 December 1895 – the anniversary of the death of the Prince Consort – the second son of the Duke and Duchess of York (later King George V and Queen Mary) was unsurprisingly christened Prince Albert Frederick Arthur George. A shy, lachrymose child, the young Prince endured considerable ill-health in boyhood, contracting gastritis as a result of his nurse's negligence and walking with his legs in splints in order to overcome incipient knock-knees. He grew up in the shade of his loving but authoritative father and also of his elder brother David (the future King Edward VIII), who seemed to have all the attributes in terms of charm, looks, confidence, sporting ability and popularity which 'Bertie', as the family nicknamed him, lacked. It is hardly surprising therefore that aged eight he developed a profound stammer.

Nor was Prince Albert bright; he entered Osborne Naval College at thirteen, but in the exams he came sixty-eighth out of sixty-eight entrants. This might have been the fault of his tutor, but at Dartmouth only a little later he only managed sixty-first out of sixty-seven. Nevertheless in 1913 he joined the fleet as a midshipman, where he developed further gastritis, complicated by seasickness. It is a great tribute to the bravery of this delicate sub-lieutenant that in May 1916, at that most terrible of naval engagements the battle of Jutland, he left his sickbed to fight in the gun turret of HMS *Collingwood*.

The next year he had to undergo an operation on an hitherto-undiagnosed duodenal ulcer. He eventually left the navy and, joining the Royal Naval Air Service, qualified as a pilot. In 1919 he went up to Trinity College, Cambridge, with his friend and cousin Lord Louis Mountbatten. As a second son he had not been closely schooled in constitutional history, but fortunately had an opportunity there to read a little about the role that unbeknownst to him would one day be forced upon him. But it was still chiefly in the field of practical jokes, jolly japes and high-spirited follies, understandable in one who had come through the Great War and who had also suffered ill-health, that the Prince excelled.

A serious side began to emerge with his interest in the welfare of the industrial workforce, which his father always feared might one day become republican. Prince Albert set up the Industrial Welfare Society, under whose auspices he visited factories and workshops, always insisting on having no red carpets or over-formality as he wanted to see the true employment situation for himself, rather than the managements' image of what was happening in the British workplace. In 1921, the year after being created Duke of York, he also inaugurated the Duke of York's camps where in an attempt to break down class barriers, public schoolboys were encouraged to spend camping and hiking weekends with inner city children of the same age. Whilst it is easy to satirise these happy campfire encounters, all sitting cross-legged singing 'Under the Spreading Chestnut Tree', they were, like the Duke himself, well intentioned, idealistic and worthy.

It was in his marriage to Lady Elizabeth Bowes-Lyon, solemnised at their wedding in Westminster Abbey on 26 April 1923, that the Duke of York made the soundest decision of his life. Marriage to a commoner was considered a modernising gesture politically, although one could hardly have found a less common commoner than the daughter of the fourteenth Earl of Strathmore. The King and Queen quickly appreciated the Duchess's gift of being able to place their son at his ease, and develop in him a self-confidence which even began to help him master his stutter. At every future crisis of his life, the Duke had beside him a strong-willed, loving and self-confident wife who also became part business-manager, part private secretary, part public relations adviser.

Living at 145 Piccadilly and Royal Lodge in Windsor Great Park, the couple, who were joined in 1926 by Princess Elizabeth (now Queen Elizabeth II) and in 1930 by Princess Margaret Rose, passed a blissful domestic life. In 1926 the Duke visited the celebrated Australian speech therapist Lionel Logue and embarked on an intensive course which helped control but never entirely eradicate his stammer. There were occasional state visits, to East Africa and the Sudan in 1924 and to New Zealand and Australia in 1927, but otherwise time passed quietly for the royal couple.

By the time of his father's death in January 1936, the Duke of York had heard rumours about his elder brother's love life, but little could prepare him for the conversation the King held with him on 17 November 1936, when he made it clear that he intended to marry Mrs Simpson even if it meant forsaking his throne in order to do so. After a series of meetings and further conversations, both with the King and with Stanley Baldwin the prime minister, Cosmo Lang the Archbishop of Canterbury and the King's confidant, lawyer and friend Walter Monckton, it became clear that nothing could be done to change his brother's mind. He wrote in his diary of 'the awful and ghastly suspense' and when he saw his mother Queen Mary on the evening of 9 December 1936, the night before the Abdication, he 'broke down and sobbed like a child'.

The next day he stood witness, along with his other brothers, to the Instrument of Abdication, which was signed at Fort Belvedere on 10 December. The next day he became King, once Parliament had approved the Instrument and the Royal Assent had been given. His Duchess, the new Queen Elizabeth, a constant rock for him throughout the crisis, was angry and hurt at what she and Queen Mary perceived as the King's dereliction of duty. She was angry too at her beloved but far from robust husband having greatness thrust upon him in this precipitate manner, but was also ready to take on the task. She always blamed her husband's relatively early death from lung cancer not on his huge cigarette consumption, but on the strains imposed upon him by Edward VIII's decision.

The swift and ruthless way in which the Duke and Duchess of Windsor were cut out of British official life was probably more due to Queen Elizabeth's innate political understanding of how they could still harm her husband's position, rather than from any sense of personal spite. How much the King, who hated personal confrontations, was pressed into action by his Queen we shall probably never exactly know. But the King informed Walter Monckton that he no longer wanted to accept his brother's telephone calls, did nothing to influence the government's

Opposite: *George VI, who reluctantly took on the responsibilities of kingship after his brother's abdication, pictured with one of the royal corgis.*

seemingly harsh decision to deny the Duchess of Windsor the title of Her Royal Highness and, most poignant of all, he refused to attend his brother's wedding in 1937. When after the outbreak of war the Duke of Windsor returned briefly to London, no attempt was made to mend fences, and the Duchess was pointedly not invited to the short interview the Duke had with the King at Buckingham Palace. The golden boy of his generation was not about to be allowed to overshadow his still-stammering younger brother.

'I could eat no breakfast,' wrote the King in his diary of the morning of his coronation on 12 May 1937, 'and had a sinking feeling inside.' The ceremony was scheduled to take place on the same day as it had originally been arranged for Edward VIII. Apart from a bishop who stood on the King's robe as he attempted to stand up – 'I had to tell him to get off it pretty sharply as I nearly fell down' – that most traditionally accident-prone of all royal pageants went off successfully.

For his title the King took his father's name, and became George VI. It had a welcome feel of continuity to it, which the more Germanic Albert would not have done. Moreover it emphasised the way in which the British establishment intended to present the eleven-month reign of Edward VIII as merely a small unfortunate tear in the silken red carpet of monarchy.

Like many other well-meaning and somewhat naive people, especially those who had fought in the Great War, he simply could not believe that the Nazi leaders could be so evil as to contemplate another war. It was a defect in him as King, but one arising from his essential goodness of heart. Fortunately his enthusiastic efforts in support of the National Government's appeasement policy – they even had to restrain him from sending messages to Mussolini and Hitler which would undoubtedly have been misinterpreted in Rome and Berlin – were easily contained.

More usefully to the government he and the Queen were sent on two important visits abroad, to France in June 1938 and to America and Canada in May and June 1939. These helped cement friendships which within months were to be tested to the utmost. An IRA plot to assassinate the King when in America was also foiled by J. Edgar Hoover's FBI. At President Roosevelt's home in Hyde Park, F. D. R. adopted an avuncular approach to the King, with whom he talked international politics until 1.30 a.m. before patting him on the knee and saying 'Time for bed, young man'. At forty-four, the King was hardly that, but he noted his appreciation of the President's friendliness, asking, 'Why don't my ministers treat me as the President did tonight?'

It was after Chamberlain returned from Munich that the King – whose constitutional duty it was not to show any political favouritism whatever – made a serious political error. By inviting Mr and Mrs Neville Chamberlain on to the balcony of Buckingham Palace under huge spotlights to wave to the crowds cheering in the rain, he gave an unmistakable sign of royal approval to the Munich Agreement.

If Chamberlain had called a snap general election, as he was being urged to do by some of his closest advisers, this public identification of royal support of the appeasement policy would have greatly helped the National Government against the Labour and Liberal parties. The distinguished political commentator John Grigg has described the King's action as 'the most unconstitutional act by a British Sovereign in the present century. Whatever the rights or wrongs of the Munich Agreement, the relevant point is that it was denounced by the Official Opposition and was to be the subject of debate in Parliament.'

Although it might be easy to see why the King and Queen wished to join with most of the rest of the nation in applauding Munich, part of the reason for having a monarchy is that an impartial power can look calmly and rationally at events in the light of precedent, and not fall for the passing enthusiasms of a fleeting hour. The dismemberment of Czechoslovakia only six months later in March 1939

Opposite: Field Marshal Montgomery and George VI in conversation during the Second World War. During the Great War George had served in both the Navy and the Air Force.

showed the King's euphoric action for the hubristic mistake it was. No commoner had ever before been invited on to the balcony at Buckingham Palace and anyhow, a great war had not been won, merely a small country let down.

Once the Second World War broke out in September 1939, the King and Queen, once again using George V and Queen Mary as their template, threw themselves into the business of maintaining national morale. They worked tirelessly from 1939 to 1945 in keeping it as high as possible, and it is chiefly for those efforts that they will always be remembered. They had the inestimable advantage over their Great War counterparts of being able to use radio, and, masking his loathing of public speaking, the King made a series of moving broadcasts, with millions of

listeners sympathetically willing him not to stutter. His most famous broadcast came at Christmas in 1939, when he made a great effect quoting a little-known poet who had written:

'I said to the man who stood at the Gate of the Year,
"Give me a light that I may tread safely into the
unknown."
And he replied: "Go out into the darkness,
And put your hand into the Hand of God.
That shall be better than light, and safer than
a known way".
May that Almighty Hand guide and uphold us all.'

In May 1940, despite personally preferring the Foreign Secretary and former appeaser Lord Halifax,

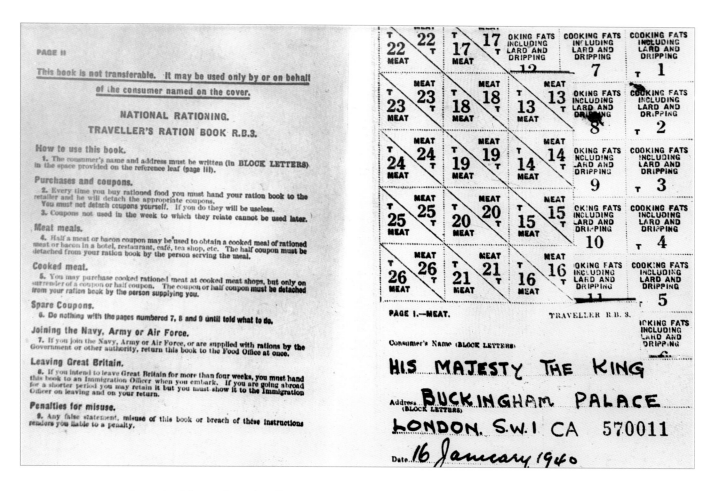

PAGE II

This book is not transferable. It may be used only by or on behalf of the consumer named on the cover.

NATIONAL RATIONING.

TRAVELLER'S RATION BOOK R.B.3.

How to use this book.

1. The consumer's name and address must be written (in BLOCK LETTERS) in the space provided on the reference leaf (page III).

Purchases and coupons.

2. Every time you buy rationed food you must hand your ration book to the retailer and he will detach the appropriate coupons. You must not detach coupons yourself. If you do they will be useless.

3. Coupons not used in the week to which they relate cannot be used later.

Meat meals.

4. Half a meat or bacon coupon may be used to obtain a cooked meal of rationed meat or bacon in a hotel, restaurant, café, tea shop, etc. The half coupon must be detached from your ration book by the person serving the meal.

Cooked meat.

5. You may purchase cooked rationed meat at cooked meat shops, but only on surrender of a coupon or half coupon. The coupon or half coupon must be detached from your ration book by the person supplying you.

Spare Coupons.

6. Do nothing with the pages numbered 7, 8 and 9 until told what to do.

Joining the Navy, Army or Air Force.

7. If you join the Navy, Army or Air Force, or are supplied with rations by the Government or other authority, return this book to the Food Office at once.

Leaving Great Britain.

8. If you intend to leave Great Britain for more than four weeks, you must hand this book to an Immigration Officer when you embark. If you are going abroad for a shorter period you may retain it but you must show it to the Immigration Officer on leaving and on your return.

Penalties for misuse.

9. Any false statement, misuse of this book or breach of these instructions renders you liable to a penalty.

PAGE I.—MEAT.   TRAVELLER R.B.3.

Consumer's Name (BLOCK LETTERS)

HIS MAJESTY THE KING

Address BUCKINGHAM PALACE (BLOCK LETTERS)

LONDON. S.W.I CA 570011

Date 16 January 1940

Opposite: The royal couple talk to occupants of London's underground shelters during the Blitz. Their own home, Buckingham Palace, was badly damaged in a daylight raid when two bombs fell on the quadrangle thirty yards from the King.
Above: King George and Queen Elizabeth were determined to share the privations of war with their subjects. This is George VI's ration book.

the King was forced to send for Winston Churchill as prime minister, after Chamberlain was humiliated in the Commons after a debate on the conduct of the campaign in Norway. As one of the only politicians of note who had publicly supported Edward VIII during the Abdication Crisis, Churchill was something of a *bête noire* to the King and Queen. This situation could easily have turned into a serious problem, but both men were too responsible to allow the past to cause difficulties during the country's perilous present. Indeed in the very interview at which the King offered Churchill the premiership he made

a bantering joke. As Churchill later recalled: 'His Majesty received me most graciously and bade me sit down. He looked at me searchingly and quizzically for some moments, and then said, "I suppose you don't know why I have sent for you?" Adopting this mood, I replied, "Sir, I simply couldn't imagine why." He laughed and said, "I want to ask you to form a government." I said I would certainly do so.'

After a few minor skirmishes over political appointments and postponed audiences, which Churchill won, the King came round to him, and by New Year's Day 1941 he fully appreciated Churchill's

Winston Churchill joins the King and Queen with Princess Elizabeth and Princess Margaret Rose on the balcony of Buckingham Palace to acknowledge the crowds on VE Day, 8 May 1945.

qualities. 'I could not have a better Prime Minister', he wrote in his diary. The relationship developed into mutual admiration and fast friendship, and Churchill ensured that the King was one of the very few people kept fully informed about both the Enigma decrypts of German telegraphs and the creation and deployment of the nuclear bomb.

On 13 September 1940 Buckingham Palace suffered by far the worst of its nine hits of the war when two bombs fell into the quadrangle during an air raid, exploding thirty yards from where the King was talking to Sir Alexander Hardinge, his Private Secretary. 'The whole thing happening in a matter of seconds,' he noted that evening in his diary, 'we all wondered why we weren't dead. Two great craters had appeared in the courtyard.' It was the occasion on which Queen Elizabeth, with her superb feel for public relations, commented that she was glad it had happened, as now she could 'look the East End in the face'.

It was their regular visits to areas of Britain devastated by bombing that gave the King the idea of instituting the George Cross and George Medal in 1940, for instances of outstanding civilian gallantry.

In an inspired move he awarded the medal, which he had personally devised and designed, to the island of Malta, so moved was he by that island's defiance of the Germans, when he visited it in 1943.

The King made few visits abroad during the war, in contrast to his father's constant travelling to the continent during the First World War, as the changing nature of warfare had made it far more dangerous than in the days of relatively static trench positions. In 1943 he visited Field Marshal Montgomery's Eighth Army in North Africa, under the *nom de guerre* General Lyon, and in the following year he visited Field Marshal Alexander's army in Italy. On D-Day plus ten he went to Normandy and toured the beaches, battlefields and field hospitals. As so many of his subjects had, the royal family experienced personal loss, when George, the Duke of Kent, was killed in a mysterious plane crash, of which there were so many in that war. It was not solely out of reasons of geographical centrality or tradition, therefore, but also out of a genuine wish to celebrate the occasion with their sovereign, that the crowds converged on Buckingham Palace to celebrate VE and VJ Days.

With peace in 1945, to the King's great surprise and irritation, came the defeat of Churchill in the general election. The King told Clement Attlee that he had heard of his victory on the six o'clock news, and advised his incoming prime minister to swap Hugh Dalton and Ernest Bevin into the posts of Chancellor of the Exchequer and Foreign Secretary respectively. Although this might have been because he wanted as little contact as possible with the Old Etonian Dalton, whose father had been tutor to his father and who he considered something of a class traitor – and although Attlee later denied the King's advice had been pivotal in the decision anyhow – it was in the best tradition of the Bagehotian constitutional duty of advice, and Bevin proved an excellent Foreign Secretary.

The King, with only the slightest regret, resigned himself to Labour's policy of stripping him of the title King–Emperor, when his cousin Lord Mountbatten oversaw India's partition and independence. He disliked but also could do nothing to halt the policy of nationalisation. 'He is of course a fairly reactionary person', wrote the Labour MP Hugh

Gaitskell after the King had told him he could not understand Aneurin Bevan's concerns over the imposition of National Health Service charges for teeth and spectacles. Yet if the holder of a feudal post the rationale of which is founded in the millennial mists of history cannot prefer stability to change, it is a cruel world. Like his father, George VI was deeply pessimistic about the likelihood of the monarchy surviving at all. 'Everything is going nowadays', he said in 1949, on hearing that the Sackville-West family were passing Knole Park, their ancestral home, to the National Trust: 'Before long, I shall have to go myself.'

The year 1947 saw both a successful tour of Southern Africa and the wedding of Princess Elizabeth to Lieutenant Philip Mountbatten, who was that day created Duke of Edinburgh. Both as a royal cousin – he was the son of Prince Andrew of Greece who had been exiled in 1922 – and as a brave young naval officer, he commended himself to the King and Queen. Showing just the same faith in his daughter and heir which Edward VII had shown his father, the King gave the Princess access to the red boxes and secret diplomatic telegrams. In the autumn of 1948 a bout of arterio-sclerosis forced the King to cancel a visit to New Zealand, and in the following March the King had to have an operation on his left leg when the blood supply to it failed. In September 1951 his entire left lung had to be removed.

The King bore all this stoically; instead it was usually trifling matters that would induce in him temper tantrums which the family called 'gnashes' and which only his wife was able successfully to defuse. His humour was heavy, his manner sometimes finickety over details. He had a fine memory for other people's errors and was constantly ticking people off for minor infringements of sartorial rules. Yet his solid religious faith and transparent decency, as well as his skill in helping bring his country through the crises of abdication and war, meant that when he died in his sleep at Sandringham in the early hours of 6 February 1952 – after a good day's hare shooting – King George VI was deeply and genuinely mourned as a monarch who, like his father but not his brother, had put duty before everything.

ELIZABETH II

r. 1952–

'I DECLARE BEFORE YOU all that my whole life, whether it be long or short, shall be devoted to your service and the service of our great Imperial family to which we all belong.' Princess Elizabeth's broadcast speech from Cape Town on 21 April 1947, to mark her twenty-first birthday, defines her reign. Like her father and grandfather,

duty has been her watchword.

Born by Caesarean section on 21 April 1926 at her maternal grandparents' Mayfair home, 17 Bruton Street, Princess Elizabeth Alexandra Mary was not expected to succeed to the throne for the first ten years of her life. This meant that the early education of the pretty girl known to the family as 'Lilibet' could be undertaken largely by her mother – with help from Queen Mary and a nurse–governess, Marion Crawford – without it becoming an issue of state. The last monarch not to go to school, she thus had a fairly relaxed, comfortable and private upbringing, which helped turn her into a tidy, somewhat methodical young woman. It was not until she was ten years old that the Abdication made her father King, and her heir to the throne.

During the war, she and her younger sister Margaret Rose (born in 1930) lived at Windsor Castle. She was taught constitutional history by Henry (later Sir Henry) Marten, Provost of Eton. When she heard of Neville Chamberlain's resignation over the radio in May 1940 she cried, but the RAF bombing of the German island of Sylt had a happier effect on her; indeed her pleasure at the news prompted her mother to wonder aloud to the Foreign Secretary Lord Halifax, whether the war would not brutalise the finer feelings of children in general. Soon the Princess was able to do her own bit for the war effort when in 1945 she joined, at her own insistence, the Auxiliary Transport Service, and

Above: *Queen Mary holds her granddaughter, the future Queen Elizabeth II, on the day of the baby's christening.*
Opposite: *An unusual study of King George VI with his eldest daughter and heir to the throne, Princess Elizabeth, aged eleven. The princesses were adored by the nation and the Commonwealth.*

Opposite: *Princess Elizabeth with her striking fiancé Lieutenant Mountbatten Royal Navy (born Prince Philip of Greece), on the occasion of their engagement.*
Above: *Shortly after her engagement to Lieutenant Philip Mountbatten Princess Elizabeth visited Southern Africa with her sister Margaret, both pictured here at a swimming party at the Victoria Falls Hotel in Rhodesia.*

somewhat incongruously became a mechanic, learning about what went on under the bonnets of trucks.

Only weeks before the war started, on 23 July 1939, aged only thirteen, the Princess had fallen in love with a handsome young naval cadet. Visiting the Royal Naval College at Dartmouth on the royal yacht *Victoria and Albert* with her parents, Princess Elizabeth met the tall, blond-haired, eighteen-year-old Prince Philip Mountbatten, nephew of her father's cousin Lord Louis Mountbatten.

At the Captain's House at Dartmouth they played together for an afternoon, Philip athletically jumping over the tennis net, which according to Miss Crawford's 1950 book *The Little Princesses*, left the little girls most impressed. '"How good he is Crawfie", said Princess Elizabeth, "How high he can jump." She never took her eyes off him the whole time.' When the royal yacht sailed off the next day, the boat he was rowing was the last to turn back. 'Damn young fool!' exclaimed the King, but his daughter had, as she later permitted a biographer of her father to confirm, fallen in love at first sight.

Whether that first meeting, and the subsequent engagement on 10 July 1947 soon after the Princess's twenty-first birthday, had been somewhat stage-managed by Lord Mountbatten is immaterial. For from their spectacular wedding on 20 November 1947, which was both broadcast and televised on the Princess's advice and for which the tight clothing ration restrictions were rightly relaxed, the marriage proved tremendously successful. Prince Philip's resilience, naval brusqueness, and occasional public gaffes are part of the national anthology, and the Queen's regard for him is undimmed.

Created the Duke of Edinburgh on the morning of the wedding service, Prince Philip swiftly adapted to court life. Originally some courtiers, such as the King's Assistant Private Secretary Sir Alan Lascelles,

dismissed him as a 'penniless foreign princeling', but he won the admiration of King George VI, not least for having been mentioned in despatches in the naval action against the Italian fleet at the battle of Cape Matapan. The son of Prince Andrew of Greece, he nevertheless took British citizenship in 1947, as soon as the extremely volatile political situation in Greece allowed him to do so. The heir to the throne, Prince Charles Philip Arthur George, was born on 14 November 1948, and was followed by Princess Anne in 1950, Prince Andrew in 1960 and in 1964 by Prince Edward.

It was when the Princess and Duke were on the initial leg of a long tour of the Empire, staying at the

Opposite: *Dressed in mourning for her father, the new Queen leaves the plane which brought her home from Kenya, to be greeted by her prime minister, Winston Churchill.*
Above: *The televised coronation of Queen Elizabeth II in June 1953 was an occasion to lift the spirits of a nation still recovering from the after-effects of war.*

Treetops Game Reserve in Kenya on 6 February 1952, that they were informed of the death of the King. He had waved them off from the airport only a week earlier, but when they returned it was a bare-headed Winston Churchill who solemnly received them. As the new Queen stepped from the aeroplane dressed in black, she inspired enormous national sympathy, both for her loss and for the fact that she had now to take on so much responsibility aged only twenty-five.

The coronation on 2 June 1953 was also televised on the Queen's insistence, and watched by twenty million Britons, and twelve million more heard it on the radio. Richard Dimbleby's splendid broadcast, the news that Edmund Hillary had conquered Everest, the end of rationing and the national rejoicing at the coronation of a beautiful young queen encouraged some enthusiasts in the press to proclaim a 'New Elizabethan Age'. In fact Britain was facing a long period of relative decline, punctuated by crises which in other countries without a monarchy might have produced constitutional upheaval. Instead of the riots, political instability and collapse of the Fourth Republic which took place in France, the British experience of the traumatic process of decolonisation, aided by the Queen's personal belief in the Commonwealth, was smooth.

There were some critics. When in 1955 Princess Margaret was dissuaded from marrying the handsome former RAF hero Group Captain Peter Townsend because he had been divorced – albeit as the innocent party – some voices were raised against the court's stuffiness and old-fashioned views. In 1957 the distinguished historian Lord Altrincham – later Mr John Grigg – wrote in the *National Review* of the Queen that 'she is out of touch with the modern world and her advisers are a tweedy entourage who know nothing of life outside the restricted circle of the establishment'. He got punched in the street for those remarks, which unfortunately probably represent the settled view of most of the British media today.

Lord Mountbatten claimed – although Anthony Eden virulently denied it – that the Queen was opposed to the military operation to recapture the Suez Canal in November 1956. If so, and it is by no means impossible, she had very little actual power to alter events, but probably instead exercised her constitutional duties to advise and warn, rather than to encourage. When Eden had to resign the following January she sent for Harold Macmillan, as was her prerogative, rather than R. A. Butler. This decision has been criticised, but ever since the previous November – when Macmillan had greatly out-performed Butler when addressing the Conservative backbench 1922 Committee during the crisis – opinion had been running Macmillan's way, and the Cabinet, which was sounded out by Lord Salisbury, was overwhelmingly for Macmillan.

More controversy was caused when the Queen had to choose a successor to Macmillan himself in October 1963, when the prime minister, who was suffering from prostate trouble, resigned. In again not sending for Butler, but plumping instead for the aristocratic Scottish landowner and personal friend the fourteenth Earl of Home, the Queen has been criticised severely by some historians. It has been alleged that she was almost an ex-officio member of what the Conservative politician Iain Macleod was to denounce as the 'magic circle' of grandees who connived at this appointment, over the head of the more popular and experienced Butler.

In fact it is not the constitutional duty of the sovereign to pick the best man for the task, merely someone who can command a majority in the House of Commons, as Home did. Had Butler refused to serve under Home, this would have been denied him, and Butler would probably have become prime minister. His nerve failed him, but that cannot be laid at the door of the Queen. Historical research has indicated that Home probably did have more support in the party at the time than Butler anyhow. Nevertheless the Queen can only have been relieved when in 1965 the Conservatives adopted rules for the future election of their own leaders.

In 1969, conscious of the 'tweedy' image that Lord Altrincham had criticised, and believing that an exercise in public relations would boost their (already great) popularity, the Queen, advised by Lord Mountbatten, his son-in-law Lord Brabourne and Prince Philip, took a step to 'let daylight in upon magic'. By sanctioning a 'fly-on-the-wall' TV programme, called *Royal Family*, in which cameras were allowed into very informal aspects of royal life, the Queen hoped to ease the family relatively painlessly into the modern world. Unrehearsed conversations were filmed between family members, the Queen was recorded making salad at a barbecue and buying bull's-eyes at the Balmoral village shop. It was very tame by modern-day standards of media intrusion, and 68 per cent of the British public watched.

Opposite: *Four months before his twenty-first birthday, Charles, the Queen's eldest son, was invested as Prince of Wales at Caernavon Castle.*

The Queen, known to have a quick wit, caught on film by Lord Lichfield in a relaxed moment during celebrations for her silver wedding anniversary in 1972.

But television tends to trivialise all it touches, and the House of Windsor was ultimately unable to prevent the liberty they had accorded it being turned into licence. 'A family on the throne is an interesting idea,' wrote Walter Bagehot in *The English Constitution* in 1867, 'it brings down the pride of sovereignty to the level of petty life.' Unfortunately for the dignity and standing of the House of Windsor the encouragement of media interest, even in the most controlled and successful way at first, gave an opportunity to a force more dangerous to the institution of monarchy than were the two world wars and the Abdication combined. In the 1980s a number of factors coalesced to make the massive public interest in the minutiae of royal life a perilously negative rather than positive phenomenon.

In 1975 there was a vivid demonstration of the prerogative powers the Queen still possesses when her Governor-General in Australia, Sir John Kerr, dismissed the democratically-elected but incompetent Labour government of Gough Whitlam, forcing a general election which was subsequently won by the Liberal Party. Kerr was acting scrupulously within his rights, but had Labour won the election it would doubtless have accelerated the movement for Australia to become a republic.

The braveness shown by George V and George VI still runs in the family. When a lunatic attempted to kidnap Princess Anne in the Mall in 1974 she showed great aplomb, escaping serious injury when her detective placed himself in the path of a bullet intended for her, receiving serious injury and the George Cross as a result. The Queen herself has also had to endure the nocturnal visit of a man named Michael Fagan to her bedroom, as well as a gun being let off at a parade. On both occasions she behaved with great dignity and calm courage.

Princess Margaret had married the photographer Anthony Armstrong-Jones, who was created Earl of Snowdon, in May 1960, but their separation in 1976 (and divorce in 1978) heralded the beginning of a number of royal splits, none of which can be blamed on the Queen, but which taken together have done much to undermine the image of the family that the *Royal Family* documentary was intended to convey. Inevitably any account of her reign must touch upon the lives of her children, and especially her daughters-in-law.

Nevertheless, the Silver Jubilee of 1977, with its massive outpouring of affection and thanks from the nation for the Queen's tireless dedication to duty, advertised the underlying fact that whoever else might bring the monarchy into controversy, its central figure was entirely above reproach. Astonishingly, considering the many thousands of royal tours and visits that she has under- taken over the past decades, the Queen has never once made a significant gaffe or embarrassing remark. If sometimes she must feel her work is taken for granted, or not appreciated by a nation and media seemingly only interested in her family's Achilles' heels, it is on occasions such as the Silver Jubilee, the Fiftieth Anniversary of VE Day in 1995 and the forthcoming Golden Jubilee in 2002 that she can be reassured.

In 1978 the Queen had to undertake one of the less agreeable sides of her job, when for economic and strategic reasons it became necessary for her to entertain the brutal dictator President Nicolae Ceaucescu of Romania, in London on a state visit, where she invested him with a British honour. The following year Sir Anthony Blunt, the Surveyor of the Queen's Pictures since 1952, was publicly unmasked as a long-standing KGB spy, a fact she had known since he had confessed to MI5 in 1964. Any action taken by her against him would, it was thought, alert the KGB to the fact that he had been 'turned', so she had to endure the presence of a traitor at Buckingham Palace until his retirement in 1972. When the truth came out in 1979 he was summarily stripped of his knighthood.

Nineteen seventy-nine also saw the callous assassination of Lord Mountbatten by the IRA, a horrific reminder of the risks associated with the Queen's position. Prince Charles, who was close to Lord Mountbatten, was particularly affected by the loss. It was Prince Charles's marriage to Lady Diana Spencer in St Paul's Cathedral on 29 July 1981 that put the royal family on a public relations roller-coaster ride, taking them further up, in terms of glamour and name-recognition, than ever before in recent times, but also at other times further down in public estimation than at any other point since Regency times. The dangers of having a Princess of Wales who was so beautiful and photogenic only became apparent when her fundamental incompatability with her husband emerged in the mid-1980s.

In 1986 Prince Andrew, the Duke of York – who had distinguished himself as a helicopter pilot during the Falklands War four years earlier – married Sarah Ferguson, the daughter of a former Life Guards officer. She turned out to be thoroughly ill-suited to royal life. A former private secretary to the Queen, Lord Charteris, even went so far as publicly to label her 'vulgar, vulgar, vulgar'. It also ended in a long separation and then divorce, as had Princess Anne's 1973 marriage to Captain Mark Phillips.

In the 1980s a number of coincidental developments tended to place the royal family, although never the Queen herself, in the most unforgiving of spotlights. The end of the deferential society, the arrival of the highly intrusive telephoto camera lens, the acrimonious collapse of the Wales's marriage, the rise of cruel, mocking television satire, and the realisation amongst newspaper editors that 'knocking copy' about the royal family would not engender libel writs but could instead vastly increase circulation, all led to an over-familiarity which soon bred contempt, at least of the younger family members.

Of many low points in that decade, the 1987 television programme, *It's a Royal Knockout*, in which the younger royals cavorted around in joke costumes, was particularly bereft of dignity. The number of holidays taken by the younger royals was held against them, as was the construction by the Duke and Duchess of York of an architecturally-challenged house near Sunningdale.

For the Queen herself, who symbolized traditional values, the divorces of her only sibling and three of her children were acutely painful on a personal as well as political level. In the year 1992 alone – the fortieth anniversary of her accession – the Prince and Princess of Wales and the Duke and Duchess of York separated, part of Windsor Castle burned to the ground, overhasty assurances by the Major government as to who should pay for its rebuilding unwittingly led to a press campaign which forced the Queen to agree to pay income tax, the 'Squidgy-gate' conversations between the Princess of Wales and James Gilbey were published and photographs appeared in the *Daily Mirror* of the Duchess of York in a compromising pedal position with someone claimed to be her 'financial adviser'. At a speech in the Guildhall on 24 November the Queen said ruefully that 'In the words of one of my more sympathetic correspondents, it has turned out to be an *annus horribilis*'.

Hitherto the Queen's desire to protect the couple's two young children, Prince William (born 21 June 1982) and Prince Harry (born in 1984), had

been paramount, but the disloyalty shown by the Princess of Wales on BBC TV's *Panorama* convinced her that the Princess, who by then had committed more than one publicised adulterous affair – was more dangerous inside the family than out. Prince Charles, who had been highly embarrassed when a tape-recording of a private conversation with his mistress, Mrs Camilla Parker-Bowles, was made public, was not himself blameless, especially as he had also publicly admitted his adultery on television to Jonathan Dimbleby. However, in order to protect their children he had repeatedly refused to allow friends to campaign against his wife.

It is impossible at present to know precisely what role the Queen played in all these events, except that she initiated the vital decision that the Prince and Princess of Wales should divorce. However, as the highly professional chief executive of what her father nicknamed 'the Firm', as well as the person who ultimately held the purse-strings, her role was undoubtedly crucial, even if it generally seems to have been reactive rather than proactive. Hailing from an earlier, pre-Freudian generation, who are not obsessed with their own feelings and reactions, the Queen is uninterested in the modern ideas of self-discovery and psychology. This perhaps made her less receptive than others to the New Age interests of her daughters-in-law. Reserved rather than cold, interested but never fascinated, regal but not unapproachable, authoritative but not bossy, she is representative of an earlier and better age.

In the early hours of 31 August 1997 Diana, Princess of Wales was killed in a car crash in a Parisian underpass. The massive outburst of national mourning was turned by popular newspapers, which were relieved not to have been blamed for the death themselves as it had been initially suggested that paparazzi photographers were at fault, into a campaign against the supposed heartlessness of the royal

Opposite: Few could have predicted the outcome of the fairytale wedding of Lady Diana Spencer and Prince Charles at St Paul's Cathedral in 1981.
Following pages: The following tragedy: Diana's sons Prince William and Prince Harry, her brother Earl Spencer, and her ex-husband Prince Charles watch the hearse bearing the coffin of Diana, Princess of Wales leaving her funeral on 6 September 1997.

family. 'Show Us You Care, Ma'am' was a representative front-page headline of a national daily paper during the week between the Princess's death and her vast funeral on 6 September 1997. The almost universal media demand was for the royal family to return to London from Balmoral and mourn 'amongst their people', as though Scotland was not in some way part of the realm.

Edmund Burke once wrote that democracy was 'the most shameless thing in the world', and the way in which two grieving adolescents, being consoled by their family in private, were dragged out into the world's media spotlight to mourn in public for the gratification of the populace, was undoubtedly the most shameless moment of the Queen's reign. But adaptability is the House of Windsor's secret weapon, and they returned to London, made tortured photocalls in front of the mountains of flowers, changed the long-standing protocol in relation to the flying of Buckingham Palace flags, and the Queen even made a television broadcast expressing her personal regret at the death.

The family behaved impeccably at the funeral for the Princess, which was watched on television by in excess of nineteen million people in the United Kingdom alone. Although the Queen shed no public tears, she did bow her head to the passing coffin, although whether in a gesture of respect to Diana or to Death is unknown, and she also left her seat to smooth the Royal Standard covering the catafalque in a touchingly maternal gesture.

Tears were shed when the royal yacht *Britannia* was decommissioned in December 1997, without any replacement being proposed by the incoming Labour government. This new era of non-republican anti-royalism – a backlash fuelled by envy and misunderstanding about the royal finances – was appeased by the Queen when she allowed it to be known that she had no objections to a Bill to allow a female child of the monarch the right to inherit the Crown if born before subsequent male children. The Queen also chairs a Way Ahead Committee which looks into further areas in which the monarchy can be adapted, and arcane practices ended. 'I must not take the easy way out' was her childhood motto.

Having never given an interview, the Queen retains a mystique denied to other more self-publicising royals. Other than preventing Prince Charles from taking part in a private Vatican Mass, we know little about her religious views, which seem to be in the mainstream of Church of England tradition, tending neither to the High nor Evangelical traditions. Her full role in grooming Juan Carlos for the Spanish throne, her opposition to the United States invasion of Grenada in 1983, her reported anxiety about the Miners' Strike of 1984–5 and her part in bringing Britain together with the Commonwealth on the issue of South African sanctions in 1986 cannot be known for certain for many years to come, but in each case she acted strictly constitutionally.

What is known for sure is that this five-foot-four ultimate professional, with her great knowledge and love both of horses – she is a keen and highly knowledgeable racehorse owner and breeder – and of dogs, especially her trademark corgis, is the very personification of Britishness. By never attempting to be the queen of people's hearts, she has nevertheless won their love and admiration. In the two months after her Internet website was launched in March 1997 it attracted no less that twelve and a half million 'hits'. Having been served by ten prime ministers, she is by far the most experienced public servant in Britain. Most have found her a useful sounding board for their hopes and ideas, and she has treated them equally. 'The Queen doesn't make fine distinctions between politicians of different parties,' Sir Godfrey Agnew, the former clerk of the Privy Council, told the Labour politician Richard Crossman, 'they all roughly belong to the same social category in her view.' Accusations of her not appreciating Margaret Thatcher are disproved by her appointment of the former prime minister both to the blue riband of the Order of the Garter and to the Order of Merit, both honours being in her personal gift. Her relations with

Opposite: Forty years on: Queen Elizabeth II in 1992. She has seen some of the greatest changes in her kingdom of any British monarch, yet remains a symbol of stability and tradition.

Tony Blair, who became Labour Prime Minister in May 1997, are believed to be good, and the prospects are excellent for the monarchy to be able to make a fresh start in recapturing some of the ground it lost during the 1980s and 1990s. As one of the few institutions to have survived the second millenium intact, the monarchy can look to the third with confidence.

Arthur Balfour once said of Queen Victoria that 'the great power of her character was from the combination of great simplicity and modesty with the dignity required by her position in the world', an estimation which could also be made of the present Queen. If the key to the House of Windsor has been in its dedication to duty, which is true of all its monarchs barring Edward VIII, then Queen Elizabeth II can take her place among her ancestors with justifiable pride. She has faithfully kept the great promise of lifelong service she made on her twenty-first birthday, over half a century ago.

INDEX

Page numbers in *italic* refer to the illustrations

Abdication Crisis, 8, 340, 344–6, 350–13, 355, 358
Aberdeen, Lord, 304, 307
Aberystwyth, 120
Acre, 56
Act of Indulgence, 252
Act of Settlement, 253
Act of Succession, 198
Act of Uniformity, 188–90
Act of Union (1707), 226, 242, 257, 258
Adam of Usk, 117–18, 119
Adela, Countess of Blois, 36
Adelaide, Queen, 294, 296
Adelaide of Louvain, 32
Agincourt, Battle of (1415), 120, 123, 126–7
Albert, Duke of Austria, 115
Albert, Prince Consort, 301, 304–11, *305*, 314, 320–2, 349
Alencon, François, Duke of, 209
Alexander I, Tsar, 299
Alexander III, King of Scotland, 86
Alexander III, Pope, 51
Alexander, Field Marshal, 357
Alexandra, Queen, 322, *322*, 324
Alfred, King of Wessex, 13, 44
Alice of France, 54, 56
American Civil War, 308–11
American Declaration of Independence, 9, 284
Anabaptists, 184
Andrew, Prince, Duke of York, 362, 367–8
Andrew, Prince of Greece, 357, 362
Anglesey, 84
Anglo-Saxon Chronicle, 32
Anjou, Counts of, 26, 32
Anjou and Angevin Empire, 20, 35, 41–66, 72, 75, 99, 123
Anne, Princess Royal, 362, 367, 368

Anne, Queen, 2, 8, 226, 242, 253, 254–8, *255*, *259*, 264, 280
Anne of Bohemia, 110
Anne of Cleves, 183, 184
Anne of Denmark, 220–22, *221*, 224
Anselm, St, Archbishop of Canterbury, 28, 30, 31–2
Antwerp, 99, 170
Aquitaine, 54, 62, 92, 102, 114, 122, 132
Aragon, 148
Arch, Joseph, 323
Argyll, Marquis of, 245
Aristotle, 10
Armada, 209–10
Armagnac, 119, 123, 126
Arminians, 229, 230
Arras, Peace of (1435), 128
Arsuf, Battle of (1191), 60
Arthur, King, 44, 94, 98, 99
Arthur, Prince of Wales, 166, *167*, 170, 171, 195
Arthur of Brittany, 64, 65
Arundel, Archbishop, 119, 120–22
Arundel, Henry, Earl of, 204
Arundel, Richard, Earl of, 106, 107–9, 110, 116, 122
Ascham, Roger, 201
Ashley, Catherine ('Kat'), 198, 201, 202
Asquith, Herbert, 324, 325, 335
Athelstan, King, 44
Atterbury, Bishop, 271
Attlee, Clement, 357
Audley, Lord, 168
Augusta, Princess of Wales, 275, 280
Australia, 343, 367
Ayscough, William, Bishop of Salisbury, 131, 133

Babington Plot, 209
Bacon, Francis, 223
badges, 192
Bagehot, Walter, 357, 366
Baldwin, Count of Flanders, 20

Baldwin, Stanley, 338, 339, 344, 350
Balfour, Arthur, 324, 374
Balliol, John, King of Scotland, 86
Balmoral, 311, 366, 372
Bamburgh, 135
Banbury, Battle of (1469), 146
Bank of England, 253
Bannockburn, Battle of (1314), 90, 92
Bari, Council of (1098), 31
Barnet, Battle of (1471), 138, 146–8, 152, 162
Basilikon Doron, 220
Beatrice, Princess, *312*
Beauchamp, Anne, 142
Beaufort, Cardinal Henry, 165
Beaufort, Henry, Bishop of Winchester, 122, 127, 128, 131
Beaufort, Joan, 142
Beaufort, Lady Margaret, 158, 162, *164*, 165, 171
Beaufort, Thomas, 122, 127
Beaufort family, 132, 165
Beaverbrook, Lord, 344
Becket, Thomas, Archbishop of Canterbury, *48*, *49*, 51–2
Bedford, John, Duke of, 127, 128
Berengaria of Navarre, 56, 60
Berkeley Castle, 93, 117
Berlin, Congress of (1878), 314
Berwick, 86, 98, 135, 156
Bevan, Aneurin, 357
Bevin, Ernest, 357
Bible, *179*, 183, 190, 220
Bill of Rights, 252
Birley, Robert, 13
Bishops' Wars, 230, 231
Black Death, 100
Blacman, John, 130–31, 135
Blair, Tony, 374
Blanche, Queen of France, 74
Blanche of Lancaster, 114
Blenheim, Battle of (1704), 257
Blount, Bessie, 176
Blunt, Sir Anthony, 367

Blunt, Dr, Bishop of Bradford, 344
Boer War, 314–15, 324
Bohemia, 223
Bohun, Mary de, 114
Boleyn, Anne, *173*, 176–7, 178, 183, 184, 192, 195, 198
Bordeaux, 132
Born, Bertrand de, 66
Boroughbridge, Battle of, 92
Bosworth, Battle of (1485), 152, 159, 162, 165
Bothmar, Baron von, 264, 266
Bothwell, Earl of, 206
Boulogne, 36
Bouvines, Battle of (1214), 65
Boyne, Battle of the (1690), 246, *250–51*
Brakespeare, Nicholas, 176
Bramham Moor, Battle of (1408), 118
Braudel, Fernand, 7
Bray, Sir Reginald, 168, 170
Breda, Declaration of (1660), 234
Brémule, Battle of (1119), 32
Brétigny, Treaty of (1360), 102
Breze, Piers de, 135
Brighton Pavilion, 290–92
British Empire, 258, 332, 333, 338, 343, 362–3
Brittany, 51, 162
Brittany, Dukes of, 131, 148
Broadhurst, Henry, 323
Brougham, Lord, 297
Brown, John, *309*, 311
Bruce, Robert, King of Scotland, 86, 89, 90, 92, 98
Brummell, George (Beau), 290, 292
Bryan, Lady, 185, 198
Buckingham, George Villiers, Duke of, *222*, 223, 224, 229–30, 236
Buckingham, Henry Stafford, Duke of, 156, 158, 159, 165
Buckingham Palace, 332, 335, 338, 348, 353–4, 356, 357, 367, 372
Burgh, Hubert de, 72, 74
Burghley, William Cecil, 1st Baron, 203–4, 206, 209, 210
Burgundy, 119, 126, 127, 138, 145–6, 148, 149, 152
Burgundy, Charles, Duke of, 146, 148
Burgundy, John the Fearless, Duke of, 122, 123, 126
Burgundy, Philip, Duke of, 126, 128
Burke, Edmund, 372
Burley, Sir Aimon, 114

Burley, Sir Robert, 103, 109
Burnell, Richard, 84
Bute, Earl of, 280, 283–4
Butler, Lady Eleanor, 145, 158
Butler, R. A., 364

Cabal, 236, 238
Cabinet, 253, 257, 270
Cabot, John and Sebastian, 170
Cade's Rebellion (1450), 132
Cadiz, 209
Cadwalader, 180
Caen, 123, 132
Calais, 100, 102, 110, 122, 123, 126, 131, 135, 146, 148, 197
Calvinism, 203, 219, 224
Cambridge, Richard, Earl of, 132
Cambridge University, 184, 349
Campbell-Bannerman, Sir Henry, 324
Campeggio, Cardinal, 177–8
Canning, Lord, 314
Canterbury, 52, 65, 96
Canterbury, Treaty of (1416), 123
Carberry Hill, Battle of (1567), 206
Carlyle, Thomas, 11
Caroline, Princess, 278
Caroline of Anspach, 268, 272, 274, 275–8
Caroline of Brunswick, 290, *290*
Castile, 107, 114
Castillon, 132, 133
Castle Rising, 94
Catesby, William, 159
Catherine of Aragon, 166, 171, 176, 177–8, *177*, 183, 190, 191, 195
Catherine of Braganza, 236, 238
Catherine of Valois, 123, 126, *126*, 128, 163
Catherine the Great, Empress of Russia, 284
Catholic Emancipation, 287, 293, 294
Caxton, William, 149
Ceaucescu, Nicolae, 367
Chamberlain, Neville, 353–4, 355, 358
Charles, Prince of Wales, 348, 362, *365*, 367, 368–72, *369–71*
Charles I, King, 8, 9, 72, 222, 223, 224–33, *225*, *233*, 234, 240
Charles II, King, *3*, 9, 10, 234–8, *235–7*, 247–8, 252, 280
Charles IV, King of France, 99
Charles V, Emperor, 175, 176, 177, 183, 197

Charles V, King of France, 102, 150
Charles VI, King of France, 122, 123, 126, 133
Charles VII, King of France, 128, 131
Charles VIII, King of France, 158
Charles of Anjou, 76
Charles Edward, Prince (Young Pretender), 279
Charlotte, Princess, 290, 294
Charlotte, Queen, *281*, 283, 285, 294
Charteris, Lord, 367–8
Chartists, 304, 307
Chastellain, 127
Chaucer, Geoffrey, 114
Cheke, John, 185, 198
Chester, 120
Chesterfield, Lord, 272
Church of England, 178, 185, 203, 204, 224–9, 231, 234, 245, 253, 254, 258, 264, 372
Churchill, Winston, 325, 344, 346, 348, 354–6, *356*, 357, *362*, 363
Civil List, 252, 274, 338
Civil War, 8, *230*, 231–3, 234
Clarence, Albert Victor, Duke of, 324, 330, 332
Clarence, George, Duke of, 146, 148–9, 155, 156
Clarence, Thomas, Duke of, 122, 123, 126, 127
Clarendon, Council of (1164), 51
Clarendon, Edward Hyde, Earl of, 234, 236, 240
Clement III, Pope, 28
Clement VII, Pope, 177
Clifford, Lord, 236, 237
Clothilde, Queen of the Franks, 150
Clovis, King of the Franks, 150
Cnut, King, 44
coats of arms, 14–15; pre–Norman kings, 44; Norman kings, 46; Edward III and Richard II, 96; fifteenth century, 150; Henry VII and Henry VIII, 180; Philip II and Elizabeth I, 192; Stuarts, 226; eighteenth century, 242; nineteenth and twentieth century, 318
Cobbett, William, 291
Cockshut, A. J., 11
Colet, John, 172
College of Arms, 44, 46, 330
Commonwealth, 318, 364, 374
Commynes, Philippe de, 145, *147*, 148

Compton, Bishop, 254
Compton, Sir Spencer, 274
Conroy, Sir John, 298, 299, 301
Conservative Party, 311, 314, 324, 344, 364
Constitutions of Clarendon, 51
Cornwall, 168
Cosne, 126
Cotentin peninsula, 99–100
Council of Regency, 184, 188, 201
Counter Reformation, 209
Covenanters, 206, 230, 232–3, 234
Coverdale, Miles, 179, 183
Cox, Richard, 185, 187
Cranmer, Thomas, Archbishop of Canterbury, 178, 183, 184, 187, 188, 197
Crawford, Marion, 358, 361
Crécy, Battle of (1346), 100, 102
Crewe, Marquis of, 335
Crimean War, 307–8
Cromwell, Oliver, 233, 234
Cromwell, Thomas, 178, 183, 184, 185, 195
Cropredy Bridge, battle of (1644), 232
Crusades, 29, 36, 54–5, 56–60, 58–9, 75–6, 80
Culpeper, Thomas, 184
Cumberland, 156
Cumberland, Ernest Augustus, Duke of, 293, 294, 318
Cumberland, William, Duke of, 278, 279
Curzon, Lord, 338
Cyprus, 56, 115

Dalton, Hugh, 357
Danby, Earl of, 238
Darnley, Lord, 206, 211, 216
Daubeney, Lord, 168
Dauphinists, 126, 127
David I, King of Scotland, 36, 42
David II, King of Scotland, 98, 100, 102
de Valera, Eamon, 338
Declaration of Indulgence (1687), 245
Dee, John, 204
Defence of the Seven Sacraments, 172–5
Derby, Henry, Earl of, 99
Derby, Robert Ferrers, Earl of, 80
Dereham, Francis, 184
Despenser, Hugh the Elder, 92
Despenser, Hugh the Younger, 91, 92

Despenser, Lord, 118
Dettingen, Battle of (1743), 276–7, 279
Diana, Princess of Wales, 343, 367, 368–72, 369, 370
Dilke, Sir Charles, 311
Disraeli, Benjamin, 310, 313–14
Dissolution of the Monasteries, 183
Domesday Book, 24, 25, 26
Douglas, Earl of, 118
Douglas-Home, Sir Alec, 364
Dover, Treaty of (1670), 236–7
Drake, Sir Francis, 209, 219
Dudley, 170, 171
Dudley Ward, Freda, 343
Duke of York's camps, 350
Dunbar, Battle of (1296), 86
Dunbar, Battle of (1650), 234
Dunbar, William, 166
Dunes, Battle of the (1658), 240
Dutch Republic, 234, 236–7, 240, 247–8, 253

Eadmer, 28–9
Eden, Anthony, 339, 364
Edgar 'The Peaceful', 44
Edgehill, Battle of (1642), 232, 234
Edinburgh, 156, 190, 268, 279, 293
Edinburgh, Treaty of (1560), 204
Edith, Queen, 30, 32
Edmund 'The Elder', 44
Edmund Ironside, 44
Edred, 44
Edward, Black Prince, 96, 98, 102, 103
Edward, Prince (son of Elizabeth II), 362
Edward, Prince (son of Henry VI), 133, 138, 148, 155, 165
Edward, Prince (son of Richard III), 155, 158
Edward I, King, 9, 72, 78, 78, 79–86, 82, 89
Edward II, King, 9–10, 84, 86, 87–93, 90, 94, 111
Edward III, King, 9, 46, 68, 92, 94–102, 95, 103, 114, 142, 169, 330
Edward IV, King, 135–8, 140, 142–9, 143, 147, 150, 152, 156, 162, 165
Edward V, King, 140, 149, 150, 156–8, 165
Edward VI, King, 8, 183, 184, 185–90, 186, 188–9, 192, 196, 198

Edward VII, King, 301, 304, 311, 316, 321, 320–25, 325, 330, 332, 333–5, 333, 340, 357
Edward VIII, King, 10, 316, 332, 339, 340–48, 341, 342, 345, 347, 349, 350–53, 355, 374
Edward the Confessor, St, 20–23, 22–3, 44, 76, 77, 78, 117
Edward 'The Martyr', 44
Edwy 'The Fair', 44
Eleanor of Aquitaine, 39, 42, 46, 54, 62
Eleanor of Castile, 79, 81
Eleanor of Provence, 74
Eliot, George, 11
Elizabeth, Queen of Bohemia, 223, 224, 229
Elizabeth, Queen Mother, 348, 350, 353, 354, 354, 356, 356, 358
Elizabeth I, Queen, 8, 13, 169, 178, 184, 185, 190, 192, 196, 197, 198–211, 199, 216
Elizabeth II, Queen, 13, 150, 318, 346, 350, 356, 357, 358–74, 358–63, 365, 366, 373
Elizabeth of York, 158, 159, 160, 162, 165–6, 169, 180
Elton, Professor, 11–12
Emma, Queen, 44
Empson, 170, 171
Entente Cordiale, 325
Erasmus, 171, 172, 185, 196
Ernest Augustus, Elector of Hanover, 264
Essex, Robert, Earl of, 208, 210
Ethelred 'The Unready', 44
Eton, 130, 131
Eustace, Prince, 39, 42
Evesham, Battle of (1265), 78, 80, 90
Exclusionists, 252

Fairfax, Thomas, 233
Falaise, 126
Falkirk, Battle of (1298), 86
Ferdinand, King of Spain, 166, 170, 175
feudalism, 85
Field of the Cloth of Gold, 176
First World War, 325, 330, 335–8, 342–3, 349, 357
Fisher, Admiral Sir John, 324
Fisher, John, Bishop of Rochester, 172, 178
fitzEmpress, Henry, 39

Fitzherbert, Maria, 288, 292
Flamank, Thomas, 168
Flambard, Ranulf, Bishop of Durham, 28, 35
Flanders, 20, 30, 100
Flanders, Counts of, 26, 32
Flodden Field, Battle of (1513), 172
Fox, Charles James, 284–5, 292–3
Foxe, Bishop, 171
Foxe, John, 197
France: coat of arms, 96, 150; Hundred Years' War, 99–102, 103, 123, 131–2, 133, 171–2; Richard II's expedition to, 110; Henry V's wars with, 122, 123–7; Truce of Picquigny, 148, 155; Treaty of Dover, 236–7; war with the Grand Alliance, 257; *Entente Cordiale*, 325; *see also* Anjou, Normandy *etc.*
Francis I, King of France, 175–6, 183
Francis II, King of France, 204
Frederick, Elector Palatinate, 223, *229*
Frederick, Prince of Wales, 274–5, 278–9, 280, 286
Frederick III, Emperor of Germany, 301
Frederick the Great, King of Prussia, 11, 279
French Revolution, 9, 287, 304
Furness, Lady, 343

Gaitskell, Hugh, 357
Gallifet, Marquis de, 323
Gambetta, 323
Gandhi, Mahatma, 338, 343
Gardiner, Stephen, Bishop of Winchester, 183–4
Garibaldi, Giuseppe, 307, 322
Gascony, 75, 79, 84, 99, 102, 132
Gaveston, Piers, 89, *90*, 92, 94, 106
General Strike (1926), 338
Genoa, 99
Geoffrey, Count of Anjou (d. 1060), 20
Geoffrey, Count of Anjou (husband of Empress Matilda), 35, 36, 38, 39, 42
Geoffrey, Prince (son of Henry II), 52, 54
George, Prince of Denmark, 254, 257
George, St, 98
George I, King, 8, 10, 242, *260*, 264–71, *265*, *266*, 274

George II, King, 270, 272–9, *273*, *276*, 280, 282, 283
George III, King, 8, 13, 280–87, 288, 294, 299, 314
George IV, King, 12, 286, 288–93, *289–91*, 294–6, 299, 318, 320
George V, King, *316*, 318, 324, 325, *328*, 330–39, *331*, *333*, *334*, *336*, *337*, 340, 343, 349, 350, 354, 357, 367
George VI, King, 8, 318, 332, 340, 346, 348, 349–57, *351*, *352*, *354–6*, 358, *359*, 361, 362–3, 367
Germany, 223, 264, 325, 330, 340, 343, 346, 348, 358
Gibbon, Edward, 9, 13
Gilbey, James, 368
Gladstone, William Ewart, 311, 314
Glanvil, Ranulf, 62
Glendower, Owen, 118, 119, 120, 122
Gloucester, Eleanor, Duchess of, 131
Gloucester, Henry, Duke of, 332
Gloucester, Humphrey, Duke of, 128, 132
Gloucester, Thomas, Duke of, 107–9, 110, 114, 116, 117
Gloucester, William, Duke of, 254
Godolphin, Francis, 257, 258
Godwin, Earl, 20, 23
Gordon, General, 314
Gordon-Cumming, Colonel Sir William, 324
Gordon Riots, 282
Gowrie, Earl of, 216
Grand Alliance, 253, 257
Grand Remonstrance, 231
Great Contract, 220
Great Exhibition (1851), 304, *306*
Great Fire of London (1666), 236
Great Northern Wars, 270
Great Seal, 150
Gregorian reform movement, 28, 31, 32
Grenville, Charles, 294
Grenville, George, 284, 287
Grey, Lady Jane, 172, 190, 196, 202
Grey, Lord, 293, 296–7, *298*
Grigg, John, 353, 364
Guise faction, 204
Gunpowder Plot, 219, 220
Gwynne, Nell, 238, *239*

Habsburg dynasty, 175–6, 184, 209, 219
Haig, Earl, 336
Hainault, 92
Halford, Sir Henry, 294–6
Halidon Hill, Battle of (1333), 98–9
Halifax, Lord, 354, 358
Hampton Court, 172, 183, 185, 196, 219–20, 233
Handel, George Frederick, 260, 268, 275
Hanover, House of, 261–315, 318; genealogical table, 262–3
Harfleur, siege of (1415), 123
Harlech Castle, 118, 135
Harley, Robert, 257, 258
Harold II, King, 23, 24, 44
Harold Hardrada, King of Norway, 23, 24
Harry, Prince of Wales, 368, *370–71*, 372
Hastings, Battle of (1066), 8, 24
Hastings, Lady Flora, 301
Hastings, Lord, 146, 156, 158, 159
Hatton, Christopher, *202*, 206, 209, 210
healing magic, 32
Henrietta, Princess, 236
Henrietta Maria, Queen, 224, *228*, 231, 234
Henry, Count of Blois, 36, 37, 39
Henry, Prince of Wales (son of James I), *220*, 222, 224
Henry, the Young King, *50*, 51, 52, 54
Henry I, King, 30–35, *31*, 36, *40*
Henry II, King of France, 20
Henry II, King, 42–52, 54, 62, 72, *43*, *53*
Henry III, King, 12, 72–8, *73*, *75*, 79–80, 99, 114
Henry IV, King, 109, 110, 111, *112*, 114–19, *115*, *116*, 120, 122, 142, 150, 158
Henry V, King, 10–11, 111, 114, 117, 119, 120–27, *121*, *124–6*, 128, 131, 150
Henry V, Emperor, 32
Henry VI, King, 10, 126, 127, 128–38, *129*, *130*, *139*, 142, 145, 146, 148, 150, 152–5, 162, 163–5, 169–70
Henry VII, King, 10, 152, 156, 158, 159, *160*, 162–70, *163*, 180, 216

Henry VIII, King, 8, 10, 11, 149, 150, 162, 168, 169, 170, 171–84, *177*, *182*, 185, 187, 190, 191, 195–6, 198–201
heraldry *see* coats of arms
hereditary kingship, 9
Hereford, Battle of (1645), 232
Hereward the Wake, 25
Herleva, 20
Hervey, Lord, 274, 275
Hewitt, Major James, 368
Hexham, Battle of (1464), 135, 145
Hitler, Adolf, 343, 346, 353
Hoare, Sir Samuel, 339
Holy Land, 54, 56–60, 75, 80
Holy League, 171
Holy Roman Empire, 175, 223, 253, 264
Hooper, Bishop of Gloucester, 197
House of Commons *see* Parliament
Howard, Catherine, 184
Howard, Frances, 222
Howard, Henrietta, 272
Hugh of Lusignan, 64–5
Huguenots, 209
Humanism, 172
Hundred Years' War, 99–102, 103, 123, 131–2, 133, 171–2, 197
Hunsdon, 206
Huntingdon, Earl of (1399), 118, 122
Hyde, Anne, 240, 254

Immortal Seven, 245–6
India, 314, 323, 324, 335, 343, 349, 357
Industrial Welfare Society, 349–50
Innocent III, Pope, *64*, 65
Innocent VIII, Pope, 165
IRA, 367
Ireland, 62, 110, 111, 117, 242, 293, 335
Irish Free State, 338
Isabella of Angoulême, 64
Isabella of France (wife of Edward II), 84, *88*, 89, 92–3, 94, 99
Isabella of France (wife of Richard II), 110, 122
Isabella of Gloucester, 64

Jacobites, 256, 266, 268–70, 271, 275
Jaffa, 56, 60, 115
James I, King, 12, 162, 166, 206, 211, *212*, 216–23, *217*, 224, 226
James I, King of Cyprus, 115

James I, King of Scotland, 118
James II, King, *3*, 8, 10, 238, 239–46, *241*, *246*, 247, 252, 254, 256
James III, King of Scotland, 156
James IV, King of Scotland, 166, 168, 201
James V, King of Scotland, 172
James Francis Edward Stuart (Old Pretender), 245–6, 264, 268
Jersey, Lady, 288
Jerusalem, 56, 60, 115
Jesuits, 238
Jews, 85, 325, 343
Joan, Queen of Sicily, 55, 56
Joan of Arc, 128
Joan of Kent, 103
John, King, 52, 54, 60, 62–6, *63*, *66*, 72
John, King of France, 102
John, Prince (son of George V), 332
John of Gaunt, Duke of Lancaster, 102, 103, 106, 107, 110, 114, 116, 117, 122, 132, 142, 165, 180
Jones, Inigo, 231
Jonson, Ben, 231
Jordan, Mrs, 294, *296*
Joseph, Michael, 168
Juan Carlos, King of Spain, 372
Julius II, Pope, 171
Jutland, battle of (1916), 349

Kelmanns, Charlotte Sophia, 268
Kendal, Duchess of, 268
Kenilworth Castle, 93
Kensington Palace, 298, 299
Kent, 106, 132
Kent, Duchess of, 298, 299
Kent, Earl of, 118
Kent, Edward, Duke of, 298, 299
Kent, George, Duke of, 332, 357
Keppel, Hon. Mrs, 324
Kerr, Sir John, 367
Kett's Rebellion, 190
KGB, 367
King's College, Cambridge, 130
'king's evil', 32, *191*
Kingston, Treaty of, 72
Kirk, 230
Kitchener, Lord, 314, 342
Knighton, Sir William, 293
Knollys, Lord, 322, 335
Königsmark, Philip von, 265–6

Labour Party, 338, 353, 357, 372

Lancaster, 62
Lancaster, Edmund, Earl of, 76, 80, 117
Lancaster, Henry, Earl of, 94
Lancaster, House of, 113–38, 162, 165, 180, 192; genealogical table, 136–7
Lancaster, Thomas, Earl of, 90, 92, 102
Lancastrians, 134–5, 145, 148, 159, 170
Lanfranc, Archbishop of Canterbury, 25, 27, 28
Lang, Cosmo, Archbishop of Canterbury, 350
Langtry, Lillie, 323, *323*
Lascelles, Sir Alan, 362
Latimer, Bishop, 185, 197
Laud, William, Archbishop of Canterbury, 230, 231
Law, Andrew Bonar, 338
Lehzen, Baroness von, 299, 301
Leicester, Robert Dudley, Earl of, *200*, 204–6, 209, 210
'Leicester House Set', 270, 275
Lennox, D'Aubigny, 216
Lennox, Lady Sarah, 280
Leo X, Pope, 175, 176
Leopold, Duke of Austria, 56, 60
Leopold I, King of the Belgians, 299
Lewes, Battle of (1264), 78, 80
Liberal Party, 311, 314, 324, 325, 335, 353
Lightfoot, Hannah, 286
Lincoln, Battle of (1141), 37, 39
Lincoln, Battle of (1217), 72
Lincoln, John de la Pole, Earl of, 166–8
Lincolnshire, 146
Lithuania, 114–15
Llewellyn ap Gruffydd, 84
Lloyd George, David, 325, 335, 336–8, 339, 340
Lollards, 127, 172
London, 65, 66, 80, 106
London, Council of (1107), 32
Long Parliament, 230–31
Longchamp, William, 62
Lords Apellant, 109–10, 114, 116
Lords Ordainers, 89
Lostwithiel, Battle of (1644), 232
Louis VI, King of France, 32
Louis VII, King of France, 42, 51, 52, 54

Louis VIII, King of France, 66, 72
Louis IX, St, King of France, 76, 77, 80
Louis XI, King of France, 135, 145, 146, 148, 149, 155, 159
Louis XII, King of France, 172, 175
Louis XIV, King of France, 247, 248, 252, 253
Louis XVI, King of France, 286
Louis Philippe, King of France, 304
Lovell, Francis, 159, 168
Lowestoft, Battle of (1665), 240
Ludlow, Battle of (1459), 135, 152
Luther, Martin, 172
Lutherans, 183, 184

Macdonald, Ramsay, 11, 338, 339
Macfarlane, Bruce, 10
Machiavelli, Niccolò, 13, 171
Macmillan, Harold, 364
Magna Carta, 65, 67, 74
Maine, 20, 28, 64, 75, 123, 131
Malplaquet, Battle of (1709), 258
Malta, 357
Mancini, Dominic, 145, 149, 155, 156, 159
Mar, Earl of, 268
March, Earl of, 111, 117, 118, 122, 123
Marcher lords, 92
Margaret (daughter of Louis VII), 51
Margaret, Maid of Norway, 86
Margaret, Princess (daughter of George VI), 350, 356, 358, 361, 364, 367
Margaret, Queen (wife of Edward I), 84
Margaret of Anjou, 131, 133, 133, 134, 135, 138, 142, 146, 148, 158
Margaret of Burgundy, 166, 168
Margaret of York, 146
Margaret Tudor, 162, 166, 172, 201
Marlborough, John Churchill, Earl of, 253, 254–7, 258, 259
Marlborough, Sarah Churchill, Duchess of, 254–6, 256, 257, 258
Marten, Sir Henry, 358
Mary, Princess (daughter of Charles I), 240
Mary, Princess (daughter of George V), 332
Mary, Princess (daughter of Henry VII), 166, 172, 190, 201

Mary, Queen (wife of George V), 331, 332, 336, 340, 343, 349, 350, 354, 358, 358
Mary, Queen of Scots, 8, 190, 204, 206–9, 211, 211, 216
Mary I, Queen, 8, 176, 183, 184, 185, 190, 191–7, 191, 202–3
Mary II, Queen, 226, 237, 247–53, 249, 254, 257
Mary of Burgundy, 148
Mary of Modena, 240, 244, 245
Masham, Abigail, 257
Matilda, Empress, 8, 32–5, 36–9, 38, 42
Matilda, wife of William I, 20, 27, 30
Matilda of Boulogne, 36, 36, 37, 39
Maximilian, Emperor, 168, 170, 175
Meaux, 126
Melbourne, Lady, 288
Melbourne, Lord, 299–301, 302–3, 304
Merchant Adventurers, 170
Merciless Parliament, 109, 110, 114
Messina, 55
Metcalfe, Major Edward, 348
Middlesex, Lionel Cranfield, Earl of, 223
Milan, Duke of, 115
Monck, General George, 236
Monckton, Walter, 346, 350
Monmouth, Duke of, 245, 252
Montagu, Lord, 135
Montfort, Simon de, 77–8, 80, 85, 90
Montfort family, 90
Montgelas, Count Albrecht von, 330
Montgomery, Field Marshal, 352, 357
Montgomery, Treaty of (1267), 84
Mordaunt, Sir Charles, 324
More, Sir Thomas, 149, 159, 166, 172, 174–5, 178
Mortain, 62
Mortimer, Anne, 132
Mortimer, Edmund, 118
Mortimer, Roger, 92, 93, 94, 117
Mortimer's Cross, Battle of (1461), 142
Morton, Andrew, 368
Morton, Archbishop, 168
Morton, 4th Earl of, 216
Mountbatten, Lord Louis, 343, 346, 348, 349, 357, 361, 362, 364, 367
Mountbatten family, 330
Mowbray, Thomas, 118

Munich Agreement (1938), 353
Mutiny Act, 252

Namur, 253
Napoleon I, Emperor, 127, 242, 293
Napoleon III, Emperor, 304, 307
Nazis, 343, 346, 349, 353
Netherlands, 170, 209
Neville, Anne, 138, 155, 158–9
Neville, Cicely, 145, 152
Neville, George, Archbishop of York, 145
Neville, Isabel, 146, 155
Neville, Ralph, 142
Neville family, 117, 134, 135
Neville's Cross, Battle of (1346), 100
Newcastle, Duke of, 278, 279, 283
Newcastle, 2nd Earl of, 234
Nicholas II, Tsar, 325, 332, 338
Nithsdale, Lady, 270
Nonsuch Palace, 178
Norfolk, 190
Norfolk, Catherine, Duchess of, 145
Norfolk, John Howard, 1st Duke of, 158
Norfolk, Thomas Howard, 3rd Duke of, 183–4, 195
Norfolk, Thomas Howard, 4th Duke of, 206
Normandy, 26, 27–8, 30, 32, 36, 39, 42, 60, 64, 65, 75, 99–100, 123–6, 131–2, 357
Normans, 8, 13, 17–39, 46; genealogical table, 18–19
Norris, Henry, 183
North, Lord Frederick, 280, 284
Northampton, Battle of (1460), 135
Northampton, Treaty of (1328), 98
Northern Rebellion (1569), 206
Northumberland, Henry Percy, 1st Earl of, 117, 118
Northumberland, Henry Percy, 4th Earl of, 159, 165
Northumberland, John Dudley, Duke of, 190, 196, 198, 202
Northumberland, John Neville, Earl of, 145, 146
Northumberland, Thomas Percy, 7th Earl of, 206
Northumberland, Robert Mowbray, Earl of, 28
Nottingham, Battle of (1469), 146
Nottingham, 2nd Earl of, 257

Nottingham, Thomas Mowbray, Earl of, 109, 110, 116–17
Nottingham Castle, 94
Nymegen, Peace of (1678), 237

Oates, Titus, 240
Odo, Bishop of Bayeux, 20, 25, 27
Order of the Garter, 98, 180, 287, 374
Orleans, Duke of, 122
Oudenarde, Battle of (1708), 257, 272, 274
Outremer, 56
Oxford, 38, 118, 238, 240
Oxford, Earls of, 122, 146, 165
Oxford, Robert de Vere, Earl of, 103–6, 109, 114
Oxford University, 184, 245, 340–42

Palmerston, Lord, 304–8, 311, 322
Paris, 115, 117, 120, 126, 127
Paris, Matthew, 44, 46, 79
Paris, Treaty of (1259), 75, 99
Parker, Matthew, Archbishop of Canterbury, 204
Parker Bowles, Camilla, 368
Parliament: Henry III and, 74, 77; under Edward I, 85; 'Good' Parliament, 102; Merciless Parliament, 109, 110, 114; and Henry IV, 119; Edward IV and, 142; Reformation Parliament, 178; Elizabeth I and, 210–11; James I and, 216, 219, 220, 223; Gunpowder Plot, 220; and Charles I, 224, 229–33; Short Parliament, 230–31; Long Parliament, 230–31; Charles II and, 236, 237–8; James II and, 245; Queen Anne and, 257, 258; George III dismisses, 284; William IV and, 296–7; constitutional crisis (1909–10), 325
Parr, Catherine, 184, 185, 187, 190, 196, 198, 201
Paston, Sir John, 146
Peasant's Revolt (1381), 106
Peel, Sir Robert, 293, 297, 301, 304
Pelham family, 279
Pembroke, Aymer de Valence, Earl of, 90
Pembroke, Jasper Tudor, Earl of, 142, 146, 162, 165, 170
Pembroke, William Herbert, Earl of, 162
Penal Act, 252

Percy, Henry (Hotspur), 118, 120
Percy, Sir Henry, 177
Percy family, 117, 118, 135, 145, 158
Pergami, Bartolomo, 290
Perrers, Alice, 102
Peter the Great, 270
Petition of Right, 229
Philip, Archduke, 168
Philip, Prince, Duke of Edinburgh, 357, 360, 361–3, 364
Philip I, King of France, 26, 27
Philip II, King of France, 52, 54, 55–6, 60, 62, 64, 65
Philip II, King of Spain, 192, 196–7, 202, 203, 204, 209–10
Philip III, King of France, 80–84, 86
Philip IV the Fair, King of France, 99
Philip VI, King of France, 99, 100, 102
Philippa of Hainault, 92
Phillips, Captain Mark, 368
Pickering, Sir William, 204
Picquigny, Truce of (1745), 148, 155
Pilgrimage of Grace, 183
Pinkie, Battle of (1547), 190
Pitt, William the Elder, 279, 283, 284
Pitt, William the Younger, 284–5, 287, 292
plague, 100, 102, 236
Plantagenets, 69–111; genealogical table, 70–71
Poitiers, 54
Poitiers, Battle of (1356), 100–101, 102
Poitou, 65
Pole, Margaret, 149
Pole, Sir Michael de la, 106, 107–9
Pole, Cardinal Reginald, 194, 196, 197, 203
Pontefract, 111, 117
Popish Plot, 238, 240, 252
Portsmouth, Duchess of, 238
Portugal, 172, 307
Prayer Book, 188–90, 203, 236
Presbyterians, 231, 232, 234
Princes in the Tower, 152, 158, 159, 168
Privy Council, 240, 245, 296, 330, 339, 374
Protestants, 190, 197, 203; see also Church of England
Puritans, 203, 216–20, 229, 231, 233
Pym, John, 231

Radcot Bridge, Battle of (1387), 109, 114
Raleigh, Sir Walter, 13, 206, 207, 209, 219, 223
Ratcliffe, Sir Richard, 159
Readeption of Henry VI, 135–8, 149
Reform Bill, 296, 297
Reformation, 8, 10, 127, 172; Edwardian, 188–90, 196
Reformation Parliament, 178
Renard, Simon, 196
Reresby, Sir John, 240
Restoration, 234, 236, 240
Reversionary Interest, 279
Revolution of 1688, 252
Rhys ap Thomas, 170
Richard, Prince (son of William I), 27
Richard I, King, 44, 46, 52, 54–60, 54, 55, 58–9, 61, 62–4, 75, 84
Richard II, King, 12, 44, 96, 102, 103–11, 107, 114, 116–17, 116, 122
Richard III, King, 10, 13, 138, 140, 145, 146, 148, 149, 150, 152–9, 153, 165
Richmond, Edmund Tudor, Earl of, 162, 180
Richmond, Henry Fitzroy, Duke of, 176
Richmond Palace, 168, 169
Ridley, Bishop, 190, 197
Ridolfi conspiracy, 206
Rivers, Anthony Woodville, Lord, 149, 156
Robert, Count of Meulan, 30
Robert, Count of Mortain, 20
Robert, Duke of Normandy (father of William I), 20
Robert, Duke of Normandy (son of William I), 26, 27–8, 30–31, 32, 34–5
Robert of Gloucester, 36, 38, 39, 42
Robethon, Jean de, 266
Robinson, Perdita, 288
Roches, Peter des, Bishop of Winchester, 74
Rochester, Earl of, 257
Rochford, Lord, 183
Rockingham, Lord, 284
Roger of Salisbury, 32, 35, 37
Roman Catholic Church, 196, 202, 203, 206–9, 216–20, 237, 238, 240, 245, 252, 287, 293, 294
Rome, Council of (1099), 31

Roosevelt, Franklin D., 353
Rouen, 32, 39, 126, 131
Royal Marriages Act, 288
Royal Navy, 294, 330–32, 349
Royalists, 233, 234, 236
Rubens, Peter Paul, 231
Runnymede, 65
Russell, Lord John, 297, 304, 308, 322
Russia, 307–8, 314, 323, 325, 338
Rye House plot, 238
Ryswick, Peace of (1697), 253

Sacheverell, Henry, 258
St Albans, Battle of (1455), 133, 135
St Albans, Battle of (1461), 135
St James's Palace, 178, 240, 247, 280, 332
St John, Henry, 258, 266, 268, 270, 274, 275
St Quentin, battle of (1557), 197
Saladin, 54, 56, 60
Salisbury, John de Montagu, 3rd Earl of, 118
Salisbury, Marquess of, 314, 324
Salisbury, Richard Neville, Earl of, 135, 142
Salisbury, Robert Cecil, Earl of, 210, 211, 216, 220
Sandringham, 323, 332, 333, 343, 349, 357
Sandwich, Battle of, 72
Saracens, 76
Saxe-Coburg-Gotha, House of, 317–25, 330; genealogical table, 326–7
Schneider, Hortense, 323
Scotland: Henry II and, 48; Edward I's campaigns, 85–6, 89; Edward II's expeditions to, 89, 90; Edward III defeats, 98–9, 100; Richard II's campaign, 106–7; Richard III's campaigns, 156; Somerset captures Edinburgh, 190; Mary, Queen of Scots, 204; union with England, 220, 226, 242, 257, 258; Covenanters, 230, 232–3, 234; Jacobite rising, 268–70
Scrope, Richard, Archbishop of York, 118
Second World War, 339, 348, 349, 354–7, 358–61
Seven Years' War, 279, 336
Seymour, Jane, 183, 185, 195

Seymour, Admiral Sir Thomas, 190, 196, 201–2
Shaftesbury, 1st Earl of, 237, 238
Shaftesbury, 7th Earl of, 304
Shakespeare, William, 114, 152
Shaw, Dr Ralph, 158
Sheen, 168
ship money, 231
Shore, Jane, 149
Short Parliament, 230–31
Shrewsbury, battle of (1403), 118, 120
Shrewsbury, Duke of, 264
Shrewsbury, Robert of Bellême, Earl of, 30, 31
Sicily, 55–6, 76, 77, 80
Sigismund, Emperor, 123
Simnel, Lambert, 166–8
Simpson, Mrs (Duchess of Windsor), 343, 344–8, 347, 350–53
Sluys, battle of (1340), 99
Smeaton, Mark, 183
Snowdon, Earl of, 367
Snowdonia, 84, 85
Socialism, 338
Solebay, Battle of (1672), 240
Somerset, Duchess of, 258
Somerset, Edmund Beaufort, Duke of, 132, 133, 134
Somerset, Edward Seymour, Duke of, 184, 187–8, 190, 198, 201
Somerset, John Beaufort, Earl of, 165
Somerset, Robert Carr, Earl of, 222–3
Sophia, Electress of Hanover, 264
Sophia Dorothea of Celle, 264–6, 267, 270, 271
South Africa, 314–15, 374
South Sea Bubble, 268, 269, 270–71
Spain, 171, 172, 192, 196–7, 209–10, 219, 223, 224
Spanish Netherlands, 247
Spencer, Earl, 370–71
Stamford Bridge, Battle of (1066), 24
Stamfordham, Lord, 330, 332, 335, 338, 339
Stanhope, 3rd Earl of, 266, 270, 271
Stanley, Lord, 159, 165
Stanley, Sir William, 168
Stephen, Count of Blois, 36
Stephen, King, 8, 35–9, 36, 40, 42, 46, 48
Stirling Bridge, battle of (1297), 86
Stoke, battle of (1487), 168
Stone of Destiny, 86
Strachey, Lytton, 11

Strafford, Earl of, 231
Strickland, Agnes, 6–7
Stuarts, 213–58; coats of arms, 226; genealogical table, 214–15
Suez Crisis (1956), 364
Suffolk, Charles Brandon, Duke of, 172
Suffolk, Edmund de la Pole, Earl of, 168
Suffolk, William de la Pole, Earl of, 131, 132, 133
Sunderland, 2nd Earl of, 245, 246
Sunderland, 3rd Earl of, 257
Surrey, Thomas Howard, Earl of, 168, 171, 172
Swein, King of Denmark, 26
Swynford, Katherine, 122, 165

Talbot, Earl of, 132, 133
Tancred, King of Sicily, 55
Tarleton, Richard, 201
Taylor, A.J.P., 10–11, 12
Test Acts, 237, 238, 240, 245, 246, 252
Teutonic Knights, 115
Tewkesbury, Battle of (1471), 138, 148, 152
Thatcher, Margaret, 374
Theobald, Archbishop of Canterbury, 39, 51
Theobald, Count of Blois, 36
Thirty Years War, 223
Tinchebrai, Battle of (1106), 31
Tories, 238, 240, 253, 257, 258, 266, 275, 278, 294, 304
Torrigiano, Pietro, 163, 169, 170
Toulouse, 51
Touraine, 60, 64
Tower of London, 106, 128, 132, 135, 138, 148, 158, 166, 203, 257
Townsend, Group Captain Peter, 364
Townshend, 266, 270
Towton, Battle of (1461), 135, 142, 148, 152
Trades Disputes Act, 324
Triennial Act, 252
'the Triumvirate', 257
Troyes, Treaty of (1420), 126
Tudor, Owen, 128, 163
Tudors, 161–211
Turkey, 314
Tyler, Wat, 106
Tyndale, William, 179, 183
Tyrwhit, Sir Robert, 202

Udall, Nicholas, 196
Ulster Unionists, 335
United States of America, 284,
    308–11, 320, 343, 353, 372
Upton, Nicholas, 46
Urban II, Pope, 28, 29
Utrecht, Treaty of (1713), 258

Valois dynasty, 175–6, 184
Venice, 115, 171
Vergil, Polydore, 158
Verneuil, 123
Vertue, Robert, 170
Vexin, 26, 28, 51
Victoria, Princess Royal, 301
Victoria, Queen, 8, 175, 298, 299–315,
    300, 302–3, 309, 310, 312, 316, 318,
    320–23, 324, 332, 340, 374
Vienna, Congress of (1815), 242
Vikings, 23, 24, 26
Vilna, siege of (1390), 115
Vives, 191

Wakefield, Battle of (1460), 135, 142
Wales: Henry II and, 48; Edward I's
    campaigns, 84–5, 86; Marcher
    lords, 92; Glendower's rebellion,
    118, 120; Henry VII and, 170; Act
    of 1536, 170; arms of the Prince of
    Wales, 318; unemployment, 344;
    Statute of (1284), 84
Wallace, William, 86
Walmoden, Madame von, 275, 278,
    279
Walpole, Horace, 268, 280
Walpole, Robert, 266, 270, 271, 274,
    275, 278–9
Walsingham, Francis, 209, 210
Walsingham, Thomas, 103, 119
Walter, Hubert, Archbishop of
    Canterbury, 60
Walter of Coutances, Archbishop of
    Rouen, 62
Warbeck, Perkin, 168

Warenne, Earl, 86
Warham, Archbishop, 171, 172
Warkworth, Henry, 138
Warren, Dr, 286
Wars of the Roses, 132, 133–8, 152,
    158, 159, 170
Warwick, Edward, Earl of, 166–8
Warwick, Richard Beauchamp, Earl
    of, 128
Warwick, Richard Neville, Earl of,
    134, 135, 138, 142–8, 162
Warwick, Thomas Beauchamp, Earl
    of, 109, 110, 116, 122
Wellington, Duke of, 292, 293, 296,
    302–3
Wenceslas, King of Bohemia, 115
Westminster, Council of (1163), 51
Westminster, Treaty of (1153), 42–3
Westminster Abbey, 75, 76, 77, 78,
    111, 135, 138, 165, 168, 169–70,
    171, 178, 197, 238, 271, 290
Westmorland, Charles Neville, 6th
    Earl of, 206
Westmorland, Ralph Neville, 1st Earl
    of, 118, 120–22
Whigs, 238, 240, 252, 253, 257–8,
    266, 270, 274, 275, 278, 283,
    293, 294, 296, 301, 304
White Ship, 32
Whitehall Palace, 178, 198, 203, 231
Whitlam, Gough, 367
Wilberforce, William, 294, 304
Wilhelmina, Princess of Prussia, 274
Wilkes, John, 284
William, Prince (son of Charles,
    Prince of Wales), 368, 370–71, 372
William, Prince (son of Henry I),
    32
William, Prince (son of Stephen), 39
William I, King, 13, 16, 20–26, 25,
    27, 30, 40
William II, Kaiser, 325, 330, 333
William II, King, 11, 27–9, 30, 31,
    40

William II, Prince of Orange, 247
William III, King, 226, 237, 245–6,
    247–53, 248, 254–7, 264
William IV, King, 294–8, 295, 297,
    299, 318, 333
William of Hainault, 115
William the Marshal, 72
William the Silent, 209, 247
Willis, Dr Francis, 286
Winchester, 29, 166
Windsor, House of, 8, 329–74;
    genealogical table, 326–7
Windsor Castle, 131, 170, 233, 287,
    290, 293, 358, 368
Witt, John de, 247
Wolsey, Cardinal Thomas, 172, 176,
    177–8, 191
Woodstock, 203, 257
Woodville, Elizabeth, Queen, 140,
    144, 145, 148, 155, 156–8, 165
Woodville, John, 145, 148
Worcester, Battle of (1651), 234
Worcester, John Toptoft, Earl of, 149
Worcester, Thomas Percy, Earl of, 118
Wyatt, Sir Thomas, 177, 196, 203

Yeomen of the Guard, 169
York, 98, 126, 155, 198
York, Edmund, Duke of, 111, 117
York, Edward, Duke of, 123
York, Cardinal Henry, 166
York, House of, 141–59, 180, 192;
    genealogical table, 136–7
York, Richard, Duke of (father of
    Edward IV), 132, 133–4, 135,
    142, 145, 152
York, Richard, Duke of (son of
    Edward IV), 156–8, 168
York, Sarah, Duchess of, 367–8
Yorkists, 133–5, 145, 155, 159, 162,
    165

Zouche, William de la, Archbishop of
    York, 100

PICTURE CREDITS